HMS ARK ROYAL

Zeal Does Not Rest
1981 – 2011

Alastair Graham and Eric Grove

Copyright © Alastair Graham and Eric Grove, 2011

Chapter 1 written by Alastair Graham and edited by Eric Grove
Chapters 2 to 9 inclusive written and edited by Alastair Graham and Eric Grove
Chapters 10 to 15 inclusive, Epilogue, Index and End Notes written and edited by Alastair Graham

First published in the United Kingdom in 2011 by
Maritime Books, Lodge Hill, Liskeard, Cornwall, PL14 4EL

The moral right of the authors have been asserted.

HMS ARK ROYAL

Zeal Does Not Rest
1981 - 2011

Hardback ISBN 978-1-904459-46-0

Set in Times New Roman 11-point by
Alastair Graham

Printed and bound in the United Kingdom by
Ashford Colour Press Ltd, Gosport
and
Hunter & Foulis Ltd, East Lothian

CONTENTS

GLOSSARY

5ATAF – 5th Alliance Tactical Air Force
AA – Anti-Air (as in missile)
AAW – Anti Air Warfare
ADAWS – Action Data Automated Weapon System
ADIMP – ADAWS Improvement Programme
AMP – Assisted Maintenance Period
AEW – Airborne Early Warning
AMRAAM – Advanced Medium Range Air-to-Air Missile
ASaC – Airborne Surveillance and Area Control
ASRAAM – Advanced Short Range Air-to-Air Missile
ASuW – Anti Surface Warfare
ASuWEX – ASuW Exercise
ASW – Anti Submarine Warfare
ASWEX – ASW Exercise
ASWSTRIKFOR – ASW Striking Force
ATG – Amphibious Task Group
AUTEC – Atlantic Underwater Test and Evaluation Centre, Andros Bahamas
AVI ORI – Aviation Operational Readiness Inspection
AWACS – Airborne Warning and Control System
BAMP – Base Assisted Maintenance Period
BD&T – Babcock Design and Technology Ltd
BOST – Basic Operational Sea Training
BRDL – Babcock Rosyth Dockyard Ltd
BRITFOR – British Force (Bosnia)
BSSL – Babcock Surface Ships Ltd
CAG – Carrier Air Group
CAH – Heavy Cruiser (Helicopter Capable)
CAP – Combat Air Patrol
CAS – Chief of the Air Staff (RAF)
CAS – Close Air Support
CASEX – Combined Anti Submarine Exercise
CB – Companion of the Order of the Bath
CDS – Chief of the Defence Staff
CGS – Chief of the General Staff (Army)
CHF – Commando Helicopter Force
CNS/1SL – Chief of the Naval Staff/First Sea Lord

CIWS – Close-In Weapon System
CLUBS – Carrier Line-Up Beacon System
COMAO – Combined Air Operations
COMATG – Commander Amphibious Task Group
COMUKTG – Commander UK Task Group
COMUKMARFOR – Commander UK Maritime Force
COMUKCSG – Commander UK Carrier Strike Group
COST – Continuation Operational Sea Training
CSH – Combat System Highway
CSS – Command Support System
CTF – Commander Task Force
CTG – Commander Task Group
CVN – Aircraft Carrier (Nuclear-Powered)
CVSA – ASW Support Aircraft Carrier (Assault)
CVSG – "   "   "   " (Guided Missile)
DAMP – Docking Assisted Maintenance Period
DAOPS – Deck Approach Optical Positioning System
DCA – Defensive Counter Air
DSC – Distinguished Service Cross
EMCON – Emissions Control
ENCOUNTEREX – Encounter Exercise
ESM – Electronic Surveillance Measures
EW – Electronic Warfare
FA-2 – Fighter Attack-2 (Sea Harrier)
FLEETEX – Fleet Exercise
FFWP – Future Fleet Working Party
FOF – Flag Officer Flotilla (1, 2, 3)
FORACS –
Fleet Operational Readiness Accuracy Check Site
FOSF – Flag Officer Surface Flotilla
FOST – Flag Officer Sea Training
FPDA – Five Powers Defence Agreement
FRS-1 – Fighter Reconnaissance Strike-1 (Harrier)
FGS – Federal German Ship
FS – French Ship
FTSP – Fleet Time Support Period
GPS – satellite Global Positioning System
GWS – Guided Weapon System

HDS – Helicopter Delivery Service
HMS – Her Majesty's Ship
HMAS – Her Majesty's Australian Ship
HMCS – Her Majesty's Canadian Ship
HNLMS – Her Netherlands Majesty's Ship
HNoMS – His Norwegian Majesty's Ship
IFF – Identification Friend of Foe
IFOR – Implementation Force (NATO Bosnia)
ITS – Italian Ship
JFH – Joint Force Harrier
JMC – Joint Maritime Conference
LGB – Laser Guided Bomb
LPD – Landing Platform Dock
LPH – Landing Platform Helicopter
LSL – Landing Ship Logistic
MADGE – Microwave Aircraft Digital Guidance Equipment
MCO – Main Communications Office
MOAR – 'Mother Of All Rehearsals' (Op TELIC)
MoD – Ministry of Defence
MRES – Marinark Rapid Evacuation System
NAAFI – Navy Army Air Force Institute
NAS – Naval Air Squadron
NATO – North Atlantic Treaty Organisation
NSR – Naval Staff Requirement
OCA – Offensive Counter Air
OPAREA – Operating Area
OPCOM – Operational Command
OPCON – Operational Control
OST – Operational Sea Training
PAAMS – Principal Anti Air Missile System
PAR – Precision Approach Radar
PASSEX – Passing Exercise
RAS – Replenishment at Sea
RCS – Reaction Control System (Harrier)
R909 – Radar Type 909 (tracker)
R992 – Radar Type 992 (MR surveillance)
R996 – Radar Type 996 (MR surveillance)
R1006/7/8 – Radar Type 1006/7/8 (navigation)
R1022 – Radar Type 1022 (LR surveillance)
RFA – Royal Fleet Auxiliary
RM – Royal Marines
RNAS – Royal Naval Air Station
SBAAT – Scottish Business Awards Trust

SDR – Strategic Defence Review
SDSR – Strategic Defence and Security Review
SFOR – Stabilisation Force (NATO Kosovo)
SKA – Sea King Assault helicopter
SKJ – Sea King Jezebel ASW helicopter
SKW – Sea King Whiskey AEW helicopter
SKU – Sea King Utility helicopter
SMP – Self Maintenance Period
SSMOB – Ship Staff Move On Board
SSBN – Ballistic Missile Nuclear Submarine
SSK – Diesel Submarine (patrol)
SSN – Nuclear Submarine (attack submarine)
SNFL – Standing Naval Force Atlantic
SNFM – Standing Naval Force Mediterranean
STOVL – Short Take Off Vertical Landing
SUCAP – Surface Combat Air Patrol
SURFEX – Surface Exercise
TACOM – Tactical Command
TACON – Tactical Control
TAG – Tailored Air Group
TF – Task Force
TG – Task Group
TLAM – Tomahawk Land Attack Missile
TVS – Thrust Vector System (Harrier)
UN – United Nations
UNHCR – UN High Commission for Refugees
UNMOVIC – UN Monitoring, Verification and Inspection Commission
UNPA – UN Protection Areas (Bosnia)
UNPROFOR – UN Protection Force
UNSCOM – UN Special Commission
UNSCR – UN Security Council Resolution
USMC – United States Marine Corps
USNS – United States Naval Ship (auxiliary)
USS – United States Ship (warship)
VETS – Vehicle Equipment Tracking System
VTOL – Vertical Take Off/Landing
WASEX – War At Sea Exercise
WESTLANT – Western Atlantic
WEU – Western European Union
WEUMARFOR – WEU Maritime Force
WMD – Weapons of Mass Destruction
WRNS – Women's Royal Naval Service
XCAS – Exercise CAS

Chapter 1

Phoenix from the ashes:
The genesis of HMS *Ark Royal* V

The history and, indeed the fate, of the fifth HMS *Ark Royal* is tied up with the struggle over British aircraft carriers that has gone on ever since the end of World War II, as the Royal Navy has fought to retain carrier capability.

By 1945 the carrier had replaced the traditional gun armed battleship as the main striking power of the fleet. In the post war era however, nuclear and, even more so, thermonuclear weapons challenged the traditional concepts of large scale war. The Admiralty had to argue a case for carriers as the British contribution to NATO's nuclear armed striking fleet and in whatever offensive role to counter the growing Soviet submarine threat or escort role would be relevant in a war of indeterminate length. More importantly, perhaps, carriers proved to be vital mobile airfields in limited conflicts. Carriers provided the only British air power deployed over Korea to stem the Communist invasion from the north. They also provided the most effective air cover for the Suez landings in 1956. The debacle of Suez forced the British government to critically reassess the state of its Armed Forces. The resulting Defence Review led by Duncan Sandys in 1957 sought to strip out post-war obsolescence and placed the priority firmly on nuclear deterrence and missiles, but the Admiralty's case for carriers was accepted, having been skilfully marshalled by that most accomplished of bureaucrat politicians, Lord Louis Mountbatten, as First Sea Lord. The Navy survived the Review with its carrier-building programme

largely intact, primarily by completing, refitting and updating the large ships started before peace in 1945. By the beginning of the 1960's, Britain thus had five fixed-wing carriers, the fleet carriers HMS *Eagle*, HMS *Victorious* and the fourth HMS *Ark Royal*, and the light fleet carriers HMS *Hermes* (only completed in 1959) and HMS *Centaur*. Two of the latter's sister ships HMS *Bulwark* and HMS *Albion* were converted into helicopter carrying 'commando carriers', making seven 'flat tops' in all.

Mountbatten's short-lived successor as First Sea Lord, Admiral of the Fleet Sir Charles Lambe, in 1959 put carriers forward as mobile floating airfields in support of amphibious forces that were to be truly joint service in character, capable of operating both RN and RAF aircraft. Given the age of the existing carriers, and the lead time for procuring replacements for at least some, the first steps to provide a new carrier were taken in 1961. The Defence Committee in February 1962 approved preliminary work to begin and four months later, four possible designs were submitted to the Board of Admiralty for the new ship, designated CVA-01. The 53,000-ton design was accepted, although Ian Orr-Ewing, the Civil Lord, expressed doubts whether any of these designs was affordable. Orr-Ewing suggested a smaller design able to operate Short Take Off Vertical Landing (STOVL) aircraft. The existing P1127 STOVL design (the forerunner of the Harrier) was subsonic and short ranged and the sailors wanted a big ship that was certain to be able to operate more capable aircraft. The proposal for a supersonic STOVL P1154 offered a potential joint way forward although the two services could not agree on the precise characteristics of the aircraft, two versions being designed.

In December 1962 at Nassau, Prime Minister Harold MacMillan committed Britain's nuclear deterrent future to Polaris. Launched from submarines, Polaris would be a replacement for the V-bomber force, transferring what had always been the RAF's fundamental role, strategic bombing, to the Royal Navy. This was the latest in a series of shadows on the RAF's horizon in the early 1960s. Mountbatten, now Chief of the Defence Staff, angled to transfer control of Coastal Command to the Admiralty under the justification of a unified anti-submarine force, better able to counter the emerging Soviet threat. The development of a UK-designed replacement 'capital' strike aircraft, the TSR-2, was also becoming prohibitively expensive and Mountbatten lobbied heavily for a cheaper but less capable alternative, the Blackburn Buccaneer. The Air Ministry asserted a strategic and global operational role for the TSR-2 as a vital factor in both its survival and, more fundamentally, the survival of the RAF as a viable and independent service. Safeguarding the RAF against further diminution would bring the Air Ministry and Admiralty into direct competition over which service should win the right to claim ownership of the key defence role of providing air power 'East of Suez'. The Navy's argument rested with carriers, while the RAF argued that global reach could be achieved with the TSR-2.

By the autumn of 1962 the problem of presenting an affordable Defence Budget was becoming crystallised into arguments over the cost effectiveness of and the need for, aircraft carriers when the existing carriers reached the end of their useful lives in some twelve to fifteen years time. In an attempt to shed some light on the arguments, Mountbatten, asked Sir Thomas Pike, Chief of the Air Staff, for his views on the matter. Pike was forthright that the RAF could do all that was required in the air, and that the cost of the carrier was disproportionate to its effectiveness. This paper was extremely prejudiced and partisan, but it was also plausible, and persuasive. The most telling point in the RAF's favour was the unsubstantiated claim that land based aircraft could do all that was required without the need for carriers, a contention which carried considerable weight with Ministers seeking economies.

The Navy neither could, nor did, try to claim that naval aircraft could cope alone without the support of land based aircraft. CAS's paper was followed in October 1962 by the Island Strategy paper, where, it was claimed, land based RAF aircraft operating from an 'island stance' east of Suez, could match the carrier's performance. Both papers proposed totally untried and probably unworkable plans to maintain global reach. Admiral of the Fleet Sir Caspar John, who had taken over as First Sea Lord in 1960, rebutted the claims, but these were the opening rounds in the battle between the dark and the light blue over carriers that would become increasingly acrimonious and last to this day.

Alternative smaller carriers were suggested that could fly STOVL aircraft in a purely ground support role and the first operational P1127 made successful trial landings on HMS *Ark Royal* IV on 8th February 1963. The Admiralty stuck to a fast fleet carrier concept with conventional jets because it was necessary for naval roles as well as joint. It had based the fighting efficiency of the fleet on the carrier, and unlike other navies, had not developed the anti-surface missile capabilities that gave the increasingly formidable Soviet Navy a significant advantage against a navy without carriers. Long range air launched anti ship missiles also required adequate long range organic air defence. To counter these threats, the carrier had to provide airborne surveillance and fixed-wing offensive anti-air and anti-surface strike; the Defence Minister, Peter Thorneycroft, who had backed a small carrier design known in Whitehall as the

'Thorneycraft', finally accepted that without a proper fleet carrier the Navy *"would have neither eyes nor teeth."* and that it was vital to the Navy's future. The Admiralty was learning how to play Whitehall games more effectively and told Thorneycroft that it would accept the RAF's single seat P1154 in return for a positive carrier decision. It knew that the P1154 was doomed because of technological difficulties and that when built the carrier would operate Buccaneers and Phantoms. The programme to build CVA-01 therefore gathered momentum, having stalled somewhat due to the limited resources in the Ministry design departments and the competing demands of designing the Resolution-class submarines destined to carry Polaris.

Progress stalled once more however as soon as the Labour administration assumed office in October 1964. Denis Healey, Thorneycroft's replacement as Secretary of State for Defence, set out to conduct a thorough review to produce viable defence forces within an extremely tight and rigid budget. It was clear from the start that the main area in which major savings might be made was in the apparently overlapping roles of land and carrier based aircraft, and for the Royal Navy Healey's review developed into a need to justify the carrier against strong RAF opposition. The review started badly for the RAF with the decision to abandon the TSR-2, on which they had pinned many of their hopes. As a result the RAF then turned to a version of the American F-111, which had an excellent low level strike capability, and based its arguments on acquiring this aircraft. Study followed study, but as the review developed, it became clear that the crux of the matter was land based versus carrier borne air power. The Navy's case was not helped by the Army view expressed by General Sir James Cassells in July 1965 that *"it can fairly be said that in terms of flexibility and sudden reaction to an emergency, the Army has learnt to place greater reliance on the RAF than on strike carriers, because RAF resources are more often available at the notice required and normally better placed for*

sustained operations." This view was clearly influential, although it did not appear to be supported by recent post war operational experience.

Mountbatten's departure as Chief of Defence Staff in July 1965, to be replaced by Field Marshal Sir Richard Hull, removed the last great protagonist in the pro-carrier camp. Sir David Luce, Caspar John's successor as First Sea Lord, was a strong advocate of the Navy's case for the carrier. But Luce lacked the doggedness of his predecessor, nor did he have the political guile of Mountbatten to employ the full range of tactics, both honourable and not so, needed to win the internecine struggle. Healey moved the goal posts commissioning innumerable studies for scenarios where success could be achieved without the carrier. Luce, realising that things were going against the carrier attempted to broaden the argument by producing a paper on sea power in general rather than concentrating on specific scenarios. This appeared at the same time as the so-called Gap Study, which analysed the special problems that would arise if the carriers were no longer available. The conclusions of the Gap Study published on 20th October 1965, were, to put it mildly, discouraging. Beyond the range of land based aircraft the Fleet would be unable to prevent detection or to detect, identify and engage missile carrying ships or aircraft outside their missile launching range, or to identify aircraft within range of ships' radars or missiles. Against air attack there would be no air defence in depth and the enemy would be opposed only by surface-to-air missiles, and then only from 1978 when a suitable and effective system (the GWS-30 Sea Dart) was expected to enter full service. Ship-borne surface-to-surface missiles would not be available before 1976 (the GWS-50 Exocet). Within range of land, shore-based aircraft could in theory perform all maritime strike roles and their range could be extended by effective air-tanker support. A combination of Phantoms and Victor tankers could provide maritime air defence by 1970, but new

Airborne Early Warning (AEW) aircraft would not be available until 1973. For strike the Fleet would have to rely on the RAF acquiring the F-111. Finally, the Fleet would have no properly equipped ships of suitable size to carry out command and control functions.

By November 1965, the writing was on the wall for CVA-01. On the 25th, Healey produced a list of provisional political decisions to be used as a basis for planning force structures. In it there were two options for and against the retention of carrier capability. The "with carriers" option, with or without the development of the Buccaneer, set out a revised building plan for two ships, delaying the delivery dates for CVA-01 and CVA-02 to 1973 and 1979 respectively and using borrowed US carriers to fill the gap. The "without carriers" option declared that the RAF would provide 36 Phantoms for maritime duties; nuclear-powered hunter-killer submarines would not receive an anti-ship missile capability but short range missiles would be fitted for surface ships (Exocet); HMS *Hermes* would be retained until 1975 for ASW cover and Fleet AEW, supported by *Tiger*-class cruisers converted as ASW helicopter ships, which would be replaced by 'escort cruisers with a significant rotary-wing air capability". The "without carriers" option pointed tantalisingly toward a future 'CAH' but in practice, at this time neither option was affordable.

On 14th January 1966 Healey tabled three major papers, one of which was "*The Future of the Carrier Force*". In it, the Secretary of State proposed to cancel CVA-01 and reduce expenditure on fixed wing naval aviation, working out the lives of the existing carriers, with a last refit of HMS *Ark Royal* to see through the carrier force until the mid-1970s, giving the Navy a chance to reshape its force structure. Despite the last-minute adjustments the target budget of £2,000 million could not be reached and so, in purely financial terms, this was the only way in which the defence budget could be balanced without over-severe repercussions on the other services. To

Healey, the RAF with the F-111 could carry out many of the tasks, particularly when these were tailored to its capabilities, and the carrier was not worth the extra money. The final decision, whereby the RAF was to be given the F-111 and the carrier force was to be phased out, was endorsed in full Cabinet on 14th February 1966 and announced the following day. Only three weeks earlier, the Admiralty Board had both optimistically and in an attempt to force Healey's hand, approved the final design for CVA-01 and named the ship "HMS *Queen Elizabeth*", but Healey was unmoved. True to his salt, Sir David Luce resigned immediately following the cancellation of HMS *Queen Elizabeth*, to be followed quickly by the Minister for the Navy, Christopher Mayhew. Luce was replaced as First Sea Lord by Admiral of the Fleet Sir Varyl Begg, one of the few Naval opponents of the carrier.

Whilst the Navy's case was more or less well presented, and strongly based both on the successful history of carrier operations and accurate predictions of future needs, the evidence suggests that the Admiralty Board and Naval Staff were missing Lord Mountbatten's formidable and ruthless Whitehall skills that had protected them for the previous decade. They were working in an unfamiliar unified Ministry of Defence environment and lacked the policy support of the old Admiralty civil service. The Naval officers' relationship with Healey was more uneasy than that between the RAF's officers and the Secretary of State who was very impressed by the apparently sophisticated form of the RAF's case as much as its content. This was a game for players with little scruple rather than reasonable gentlemen. The whole long term viability of the East of Suez role was also coming under increasing pressure and expensive carriers based primarily on this scenario seemed a bad investment. A capability that would fade away in the mid 1970s would do. The progressive speeding up of East of Suez withdrawal with the 1968 decision to withdraw by 1971 meant the scrapping of all carriers (including the recently modernised *Ark Royal*) was brought forward to this earlier date.

Undoubtedly the 'complimentary' escort cruiser concept did little to help the argument for CVA-01, since it highlighted the vulnerability of the Fleet Carrier without rotary-wing anti-submarine helicopters or escorts armed with effective anti-air missiles, such as the *Type-82* destroyer. Even the largest carriers that would fit into British dockyards would be hard pressed to operate large anti-submarine helicopters in addition to the expected high performance fixed wing types of the future. It was thought, therefore, that a cruiser type ship with a hangar and flight deck would provide a valuable complimentary capability while also providing a useful extra command platform. The first direction from the Admiralty Board came on 28th July 1960 to investigate options for a small helicopter carrier that would be useful in both 'hot' and 'cold' war situations, with outline plans to be presented the following year. But these plans were muddled; in part due to the broad requirement set by the Admiralty Board for a new design that would be *"valuable for its own versatile capabilities and not depending for its justification simply, or even predominantly, on the carriage of ASW helicopters."* Numerous iterations were provided in the following years, with variations on the themes of escort cruisers/helicopter carriers, some of which were beginning to look, and sound, too much like proper carriers to assist the case for CVA-01.

The cruiser project was delayed by the Polaris programme, which led to two of the existing *Tiger*-class cruisers being converted to the new role. By the time drawing office staff could be redeployed to the project in the mid to late 1960s the ship had acquired a whole new significance. The Navy's future planners made the point that the loss of CVA-01 would greatly diminish the operational flexibility of the fleet but there were strong elements within the service, led by Varyl Begg, that were anxious not to reopen the carrier controversy. Begg set in train a Future Fleet

Working Party (FFWP) to investigate the possibility of creating a fleet without carriers by the mid-1970's when the current ships were expected to reach the end of their useful lives.

The FFWP was led by Rear Admiral John Adams, newly-promoted as the Assistant Chief of Naval Staff (Policy). Adams arrived at the Ministry of Defence a few months after Denis Healey cancelled CVA-01, having just finished a highly successful sea-command in the commando carrier HMS *Albion*, based in the Far East. Adams's *Albion* had the knack of being wherever there was a crisis, however minor, which led to the carrier being nicknamed 'The Old Grey Ghost'. The demand for her services and the wide range of her operations over thousands of miles of ocean convinced Adams of the versatility of such ships. Reporting directly to the First Sea Lord, Adams had both the Directors of Naval Plans and, to provide perspective, the Naval Historical Branch subordinated to him in order to reassess the role and structure of the Royal Navy. But when his working party recommended flat topped ships which would deploy helicopters and vertical take-off fighters, Begg was adamant that he did not want this. Adams insisted that it was the logical outcome of his inquiry, and Begg exploded with rage. He publicly rejected Adams's report, and privately told him that he would never be employed again. Adams was appointed CB and retired in 1968, but he was invited to the launch of *Invincible* in 1977, and his ideas for the shape and size of the fleet were vindicated over the next quarter-century.

Adams's conclusions echoed closely those of the 1965 Gap Study and of earlier studies in 1962, which had determined the need for CVA-01. Immediate response to the report suggested however that the Navy understood the different reality it faced over the coming decades. In an extraordinary about-face, within days of CVA-01's cancellation, the case for embarked aviation was voiced in terms that showed the Naval Staff had learned valuable lessons from the bruising Healey review. Captain Raymond Lygo, the Deputy Director Naval Air Warfare, in March 1966, wrote *"Progress in aeronautics had been such that future aircraft were expected to reduce in weight and complexity for any given staff requirement; AEW was the most important embarked role* and *VTOL strike fighters were now seen as having the potential to carry out their roles successfully from ships other than conventional carriers."*

The first recognisable designs for a "Commando Cruiser" (66)/75B, were presented to the FFWP on 24th April 1966 and resembled a scaled-down CVA-01. Costing about £30 million the ship was 645ft long, has a 100ft beam and displaced 15,000 tons. The main sensors were the Anglo-Dutch Type 988 surveillance radar and Type 909 trackers for directing the medium range GWS 30 Sea Dart anti-air missile system mounted aft of the flight deck. Other armament included the short range Sea Wolf missile mounted on the aft island and a Mark-8 4.5" gun mounted forward. An extended starboard island incorporated the hangar and the ship could operate six Sea King or four P1127 Kestrels and two helicopters. It also had the capacity to carry a Commando unit of 600 men and sufficient command and control facilities to act as a grade II flagship. The FFWP noted the design and called for further work to address its weaknesses. The main resulting changes were to be an increase in the number of aircraft from six to eighteen, allowing for some growth in aircraft weight, which required an internal hangar on four-deck accessed by an 'over-edge' aircraft lift aft. This change meant the Sea Dart launcher had to move forward, taking the place of the 4.5" gun which was struck from the design. Capacity also increased to 650 embarked marines and with greater range, speed and ballistic protection, the displacement crept past 17,000 tons and the revised cost leapt to £38 million. The plans continued to evolve but caused disquiet among the senior echelons of the Navy who could not reconcile the increasing cost of the Commando Cruiser and far less capability it offered versus the comparative value-for-money (£60 million), but cancelled, CVA-01.

It was not until Sir Michael le Fanu replaced Varyl Begg as First Sea Lord in 1968 that sufficient confidence returned to champion the ideas for a carrier-cruiser. Le Fanu, who had been Controller of the Navy in 1966 and a strong supporter of CVA-01 when it was cancelled, steered the cruiser design away from smaller, less capable ships toward larger designs with an unobstructed flight deck and starboard island, capable of operating STOVL aircraft. The latter, now known in its fully developed form as the Harrier, would be a vital asset in order to 'hack' shadowing aircraft, probe for surface targets and provide organic combat air power. There was no question of putting this suggestion forward as yet, however, as it would not have received support at the Chiefs of Staff level.

In keeping with their manifesto promise, the Conservative government of 1970 called for an evaluation into the feasibility of running-on the Navy's legacy fixed wing carriers. In truth, the offer came with no additional resources and so the review became an exercise in managing a wasting asset. HMS *Eagle* and HMS *Ark Royal* were to run onto 1979 and HMS *Hermes* was to convert to the commando carrier role after 1970. In the event, the Admiralty Board considered that the cost of delivering this plan would have delayed work on the command cruiser and so the decision was taken to extend only *Ark Royal*, which had recently been converted to operate Phantoms. HMS *Eagle*, in every way a better ship, was to be discarded: she was in need of an expensive and large refit for which the funds were not immediately available and the Navy could not afford the gap.

With the fate of the existing carrier force decided, attention returned to the command cruiser. The Board felt unable to seek political approval to design and build a true carrier and as the command cruiser seemed the only viable option, work on the design proceeded with some urgency. Naval Staff Requirement NSR7097, issued in its first definitive form in 1970, set out the requirement for the new ship. The ship was to: be capable of commanding a task force and controlling the operation of land-based aircraft; provide a flagship for a Force ASW commander of a NATO task group; be able to operate large helicopters for area anti-submarine defence, with organic air defence provided by an 'area' defence missile system. It must also be able to deploy STOVL aircraft providing a quick reaction contribution to limited air defence, probe and strike capabilities. In peacetime the NSR expected the ship to "*be deployed to provide a maritime presence for exercises and training throughout the NATO area, and as the flagship of Task Forces visiting other parts of the world*".

In general outline NSR7097 called for modest capabilities but very much a product of the late 1960's, the authors went into small detail that resulted in some shortcomings, which hamstrung the class in service. In particular, focussing on 'transition to war' rather than 'war fighting' itself left capacity constraints of ammunition stocks and types that could be stowed, with tedious limitations on flexibility.

The plans developed to meet NSR7097 eventually resulted in the *Invincible*-class. The design allowed a long hangar on four-deck able to accommodate the Sea King and its replacement expected in 1975; an unobstructed flight deck and the possibility of operating Harriers with sufficient uncommitted space for the design to 'absorb' them. The design finally emerged as a 19,500 ton ship with an excessively large starboard island and narrow flight deck, just big enough to allow the launch and recovery of STOVL aircraft. Unlike previous cruiser options, the round down over an enclosed bow was replaced by an open forecastle on which was installed an anti-ship battery with Exocet. Above this, a Sea Dart launcher was located in the most inconvenient place relative to the aircraft parking area forward of the island.

The ship was to be capable of operating nine Sea Kings and five Harriers, all of which could be stowed in the hangar; although this complement grew steadily through the design phase such that the final tally was 22 mixed aircraft stowed in the hangar and on the flight deck. The lack of hangar space and personnel accommodation caused AEW, described in 1966 as the most important role, to be deleted from the requirement during the design phase. Early experience was to show how short sighted this decision was. Politically, the displacement was limited below 20,000 tons which meant having to design a very light structure to enclose the ship's relatively voluminous envelope. The heavy 'over-edge' aircraft lifts gave way to novel, lightweight internal lifts (one of the few original design features retained from CVA-01) but these took up considerable volume in the hangar. Four Rolls-Royce Olympus TM3B gas turbines, marine variants of those used in Concorde, provided the power through huge reversing gearboxes driving two shafts, making the class the most powerful warship (per shaft) ever built for the Navy. The engines offered a common solution with contemporary frigate and destroyer propulsion designs, but at the expense of requiring uptakes five-times the cross sectional area of the equivalent steam or diesel-electric plants. The twin-funnel arrangement produced a disproportionately long island while the encroachment of the machinery lifts and uptakes gave the hangar a 'wasp-waisted' layout. The most unsatisfactory feature of the design however was the diminutive flight deck, further limited by the intrusive and notoriously unreliable lifts. The need for a wide deck to allow vertical landings, by fighters or helicopters, at any angle across the deck with the ship 'out of wind' was clearly understood from early designs in 1956, but inexplicably never incorporated in the final design. As a result, like all earlier carriers, the CAH would be forced to turn into wind for virtually every recovery.

Just before leaving office in 1970, Denis Healey approved the first of the new cruisers and a public announcement was made in February 1971. The designation "through deck cruiser" was given to the ship, but was immediately seized upon by the RAF as a "see through carrier", with senior officers ridiculing the contortions undertaken to avoid using the politically emotive term "carrier". The change of government meant that the idea had to be sold over again to his Conservative successor, Lord Carrington. This was done, but in the context of the financial climate of the early years of the Heath administration it was a harder job selling the idea to the Treasury. It was not until 17th April 1973 that the first ship, HMS *Invincible*, was ordered from Vickers Shipbuilding at Barrow-in-Furness. By 1973, the decision to operate the new Sea Harrier had led to the removal of the Exocet battery and the MOD's 1973 model more closely resembled the ship as completed than did successive Vickers publicity drawings. The only major difference between the MoD design of 1973 and the ship that entered service five years later was the introduction of the 'ski-jump', an idea of Lieutenant Commander Doug Taylor. However, it took a further two years and some hard advocacy by the new First Sea Lord, Admiral of the Fleet Sir Edward Ashmore, before he could convince the Wilson Government to actually order the aircraft. Ashmore was however unwilling to create a crisis with the RAF over organic AEW as he feared that if he did the RAF would oppose the new anti-submarine helicopter destined for service by the mid 1970s.

The second ship of the class, ordered on 14th May 1976, received another old carrier name: "*Illustrious*". The third of the class was to have been "*Indomitable*", but public outcry at the demise of the old *Ark Royal* caused a change of heart by the Admiralty Board. On 30th November 1978, the Board signalled Captain Anson in *Ark Royal* IV as she returned to Portsmouth for the final time to pay off, to tell him their decision "*that CAH-03 shall be named Ark Royal.*"

Two days later, Fred Mulley, the Minister of Defence announced the order for the fifth HMS *Ark Royal*, to be built on the Tyne. The retention of the famous old name carefully spiked the guns of the preservation lobby that was keen to preserve the old *Ark Royal* in some capacity or another. The original NATO designation for the class was 'CAH' however following the decision to operate the Sea Harrier from the deck and the tacit acceptance that it was in fact an aircraft carrier, by the time of HMS *Invincible*'s commissioning in 1981, the official designation became 'CVS', for 'ASW Support Aircraft Carrier'. By the mid-1980's, the designator 'CVSA' came into vogue, reflecting the ships' utility as attack/assault assets depending on the type of air group embarked. Latterly, however, the designation settled down as 'CVSG', the 'G' standing for 'Guided Missile' and reflecting retention of a Sea Dart area defence anti-air guided missile capability, a relic of the original cruiser concept.

HMS *Ark Royal* V began life on 9th December 1978 when the first section of the keel was laid in the Wallsend Yard of Swan Hunter Shipbuilders Ltd. The official keel-laying ceremony took place five days later. Over the next 18 months sections which had been prefabricated were moved onto the berth and the ship began to take shape. By mid 1981 the hull was complete and most of the masts and superstructure were in place. The new *Ark Royal* was launched by Her Majesty Queen Elizabeth the Queen Mother on 2nd June 1981, to the delight of thousands of Tynesiders. As sponsor of *Ark Royal* IV, Her Majesty had always taken a great interest in the Fleet Air Arm visiting the ship as often as possible, and she wished to maintain this close relationship with the new ship also.

The future of the new aircraft carriers was examined in the defence review led by Secretary of State John Nott in 1981, following Mrs Thatcher's order that the country's defence policy had to be brought under some kind of financial discipline. Nott quickly lost faith in the Naval Staff's approach to the review and was advised that the best way of carrying out the primary NATO role of anti-submarine warfare in the North Atlantic would be by hunter-killer submarines and towed array frigates, supported by RAF Nimrod maritime patrol aircraft. The Government was however committed to placing a greater emphasis on contingencies outside the NATO area and these commitments would be undertaken by a reduced CVS force of two ships. In early 1981, Nott refused to give a commitment that *Ark Royal* would go into service, admitting that the ship would never have been ordered had the decision been taken in 1981, giving rise to speculation that the ship might not be completed or would go immediately into reserve. By the time of *Ark*'s launch, Nott grudgingly confirmed that she would *"proceed to completion"* but rumours of a planned sale of at least one CVS to Australia were rife. In December 1981, the government was forced to confirm that official talks with Australian officials had taken place.

The Argentine invasion of the Falkland Islands in April 1982 caused a change in policy. The Argentines, like many commentators, had clearly not read the Nott Review statement, 'The Way Forward' which stated the intention to periodically deploy the new carriers in the South Atlantic. *Invincible*, along with the old *Hermes* now operating as an interim CVS, were the keys to the islands being retaken. It was therefore decided to retain all three carriers in order to be sure of deploying two.

HMS *Ark Royal* was thus finally safeguarded and the massive task of outfitting her compartments continued apace at Wallsend. In September 1982 the ship docked for five weeks to install the propellers, rudders and stabilisers. Emerging from dock in November, *Ark* remained at Wallsend until May 1983 when a move up river to Walker Yard was undertaken to vacate her berth for the new MV *Atlantic Conveyor*, ordered as a replacement for the ship that had been sunk in the South Atlantic a year earlier. Fitting out was extended both to delay *Ark*'s final delivery, in order to re-profile the project cost, but also to incorporate all of the design lessons identified during the Falklands conflict. The ski jump originally fitted in *Invincible* and *Illustrious* had a 7-degree angle, but the 12-degree ramp in HMS *Hermes* proved to be more effective, giving the Sea Harrier a greater take-off weight and so a larger ramp was fitted to *Ark*. AEW was, finally, considered an 'essential' capability and changes to the hangar, planning and briefing rooms and accommodation were needed for the squadron staff and aircrews to operate Sea King AEW helicopters.

The Falklands War had highlighted the need for effective defence against anti-ship missile attack and this was to be provided by a Close-In Weapons System. HMS *Invincible* and HMS *Illustrious* were hastily fitted with Vulcan Phalanx guns on the fo'c'sle and starboard aft corner of the flight deck; *Ark Royal* had her mounts designed on purpose built sponsons. The forward mount, situated up on the bow in front of the Sea Dart launcher required weather protection and so a larger swept bulwark was fitted. The Flying Control (FlyCo) position on the port side of the bridge was cramped and so a revised and enlarged FlyCo was built. Accommodation, hangar and workshop spaces were also improved. In accordance with contemporary policy, *Ark Royal* was fitted to carry the WE-177 nuclear weapon although, in keeping with the policy of the time, it was never confirmed or denied that she was actually in possession of these. This later led to various demonstrations against the ship during port visits and, coupled with the extra security measures the weapons demanded, made them perhaps more trouble that they were worth.

In Walker Yard the ship slowly came alive. Machinery started to run, installed lighting and ventilation were commissioned and the web of temporary pipes, trunks and hoses began to be withdrawn. The main engines were turned tentatively for the first time on 3rd May 1984. In July, the ship was docked for the second time to allow a complete shot blasting of the hull and the application of the distinctive plum and grey underwater paint.

The Ship's Company, led initially by Commander H R Evans, joined from June 1982 and by mid-1984 their numbers reached fifty. Among the first was Warrant Officer David Blackburn, a veteran of the previous *Ark Royal*, who joined as the Warrant Officer Shipwright and became the first President of the Warrant Officers and Senior Rates Mess, such as it was. The first mess was formed in the rented house in Cullercoats occupied by the three Marine Engineering Warrant Officers, but these humble beginnings did not stop the '*Ark* spirit' being reignited, with very strong relations built with the Swan Hunter workers. When the ship sailed on 19th October 1984 for Contractor's Sea Trials, 111 Ship's Company were onboard working alongside the shipbuilders and Naval Overseers. The sea trials were a resounding success, completed in two weeks instead of the programmed three. In addition to the official programme, a number of other milestones were achieved, including the first fifty deck landings; the inaugural Wardroom Trafalgar Night Dinner and a Ship's Operatic and Drama Society – "SODS" – Opera, staged in the hangar. Most of the shipyard workers turned cabaret acts for the evening, but the Ship's Company played their part, led by the "Singing Warrant Officers" (Messrs Gibson, Griffiths, Hamilton and Blackburn) who composed 'The Swan Song', sung to the tune of the Eton Boating Song.

On completion of sea trials the ship returned to Walker Yard with eight months remaining to finish 1400 compartments, set to work and test the machinery and weapon systems, and tune and balance the multitude of independent water, air and power plants. The last docking at Hebburn Dock was followed by the Final Machinery Trials period in early 1985, to prove again that the ship's propulsion machinery was in peak condition. The weapon sensors and communications systems were also brought to acceptance standard, although Phalanx was not yet fitted, nor had Sea Dart been fired in anger. Work toward final inspection continued at an ever increasing pace. Over a thousand personnel inspected, cleaned and polished the ship so that it could leave the Swan Hunter yard on time. In part, the urgency to meet the deadline was caused by nervousness that the Board planned to close the Walker Yard as soon as *Ark Royal* was finished and that if delayed, the ship may end up in the middle of an unsightly dispute between management, unions and the workforce. The ship was ready to sail by the end of June 1985, but only just. She left Tyneside on 28th June for her new home at Portsmouth. On route, the Commodore Naval Ship Acceptance and his staff inspected the 'finished' article. Despite the countless unfinished jobs and minor teething troubles, he declared himself content: on 1st July 1985 HMS *Ark Royal* was ready to join the Fleet and formally accepted into Naval service.

Vice Admiral Sir James Weatherall KCVO KCB DL

(Commanding Officer 1985 – 1987)

In late 1983, while Captain F8 driving HMS *Andromeda* I was told that, all things being equal, I would be the first Captain of the fifth HMS *Ark Royal*. Having been the Commander of the much loved fourth this was great news indeed. After the short rest in between I led the Royal Navy Presentation Team while the Commander, Nigel Essenhigh, "specially selected for the job", brought the *Ark* out of build. One hundred presentations, fifty radio and twenty television interviews later I arrived (fresh as paint) at the last possible moment to prise the *Ark* out of Nigel's extremely capable and very reluctant grasp!

After basic completion of the build, sea trials and with every help from Swan Hunter in very difficult circumstances, we accepted the ship with her internal state still far from beautiful (as Neil Rankin will well remember – his face was a picture!) It was a calculated risk and proved to be the right decision. We had already set ourselves the hugely ambitious target of New York, 4th July 1986 for the re-unveiling of the Statue of Liberty.

The trials period and work-up all had to be completed first however. The programme was brilliantly masterminded, squeezed and managed by Rees Ward, Commander (WE). With Nigel's planning, drive and initiative and Doug Lewis' special talent for "fixing" everything as Commander (S) we kept on track; but only just. We drove the *Ark* like a frigate and enjoyed ourselves enormously.

Compared with our sisters we had much youth and inexperience, particularly among the officers. What was missing in professional expertise was made up for in sheer hard work and fierce, joyous enthusiasm. The very name *Ark Royal* conjured up an amazingly happy and determined team spirit which was almost inspirational.

At the anniversary officers' dinner five years later after our headlong sprint start, John Brigstocke, then in command, asked me with a smile how on earth I ran the ship with this motley lot. Seeing them at play just as they were five years before I can quite see why! We were living proof that a mixed bag of delightful characters of varying ability plus a few absolutely outstanding people can achieve truly great results. The Ship's Company responded well to huge pressure and we all supported each other. We made New York in tremendous style and achieved much more besides. I believe we gave the *Ark* the cracking start she needed and deserved.

Chapter 2

1985 – 1987:
A new ship and a new beginning

To fanfares of welcome and huge publicity, HMS *Ark Royal* arrived at Portsmouth for the first time on 1st July 1985. Honoured by a flypast of the Fleet Air Arm Historic Flight, a Sea Harrier and Sea King helicopters that would later embark as her air wing, and with her Ship's Company marched onboard in the traditional manner, she was accepted into service the same day.

The ship looked outwardly impressive, but beneath the surface she hid over 10,000 defects that had not been cleared during build at Swan Hunter's and her first Commanding Officer, Captain James Weatherall, recognised before sailing from Tyneside that he had a significant task on his hands to bring the ship up to in-service standard. To achieve it, some 140 Swan Hunter employees, including forty women cleaners remained at work on the ship for the next two weeks, while the Ship's Company undertook an intensive training programme to prepare the new carrier for trials and safety assessment. Much good will, hard work and tolerance on both sides achieved the required standard, readying *Ark Royal* to sail on 15th July for an arduous series of sea acceptance trials and shakedown. The initial aviation trials involving two Sea Harriers and four Sea Kings, designed to prove the ship's aircraft landing aids and communications, were completed successfully followed by a well-deserved stand-off for the Ship's Company at anchor in Torbay. Flag Officer Sea Training staff embarked at Torbay to conduct a two-week Safety Operational Sea Training (SOST) package. SOST proved that the Ship's Company could effectively respond to peacetime emergencies onboard and as such was a necessary milestone for them to achieve clearance to commence the more intensive Part IV sea trials following summer leave.

Media interest in *Ark Royal* remained intense throughout the summer, as television, radio and print outlets clamoured for access to the Royal Navy's newest carrier. The BBC's "Tomorrow's World" and ITV's "Game for a Laugh" both recorded onboard, as did every major British television news programme. Print articles appeared in The Times, Daily Telegraph, Daily Mail and Daily Mirror, as well as over 30 regional newspapers as far North as Glasgow, while visitors from across the country were welcomed onboard by the Ship's Company who enthusiastically embraced their new found celebrity. The ship formed the star attraction at Navy Days in August, opening her gangways to 32,000 visitors over two days. She was also the showpiece for the Royal Navy Equipment Exhibition held at Portsmouth in September.

Swan Hunter's staff again swarmed over the ship to remedy outstanding defects, reducing the outstanding number to about 800. Acceptance trials followed in late October, to assess the performance of the ship's combat system, the Action Data Automation Weapons System, or ADAWS for short. Most of *Ark*'s combat system was shared with the *Type-42* destroyer, including the same principal weapon, the Sea Dart guided missile system, the same radars in R1022, R992 and R909 and the same hull-mounted sonar in S2016. Sadly, ADAWS proved no more reliable in *Ark* than it was in the destroyers and its trials had to be cut short due to software problems. Unusually for the time of year, doldrums in the exercise area meant that trials to model wind patterns across the flight deck, needed to understand the launch and recovery limitations for aircraft taking off and landing also had to be curtailed; the ship thus returned to Portsmouth on 23rd to try to fix ADAWS and to prepare for her commissioning.

HMS *Ark Royal* was commissioned on 1st November 1985 at Portsmouth in the presence of Her Majesty Queen Elizabeth the Queen Mother and with every surviving Commanding Officer of the ship's forebears keeping a watchful eye over proceedings; Captain Weatherall reported confidently that *Ark Royal* already showed "*much to give encouragement for the future*". Having achieved this significant milestone, thoughts now turned to the next key target: New York on 4th July 1986, to mark the unveiling of the newly refurbished Statue of Liberty. This had been Captain Weatherall's target since joining and the Heads of Department were firmly on track to meet it.

Three days after commissioning, *Ark Royal* sailed for the Mediterranean to take advantage of the good weather to be expected there to continue sea trials. First-of-Class Flying Trials of the unique twelve-degree ski ramp took up most of November with two Sea Harriers completing over fifty sorties to prove the design that would be retrofitted in HMS *Invincible* and HMS *Illustrious*, and the new aircraft landing aid 'MADGE', which had been the subject of the "Tomorrow's World" broadcast earlier in the year. On 13th November, the ship made a poignant rendezvous off Gibraltar, near the spot where *Ark Royal* III sank having been attacked by the German submarine U-81 on the same date in 1941. The Ship's Company held a

short commemorative service and laid a wreath, perhaps for the first time reflecting on the legacy they had inherited from their predecessors and the Spirit of the Ark that now lived on in them.

From Gibraltar, which matelots never consider as a proper foreign run-ashore, HMS *Ark Royal* called at Marseilles at the end of November, for her first oversees visit. The Consul General, David Gladstone was keen to make the most of *Ark Royal*'s presence and set a very hot pace of diplomatic engagements. Next stop on the short Mediterranean adventure was Crete, for the ship to undertake ranging at the NATO FORACS range at Souda Bay. The ship made her first "*opposed berthing*", Captain Weatherall "*brushing aside the efforts of four determined Greek tugs which posed a serious menace to ships handling, in to a tightly restrained, badly fendered, angled jetty.*" Careful diplomacy with the Greek authorities ensured that everyone enjoyed Crete to its fullest extent. The island provided a welcome diversion for the Ship's Company who shirked off the winter blues at home with an out-of-season opportunity to don tropical rig. Only a few casualties were sustained, mostly from scooter accidents. As one sailor admitted to Captain Weatherall, he "*was looking at the very pretty girl instead of the pot holes!*" In general, the deployment to Crete and back was a great success, not least in consolidating a strong sense of team spirit among the Ship's Company and in the view of the Captain, the trip taught "*a lot of very young men how to live in a ship at sea*".

After Christmas leave the last series of equipment trials, this time on the Type 909 tracking radars and the still troublesome ADAWS were completed in home waters. A port visit to Amsterdam in early February allowed for much serious diplomacy with the Royal Netherlands Navy at the higher level, whereas further down the city offered its excellent facilities to suit all tastes. With the final trials and some last-minute defect repairs completed in Portsmouth, on 20th February 1986, HMS *Ark Royal* passed her Operational Date Material Assessment and could be declared fully operational.

The eight-month period since leaving Swan Hunter's had bonded the Ship's Company into a coherent fighting unit; in Captain Weatherall's view *"what Ark Royal lacks in experience (which is quite a lot) she compensates for in her enthusiasm and I believe she is ready to move on in good material state to join the Fleet."* The opportunity to prove this decisively came straight away, when *Ark Royal* embarked her aircraft - 801 Squadron with six Sea Harriers and 820 Squadron with nine Sea King 'Jezebel' (SKJ) anti-submarine variants - and sailed to Portland for Basic Operational Sea Training. Four weeks later, Flag Officer Sea Training gave the ship a "Satisfactory" assessment, leaving the Commanders to reflect on their individual department performances, which ranged from "Good" to "Below Standard".

HMS *Ark Royal* once again attracted media attention throughout the spring. The then fledgling TV-AM featured the ship on 24th to 26th February while on passage to Portland. A half-page feature on the ship appeared in The Radio Times on 3rd April and on 7th April the BBC "Pebble Mill at One" programme was filmed onboard, attracting an audience of over four million viewers, while BBC Radio 2 broadcast live from the ship throughout the day. The following day, The Queen Mother paid a private visit to the ship to witness the air group embarkation, before flying off by helicopter in the afternoon. The ship then proceeded north through the Irish Sea into the North West Approaches, to conduct the final and most important phase of training and assessment: Air Group Work Up.

Under the eye of the staff from the Third Flotilla, the Sea Harriers provided continuous air patrols while the SKJs hunted the nuclear-powered attack submarines HMS *Churchill* and HMS *Superb*, both squadrons working against cold and variable weather in as realistic a warfare environment as could be achieved in peacetime. In these challenging conditions, *Ark* suffered her first aircraft casualty. Sea Harrier XZ491, flown by

Lieutenant Commander Andy Sinclair RN who had been seconded from 800 Squadron for the Work Up, crashed into the sea off Benbecula, some 55 miles from the ship. Following navigation instrument failure and misdirection back to the ship, Sinclair's aircraft ran out of fuel and he was forced to ditch; thankfully he was recovered safely. Despite this setback the rest of Work Up proceeded well and on 23rd April, *Ark* achieved a "Satisfactory" assessment at her Operational Readiness Inspection. Her air group disembarked and the ship returned to Portsmouth for early summer leave and a Base Assisted Maintenance Period.

During the period alongside, the final notable addition to *Ark*'s weapons fit was completed with the installation of the three Vulcan Phalanx Close-In Weapons Systems. What Captain Weatherall described as *"confidence-lowering"* cracks found in a hull sea chest in the Aft Engine Room were repaired in dock, while the SCOT II satellite communications domes were also strengthened. With the last repairs completed, the final reading of the D448 took place on 10th June 1986, formally severing the ship's ties with Swan Hunter. Captain Weatherall reported on an excellent meeting with the ship's builder; it had been a reaffirmation of the *"strong and happy liaison"* with the company.

On 17th June 1986, HMS *Ark Royal* sailed from Portsmouth for her first deployment. She embarked her full air group for the first time as 801 Squadron and 820 Squadron were now joined by three AEW Sea King 'Whiskey' (SKW) helicopters from 849 'B' Flight. The SKWs were more commonly referred to as the 'Bags' on account of the ungainly inflatable radar dome fixed to the starboard side of the aircraft that was rotated into position once in-flight. Three days were spent conducting trials of the Phalanx mounts while hosting a series of visiting VIPs, including George Younger, the Secretary of State for Defence. Having said "goodbye" to the 'tourists', *Ark Royal* said "hello" to her task group; the *Leander*-class frigates HMS *Cleopatra* and HMS *Sirius* and the Royal Fleet

Auxiliaries *Resource* and *Olna*, for Exercise LIBERTY TRAIN, en-route to New York. Joined also by the hunter-killer submarine HMS *Churchill* in the deep water of the South West Approaches, the task group conducted four days of Anti-Submarine Warfare (ASW) exercises before *Churchill* departed and the surface units made a fast passage West from the Azores.

HMS *Ark Royal* arrived in New York, as planned over a year earlier, on 28th June 1986 and the Ship's Company enjoyed eight days in the heart of Manhattan. On 2nd July *Ark* sailed to regroup with her escorts before making a ceremonial re-entry the following day to her anchorage, in preparation for the unveiling of the Statue of Liberty and the International Fleet Review. The ship played host to the American Secretary of Defence, Mr Caspar Weinberger, at dinner that evening, who was accompanied by the British Ambassador. Independence Day was the spectacle the Ship's Company had hoped it would be and represented repayment in full for the year-long trials and tribulations they had gone through to get the ship there on time. In the fine traditions of the Fleet Air Arm and as only the Sea Harrier could do, two jets from 801 Squadron provided a unique spectacle ahead of the main flypast including hovering in front of the grand lady and 'bowing' to her, to the delight of the American audience. *Ark* sailed from New York on 8th July, having fittingly ended the first year of the ship's life in the style that would become her hallmark.

The main war role of the CVS in the 1980s and early 1990s was to act as an anti-submarine Command Platform for NATO's recently re-designated Anti Submarine Warfare Striking Force (ASWSTRIKFOR), then under the command of Flag Officer Third Flotilla, Vice Admiral Julian Oswald. The new emphasis on deep field ASW in support of the NATO Striking Fleet was facilitated by the deployment in RN frigates of highly effective passive towed array sonar systems, with helicopter-borne torpedoes and depth charges used to attack the submarines. Consequently, *Ark*'s

largest element of her air wing comprised of nine SKJ ASW helicopters, with the three SKWs and six Sea Harriers borne primarily for airborne surveillance and self-defence of the task group. The remainder of 1986 would see a series of increasingly challenging ASW exercises on both sides of the Atlantic, to provide *Ark*'s crew the opportunity to hone their ASW skills and smooth the interfaces between them and FOF3's command staff.

ASWEX 1/86 en-route from New York to Fort Lauderdale; Trial BASTE 86 at the Atlantic Underwater Test and Evaluation Centre (AUTEC) off Andros Island in the Bahamas, and finally Exercise NORTHERN ENGAGEMENT on the return Atlantic crossing all offered a chance to develop the ASW expertise and allow confidence to grow between the units and the command team. In between, the Ship's Company made the most of the last stops in the USA, at Fort Lauderdale at the end of July, and Norfolk in the middle of August. These exercises were the prelude to the year's major NATO exercise NORTHERN WEDDING. *Ark Royal* and her group made a fast and silent passage to the Greenland-Iceland-UK-Gaps (the GRIUK), and then stayed in theatre for four weeks, avoiding enemy contact through emission control of the ships' transmitters and radars and by the use of operational deception. Operations began to sanitise the GRIUK of nearby submarines, to open a passage for the ships following in the main Striking Fleet. Sea Harrier availability was disappointing and the spares required to keep them airborne stretched the supply lines to breaking point, however an air bridge to Norway helped the air wing achieve its missions of hunting the submarines while keeping *Ark* and the striking force safe from air attack. This strategy and the dispersion of the task group ships placed a great strain on air defence. The ASW operations were, however, a great success, giving confidence that the group could take on and defeat the Soviet submarine force that would be drawn out to engage the Striking Fleet as a whole. *Ark Royal*'s Captain considered the ship had done well and that the exercise had shown that *"we had finished the process of growing up and were a fully paid up member of the team"*. The Ship's Company made the most of the task group visit to Amsterdam while the various command teams engaged with the NATO commander in the usual 'back-slapping' at the post-exercise wash-up.

Following a short maintenance period, *Ark* sailed from Portsmouth on 13th October for Exercise AUTUMN TRAIN under the Command of Rear Admiral Richard Thomas, Flag Officer Second Flotilla, flying his flag in the HMS *Bristol* the only *Type-82* destroyer ever built of the aborted escorts for CVA-01. AUTUMN TRAIN consisted of more anti-submarine serials under the guise of ASWEX 2/86 combined with a significant anti-air warfare element, with a high percentage of 'in-contact' time and unalerted detections at considerable ranges. The Sea Dart system successfully completed a High Seas Firing giving confidence to the operators and maintainers alike, and the exercise was marred only by the loss of Sea King HAS-5 ZD632 from 820 Squadron, piloted by Lieutenant Phillip Thicknesse, which ditched after an engine explosion while recovering from a check test flight. Lieutenant Thicknesse and his two crewmates escaped from the wreckage and were winched to safety but the helicopter sank rapidly before salvage could be effected.

A standoff at Gibraltar from 23rd to 27th October saw *Ark Royal* transformed into a concert venue for filming "*Ark Royal – The Rock Show*" to be shown by Granada TV as part of their Christmas Day schedule. Aircraft handlers turned roadies and stewards turned backing singers and dancers for Bob Geldof, Paul Young, Alison Moyet and Cindy Lauper, in the way only matelots can. With a 'wrap' declared on Sunday evening, the staging and equipment were dismantled through the night, and before dawn the following morning *Ark Royal* sailed for Lisbon for a goodwill visit and a few days rest prior to the next exercise.

From ASW Strike, HMS *Ark Royal* hastily regrouped to exercise her secondary role as an interim amphibious helicopter assault ship or 'LPH', standing for 'Landing Platform Helicopter' in UK-parlance. Two days after leaving Lisbon, *Ark* took up station off Cornwall to disembark 820 Squadron's SKJs to Culdrose and to pick up the Sea King Mk4s of 845 Squadron, as well as the Commodore Amphibious Warfare, Commodore Jeremy Larkin, before heading up the Irish Sea. Sailing up the Clyde, *Ark* operated off the Tail O' the Bank while the Dutch First Amphibious Combat Group embarked by helicopter from Garelochhead. The exercise, HIGH TIDE, demonstrated the flexibility of the CVS to undertake its alternative role, and also its ability to adapt to prevailing conditions. Responding to bad weather on the west coast that stopped the exercise, the ship sailed round the north of Scotland and instead landed the troops near Arbroath. At the end of HIGH TIDE the Dutch marines went ashore at Valkenburg in the Netherlands and the ship continued on for a pre-Christmas visit to Hamburg. Although most took full benefit of the city, a few ventured further afield including the first organised visit by the the 17th/21st Lancers, *Ark*'s affiliated Army regiment, then based at Munster.

Back in her core ASW role by the start of 1987, HMS *Ark Royal*'s first effort of the year was Exercise CARIBTRAIN in the West Indies. Sailing on 6th January she tried to leave behind a country in the grip of the "Big Freeze". Sadly, events conspired against the ship and the squadrons of her air group could not so easily free themselves from the wintry conditions. 820 Squadron and 849 'B' Flight were both grounded by heavy snow at Culdrose and *Ark* had to make a hasty return to Portsmouth to rectify the aft aircraft lift that had failed leaving it stuck at an angle of twenty-degrees and closing the flight deck. Second time lucky, *Ark* embarked her helicopters and made it safely out of Portsmouth, making best speed to the exercise areas. Once there, she met up with her by now familiar playmate HMS *Churchill* and the towed array *Leander*-class frigate, HMS *Argonaut* and then struggled through very bad weather to make the most of ASWEX 1/87 Part 1. Putting west on 21st January, *Ark* battled through the Atlantic at its wintry worst with her escorts in company, heading for Barbados.

Passing the Azores on 26th January the ship suddenly experienced flooding forward in Alpha section. The heavy seas had forced off a section of plating in the bow. Emergency response teams acted quickly to contain the flooding and the ship was able to continue to Barbados for temporary repairs.

Despite the last-minute excitement of the transatlantic passage, Captain Weatherall had brought the ship to an enviable level of operational capability. Nearly at the end of his period in command, he reviewed what had been achieved and gave a prescient assessment of the public perception of *Ark Royal* that remained true throughout her life: *"The ship continues to be the centre of attention wherever she goes, the fan mail arrives with every post bag and public relations and visitors occupy much time and effort. Provided we keep our balance and make certain that our professional standards are of a first class order, I believe that we should continue to give a high priority to showing the World that the Royal Navy is effective, efficient, smart and cheerful and has a real role to play in the defence of our country and our alliance. It is just as important to give taxpayers the correct impression as it is to convince ministers. We need all the support we can get."*

Rear Admiral M G T Harris BA JP

(Commanding Officer 1987 – 1989)

As I sit down in April 2010 to reflect again on my time in command of *Ark Royal*, it is now 21 years to the day that I left her and over 18 since I left the Royal Navy. From a busy life 'outside' it is difficult to look back and recall the detail of what went on between February 1987 when I joined in Barbados and April 1989 when I left. What is easy to remember though is that command of the *Ark* is the finest job in the Royal Navy and that those two years marked the real beginning of her operational life as a new ship. We worked hard but, in doing so, had the satisfaction of seeing the world rather more than most of the Navy of the eighties. The West Indies, the USA, Northern Europe, the Mediterranean, Suez, the Indian Ocean, the Far East and Australia all saw the *Ark* in that period.

In trying to pick out the highlights I hope I can help others who read this to recall their own particular memories of their time in the Navy's greatest ship, taken against a background of the highest standard of operating by all twelve hundred people onboard which never wavered. Having said that, the Tortola Banyan Fiasco, as it was called, was quite a challenge. Landing 600 people a day on a remote beach for a barbeque from a big ship with few boats takes some doing but the results were spectacular in terms of rest, recreation and suntans. June 1987 saw us moored off Deptford where the first *Ark* had been launched 400 years before. Negotiating the Thames Barrier left me feeling like the driver of a car who has just survived a foolishly narrow escape: he is determined not to repeat it. On this occasion we had to, but not until we had hosted a huge White Ensign Association dinner in the hangar for 700 guests including Princess Alexandra and dozens of other VIPs.

Another incident in 1987 that springs to mind, which lasted two hours from start to finish, began on a beautiful summer's evening off the Orkneys as we were coming home at the end of our Aviation Workup. The Coastguard reported that a German trawler was taking in water off the Pentland Firth. Helicopters with damage control parties were launched and the ship followed as fast as she could. The Hessen had actually struck a rock and was mortally wounded. The teams did what they could and ensured the crew got off. *Ark* arrived to see the skipper being winched off as his ship sank beneath him. Warrant Officer Benton was left to swim gently off in a dignified fashion before he too was rescued. Minutes later there was nothing to be seen except for the calm sunlit sea.

8th February 1988 was the 25th anniversary of the first STOVL landing and take off on the fourth *Ark Royal* and it was a pleasure to welcome onboard the original test pilot, Bill Bedford, who was flown out in a 2-seat Harrier for the day. His aircraft also allowed me to experience a launch and landing, a unique experience for a submariner in an era of single seat jet aircraft. 1988 was also the year when the Admiral's dining cabin finally looked like one thanks to the generosity of Sir Donald Gosling who has been a benefactor to the ship in all sorts of ways. The timing was excellent as that was the year of the Australian Bicentennial celebrations to which we had been invited. We were away from June to December and, apart from the highlight of the spectacular Naval Salute in Sydney in October, we visited Malta (St. Paul's Bay because of political problems), Singapore (Station leave and Mrs Thatcher for lunch), Subic Bay (USS *New Jersey*'s 16-inch broadside fired), Hong Kong (vibrant), Brisbane (Expo '88), Fremantle (recover from Sydney), Bombay (wealth and poverty) and Gibraltar (rabbits). On arrival at Fremantle after we had been prevented from entering Melbourne by some Union antics the Press wanted to know what I thought of it. They enjoyed the answer: "Melbourne, where's that?"

It was my greatest privilege to have commanded *Ark*, not least to have served with so many wonderful people. There is, of course, a great sense of history bound up with the name, the first ship becoming *Royal* because she was bought from Sir Walter Raleigh by Her Majesty Queen Elizabeth I to help fend off the Spanish Armada. For me this was epitomised during my first visit to the ship of our sponsor, Her Majesty Queen Elizabeth the Queen Mother, when she said to me by means of casual conversation, "*of course, I have launched the last two Ark Royals*". There is no answer to that!

Chapter 3

1987 - 1989:
Down to business – Out and Back!

During the impromptu repairs at Barbados, on 3rd February 1987, Captain Mike Harris, a former submarine commander who joined the ship from a posting on the Central Staff in the Ministry of Defence, succeeded Captain Weatherall in command of HMS *Ark Royal*.

Captain Harris quickly brought his submarine experience to bear as the series of exercises under the CARIBTRAIN 'umbrella' continued. He took the ship out on 9th February for ASWEX 1/87 Parts 2 and 3, either side of a major FLEETEX with the United States Navy and weapon tests at AUTEC Bahamas, under Trial PUNISH.

FLEETEX commenced for the UK contingent on 13th February 1987, with High Seas Firings against a variety of airborne craft, including for the first time Sea Dart going up against the new, very high speed Petrel target, with further firings against Chukar and Stiletto targets. In the event, *Ark Royal* did not get the chance to engage the Petrel, but at least the ship's R909 radars tracked it successfully during its flight in a very demanding geometry. *Ark*'s Sea Dart scored a notable success in downing a Chukar target that had survived five American Standard missiles, but the missiles fired subsequently against the Stiletto malfunctioned and splashed before they engaged.

Overall, the CARIBTRAIN exercise provided a good variety and balance of weapon training and flying including some spectacularly accurate live 1,000-lb bombing by 801 Squadron on the Vieques bomb range. Between actions the ship visited Tortola in the British Virgin Islands, San Juan in American-owned Puerto Rico; Mayport, the American carrier home port in Florida and Charleston, South Carolina. The visit to San Juan was an especially important piece of 'flag waving' diplomacy; *Ark Royal*'s presence as an ambassador helping to promote better trade relations between Puerto Rico and the United Kingdom.

Ark's teething troubles continued, however. On 18th March, as she was taking part in Trial PUNISH, the port outer Olympus gas turbine failed catastrophically and spectacularly, with smashed turbine blades being projected through the funnel uptakes and onto the flight deck. The engine was replaced at sea. The hole in *Ark*'s bow received remedial attention at an emergency docking on her return to Portsmouth in late April, but the repair could not be completed until *Ark* was scheduled to dock as part of her major maintenance period in July, and in the interim she soldiered on through a busy late-spring programme back in UK waters.

The new Flag Officer Third Flotilla, Rear Admiral Hugo White, embarked in May for two weeks of ASW exercises in the North Western Approaches. *Ark* then formed the centrepiece of Staff College Sea Days under the command of Rear Admiral Kerr, Flag Officer First Flotilla, before heading up the Thames in early June for an official visit to London. Berthing just upstream from the Royal Naval College, at Greenwich, Captain Harris gingerly navigated *Ark* through the Thames Barrier at Woolwich, the ship's 115 feet beam leaving very little room for manoeuvre between the 200 feet navigable span between the iconic flood gates. The purpose of the visit was to provide a venue for a fundraising banquet on 8th June organised by the White Ensign Association. A huge marquee was erected over a dance floor created on the flight deck and tables and chairs for 800 guests were laid out in the hangar. HRH Princess Alexandra was the guest of honour, accompanied by the great and good of British government and industry. Other guests included Lord Lewin, Denis Thatcher (the Prime Minister being pre-occupied with the forthcoming general election), Lord Trefgarne, the Minister of State, Lord King of British Airways, Virginia Wade and John Lehman, former US Secretary of the Navy. The evening was spectacular, accompanied by flying display; a Royal Marines beat retreat, fireworks and the unmistakeable jangle of very expensive jewellery around the marquee dance floor.

For the remainder of the visit the Ship's Company took advantage of dozens of organised sporting and social visits, free entry to a host of London tourist sites, and the other obvious attractions that the city had to offer. The highlight for many though was a visit by The Queen Mother to "her" ship on 9th June. Neither atrocious weather, nor the fatigue of a transatlantic flight from Canada the previous day, could dull the twinkle in Her Majesty's eye and obvious enjoyment as she met the crew. The visit provided a fitting climax to Ark's first call on the capital.

On proceeding down river on 10th June, Ark Royal pointed her bows northwards for Rosyth, first for Navy Days, which attracted over 15,000 visitors and then for Joint Maritime Course (JMC) 87-2. The JMC was designed to exercise the ships and aircraft of different Allied nations in joint and combined operations, with the exercise split into two phases. During the four day work up Harrier GR-3s from No.1 (F) Squadron RAF embarked for Exercise HARDY CRAB, the RAF's periodic foray into Harrier operations at sea that prepared the squadron for further exercises later in the autumn. The work up phase was followed between by a "free play" battle from 20th to 26th June, during which Ark avoided detection for 48 hours. Those convinced of the supposed "vulnerability" of carriers usually ignored the remarkable facility of even large ships to disappear into the wide-open spaces of the ocean. During the free play, Ark's warfare team had the chance to control RAF Tornado F-3s from 229 Operational Conversion Unit, based at RAF Coningsby; the first time the ship had worked with the type of aircraft.

Just as the exercise came to an end, at 20:15 on 25th June a distress call was received from the German trawler MV Hessen via Wick radio. The vessel was reported as sinking close to Ark Royal's position. Ark arrived on the scene at 21:00 and two 820 Squadron Sea Kings were launched with a salvage team led by Warrant Officer A R S Benton. The Hessen had taken too much water however to be salvaged and the team and the crew had to be taken off before it sank.

Ark Royal had been on passage to her next commitment, Exercise HADRIAN's WALL, a Special Forces insertion exercise in the border area. The ship spent much of the time anchored off St Andrews as her detachment of SBS, SAS and American Delta Force was late arriving as a result of the Hessen affair. The detachment eventually arrived with their helicopters, were briefed and taken to their launch point.

On completion of the exercise at the end of June Ark proceeded south to Portsmouth, Families and Navy days and the docking for the Base AMP. She entered 'D' Lock at Portsmouth on 13th July where full repairs were finally achieved in the compartment that had flooded during the Azores incident, several weapon enhancements were completed and the aft R909 tracker was replaced due to serious oil leak. In August the Ship's Company held a memorial service in the chapel for Squadron Commander E H Dunning DSC RNAS to mark the 70th anniversary of the first landing on the deck of a moving ship (HMS Furious) on 2nd

August 1917. Five days later Dunning made another landing but was killed when his aircraft was blown over the side.

HMS *Ark Royal* was again the star attraction at Portsmouth Navy Days at the end of August, although the crowds of visitors were less than impressed by the fact that the flight deck was out of bounds because the paint applied to it during the maintenance period was still wet! *Ark* began her post-maintenance trials on 1st September. These were compressed into three days as the ship was needed for the Royal Navy Equipment Exhibition during which she was visited by HRH Prince Michael of Kent. On 14th September the ship sailed to begin a week's preparations for COST (Continuation Operational Sea Training), the ship's periodical subjection to the demands of the staff of Flag Officer Sea Training at Portland. This was again rather compressed because of the ship's intended programme and the final sea assessment was conducted in the Western Approaches on passage to the Northern Fleet Exercise Areas for aviation work up. During the COST period, *Ark Royal* took on her full outfit of explosives stores at sea from RFA *Fort Austin*, saving a great deal of time in the downstream programme by avoiding the need to use lighters at the Up-Harbour Ammunition Facility at Portsmouth.

On 10th October the ship conducted live Sea Dart firings, proving the new aft R909 tracking radar fitted during the AMP. At the final inspection the following day, FOST awarded a "Very Satisfactory" assessment to the ship; more time would have achieved still higher marks. Aviation work up began on 14th October but started badly: on the second day, Lieutenant Dale O'Meara of 801 Squadron, flying Sea Harrier ZA190 suffered a bird strike while engaged in a low-level sortie over the sea and crashed 85 nautical miles South West of Tiree. Lieutenant O'Meara ejected safely and was recovered back to mother by helicopter. With tongues firmly in cheeks, O'Meara's reception committee informed him that Captain Harris (a keen ornithologist) on hearing of the demise of the

bird had taken some persuading to launch the rescue aircraft. ZA190 was a Falklands veteran in HMS *Invincible*, flown by Lieutenant Steve Thomas who shot down two Argentine Daggers with Sidewinder missiles on 21st May 1982. Work-up continued despite this setback and the pressure was high on the Ship's Company with long periods of operational or full defence watches.

Rear Admiral White appeared on Trafalgar Day to conduct his Operational Readiness Inspection, accompanied by a BBC film crew recording material for a programme inaptly titled "Hitting the Deck", and made his final assessment two days later. He complimented the ship both on "*it's most creditable all round standards*" and on the "*positive attitude and good humour amongst a manifestly well led and happy Ship's Company.*" *Ark Royal* then returned to Portsmouth for a short period of self maintenance, again attracting media interest with visits from Michaela Strachan of TV-AM's "Wide-Awake Club" and an editorial feature for Car Magazine with their "Top Ten Cars of 1987" (three Citroens, two Lancias, a Renault, Bentley, Porsche, Range Rover and Jaguar making the line-up) embarked on the flight deck; several wags commenting that Sir Donald Gosling had finally turned the ship into an NCP car-park! The ship also became a stage for the Didcot Phoenix Amateur Dramatic Society's production of "Lysistrata"; just another example of the utility of the ship and the tireless flexibility of her crew.

On 3rd November HMS *Ark Royal* sailed for Exercise PURPLE WARRIOR, the biggest single maritime operation for British forces since the Falklands War and the main factor compressing her lead-up programme. PURPLE WARRIOR was designed to test the ability of the United Kingdom task group to protect and evacuate UK nationals from a distant shore. With HMS *Illustrious* carrying the commando helicopters in the LPH role, *Ark Royal* was to act both as command ship and air defence and attack carrier (CVA), providing mobile air support with three Harrier squadrons. Space onboard was tight! Twelve Sea

Harriers of 800 and 801 Squadrons, six RAF Harrier GR-3s from No.1 (F) Squadron, three AEW Sea Kings of 849 'B' Flight supplemented by a fourth aircraft from 849 'A' Flight to achieve 24-hour airborne surveillance, and a flight of two SKJs of 826 Squadron carried for helicopter delivery service (HDS), filled the hangar and flight deck to bursting point. With the extra staffs of both the Joint Forces Headquarters and the Third Flotilla also embarked, the ship's complement grew to over 1,500. Accommodation for the guests was arranged by converting some passageways and electrical spaces into cabins and mess decks.

Rear Admiral White and Major General Nick Vaux rejoined their staffs on 4th November and the ship stayed in the Channel while rehearsal landings were carried out on the South Coast. The force then proceeded to the exercise areas off southwest Scotland where it arrived on the 8th, despite the catastrophic failure of *Ark*'s port inner gas turbine, which limited her speed to 25 knots. The first landings were made on the 9th and the JFHQ staff went ashore on 11th November after a forward base had been established. The Sea Harriers provided combat air patrol over both the ships and shore emplacements while the GR-3s reconnoitred the landing areas. The threat was from RAF Buccaneers from the northwest and Jaguars from the east but rules of engagement would not allow offensive operations until 'hostile action' commenced on the 11th. The GR-3s went ashore the day after the JFHQ staff; their joint departure helping to relieve pressure on *Ark Royal*'s accommodation spaces. The Sea Harriers were kept busy defending against the Buccaneers, Jaguars and USAF F-111s, and 'hacking' shadowing Nimrods. A 'four over four'-by-day and 'two over two'-by-night flying programme was maintained and on 16th November alone *Ark Royal* launched no less than 52 fixed-wing sorties. With some help from RAF Phantoms, continuous cover was thus provided throughout PURPLE WARRIOR. As the main exercise closed, on the 17th the ship moved into Loch Lhinnie, to

experiment with air defence in coastal waters surrounded by mountains and to practice operating RAF Chinook helicopters. One notable event of this coastal phase was the unscheduled first attempt by a Chinook to lift a CVS. If it hadn't been for some weak deck lashings it could have proved successful, but the pilot had to make do with 'kidnapping' a member of *Ark*'s flight deck crew and the Air Force Cross. Admiral Sir Julian Oswald, the Commander in Chief Fleet, congratulated the ship on having risen to the challenge of PURPLE WARRIOR with great style, thanking the Ship's Company *"for your enthusiasm, your hard work and professionalism, for your cheerfulness in the face of some pretty bloody weather and, in sum, for your contribution to an outstanding success. Well done"*. Most of *Ark*'s enhanced air group disembarked to Yeovilton by the 19th and the ship paid a routine visit to Cherbourg, the majority of the Ship's Company overcoming their initial scepticism that the French could provide a decent 'run ashore', to visit Paris, Bayeux and the D-Day beaches, as well as stock up early on presents for Christmas.

Back home in Portsmouth, *Ark Royal* was used to show off her latest piece of electronic command and control equipment to each of the Flotilla staffs who would come to use it in anger. The Joint Operational Tactical System, known by its acronym "JOTS" was an American device based around desk top computers and satellite communications that provided a constantly updated picture of the positions of various units. The port inner gas turbine damaged during PURPLE WARRIOR was also replaced.

Ark Royal was off again after Christmas, for shakedown and preparations for JMC 88-1, before visiting her birth place in Newcastle. On the cold and snowy morning of 29th January 1988 thousands of Tynesiders lined the banks of the river to see their ship return home. 33,000 people then poured over the gangway during two days of Ships Open to Visitors, the chaos captured by the Navy's cartoonist 'Tugg', while many of the

Ship's Company visited their old haunts in Newcastle and North Shields. The memories of the Scottish and Newcastle Brewery and the Tuxedo Princess would last through 1988, despite the exotica promised by the global OUTBACK '88 deployment announced in Parliament to coincide with *Ark*'s visit to the Tyne.

The air group embarked after *Ark* left Newcastle, with a full complement intended for the ship: nine SKJs, three SKWs and eight Sea Harriers. The opportunity was taken for a great deal of flying and air defence training with RAF Tornados and Phantoms, helping protect against RAF Buccaneers and USAF F-111s, covered by RAF Canberra electronic warfare aircraft. All of these activities were captured by another BBC film crew, this time filming "Reach for the Sky". On 8th February, former Hawker test pilot Bill Bedford landed a Harrier T4 twin-seat trainer onboard to mark the 25th Anniversary of his first landing in 1963 of the then experimental P1127 on *Ark Royal*'s forebear. Many in the Navy of the early 1960s had doubts about the concept of STOVL and the performance limitations of the little aircraft compared with the large conventional jets of the time. However, the cancellation of CVA-01 and the ensuing formidable account given by the Harrier in the Falklands proved the doubters wrong and heralded the shape of things to come. The T4 also provided a rare opportunity for a submariner to experience carrier aviation first hand; Bill Bedford taking Captain Harris for a circuit from *Ark Royal*'s flight deck.

JMC 88-1 lasted until 26th February 1988 and proceeded without incident, except for an influenza epidemic that affected almost everyone on board, providing good training in all warfare areas. *Ark Royal* carried out a Passing Exercise (PASSEX) with her sister *Illustrious* on 1st March and then made for Hamburg for a visit in which she acted as Sir Julian Oswald's flagship. Twenty five of the Ship's Company visited West Berlin as guests of the 14th/20th Hussars, crossing the Wall at Checkpoint Charlie and coming face to face with

Soviet army personnel on the eastern side. The remainder enjoyed the various sites and nocturnal offerings of Hamburg; souvenir shopping proving expensive while window shopping of a different kind provided an enlightening eyeful for the more naïve sailors! What had been a successful visit was marred by the death of MEM Barry Cooney who died following an incident on the last night and a memorial service was held off Scarborough to mark his loss. Six of 820's SKJs departed to Culdrose for ASW training, while *Ark Royal* started Exercise MALLET HAMMER, an air interception exercise with the carrier acting as an offshore picket and control centre for UK Air Defence Region. Bad weather prevented the RAF flying for much of the time but 801 Squadron continued in action throughout and on 17th March carried out 104 interceptions in 25 sorties (80 hours flying). Another visit to mainland Europe, this time to Rotterdam, ended *Ark Royal*'s last programme in home waters for some time. After arriving at Portsmouth on 23rd March, she immediately docked for a Base Assisted Maintenance Period, eleven weeks of crew leave and preparations for her most extended deployment yet, which would take her to the other side of the world.

The withdrawal from East of Suez in 1971 did not mean the end of periodical naval forays out of the NATO area. Governments considered it useful to deploy naval forces wherever Britain retained various defence commitments and to countries to whom she wished to sell military and naval equipment. The Royal Navy was only too ready to take advantage of these opportunities to send groups of ships on deployments to provide useful training and experience of ships and their crews, to maintain links with traditional friends and, more generally, to demonstrate the service's continued global reach should circumstances demand it.

By 1988 it had been decided that the group deployment should centre around Australia's bi-centennial. HMS *Ark Royal* would lead a group out to take part in the celebrations, coming back the same way rather than continuing round the world; hence the name: OUTBACK '88. The maximum number of visits and exercises would be crammed in during the deployment that was to take six months.

Extensive preparations were required, both for the ship and her crew. *Ark Royal* had undocked to the North Wall at Portsmouth on 15th April 1988, but the maintenance period continued until 27th May. Two Olympus gas turbines and a diesel generator were replaced, the flight deck was refurbished and the ship generally spruced up. Thanks to Swan Hunter the ship's chapel was fitted out with wood panelling and new carpets. Between 25th March and 18th April and 13th and 22nd May, the ship granted 80% leave giving everyone onboard the chance to use up their Easter and summer leave allowances before departure. On 1st June the ship carried out a fast cruise to prove her routines at sea and then took on ammunition up-harbour. Families Day was held on the 3rd giving 2,500 family and friends of the Ship's Company the chance to experience life at sea, albeit briefly. Three days after that, the ship sailed for a week's shakedown at the end of which Rear Admiral White visited the ship to hand her over to the Flag Officer whose staff would command Task Group 318.1, Rear Admiral Peter Woodhead, Flag Officer Second Flotilla. Captain Harris assessed this period as having been *"a good and settling pre-deployment phase which left the ship and her men well prepared for the months ahead."*

With a detachment of Royal Marines onboard and her air group increased to 22 aircraft by two Commando Sea Kings from 845 Squadron, on 13th June, *Ark Royal* slipped and proceeded from Portsmouth for her long odyssey. The increased complement of over 1200 men required the gymnasium to be converted to a makeshift mess deck, while every available space was crammed with spares and defence sales equipment. The other members of TG318.1 were the *Type-42* destroyer HMS *Edinburgh*, the towed array Leander-class frigate HMS *Sirius* and the three RFAs *Olwen*, *Orangeleaf* and *Fort Grange*.

No sooner was the group at sea than exercises were being carried out in the Bay of Biscay with both the French Navy, in the shape of the frigate ACONIT, Super Etendard fighter bombers and Atlantique patrol aircraft, and the RAF with Nimrods of No.42 Squadron. On 16th June, HMS *Ark Royal* met up with SS *Canberra*, the 'great white whale' of the Falklands War, 45 miles off Lisbon. The two ships sailed in company for a quarter of an hour, making the customary exchange of dipping ensigns and sounding their sirens. The encounter marked a personal reunion for the captains of both ships, last together in 1982 during the Falklands War. Mike Harris then commanding HMS *Cardiff* and James Weatherall in HMS *Andromeda* had escorted Commodore Mike Bradford in SS *Canberra* into Port Stanley to take off Argentine prisoners.

The following day *Ark* began ASW Exercise JOLLY ROGER that allowed the task group to shake down together and the 820 SKJs, working hard in continuous ripple mode, to practice cooperation with the towed array frigate. On the first day 801 Squadron also had a trade in the shape of Spanish EAV-8B Matadors and Mirage aircraft. On entering the Mediterranean, *Ark Royal*'s group met with an Italian task group led by the carrier ITS *Giuseppe Garibaldi*. A PASSEX was held in which two 801 Sea Harriers, supported by a party of maintainers, deck crew and supervisors, operated from the Italian ship. Because of the Italian Navy's legal difficulties with operating fixed wing aircraft their procurement of STOVL aircraft had been delayed for the *Giuseppe Garibaldi* and the Italians found the experience most useful. Two days later *Ark Royal* met another aviation ship, the latest Soviet aircraft carrying cruiser, the BAKU close to the Hammamet anchorage and the two ships sailed in company for over an hour. The Russians seemed anxious to show off their prowess in the STOVL mode of operating their normally VTOL Forgers and one of the few observed running take-offs with the type was observed.

Malta was the next port of call, the former main base of the British Mediterranean Fleet but recently out of bounds because of political differences with the Maltese Government. Relations were now much better, as indicated by the planned visit, but the opposition Labour Party and its associated trade unions came out against it, given the excuse provided by *Ark Royal*'s nuclear capability. A tanker was hijacked to block the entrance to Grand Harbour. The task group therefore put into St Paul's Bay to a great welcome by a flotilla of small boats full of cheering well wishers. Another welcoming crowd on the jetty at Birzeobuga and a firework display completed a very Maltese welcome. Despite intimidation of the ship's local agent and delays in obtaining provisions, *Ark Royal*'s Ship's Company were treated with both warmth and hospitality when ashore and the Maltese Prime Minister and other government officials were hosted onboard. Defence sales presentations were both rehearsed and carried out. Ten members of the crew were reunited with the ship having taken a more arduous route to Malta: the 'Euro-cycle '88' team had cycled the 1,730 miles through France, over the Alps and then down the length of Italy to raise £4,500 for the Great Ormond Street Hospital appeal.

When *Ark Royal* sailed on 29th June she was surrounded by another throng of well wishers. Joining the Ship's Company were ten members of the Swiss Reserve Officers Association who stayed onboard for two days before transferring to the Swiss ketch *Colombaio V*. The evolution, 300 miles west of Port Said was complicated by bad weather but the transfer conducted by rigid inflatable boat was achieved safely. Then, for some reason, the ketch swerved into the side of the carrier denting both itself and *Ark*'s plating. Having been assured that there were no injuries onboard the Swiss vessel, *Ark* continued east, to exercise with the USN submarine USS *Cincinnati* and RAF aircraft from Cyprus. The exercise had to

be cut short however when an emergency call was received from the American auxiliary USNS *Waccamaw*. One of the ship's deckhands had been hurt in an accident onboard, sustaining serious head and neck injuries that required urgent medical attention. The deckhand was evacuated by one of 820's Sea Kings and given emergency treatment in the ship's Sick Bay. The casualty was resuscitated and later transferred to Haifa.

On 2nd July, *Ark Royal* arrived at Port Said for the transit of the Suez Canal that began the same day. Anchoring briefly in the Bitter Lakes the transit through the Canal was completed the following day, allowing 152 of the Ship's Company the opportunity to sightsee in Cairo before the task group set off down the Red Sea. "Pharaoh's Revenge", as it became known, embarked with the day-trippers keeping the sick bay staff busy as the ship headed south. Temperatures passed the 40°C mark and the sand-laden atmosphere turned the weather decks and ranged aircraft brown. It was not until the ship passed through the Bab-el-Mandeb and entered the Indian Ocean that a fortuitous and rare rain shower eventually washed off the deposits picked up in the Red Sea. An arranged Passing Exercise with the French Navy proved an anticlimax as the planned Sea Dart firings had to be aborted due to bad weather, but the ship pressed on south towards the Indian sub-continent. Two weeks after Suez, the ship rounded the southern tip of India and on 16th July a major helicopter delivery service (HDS) operation was carried out using the two SKAs 'leapfrogging' from *Ark Royal* via RFA *Fort Grange* and HMS *Edinburgh* to Colombo in Sri Lanka, a total distance of 320 miles. This was an especially notable achievement as the pilots of the Commando Sea Kings had to rely on dead reckoning for navigation.

The ship continued its passage east, heading down the Straits of Malacca toward Singapore. 820 Squadron flew off to take part in Exercise STARFISH, an annual event carried out under the auspices of the Five Power Defence Agreement of

1971. Under this agreement Britain has obligations to consult with Australia, New Zealand, Malaysia and Singapore if the security of the latter two is threatened. Flying from the Royal Malaysian Air Force airfield at Kuantan, the Sea Kings demonstrated their active dipping sonar capability at ranges over 100 miles from base. The target was the Australian *Oberon*-class submarine HMAS *Oxley*. While this was in progress, five of 801's Sea Harriers flew off to Paya Lebar airfield in Singapore, staying ashore for fourteen days while carrying out a varied training programme with local A-4s, Hunters and F-5s.

On 23rd July HMS *Ark Royal* reached Singapore, and just prior to arrival the Ship's Company were mustered on the flight deck to spell out "OUTBACK 88" for the deployment photograph. 'Flat-tops' had a long tradition of signing messages using the crew and "OUTBACK 88" was the first of many to be sent throughout the ship's life. Berthing at the old naval base at Sembawang was a nostalgic event for some who had served there in the days of the Far East Fleet, although the enormous and rapid development of Singapore since 1971 that swept aside the old shanty towns near the docks and at Neesoon proved impressive to all. While some of the enjoyed the sights of the island, others sampled the myriad of stalls in Newton Circus and on the Padang, and others ventured further a field, the engineers were left onboard to complete a two-week maintenance period assisted by a Fleet Maintenance Unit from HMS *Defiance* in Plymouth. Captain Harris was also preoccupied by the first visit to the ship of a serving Prime Minister; Margaret Thatcher lunching onboard on 31st July as part of whirlwind diplomatic tour supporting UK industry in the Far East.

On 8th August the ship sailed for the Philippines and the American naval base at Subic Bay, where she docked astern of the battleship USS *New Jersey*. A relic of World War II, she had nevertheless been updated to carry the Tomahawk land attack missile, and like *Ark* was now armed with Phalanx, but it was her nine 16-inch guns that still provided a jaw-dropping sight. *New Jersey* escorted *Ark Royal* as she departed from Subic Bay on 12th and once in the local exercise area and stationed astern of the carrier, she showed off her firepower. Two broadsides fired with maximum flash effect provided an awesome spectacle, not often witnessed by Royal Navy personnel whose ships had long since swapped guns for missile systems. While the demonstration was undoubtedly impressive, the die-hard aviators in *Ark* could not help reflecting that the carrier and its aircraft had long gained the upper hand over the relics of a bygone era in naval warfare.

After this firework display the serious training in modern naval warfare began. The American nuclear submarine USS *Haddock* provided a demanding ASW target in the water conditions, but SKJ co-operation with HMS *Sirius* improved still further and the 'fighting pair' Sea King concept was vindicated. USN P-3C Orions also gave support. Sea Dart firings against Petrel targets were less successful and after the failure in the Indian Ocean the previous month, studies began on how to make it 'third time lucky' as *Ark Royal* pointed her bow towards Hong Kong. She carried out a PASSEX with the Hong Kong Squadron patrol vessels on the 23rd, before the ship berthed at HMS *Tamar* later that day.

After some busy days for her Ship's Company enjoying the sights of Hong Kong, *Ark Royal* sailed for Brunei. On the passage south one of the AEW Sea Kings spotted a small boat drifting alone that was full of 26 Vietnamese boat people. At least one person had already died, a woman had given birth and as the boat had no power, no food and no water, it was unlikely that any of the others would survive without help. HMS *Edinburgh* conducted the rescue, transferring the survivors to RFA *Olwen*. Although it was only August, the Ship's Companies of the task group decided that Christmas should come early, so shipwrights made wooden toys and those who had bought souvenirs along the way donated them to the cause. Santa

Claus then transferred to *Olwen* with his sacks and brought a little cheer to the refugee children; despite the language barrier, their smiles said it all. Eventually they were landed in Singapore to begin a new life.

Exercise SETHIA KAWAN, designed to test British support for the Sultan of Brunei, who jealously guarded his independence from Malaysia, was the next activity. Troops from the British garrisons in Brunei and Hong Kong exercised ashore with the Brunei armed forces while *Ark* acted as flagship and landing platform for the naval task force. Her principal contribution to the exercise was to land 250 Bruneian assault troops from the ship while the Sea Harriers carried out reconnaissance and ground attack missions under the control of forward air controllers. On 3rd September the Sultan himself visited the ship to meet the crew and witness their interaction with his personnel. From Brunei, the next event was another 'Five Power Defence Agreement' exercise, this one Exercise LIMA BERSATU, designed to integrate the participating maritime and air forces. Two days of air operations against Malaysian and Singaporean aircraft were followed by a similar period of attack operations against land targets in both countries. RAF Tornado aircraft deployed from UK also provided air cover. The defence ministers of the Five Powers met on board the ship on 6th September, with Britain represented by Archie Hamilton, the Minister for the Armed Forces.

Defence sales were not forgotten. During the Bruneian operations 849 'B' Flight demonstrated the potential of the Searchwater radar fitted in the SKW for the locals. Then, after the equator had been crossed with all due ceremony, on 11th September, an Indonesian delegation led by the Chief of the Indonesian Naval Staff were treated to a defence Export Support Day; the ship showing off the capabilities of her air group in what was now a well rehearsed demonstration by her Combined Air Group. As the ship neared Australia she was "attacked" by RAAF Mirages in their last weeks in service. This provided useful practice for *Ark*'s air defence team and her Sea Harriers flying Combat Air Patrol, while PASSEXs were held with HMAS *Geelong* and HMAS *Gawler*, two patrol craft of the Australian northern flotilla.

On 17th September, Captain Harris and around thirty of his Ship's Company landed on Possession Island to unveil a plaque re-dedicating the memorial to the first landing by Captain Cook 218 years before. The next four days saw *Ark Royal* on passage inside the Great Barrier Reef with 820 Squadron providing tourist flights for many to see this natural wonder from the air. After this excursion it was back to work with more exercises with the Australians, including an air defence exercise against RAAF F-111s and some live bombing by the Sea Harriers on the Halifax Bay range, near Townsville. Five 801 Squadron aircraft later detached to RAAF airfields at Williamstown and Amberley and on the 21st, two more 820 Squadron aircraft and one each from the Sea King flights disembarked to Amberley while the ship berthed at Brisbane.

Brisbane was in the middle of EXPO '88 that drew many members of the Ship's Company while others were press-ganged into a platoon that took part in the multi-national bicentennial march that passed through both the city and the exhibition site. The locals were most hospitable, the only discordant note being struck by an anti-nuclear Senator who used her position to get on board and had to be escorted off before a press conference.

On 25th September, with press on board, *Ark Royal* sailed for Sydney and the great Bicentennial Naval Review, the high spot of the whole deployment. The Governor of New South Wales, Sir James Rowland, embarked for the entry to Sydney Harbour and the ship was met by a mixed bag of friendly, cheering well-wishers and anti-nuclear protestors. Judicious ship handling by Captain Harris prevented any collisions and *Ark Royal* berthed safely at the Sydney Cove passenger terminal between the Opera House and the Harbour Bridge. The ship was soon immersed in a social and sporting programme of massive proportions, where over 10,000 visitors were hosted on board. On 29th September, the Ship's Company, now well-practiced in marching, took part in a march past of about 8,000 personnel from the international group attending the review. *Ark* then took up position moored in the inner harbour close by USS *New Jersey* and the cruiser FS *Colbert*. On 1st October, HRH The Duke of York embarked in HMAS *Cook* conducted the Fleet Review on behalf of The Queen. Four of 801's Sea Harriers, two of 820's Sea Kings and an SKW of 849 'B' Flight took part in the fly past. Various aircraft also detached ashore, to a historic air fair at Bankstown and the Australian Navy airfield at Nowra. Not forgetting UK Industry, on the penultimate day of the visit *Ark* held another Defence Export Sales Day.

HMS *Ark Royal* sailed from Sydney on 7th October and it was straight back to business with evolutions in the Jervis Bay exercise areas. The participants in SURFEX 429 were the ships that had taken part in the review from Australia, New Zealand, the Netherlands, France, Italy and Malaysia as well as the UK ships of Task Group 318.1. Two RAN Sea Kings embarked for carrier experience and 820 had considerable success in active operations against the Australian submarines HMAS *Onslow* and HMAS *Orion*. For *Ark* the high spot of the exercise came on 8th October when her Sea Harriers sank the old patrol boat HMAS *Buccaneer* with 1,000-lb bombs. Air defence exercises were also held with the enemy being provided by RAAF Learjets, Macchis and F-18s. The Harriers did their share of attacking, providing an air threat to test the crews of both USS *Ingersoll* and HMS *Sirius*.

HMS *Ark Royal* was bound for Melbourne, but the ship's latent nuclear capability again caused political problems; the most vociferous yet. The Seamen's Union announced a boycott of *Ark* and RFA *Fort Grange* which prevented the harbour tugs from sailing out to assist their entry. The assigned berth for the carrier was alongside Prince's Pier up a narrow straight channel followed by a complete 180-degree turn. This was tricky enough at the best of times without tugs but high winds ruled out an unassisted berthing completely. Neither ship could go alongside, instead remaining under way in the Bay of Port Philip. There they waited three days for reason to prevail but despite the best efforts of Admiral Woodhead, Royal Australian Navy officials and the British High Commissioner, the unions supported by the State Premier remained intransigent. With the stalemate unbroken, *Ark* and her auxiliary had no alternative but to sail away on 16th October, with Fremantle in Western Australia the next port of call. The only personnel to make it ashore during the Melbourne stand-off were the crews of two Sea Kings which disembarked to RAAF Laverton.

Poor weather with 60-70 knot winds added to the general gloom but after five days at sea the ship berthed at her next port of call, Fremantle. Again the nuclear issue raised its ugly head and this time the crane drivers' union boycotted the ship. This necessitated boat transfers of personnel rather than the use of brows, but the boycott was lifted on 24th November, which also happened to be the day of the visit of the Australian Defence Minister Kim Beazley. A full social and sporting programme was enjoyed by all in excellent weather and the visit was a fitting culmination to what had been, despite some glitches, a very successful six weeks.

Ark Royal recovered those aircraft still ashore on 31st October and sailed for Bombay two days later, a turn for the worse in the weather symbolising the ship's northern destination. Air defence exercises were held as the ship headed for Bombay and the Sea Dart firings were at last carried out successfully. Eight Petrels were fired, the first two of which were successfully engaged by *Ark* and *Edinburgh*. The remaining drones sent in a stream attack escaped interception but much was learned about the performance of the ships' systems against very demanding ultra high speed (Mach 4) targets.

The task group kept itself busy over the

following days, with surface, ASW and air defence exercises. On 15th November the ships reached Bombay and conducted Defence Export Days on the 18th and 19th; the first in harbour and the second at sea after the ship had left Bombay for Suez. *Ark Royal* was not the only flat-top in the Indian Ocean in late 1988 with the Iran/Iraq war demanding the presence of the USS *Nimitz* battle group. This allowed useful training opportunities and on 22nd November a major War At Sea Exercise (WASEX) was conducted. The super carrier's aircraft provided a formidable 'threat' and valuable insights into the tactics of the USN. The task group's layered air defence with Sea Harriers, Sea King Whiskeys, Sea Dart and Vulcan Phalanx proved reassuringly effective, even against such high quality opposition. The defences succeeded in inflicting significant attrition even against considerable numerical odds. It was assessed that only exercise rules had prevented the Sea Harrier/Sea King Whiskey combination achieving even better results, especially in the early detection and destruction of shadowing aircraft. On the 24th *Ark Royal* exercised her own offensive potential when the Sea Harriers dropped 22 1,000-lb bombs on smoke flare targets.

It was not all work, however. A Ship's Company cabaret was held on the 26th in the hangar and the following day a 100 mile relay race was held on the flight deck. The ship reached Suez on 1st December and this allowed 300 sailors to be landed from the whole group to enjoy the sights of Egypt. The task group transited the canal on the 2nd and after recovering the tourists, set sail westwards. The 5th of December saw another carrier battle fought out, this time against the French carrier FS *Clemenceau*. The latter operated her F-8 fighters and Super Etendard attack aircraft against the British group which received the vital extra support of a NATO AWACS E-3A. This extra cover allowed a strike of six Super Etendard to be engaged by Sea Harriers at ranges of 110 and 70 miles, keeping the Falklands-proven attack aircraft safely at arm's length before the ship came

within range of their Exocet missiles. On the 8th, French opposition was replaced by American, this time from USS *John F Kennedy* and again the Group demonstrated what could be achieved by a small task group with its own modest organic air power against sophisticated and numerically superior forces.

HMS *Ark Royal* berthed at Gibraltar on 9th December prior to the last lap home and she embarked pressmen and eighteen sons, nephews and brothers as part of the "sons at sea" programme. While at Gibraltar, the ship's athletes achieved the fastest ship's time in the "Top of the Rock" race. When the ship sailed on the 11th the Governor embarked for a short sea passage, being returned to the Rock by helicopter. *Ark* conducted a full power trial on 12th December and the following day, as 801's Sea Harriers disembarked, she met up with her sister HMS *Illustrious* in the Bay of Biscay. The ships remained in company sailing north while conducting joint ASW exercises. Arriving in the West Country, *Ark* anchored briefly in Mount's Bay so that her helicopters could fly off to Culdrose and Yeovilton. The final landmark of the cruise was the first ever meeting between all three carriers, HMS *Invincible*, fresh from refit, meeting her younger sisters south of Start Point. As the three ships steamed in close company the event was duly recorded in a unique photograph. By evening *Ark Royal* was at anchor at Spithead. After a final clean up and with more press embarked she finally came home on 15th December 1988, berthing at the South Railway Jetty. Families were soon reunited after six months separation. The global deployment had been a great success. Captain Harris reported that OUTBACK '88 had been "*a happy though busy time which undoubtedly provided all concerned with a rich, varied and rewarding experience.*" The Ship's Company had been honed into an even more professional and tightly knit team than normal. Rarely had a period of Christmas leave been better earned. After her voyage half way round the world and back, *Ark*

Royal returned home to a more normal programme of NATO exercises. After maintenance in Portsmouth, *Ark* began her Area Capability Tests in early February 1989. The ship was operating a somewhat reduced air group of seven Sea Harriers, two SKWs and six SKJs; the shortfall in airframes caused by a mixture of deep maintenance requirements, major unserviceability and re-allocation to higher priorities. At least, however it meant that what aircraft were available were kept at higher states of availability than normal and the 820 SKJs in particular were able to make particularly profitable use of real submarine targets.

Ark began conversion to her secondary LPH role on 17th February 1989, in preparations for Exercise COLD WINTER off Norway. The Navy no longer had bespoke commando carriers, the last to leave service being HMS *Hermes*, the Falkland war-horse, sold to India in the mid-1980s. It seemed natural therefore to press the CVSG into service periodically in this role. Since the late 1960's the Royal Marines had emphasised their role as reinforcements to NATO's Northern Flank. *Ark* would provide helicopter spots to supplement those on the amphibious ship HMS *Intrepid*. Fourteen Sea King 4 helicopters (SKAs) of 845 and 846 Squadrons were embarked and maintained in the aft section of the hangar. The forward part of this space became a crowded mess deck for the embarked force of almost 400 extra personnel from 42 and 45 Commandos and 29 Battery Royal Artillery. There was also a detachment of Dutch marines. COLD WINTER did not live up to its name: the weather was remarkably mild for the latitudes and time of year and created no problems. The highlight of the exercise was a twelve-aircraft assault near Tromso. The ship then returned south bringing home 45 Commando, who disembarked by helicopter off Arbroath on 16th March. The SKAs disembarked to Yeovilton the following day, when *Ark Royal* returned to Portsmouth.

Although successful, Exercise COLD WINTER provided little operational benefit to the ship, the impact being that her CAG remained disembarked for all but ten days of first three months of the year. The annual SPRINGTRAIN exercise that followed COLD WINTER, which should have been fully integrated high intensity flying operations, was thus reduced to a basic training and recovery exercise. This proved frustrating to Mike Harris, who commented tersely that *"to survive in war, the ship and her CAG must be an indivisible whole."* Sadly, this would provide a model for much of the CVS's future operations where limited aircraft and competing priorities meant that months and even years would go by between fixed-wing embarkations in *Ark Royal*.

SPRINGTRAIN in the South Western Approaches and west of Gibraltar began on April Fool's Day 1989 and consisted of the usual air group activities. Poor serviceability dogged both the Sea Harriers and SKJs, but the majority of tasking requirements were met. Sea Dart firings were carried out and although the Petrel targets once again proved troublesome, *Ark Royal's* missile system worked well, downing a Chukar target on 9th April. The exercises went on until 21st April when the ship put in for three days well-earned leave at Gibraltar. The tempo throughout the spring had been extremely high, and only three days in Gibraltar following four weeks at sea seemed to Captain Harris to be little reward for his Ship's Company, noting ruefully in his subsequent Report of Proceedings that *"too much work and no play makes Jack a dull boy."* But the tempo was only to increase further and, with it, came a new man in charge; Mike Harris handing over command to John Brigstocke at Portsmouth on 27th April 1989. Without doubt, Captain Harris could reflect that the ship had finally escaped the 'new build' mindset and justifiably call itself a fully worked-up member of the team.

Admiral Sir John Brigstocke KCB

(Commanding Officer 1989 – 1990)

The attachment of a Commanding Officer to his ship is always deep and emotional; that is the way it should be. In HMS *Ark Royal* I found such attachment at every level; that is unusual, and the key to the ship's unique spirit, style and efficiency. Thus my abiding memory of eighteen months in command is of all who served with me, and who made things happen with such willing energy, enthusiasm, humour and determination to do everything well.

And a lot did happen. Events were too numerous to catalogue, but included six major exercises for which we flew the flags of every seagoing Flag Officer (who all departed well pleased!), a major DAMP which culminated in a highly successful Continuation Material Assessment, a "Good" Work-up and Operational Readiness Inspection in the worst weather I can ever remember, and a particularly enjoyable and worthwhile WESTLANT deployment.

But I must return again to people. So many of you spring to mind, so I will confine myself to just three as no more than an illustration of typical *Ark Royal* commitment: Chief Petty Officer (Air Handler) Bearcroft who led the Flight Deck team through weeks of work-up flying at the very limits, indeed on several occasions beyond the limits, of weather safety; Mr Alan Kendall who completed 47 years at sea with NAAFI, of which the last five were in *Ark Royal*, and Chief Petty Officer (Mechanic) Price who was awarded the British Empire Medal for his outstandingly effective contribution in NBCD, culminating in the first ever Portland "Good" for a CVSG in damage control.

I will finish with a quote from "Noah's News", *"Be nice to them when they return home – they will have had a few laughs, spun a few yarns around a can or two, moaned a bit, missed their families a lot, but always dug out when it mattered to enable the ship to be what she is: 'Britain's Best'."*

She certainly was the best, remained so when I was privileged to fly my Flag in her as CTG 323.2 supporting the Tomahawk armed USS *Virginia*, *Spruance* and *Philippine Sea* in the Eastern Mediterranean during the 1st Gulf War, and later as CTG of all RN forces in the Adriatic during operations in former Yugoslavia. From all I hear, she remained the best.

My very sincerest thanks to all who served with me when I was in command, and who supported me and my staff so well, as an embarked task group Commander, during two important operational deployments.

Chapter 4

1989 – 1990:
The End of the Cold War

Captain John Brigstocke was one of the last traditional "gunners" in the Navy, having come top in the last Long Course at HMS *Excellent* at Whale Island, and his dynamism and force of character would help carry the ship through an extremely busy period, with no immediate respite in sight for the Ship's Company.

The first event of John Brigstocke's command was Exercise MINIBUS, held from 1st to 5th May. The Duke of Edinburgh, accompanied by the First Sea Lord, Admiral Sir William Stavely, visited the ship on sailing to celebrate His Royal Highness's fiftieth anniversary of joining the Royal Navy, and was entertained by a capability demonstration from *Ark*'s CAG, despite the marginal weather conditions. MINIBUS completed and following five days to reset at Portsmouth, *Ark Royal* sailed for the North Sea to conduct Air Defence Exercises with the Royal Netherlands Navy, under the codename SQUARE NUT. The Sea Harriers from 801 Squadron enjoyed their operations with the Dutch fighter controllers, against a varied threat of Dutch and Belgian F-16s, RAF Buccaneers and Belgian Mirages. From exercises, the ship paid a six-day visit to Hamburg, a re-acquaintance for most of the Ship's Company, who had enjoyed all the city had to offer the previous March. This Hamburg visit however faced a greater than usual contingent of anti-nuclear protestors and *Ark Royal*'s men received praise from the German press for the way they dealt with the demonstrators.

Following Hamburg, the ship became the flagship of Vice Admiral Alan Grose, Flag Officer Third Flotilla and played host to Harrier GR-3s from No.4 Squadron RAF which embarked for two days of flight deck operations; five of 801 NAS's aircraft disembarked to Lossiemouth to make room. As well as being Flag Officer of the Royal Navy's third flotilla, Vice Admiral Grose was also the commander of NATO's ASW Striking Force (ASWSTRIKFOR) and his staff would take the lead role in the next exercise, VENDETTA. Although not the main effort for the year to develop the Alliance's Concept of Maritime Operations, VENDETTA was nevertheless an iteration of its Forward Maritime Strategy, designed to continue putting pressure on the Soviets, reassure Norway and improve ASW tactical skills even further. Conducted in the Norwegian Sea, VENDETTA began on 22nd May with *Ark Royal* leading an ASW striking force of towed array ships formed off the North of Scotland. Most of the group comprised the NATO Standing Naval Force Atlantic (SNFL), including HMS *Boxer*, USS *Mahan* and USS *Preble* (USA), HMCS *Saguenay* (Canada), NRP *Roberto Ivens* (Portugal) and HNLMS *Bloys Von Treslong* (Netherlands), under the command of Rear Admiral Klaus Laudien FGN, embarked in FGS *Rheinland-Phalz*.

The "tails" worked in close liaison with the SKJs of 820 Squadron while the Sea Harriers of 801 Squadron, supported by 849 'B' Flight's Sea King Whiskeys kept 'orange-force' Buccaneers at bay. USS *Preble* conducted around-the-clock flight operations as refuelling station for *Ark*'s helicopters and on 27th May, led the force into the Arctic Circle; the event marked by the USN's traditional "Blue Nose" ceremony. As had become customary, once Norway was reached the exercise concentrated on operating in fjord "bastions" where submarines were pressurized not only by 820's "pingers" but also by the Searchwater radars of 849's "bags" flooding the area and pinning the 'enemy' submarines down, at least below periscope depth. Soviet Badger Delta surveillance aircraft provided live interception targets for 801's Harriers; an opportunity that would 'soon be unavailable with the fast changing world situation (that was reflected in the Soviet surveillance assets shying away from contact). In the midst of the real interceptions, while *Ark* was in the fjord, 801's jets also intercepted attacking fast patrol boats, conducted combat air patrols, probe missions in land and reconnaissance sorties further afield. VENDETTA ended on 1st June and *Ark Royal* returned to Portsmouth three days later.

No sooner alongside, than *Ark* was out again on 5th June as the flagship for Staff College Sea Days, first for Vice Admiral Coward, Flag Officer First Flotilla, and then his counterpart in the Second Flotilla, Rear Admiral Peter Woodhead. Sea Days led straight into another period on show with Rosyth Navy Days followed by JMC 89-2 from 20th to 30th June, with Vice Admiral Coward once again embarked. High point of the JMC was a live Sea Dart firing on the 27th, while the low point came from the use of civilian helicopters for logistics support, a development designed to save money but which ultimately proved less than satisfactory. On the way back to Portsmouth in early July the ship operated with the AV8-B Matadors of the Spanish Navy's 9th Escuadrilla. 801 Squadron had forged the contact by operating four of its aircraft from the new Spanish carrier SNS *Principe de Asturias* in the Mediterranean in June and this was the Spaniard's turn to cross-deck. The Spanish Harriers flew to the ship via Yeovilton to where five of 801's aircraft were detached. More

powerful than the UK FRS-1, the AV-8B showed impressive power and endurance as they exercised with the remaining 801 jets and 849's helicopters. Mixed pairs of aircraft were pitted against attacks by RAF Phantoms and Buccaneers and Italian Air Force F-104s.

Ark Royal returned to Portsmouth on 7th July, for the Ship's Company to enjoy summer leave and carry out a self-maintenance period. The most important repair amidst a considerable package of maintenance and defect rectification was to the port gearbox that had shed a tooth during previous operations. Extensive use was made of the FLAGO painting and cleaning fund – a new contract designed to streamline ships' husbandry in Portsmouth – to capitalize on the excellent summer weather. A substantial amount of the ship's side and flight deck was represerved in favourable conditions, helped by the easier application of a new silicon alkyl grey paint scheme. Although the FLAGO contract did little to reduce the 'harbour hassle' among the middle management during the maintenance period, it was responsive and helped ensure the ship looked pristine for Navy Days in August, where she starred alongside her elder sister, *Invincible*.

Rear Admiral Peter Abbot assumed command of the Second Flotilla while *Ark* underwent her maintenance period, and his first outing in her came at the beginning of September, with the major NATO exercise of the year, codenamed SHARP SPEAR. Involving more than 250 ships and 350 aircraft from ten countries, SHARP SPEAR tested the 'Shallow Seas' campaign in NATO's concept of operations, that is, operations in the Baltic, Baltic Approaches, North Sea and the waters surrounding the British Isles. The central part of the exercise was the protection of a merchant convoy that left Loch Ewe on 14th September and would link up with the carrier force off the North coast of Scotland before being escorted to its final destination at Stavanger in Norway. HMS *Ark Royal*'s contribution was to maintain sea control in the Western Approaches and she operated with

Spanish and Dutch task groups, the former led by SNS *Principe de Asturias*. The Spanish Matadors and 801's Sea Harriers joined in an attack on the hulk of the old frigate HMS *Leander*, which was finally finished off by 801 with three direct bomb hits after three close misses. As the ships passed around the North of Scotland and into the North Sea attacks on *Ark*'s group were carried out by a range of aircraft, including American B-52s and F-16s, RAF Tornados, Buccaneers and Jaguars; Dutch, Belgian, Danish and Norwegian F-16s, and Danish Drakens. 801 Squadron had great success splashing up to fourteen enemy aircraft in each sortie, making full use of the exercise artificiality of in-flight weapon reloads.

With the SHARP SPEAR battle won, *Ark Royal* returned to Portsmouth at the end of September where she hosted the Spanish carrier during a visit to the city by her battle group. Back at sea on 4th October, *Ark Royal* hosted the North Atlantic Council, with the Commander in Chief Fleet, Admiral Sir Benjamin Bathurst embarked. The combined air group put on its usual and well-rehearsed display. Sadly however, Lieutenant Paul Simmonds-Short flying Sea Harrier ZA191 misjudged a high-speed low-level approach over the ship and struck the top of R992 radar antenna situated on the main mast. He could not maintain control of the jet and it crashed ten miles off Lyme Regis. Lieutenant Simmonds-Short ejected and was safely recovered so that he could explain his actions to a very interested Commander in Chief.

After this unplanned excitement, *Ark Royal* sailed to Brest with Admiral Bathurst still embarked so that he could hold bilateral talks with his French counterpart. The commander of the French Atlantic Fleet described the conduct of *Ark*'s Ship's Company during their visit as exemplary, but the subsequent visit to Lisbon a week later did not go so smoothly. On the first night ashore, some of the Ship's Company became entangled in a riot between American personnel from a visiting amphibious group and the Portuguese authorities, themselves becoming a target for the police. Some sailors were assaulted and injured while others were caught in a cordon operation and arrested. Innocent bystanders in the wrong place at the wrong time, *Ark*'s men showed considerable restraint and were subsequently exonerated by the Superintendent of Police. The British Ambassador to Lisbon in a personal letter to Captain Brigstocke thanked them *"for their excellent conduct in what were clearly very difficult circumstances."* As a precaution, Captain Brigstocke cut short the visit and sailed the following morning, preferring instead the relative safety of a long weekend in Portsmouth.

A Families Day on 20th October helped restore spirits as did the cancellation of Exercise AUTUMN TRAIN that relieved an altogether too-crowded programme. The ship could therefore begin a Docking Assisted Maintenance Period (DAMP) at Portsmouth on 23rd October. Two diesel generators and two auxiliary boilers that had proved extremely temperamental during the summer exercises were replaced and modifications made to the aircraft lifts. A large package of painting and preservation was also undertaken, as was work on the ship's undersides. The ship was refitted to operate the latest Mk6 version of the Sea King ASW helicopter with which 820 Squadron was gradually re-equipping. The only problem during the DAMP was the inability to carry out budgeted alterations and additions because of delays in the required paperwork. During this period alongside, on 16th November the Ship's Company exercised the Freedom of the City of Leeds, marching through their affiliated city with bayonets fixed, drums beating and Colour flying.

On completion of the DAMP, on 12th January 1990 HMS *Ark Royal* passed her Fleet Material Inspection and after re-ammunitioning, she sailed for her shakedown cruise that lasted until the 23rd. Shakedown and a short defect rectification period provided little preparation for the ship's first hurdle of 1990: to pass Continuation Operational Sea Training. The ship was welcomed into FOST's embrace on 5th February and stayed at Portland for three weeks. Work-Up went very smoothly and included the notable first for a CVS in achieving a 'Good' assessment for her Damage Control efforts and a successful Sea Dart firing. From Portland, the ship stopped briefly at Copenhagen before starting Aviation Work Up in the Moray Firth; the milestone of the Operational Readiness Inspection being completed on 15th March. 800 Squadron, the Sea Harriers operating for the first time from Yeovilton with RAF Tri-Star tanker support, attacked the ship. 820 Squadron exercised the capability of their new SKJ Mk6 aircraft to deploy eight sono-buoys against submarine targets. Atrocious weather badly affected proceedings, with severe gales and heavy seas damaging both the ship's fittings and her hull. The heavy seas washed a flight deck tractor overboard, damaged a helicopter and gave the forward Vulcan Phalanx a particularly heavy battering, which forced the subsequent fitting of a replacement mount. Notwithstanding the weather, COST and ORI were both assessed as "Very Satisfactory" and Captain Brigstocke was encouraged by the high morale of his Ship's Company.

Certified ready for operations, HMS *Ark Royal* berthed at Portsmouth on 17th March to prepare for WESTLANT '90, an extended deployment of several ships to the United States and Canada. Rear Admiral the Honourable Nicholas Hill-Norton had succeeded Alan Grose as Flag Officer Third Flotilla and he would fly his flag in *Ark* at the head of Task Group 318.5. TG 318.5 included the Type-42 destroyer HMS *Glasgow*, Type-22 frigates HMS *Cumberland* and HMS *Brave* and the RFAs *Fort Grange* and *Olna*. The deployment began on 18th April when *Ark* with the Type-22s sailed for Exercise JOLLY ROGER, which would give useful anti-submarine practice with "live" targets and the crews from 820 Squadron the opportunity to gain experience of the tactical potential of their new aircraft. On 1st May, the three ships exercised with the American nuclear submarine USS *Providence* and then joined by RFA *Olna* rendezvoused with French Task Force 471 led by the carrier FS *Foch*

for a major PASSEX. The British and French air groups were to provide the threat in a joint air defence exercise but as it was, bad weather and heavy seas prevented the full plans coming to fruition. The very tight limits of pitch for operations by the French carrier restricted her catapult-launched aircraft getting off the deck, but *Ark*'s more adaptable Sea Harriers and helicopters managed to cross deck and invitations to lunch were exchanged. In all, the old Entente Cordiale was reasserted in no uncertain manner.

HMS *Brave* rejoined the task group on 6th May and HMS *Glasgow* linked up two days later, when *Ark* again became Admiral Hill-Norton's flagship. The following day the ships entered New York harbour for a successful five day flag visit. Following the visit, the task group dispersed temporarily. RFA *Fort Grange* arrived in New Jersey on the 11th and following a brief rendezvous at sea with the carrier left again to visit Charleston on the 18th. The three escorts left for their own programme in Canada, visiting Toronto, Hamilton and St John's. *Ark Royal*, in company with *Olna*, turned south for a visit and self maintenance period at Mayport in Florida. During the two-week stay, relations with the Americans were maintained and strengthened through official and private functions, sports, and organized visits. Many officers and men took the opportunity to reunite with their families who flew over for the occasion. It was with rather heavy hearts among her Ship's Company that *Ark* sailed from the 'palm tree and white sands paradise' of Mayport on 30th May to concentrate with the rest of the ships for Exercise MARCOT.

MARCOT was an exercise with the Royal Canadian Navy, whose assets formed a key component of the NATO Striking Fleet. The ships operated under the command of the Canadian Task Force 301 based in Bermuda and the 5th Destroyer Squadron led by the helicopter-carrying destroyer HMCS *Athabaskan*. The lack of a submarine target limited ASW training opportunities but aircraft based in Bermuda provided excellent AAW training for the Sea Harriers and the 'Bags'. The aircraft crews also honed their skills as an anti-surface unit team. The exercise continued as the force moved northwards from Bermuda, and the task group acquired a good understanding of both the strengths and weaknesses (especially in the AAW area) of the Canadian Navy. The ships arrived at Halifax on 15th June under a blanket of thick fog. *Ark Royal*'s nuclear capability was a focus for Greenpeace demonstrators who used small rubber boats to attempt to paint radiation symbols on the carrier's hull. They also unfurled a large anti-nuclear banner from the bridge close to the ship's berth, although it could hardly be seen in the mist. Most of the demonstrators were not local and the vast majority of Halifax's citizens gave a very friendly reception to the British matelots. From Halifax, *Ark* next sailed alone to Boston where the anti-nuclear demonstration was less prominent and the real welcome just as warm. During the passage to Boston the port outer gas turbine was changed; this was the second such failure in twelve months, highlighting a worrying negative trend in the reliability of *Ark*'s engines.

Boston was the last stop for *Ark Royal* during WESTLANT '90, the ship berthing at the commercial wharfs that lay directly under the flight path for airliners arriving at Logan International Airport. From Boston, Ark headed home, arriving at Portsmouth on 4th July to start a Base Assisted Maintenance Period (BAMP) and take summer leave. The BAMP proved a significant stage in *Ark*'s career with upgrades to the accommodation on two-deck marking the first phase of her conversion to carry female personnel. Along with this work, accommodation was increased for both officers and junior ratings, the ship's waste disposal system was improved, a large area of the flight deck represerved, the troublesome auxiliary boilers repaired, again. The software in the by now much more reliable ADAWS command system was also updated. The Lord Mayor of Leeds paid a reciprocal visit to the ship on 21st August following the Freedom of the City the previous November. *Ark* briefly put to sea for a couple of days for post-BAMP shakedown but she was soon back alongside by 23rd August to star first in a live BBC "South Today" programme and then Portsmouth Navy Days from 25th to 27th August.

On 3rd September HMS *Ark Royal* sailed as Rear Admiral Hill-Norton's flagship for Exercise TEAMWORK '90; another demonstration of the NATO ASW plan in the key Norwegian Sea campaign. NATO's plan acquired particular importance with the emphasis on forward operations in the 1980s, but by 1990 the exercise had been rather overtaken by events out of NATO's area. Not only had relations with the Soviet Union been transformed but, more importantly, a new threat had appeared in the shape of Saddam Hussein who had invaded Kuwait. All American assets bound for TEAMWORK '90 were diverted to Operation DESERT SHIELD, the build up in the Middle East designed to put pressure on Saddam to withdraw his forces and to protect Saudi Arabia. TEAMWORK '90 went ahead but with reduced forces and a foreshortened programme between 6th and 17th September. There was an increased emphasis on the role of the British CVSGs with HMS *Invincible* also taking part. *Ark Royal* covered the movement of an amphibious force to carry out landings at Namsos in Northern Norway. She was carrying a slightly reduced air group with one Sea Harrier and one SKJ less than normal complement. 820 Squadron suffered further losses when two more of its helicopters were damaged and had to be craned off the ship for repairs. In part to placate the Norwegians slightly alarmed by their apparent rapid downgrading as a NATO priority in the face of the Gulf build-up, *Ark Royal* visited Oslo at the end of TEAMWORK '90 with Admiral Hill-Norton making numerous visits and meetings to cement relations. The Oslo visit also proved highly enjoyable for *Ark*'s Ship's Company, somewhat to their surprise given the expectation of the high cost of living and 'Viking' character of the locals.

HMS *Ark Royal* left the Norwegian capital on 24th September and arrived at her base port two days later. A busy period of maintenance and planning ensued, to put her at thirty-days notice to deploy to the Gulf. Britain had codenamed its contribution to the Middle East crisis Operation GRANBY and *Ark Royal* was nominated as the contingency CVSG. On 15th October it looked like she might actually deploy as she sailed from Portsmouth and embarked her CAG. 801 Squadron was at full strength in pilots for the first time since the Falklands War and operated eight Sea Harriers worked-up during the passage south. 820 Squadron was still minus the two TEAMWORK '90 casualties but nevertheless exercised surface search, fighter evasion and assault operations with 849 'B' which was also still minus one aircraft.

A new era in the ship's operational role was beginning, symbolized by the departure of Captain Brigstocke at Gibraltar on 23rd October to be replaced by the first aviator in command, Captain Neil Rankin CBE.

Rear Admiral N E Rankin CB CBE JP

(Commanding Officer 1990 – 1992)

Aside from being professionally the best command in the Royal Navy, HMS *Ark Royal* enjoys a National profile of public affection that imbues a sense of cohesion and spirit amongst her Ship's Company that lives beyond a commission – shipmates remain friends.

A carrier's programme is invariably crowded with operational and recreational interest, and my time in our Ship was no exception. It spanned a gamut of experiences; minding United States TLAM shooters in the Eastern Mediterranean during the Gulf War, later rewarded by visits to Naples, Piraeus sans mortars, Majorca and the spectacular sights of Stromboli, Santorini et al; the WESTLANT deployment with a salmonella outbreak between Fort Lauderdale and Mayport, and memories of the Buffer off the Azores trading in his rigging knife for fourteen serious swordfish; the successes of the round Britain SHOPWINDOW '92, with its highlights of the SBAAT luncheon in Leith (the toppled lock lamp-post on departure, which I still prefer to look on as eleven left standing!); La Pallice, Copenhagen, Gibraltar, and Amsterdam that never was; the miscellany of professional achievements – COST, SCSD, AUTEC, JMC, Ex *Ocean* SAFARI, to name but a few.

Indeed, my time in the mighty *Ark* was a kaleidoscope of nothing but wonderful memories of people, events and places but none more enduring that that of the visit of Queen Elizabeth The Queen Mother; I am sure that it is Her Majesty's association with, and interest in, *Ark Royal* that makes us feel so special to be a member of the Ship's Company, whether past or present.

(page 2, see also page 25)

The shape of things to come: the first deck landing of the P1127 Kestrel, piloted by Bill Bedford, onboard HMS *Ark Royal* IV, 8th February 1963.

(page 8)
HMS *Ark Royal* V, under construction at Wallsend
Yard, Swan Hunter Shipbuilders Ltd during 1980
with HMS *Illustrious* in the background fitting out.
(Crown Copyright/MoD 1980)

(page 8)
Fitting the port Gear Box in
HMS *Ark Royal*, 1980.
(Crown Copyright/MoD 1980)

(page 8)
Craning on the 12° ski ramp onto
HMS *Ark Royal*, Spring 1981.
(Crown Copyright/MoD 1981)

(page 8)
HM Queen Elizabeth The Queen Mother at the
Naming Ceremony for HMS *Ark Royal V*, 2nd June 1981.
(Crown Copyright/MoD 1981)

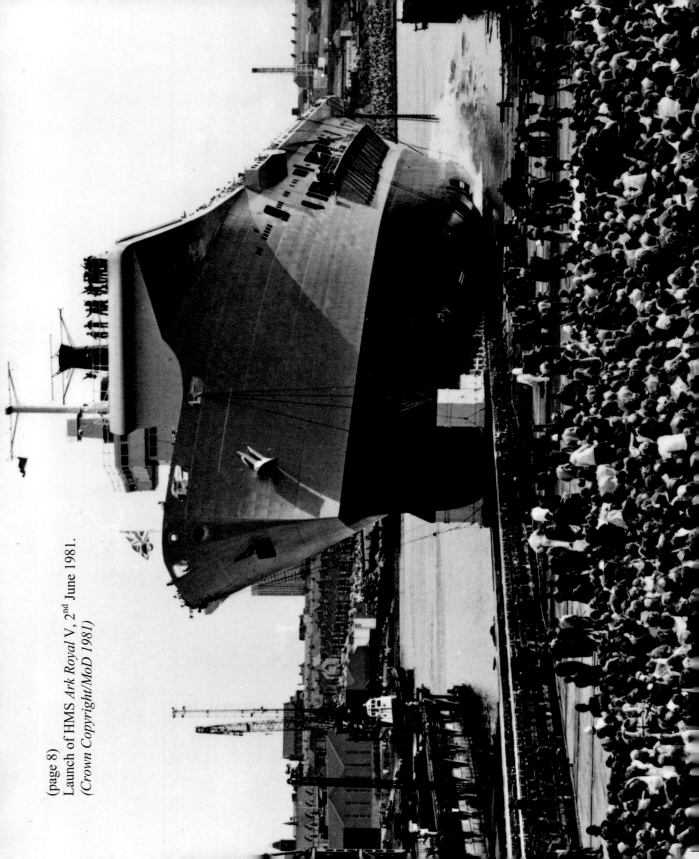

(page 8)
Launch of HMS *Ark Royal V*, 2nd June 1981.
(Crown Copyright/MoD 1981)

(pages 9-10)
Fitting Out of HMS *Ark Royal*, at Walker Yard,
Swan Hunter Shipbuilders Ltd, 1983
(Crown Copyright/MoD 1983)

(page 10)
Rendezvous with HMS *Illustrious* in the South
Western Approaches during HMS *Ark Royal*'s
Contractors Sea Trials, 1984.
(Crown Copyright/MoD 1984).

(page 10)

HMS *Ark Royal* leaves North Shields for Portsmouth
28th June 1985. A Fairey Swordfish is parked at No.1
Spot on the Flight Deck.
(*Crown Copyright/MoD 1985*)

(page 13)
HMS *Ark Royal* arrives at Portsmouth, 1st July 1985.
The Fairey Swordfish is joined onboard by Sea
Harrier XZ494 flown by Lt Cdr Hugh Slade 899
NAS with 820 NAS Sea Kings providing a fly past.
(Crown Copyright/MoD 1985)

(page 14)
HM Queen Elizabeth The Queen Mother
at HMS *Ark Royal's* Commissioning
Ceremony, 1st November 1985.
(Crown Copyright/MoD 1985)

(page 16)
HMS *Ark Royal* sails past Governor's Island outbound from New York City, 8th July 1986, following her participation in the Centenary unveiling of the Statue of Liberty.
(Crown Copyright/MoD 1986)

(page 17)
FOF2's task group for Exercise AUTUMN TRAIN 86, Rear Admiral
Richard Thomas flying his flag in HMS *Bristol* (lead ship).
(Crown Copyright/MoD 1986)

(page 17)
HMS *Ark Royal* off Gibraltar, during Exercise
AUTUMN TRAIN 86, October 1986.
(Crown Copyright/MoD 1986)

(page 17)
Sea Dart High Seas Firing, during Exercise
AUTUMN TRAIN. October 1986.
(Crown Copyright/MoD 1986)

(pages 21-22)
HMS *Ark Royal* negotiates the Thames Barrier,
en route to Greenwich, 4th June 1987,
(Crown Copyright/MoD 1987)

(page 22)
820 NAS Sea King winches WO A R S Benton clear of the stricken MV *Hessen*, 25th June 1987.
(Crown Copyright/MoD 1987)

(page 23)
Lt Dale O'Meara recovered by 820 NAS Sea King to HMS *Ark Royal* after ditching Sea Harrier ZA190 south west of Tiree, 15th October 1987.
(Crown Copyright/MoD 1987)

(pages 23-24)
Harrier GR-3s from No.1 Squadron and
Sea Harriers from 800 and 801 NAS
operating from HMS *Ark Royal* during
Exercise PURPLE WARRIOR,
November 1987.
(Crown Copyright/MoD 1987)

'NEVER MIND ALL THAT RUBBISH! WHERE DID ROD STEWART SING 'I AM SAILING'?'

(pages 26-32)
HMS *Ark Royal*'s only global deployment – OUTBACK '88
(photograph taken off Singapore, 23rd July 1988).
(Crown Copyright/MoD 1988)

(page 26)
SS *Canberra* and HMS *Ark Royal* rendezvous in the eastern Atlantic, off Lisbon, 16th June 1988.
(Crown Copyright/MoD 1988)

(page 26)
HMS *Ark Royal* meets Italian task group led by
the carrier ITS *Guiseppe Garibaldi* in the western
Mediterranean.
(Crown Copyright/MoD 1988)

(page 28)
USS *New Jersey* fires a broadside with maximum flash effect in company astern of HMS *Ark Royal*. Subic Bay exercise area. 12th August 1988.
(Crown Copyright/MoD 1988)

(page 28)
HMS *Ark Royal* arrives at Hong Kong, 23rd August 1988.
(Crown Copyright/MoD 1988)

(page 30)
HMS *Ark Royal* berths next to the Opera House, Sydney, Australia, 27th September 1988.
(Crown Copyright/MoD 1988)

(page 31)
The only ever meeting of all three CVSs at sea - HMS *Ark Royal* (foreground), HMS *Illustrious* (middle), HMS *Invincible* (rear, fresh from refit), rendezvous off Start Point 14th December 1988. (*Crown Copyright/MoD 1988*)

(page 36)
UK FRS-1s and Spanish Matador AV8-Bs operate from the deck of
HMS *Ark Royal*, during Exercise SHARP SPEAR September 1989.
(Crown Copyright/MoD 1989)

HMS *Ark Royal* arrives at Lisbon Portugal for an ill-fated visit

(page 38)
HMS *Ark Royal* during Self Maintenance Period, Mayport Florida, during
WESTLANT '90, May 1990. In port with *Ark Royal* are the US conventional
carriers USS *Saratoga* and USS *Forrestal*
(Crown Copyright/MoD 1990)

(page 38)
HMS *Ark Royal* passing the Twin
Towers, New York, 9th May 1990
(Crown Copyright/MoD 1990)

(page 39)
HMS *Ark Royal* last port visit during
WESTLANT '90; arriving at Boston
under the flight path into Logan Airport
(Crown Copyright/MoD 1990)

Chapter 5

1990 – 1992:
GRANBY, *Gloucester* and girls at sea

Captain Neil Rankin CBE had spent a varied career with the Royal Navy and the Royal Air Force. Experienced with both rotary and fixed-wing aircraft, he was the first Royal Navy pilot to fly the Harrier and went on to command three *Leander*-class frigates: HMS *Achilles*, HMS *Bacchante* and latterly HMS *Andromeda* as Captain F8, during which the ship had been busy protecting UK-registered oil tankers operating in the Arabian Gulf, under the auspices of Operation ARMILLA. The first Commander Air in HMS *Invincible*, he was no stranger to CVS operations, or to the regional tensions caused by the fall-out of the Iran-Iraq War. As such, Captain Rankin was ideally suited to lead *Ark Royal* into combat.

In the event however, the Government decided that a CVS was not immediately required and instead of deploying east from Gibraltar, *Ark Royal* sailed for home on the 25th October, carrying out altogether more mundane self-noise trials at Portland before arriving at Portsmouth on 1st November. There followed a period of uncertainty and contingency planning largely spent alongside in the ship's homeport while the debate continued over whether a CVS was an appropriate augmentation of Britain's Gulf forces. While keeping herself in readiness for deployment in some form or other the ship was available for work close to home. On 7th November she embarked two 820 SKJs and sailed for the South Western Approaches where two prototype Sea Harriers FRS-2 variants from Boscombe Down carried out

sea trials from the ship, while 801 Squadron also exercised with the ship as part of their GRANBY preparations.

After the short period at sea, *Ark*'s waiting game at Portsmouth began again on 16th November and continued through Christmas but, in early January 1991, the plans for JMC 91-1 were suddenly cancelled six days prior to the start of the exercise. With a military offensive about to take place to dislodge Iraqi forces occupying Kuwait, the Government belatedly took the decision to send a carrier to the Gulf, ordering HMS *Ark Royal* to deploy with all speed. The ship sailed from Portsmouth on 10th January 1991, for GRANBY duties as flagship of Task Group 323.2, with the *Type-22* frigate HMS *Sheffield* and the Royal Fleet Auxiliaries RFA *Olmeda* and RFA *Regent*. The following day *Ark Royal* embarked her own air group that had been tailored into a GRANBY configuration that reflected the expected operational profile of the ship. The eight Sea Harriers of 801 Squadron were supplemented by four normal SKJs from 820 Squadron, and six more stripped of sonar for use in the utility role (coded SKU). One or two of the latter usually flew from *Olmeda*. The 'pinger' helicopters provided protection from possible submarine threats, notably from Libya, while the SKUs were used for boarding operations in support of sanctions. Three SKWs of 849 'B' Flight provided radar cover. On the third day of the southern transit, *Ark Royal* met the *Type-42* destroyers HMS *Exeter* and HMS

Manchester for all three ships to conduct Sea Dart test firings, which was part of an intensive weapons training and work-up programme run by the combined staffs of the First and Third Flotillas. HMS *Manchester* remained with the task group and continued south with the other ships. Fast roping drills for boarding parties were conceived and practiced, using the RFAs as targets after initial trials on *Ark*'s flight deck. Meanwhile, the ship's command team also familiarised itself with the use of an enhanced satellite communications fit that included an INMARSAT telephone link. Off Gibraltar, the work up staff departed by 820 SKU just before the newly promoted Rear Admiral John Brigstocke, now the Flag Officer Second Flotilla, arrived to use his former command as flagship of the task group. The staff from Flag Officer Naval Aviation also arrived to assist in training up the air group as the ship transited the Mediterranean.

On 17th January 1991, Operation DESERT SHIELD became Operation DESERT STORM as American and British air and naval forces began offensive bombardment of Iraq. As the fighting started, *Ark Royal*'s posture escalated with the Ship's Company going into defence watches and the Sea Harriers moving to "Alert-5" for Combat Air Patrol, each armed with four AIM-9L Sidewinder missiles. In order to avoid any unnecessary escalation of tensions, given both the instability of Colonel Gaddafi and the uncertainty of his support for Saddam Hussein, flying was temporarily curtailed on the 18th as the task group sailed past the Libyan coast.

HMS *Ark Royal* arrived off Cyprus on 22nd January and immediately adopted a holding pattern while it was decided what her next step should be. Having spent weeks training and even longer waiting, *Ark*'s Ship's Company were keen to enter the mix. In the event however, *Ark* would go no further as there seemed to be opposition in London to her playing a more forward role. Reportedly the US Navy would have liked her to come at least into the Red Sea to lead the continued sanctions operations and to release American assets for more

offensive deployment. But it was not to be and of Admiral Brigstocke's ships only HMS *Manchester* went onward through the Suez Canal. Admiral Brigstocke and the remainder of his group took up the important but rather frustrating role of surveillance of the vital Mediterranean lines of communication upon which the coalition forces in the Gulf depended. *Ark Royal* and her aircraft undertook the major share of the surveillance task, maintaining a comprehensive air and surface picture of the eastern Mediterranean. The ship also acted as anti-air warfare controller of the eastern sector of the US Sixth Fleet's defensive organisation, one of three such coordinated controllers covering the entire sea, as well as the Force controller 'Over the Horizon' Tactical aircraft deployments. NATO's Southern Naval and Air Commanders based in Naples attempted to build a coherent alliance-level surveillance organization. While this was established the task group took interim lead in providing a network-enabled picture of surface and air traffic to the NATO headquarters, using JOTS.

849 'B' Flight had to fly up to five sorties a day to fulfil the important role of providing daylight AEW cover for the force, but the emergent presence of NATO E-3A AWACs aircraft reduced the pressure on the squadron after 29th January. During February, the SKWs flew AEW missions only at dawn and dusk and were able to be used more in the surface surveillance and targeting roles. 801 Squadron concentrated on combat air patrol against the possibility of Iraqi attack with an intensive flying programme at times. For two periods of 36 hours each, the squadron achieved a two-over-two flying programme of Sea Harriers on CAP by day and one-over-one by night. 820 Squadron was also kept busy with helicopter delivery service and replenishment tasks as well as surface search and probe missions. A weekly flight was maintained with RAF Akrotiri in Cyprus for fresh provisions, incoming stores and mail.

RAF Phantoms based in Cyprus were frequent visitors for air defence exercises. The closest touch was kept with the Americans with a direct FLEET SATCOM secure satellite link established with the flagship of the Sixth Fleet, the cruiser USS *Belknap*. This was backed up by a portable satellite communications terminal specially obtained from the US Navy at Rota in southern Spain, complete with a USN Chief Petty Officer to instruct *Ark*'s communicators in its workings. The group operated with three US warships, the destroyer USS *Spruance* and Ticonderoga-class Aegis cruiser USS *Philippine Sea*, together with the nuclear-powered cruiser USS *Virginia* that was an active participant in the Desert Storm strategic air campaign with her Tomahawk cruise missiles.

HMS *Charybdis*, a Sea Wolf *Leander*-class frigate, nicknamed the "Cherry-B", relieved HMS *Manchester* as *Ark Royal*'s air-defence goalkeeper on 7th February and the opportunity was taken during the handover to carry out an anti-surface exercise with the additional ship. The following day a ceasefire was announced but it was not until the 19th that the situation was assessed as stable enough for *Ark Royal* to revert to thirty minutes notice for action. As the de-escalation continued for a further five days, the tactical situation allowed TG 323.2 to depart the Cyprus area for Naples and following a relaxation in the Rules of Engagement, for the Ship's Company to revert to cruising watches. On 25th February the Task Group exercised with the German Task Group 501 of four destroyers and frigates, with two support ships, that had been sent to the Mediterranean to relieve other assets sent to the Gulf. 801's Sea Harriers carried out a most encouraging undetected exercise Sea Eagle attack on the German ships. As the German ships kept company, a Greek submarine provided a target for 820 Squadron's rather under-used SKJs. Combined air defence exercises in the Ionian Sea were organised at the last minute by the Sixth Fleet for the following two days, which delayed *Ark Royal*'s passage north but she passed through the straits of Messina for a well earned rest in Naples that began on 1st March.

That day, Admiral Brigstocke delegated

conduct of the Task Group to Captain Rankin under the operational control of the Commander in Chief Fleet and he hauled down his flag two days later. *Ark Royal* sailed with RFA *Regent* from Naples on 7th March and the task group reformed briefly the following day. NATO high command lowered the surveillance level and the Sixth Fleet disbanded the AAW control system shortly after; the impressive Mediterranean-wide air and sea surveillance picture faded away and *Ark* could find nothing on the frequencies that had once been so busy.

Operational efficiency was maintained by exercises, including two with the SSNs HMS *Torbay* and USS *Grayling* while air defence serials also continued to exploit the opportunities for data exchange with shore stations. There was no doubt that the preceding weeks had seen an impressive demonstration of NATO's ability to conduct integrated maritime operations in the Mediterranean. To provide relaxation after the tensions of long hours at advanced states of readiness, *Ark Royal* visited Piraeus from 15th to 20th March and then Palma from 27th March to 3rd April. "Cherry-B" detached from the Group on 11th March to go under the control of NATO, but the rest of the ships rendezvoused South of Ibiza on 4th April for a four-ship replenishment at sea. They then transited the Straits of Gibraltar the following day and finally *Ark* formally reverted to organic surveillance and link procedures. Four days later TG 323.2 began to dissolve as HMS *Sheffield* and RFA *Regent* detached to Devonport, RFA *Olmeda* headed east to Portland and the Sea Harriers flew off to Yeovilton. HMS *Ark Royal* sailed back to Portsmouth alone. The thwarted GRANBY deployment was finally over.

HMS *Ark Royal* now began a much-needed period of maintenance through April and May, and the Ship's Company was granted Easter leave. Having come unscathed through the deployment, the period was marred by the death of MEM Peter Peers in a road accident while on leave. The ship was in good material state when she sailed on 30th

May for first shakedown and then JMC 91-2. The air group shakedown was particularly valuable with very heavy interaction between the Sea Harriers and shore-based aircraft from various units. Shake down led straight into Exercise *Ocean* SAFARI, the traditional periodic exercise of NATO's Atlantic Lifelines campaign that began on 6th June.

With the USSR in dissolution and the Gulf situation absorbing the efforts of the European-based US carrier battle groups, the exercise did not have a forward operations component. Instead of leading the Striking Fleet through the GRIUK gaps into the Norwegian Sea, *Ark Royal*'s group conducted ASW precursor operations in the South Western Approaches before transiting south to commence convoy escort operations in the Bay of Biscay. The carrier remained detached from the rest of the group in radio silence and without transmitting her radars, instead receiving the tactical picture by link from the escorts while providing cover both to them and the convoy with her air group. The exercise was a "free play" evolution and the carrier completely escaped submarine attack by this tactic and there were only a few air attacks, which the SKW/Sea Harrier CAP combination proved very effective in handling. Nevertheless, the Sea Harriers were plagued with technical problems.

The Sea Harrier was the most manoeuvrable fixed wing aircraft in the world, but the necessary understanding and skills needed to pilot it were considerable. In addition to being able to fly the Harrier in forward flight (above stall speed when it behaved in the manner of a typical fixed-wing aircraft), it was necessary to maintain control during STOVL manoeuvres when the lift and control surfaces did not work. Two control elements were fitted to achieve this that a fixed wing aircraft did not normally have; namely the Thrust Vector System (TVS) and the Reaction Control System (RCS). TVS adjusted the angle of the four engine nozzles between 0° (horizontal, pointing straight back) and 98° (pointing

downwards and slightly forward), with the 90° position generally used for vertical take-off and landing. RCS was similar in action to the cyclic control of a helicopter, and while irrelevant during forward flight mode, it maintained critical control during vertical and slow-speed hovering manoeuvres. During the ascent and hover, RCS was continuously adjusted to maintain position over the patch of ground, much as it was with a helicopter. Wind direction and the orientation of the aircraft to this was also critically-important since the aircraft had to face into the wind when taking off in this way and a side wind would cause the aircraft to pitch away from the lee side. This would alter the thrust vector away from vertical and cause the aircraft to slew sideways, which was hard to control and dangerous, in severe cases the aircraft could settle with power while moving to the side.

For 801's pilots, the performance of the RCS was causing severe doubts about their ability to land the aircraft safely, limiting their operations to all but the most benign and optimal weather conditions. These doubts led the following month to the removal and overhaul of the engine from all aircraft. The ship also suffered her own difficulties with the catastrophic failure of the port outer Olympus gas turbine.

Ocean SAFARI terminated on 18th June, when Admiral Brigstocke and his staff disembarked and ship made for La Pallice for a little 'rest and recuperation'. Ten days later, *Ark Royal* was back in Portsmouth to begin a self-maintenance and leave period that lasted until 21st August. This included repairs to the engine and completion of the work to make the ship able to carry the first female personnel, due to embark in November. All of 801 Squadron's Sea Harriers were successfully reworked and remedial treatment on the airframes of 820 Squadron's newly upgraded Mk6 SKJs was completed after cracks had been discovered during following their conversion. Sadly during the leave period, the ship's Chinese cobbler, Lam Fat Ting, succumbed to serious illness and died before he could be repatriated to Hong Kong.

At the end of Summer leave, HMS *Ark Royal* dutifully carried out the usual early autumn round of public engagements: at Devonport Navy Days, a Families Day from Portsmouth and then the Royal Navy Equipment Exhibition. The ship embarked a pre-production Merlin helicopter and hosted the opening-day press conference given by Tom King, the Secretary of State for Defence, where he announced the order for 44 of the aircraft as successors to the trusty SKJ. Many visitors were hosted onboard including a senior Omani delegation. Just over a week later, on 10th September the ship was at sea once more for another WESTLANT Task Group deployment. The departure was an especially sad one as AEM Gareth James collapsed on the flight deck from a brain haemorrhage and died a few days later in the Royal Naval Hospital Haslar.

Task Group 313.1 consisted of HMS *Ark Royal*, once again flying the flag of Rear Admiral Brigstocke, the *Type-42* destroyer HMS *Gloucester* which had earlier in the year shot down an Iraqi Silkworm missile, earning its Commanding Officer Phillip Willcocks a DSC, the *Type-22* frigate HMS *London* commanded by Captain Mark Stanhope and *Ark*'s trusted and regular RFAs, *Olna* and *Regent*. HMS *Talent* attached to the group during the transatlantic crossing to exercise with the seven SKJs embarked from 820 NAS, in preparation for the mutual tactical development trials that would follow at AUTEC, under the codename Trial WOKING. The ship also carried a reduced air group of six Sea Harriers and three SKWs. Flag Officer Second Flotilla left as the ship passed Bermuda on the 20th and *Ark Royal* put into Fort Lauderdale, Florida. In the midst of conducting pre-AUTEC briefings for the command teams and modifying the SKJs so that they could be tracked on the American weapon ranges in the Bahamas, most of the Ship's Company had time to enjoy some rest and relaxation. An even greater number of locals took advantage of the ship being open to visitors, to 'goof' at the UK's flagship and the 250,000th visitor since commissioning was received onboard.

HMS *Ark Royal* sailed for Andros on 28th September and Trial WOKING began three days later. The main objective of the trial was to develop the tactics used by the SKJ Mk6s and the Stingray torpedo against fast, deep-diving nuclear submarines. The SKJs worked intensively, flying 250 hours in the air and achieving 143 hours of 'in-contact' time with HMS *Talent*, which included launching nine Stingray exercise torpedoes against the submarine. The WOKING trials equipment filled each SKJ leaving only one spare seat in the cabin and little or no room to conduct helicopter delivery services; nevertheless they were pressed into service but this hampered the exercise significantly. Hopes of the Ship's Company enjoying the tropical beaches on Andros and the Bahamas were thwarted by an outbreak of salmonella food poisoning that affected 200 people and led to a quarantine being imposed onboard. Stringent hygiene and movement measures contained the epidemic and the ship remained operational throughout. 849 'B' Flight escaped the quarantine by flying to RFA *Olna*, assisting HMS *London*'s support of US Coast Guard drug interdiction operations near the Turks and Caicos Islands. This was the first time *Ark*'s assets had been used in this role, an important new dimension of naval operations. Despite the minor difficulties encountered, WOKING was a great success and the task group rendezvoused northeast of the Bahamas on 6th October for three days of combined training. Sea Dart high seas firings were the highpoint; *Gloucester* scoring two hits in the first session while *Ark* tried to rectify a fault with one of the hydraulic rams in her magazine and repair the forward R909 tracker. The system recovered just in time. *Ark* scored two hits during her own twin-target engagement; equalling the score against the war-proven *Type-42*.

The Task Group then put into Mayport on 11th October, first for a flag visit and then for an extended port visit. Over a hundred friends and family members of the Ship's Company crossed the Atlantic to enjoy Florida and take an early opportunity for Christmas shopping. Many personnel took advantage of the very favourable Government exchange rate offered onboard, judging by the business done by the Chief Writer who cashed over $1 million dollars between the Fort Lauderdale and Mayport visits. 801 Squadron detached six Sea Harriers to Cecil Field Naval Air Station where combat training was carried out against American F-15s, F-16s and F-18s, while 820 Squadron disembarked four SKJs to the US air station at Mayport for continuation flying training.

Her American exploits over for another year, HMS *Ark Royal* sailed for Gibraltar on 22nd October and filled the Atlantic passage with ship and departmental training drills. The relatively small air group had generally relieved pressure on both flight deck and hangar operations and maintenance but now the pressures of the limited helicopter service at Andros, poor mail delivery to the USA and spares shortages during the preceding weeks began to tell, with the aircraft and ship's equipment alike starting to fail. The highlight of the passage was a three-day passing exercise with French Task Group 450.1 under the command of Rear Admiral Christian Rouyer, with the ASW frigates FS *Tourville* and FS *La Motte-Picquet*, together with the auxiliary *Durance* and the nuclear-powered submarine *Emeraude*. The French welcomed *Ark*'s participation and there was a healthy exchange of officers between ships. 801's aircraft had good Sea Eagle practice in ASuW serials while *Emeraude* provided a live target for the SKJs.

On arrival at Gibraltar on 4th November, HMS *Ark Royal*'s air engineers rigged the hangar for a television recording for Central Television's "Frankie's On...Board!" starring the comedian Frankie Howerd. Howerd had made several such "concert" type programmes throughout his career, and the planned six-part series "Frankie's On..." took his unique brand of comedy to various audiences, including coal miners and medical students in Nottingham ("Frankie's On...The Coals!" and "Frankie's On...Call!") and fire fighters in Gloucester ("Frankie's On... Fire!") Frankie was clearly in his element in front of *Ark*'s Ship's Company and he was more than happy to look out and see wall-to-wall sailors, all laughing at every line of vintage Howerd. One sailor caught his eye and during an exchange he chastised him for, "*Being naughty! Now return to your cabin - alone!*" Howerd's humour did not appeal to all however; Captain Rankin 'tittering ye not' as he remarked wryly in his subsequent report of proceedings that the show was "*...unlikely to break box office records when it is transmitted later this year.*" As it was, the show turned out to be Howerd's last television performance. The comedian died in April 1992 before the final two shows were recorded and his appearance onboard *Ark* aired on 21st June. Sadly also, Captain Rankin's prediction came true - the show failing to make the top-ten ratings.

Back to more routine matters, the ship sailed from Gibraltar for more aircraft trials. This time, the team from Boscombe Down wanted to expand the Ship Helicopter Operating Limits of the Chinook heavy lift helicopter, requiring many hours of data to be gathered on the performance of the helicopter as it launched and recovered to the deck in various geometries and wind conditions. The trials revealed significant limitations on other simultaneous deck operations, for example, embarked aircraft could only be parked forward of two-spot while the Chinook operated to the deck. The trials team soon exhausted the options available in the calm weather conditions off Gibraltar. Rather than tarrying too long in the warmer Mediterranean climes, the ship sought rougher weather in the South Western Approaches and a demanding trials schedule was achieved with eighty hours of flying in nine days involving 400 deck landings. During the first half of the exercise while the ship was still in the Gibraltar area, useful AAW training was carried out with detachments of Tornado GR-1 and F-4 Phantoms from No.27 and

No.74 Squadrons RAF, respectively. On the way home a long-range encounter exercise was also carried out with HMS *Invincible*, providing useful experience for the Ops Room team and the reduced CAG.

The reduced flying by the carrier air group enforced by the Chinook trials allowed an advance party of sixty to be flown home early in a C-130 to RAF Lyneham, but for the rest of the Ship's Company, they arrived home on 18th November 1991. The following day, The Queen Mother paid another very welcome visit to her ship to belatedly celebrate the tenth anniversary of its launching at Swan Hunter, meeting a cross section of officers, men and their families during a reception in the hangar and over lunch in the wardroom. This was the last time that Her Majesty would meet an all-male crew, for on 25th November, the ship received its first draft of 73 WRNS. The new female members of the Ship's Company immediately settled in, overcoming the significant challenge of finding her in deep maintenance with the domestic facilities on the jetty and hotel services provided on a floating barge moored alongside.

HMS *Ark Royal* docked down from 28th November 1991 until 4th February 1992, during which time several important upgrades were completed. A reverse osmosis water making plant was installed to increase the water making capacity of the ship to cope with the increases in the ships complement over the original design capacity. The OASIS4 computerised stores inventory and data handling system, with three central processors and seventy access terminals used by the ship's supply department, was also installed to help improve their service to the engineers. The system was not without its teething troubles however and despite the Jack Dusty's "willingness" to assist would-be customers, all too often the computers said 'no'. The midships and aft Phalanx mounts were also removed to go for refurbishment and replaced by units taken from HMS *Manchester*. The replacement midships Phalanx proved unusually temperamental and it would be some weeks before

the gun was finally set to work. The enormous work package was only completed thanks to some unseasonably mild weather that allowed access to the superstructure for husbandry and ensured the flight deck paint dried on time. *Ark Royal* sailed on time for post-DAMP trials on 12th February, which were largely successful save for a serious problem with the propulsion plant caused by overheating of the new bearings fitted in the main gearboxes. The ship put back a day early, on the 20th, to rectify the problem.

During this period alongside, the WRNS attracted their first royal visitor. On 28th February 1992, HRH The Princess Royal, in her capacity as Chief Commandant, visited the ship to see how the wrens were settling into life at sea. Her Royal Highness was met by Vice Admiral The Hon Sir Nicholas Hill-Norton, Flag Officer Third Flotilla, and toured the ship meeting female personnel in their working spaces.

With repairs to the gearbox bearings complete the ship sailed for shakedown and weapon training on 4th March and work continued on the troublesome Phalanx system. The shakedown was particularly important since the wrens were not the only new personnel on board. In fact, almost a third of the Ship's Company was new to the ship since the start of DAMP and everyone needed working up to full efficiency; Captain Rankin and his officers instigating an intensive training programme to achieve just that. Sadly, the Ship's Company's anticipated reward for both the DAMP and the intensive shake-down – a routine visit to Amsterdam – had to be cancelled due to extremely bad weather, and much to the Captain's regret, the ship arrived back at Portsmouth on 14th March.

HMS *Ark Royal*'s still rather raw Ship's Company could now look forward to another of those most demanding periods in a ship's life, operational sea training, that would work them up into a fully honed team. Bar a few lingering and stubborn defects, the ship itself was in generally good material shape as she left for another week of shakedown and weapon training before arriving at

Portland. In the middle of shakedown, on 26th March, Admiral Sir Julian Oswald, now First Sea Lord, felt sufficiently confident in *Ark*'s progress to host his French opposite number, Admiral Coatanea, onboard.

The harbour week of Continuation Operational Sea Training (COST) began on 30th March 1992. Normally a warship would be in immaculate condition both materially and cosmetically for FOST's inspection, but for the Marine Engineers this proved impossible. Two bearings on the high speed line from the port inner Olympus engine to the port main gearbox, needed to be replaced and work had to go on in the midst of the inspection, with Commander (ME) carefully managing the expectations of his FOST opposite number. With the repair completed, COST began in earnest in the Portland sea areas on 6th April and continued until the 16th. The assessment included live Sea Dart firings, and the usual series of increasingly difficult damage control scenarios, which the Ship's Company managed to deal with. After the ship had been put through its paces, next in the firing line was her air group.

The air group was specially configured with reduced numbers during the lead into COST to enable squadron work up ashore to continue in parallel to the work up of the ship. The full CAG only embarked temporarily a week before the Staff Sea Check. During COST harbour week, 820 Squadron disembarked to continue ASW training while 801 Squadron and 849 'B' Flight remained ashore at Yeovilton until 10th April. Confidence quickly built among *Ark*'s men and women, and morale improved noticeably as everyone learned their function and teamwork grew. This was despite a very serious accident that took place on 20th April, Easter Monday, during the air group work up to ORI. The Sea Harriers were lobbing 28-lb practice bombs at a splash target astern. Due to a software failure the correct "aim off" was not applied to one bomb that landed on the flight deck, detonating as it penetrated into 2L2 mess deck where it injured five people. The most badly injured sailor suffered burns and injuries to his hand and stomach. This is how one anonymous messmate saw it: "*There was an explosion in the mess deck and it was all white smoke. I got out of my bunk, saw my mate and got him out. I went back but couldn't see anyone else. Meanwhile I was shouting, 'Fire! Fire! Fire!' It could have been worse, someone could have died.*"

The Principal Medical Officer, Surgeon Commander Andrew Burgess, assisted by Surgeon Lieutenant Commander Patrick Loxdale, assessed the casualties and dealt with the most serious first. In the midst of all this, one of the female members of the ship's company developed acute appendicitis and had to be operated on. The casualties were stabilised overnight before being transferred by RAF aero-medical evacuation team to the Royal Naval Hospital at Haslar. Captain Rankin had every reason to be proud of his Ship's Company and the way they coped with the incident. Flag Officer Sea Training complimented the ship on its reaction; "*the response teams, already sharpened up, acted with impressive speed and efficiency, preventing further tragedy.*" The initial treatment the casualties had received onboard was described as "*exemplary*" by the staff at RNH Haslar. The reaction to the emergency underpinned how far the team had developed together. With so many new personnel, many in key positions, it was a considerable achievement for *Ark Royal* to emerge from COST and ORI with a "Very Satisfactory" overall assessment.

Having worked through Easter the ship appreciated a five-day visit to Greenock at the beginning of May. *Ark* then made a rapid passage to Portsmouth for a self-maintenance period that began on the 6th. The gearbox problem on the port inner drive train was finally solved and the damaged mess deck repaired as the Ship's Company took delayed Easter leave. Communications were also enhanced for the carrier's planned role as a floating Joint Force headquarters in Exercise PURPLE MONARCH. The 1st June saw *Ark* once again take centre stage during Staff College Sea Days before continuing her showpiece role as she led a ship-tour around the UK in Exercise SHOP WNDOW. This was an attempt to sell the Navy to the widest and most influential audience possible; to explain that even with the end of the Cold War it was as useful as ever in a wider range of roles in an unstable world. Captain Rankin was pleased to be able "*to reach a lot of people who would otherwise not get the opportunity to meet the Navy, who live too far away from Navy Days ports.*"

The SHOP WINDOW Group included the destroyer HMS *Gloucester*, the single role mine hunter HMS *Cromer* and the diesel submarine HMS *Oracle*, supported by RFA *Olmeda*. Commando Sea Kings were embarked to transport the visitors to and from the ship. The first dress rehearsal took place off Portsmouth with the Commander in Chief Fleet, Admiral Sir Jock Slater, using the opportunity as his annual VIP day. Then it was off to the Bristol Channel where on 6th June the Sea Kings picked up visitors from both Bristol and Cardiff Airports. Onboard the carrier they were welcomed by the newly designated Flag Officer Surface Flotilla, Vice Admiral Sir Nicholas Hill-Norton (formerly Flag Officer Third Flotilla), and then given a series of presentations and a tour of the ship before witnessing an air display by the embarked aircraft and *Gloucester*'s Lynx. The SKAs were able to show off the rapid roping techniques, developed onboard during Operation GRANBY, while a replenishment with RFA *Olmeda* demonstrated the deft ship-handling ability of the big ships' command teams. The public display was repeated two days later off Liverpool for visitors from the northwest of England and then again on the 10th for Scottish visitors, with the units taking part in JMC 93-2 in the Firth of Forth.

The opportunity was taken of an informal visit to Leith during which period Admiral Hill-Norton disembarked and Sir Jock Slater hosted a dinner. The Ship's Company made the most of the Scottish capitol, while Captain Rankin enjoyed the hospitality of the Scottish Business Awards Achievement Trust at their annual awards ceremony in Leith, in the presence of HRH The Princess Royal. When the ship sailed on the 15th, Admiral Hill Norton's chief of staff became the principal host, but the routine was much the same as "Event Days" were held off Newcastle and Hull on the 16th and 17th. After this sustained public relations effort the Ship's Company was especially happy to relax in the congenial surroundings of Copenhagen from 19th to 23rd June, the ship making its first foreign visit since October 1991. Then it was back to Portsmouth for a short period alongside before embarking the Commander UK Task Group (as Rear Admiral Brigstocke, had now been retitled) for Exercise PURPLE MONARCH.

Exercise PURPLE MONARCH started ashore at the end of June and over the weekend of 27th - 28th COMUKTG's Joint Force Operations Staff embarked in the ship. *Ark Royal* sailed for Gibraltar the following day giving the flag staff the opportunity to familiarise themselves with their new surroundings. For the Ship's Company, much of this activity was invisible: no CAG was embarked save for four Chinooks carried on the flight deck and one fifth of the crew were given sea-leave, resolving any accommodation shortages caused by the presence of the flag staff. The exercise preparations were delayed by unseasonal foggy weather but all the passage and exercise procedures ran smoothly before the Staff were transferred at Gibraltar to the amphibious landing ship, HMS *Fearless*, or ashore to continue the exercise.

Ark came alongside in Gibraltar on 2nd July, and once again hosted Admiral Slater who had come onboard to view the exercise festivities. For the Ship's Company however, a far more significant senior officer arrived six days later, in the shape of their new commanding officer, Captain Jeremy Blackham. Captain Rankin had overseen many significant changes in *Ark Royal* during his period in command and through the highs and lows of deployments, DAMP, work-up and 'window dressing' had forged a strong team. But he also recognised that the recent programme and lack of aviation assets had taken some toll on the operational efficiency of the ship since COST and that a major work-up package would be needed to prepare the Ship's Company for the busy and challenging autumn programme. This would be Captain Blackham's first challenge, the first of many.

Vice Admiral Sir Jeremy Blackham KCB MA

(Commanding Officer 1992 – 1993)

My period in command of HMS *Ark Royal* was brief, July 1992 to April 1993, but it was certainly varied, exciting, and very much in the limelight. The autumn 1992 deployment had us dodging hurricanes, meeting and exercising with, and establishing close friendships with the USS *John F Kennedy* and her battle group – something that was to stand us in very good stead later. We managed a relaxing maintenance period in Mayport and first rate visit to Nassau where the Ship's Company, not for the first time, impressed everyone with their conduct ashore.

On our return home in November 1992 we were privileged to be the venue for the Admiralty Board's Dinner for Her Majesty the Queen to celebrate the 40th anniversary of her Accession. This was a glittering occasion, the highlight of a busy year and showed again how well *Ark* and her Ship's Company could rise to any occasion. Once again she proved herself to be a worthy Fleet Flagship.

As if all that was not enough, immediately after Christmas we were sailed at short notice for the Adriatic in order to support the British and UN forces in Bosnia. Once again *Ark* rose to the occasion as we established what was to become a long running RN presence in the area, and took the lead in setting up the maritime arrangements under which several maritime nations operated. Amongst our allies was the USS *John F Kennedy* and the value of our good friendship and previous experience with them was proven over and over again. This was a testing period but, as always, the professional skill, teamwork, enthusiasm and good humour of the Ship's Company stood out.

I left *Ark* with great sadness halfway through her first Adriatic deployment, but with a great sense of privilege and pride at having commanded her, and a great affection for the ship and for her crew which remains with me 17 years later and always will. She is certainly a very special ship and able to deal with anything thrown at her.

Chapter 6

1992 – 1993:
New World Order – the UN and the Adriatic

Captain Jeremy Blackham had extensive sea experience, having commanded the *Ton*-class mine hunter HMS *Beachampton* based in the Gulf during the late 1960s and the *Tribal*-class frigate HMS *Ashanti* a decade later, served as the Executive Officer in HMS *Hermes* after the Falklands War and, most recently, been CO of the *Type-42* destroyer HMS *Nottingham*. He joined HMS *Ark Royal* following two one-star shore appointments as Commandant of the Royal Naval Staff College at Greenwich and then the Director of Naval Plans and Programmes within the Ministry of Defence. An intellectual officer with a first-class degree in philosophy, it was likely that he would quickly be promoted to Flag Rank and his time in command of *Ark Royal* might be short. It was essential for him therefore to make every day count.

Taking command at Gibraltar on 8th July 1992, Captain Blackham inherited a ship whose operational efficiency had diminished from the very high levels achieved at COST and Area Capability Training in the spring, because of lack of aviation assets and a weak programme. Materially, *Ark* also needed a maintenance period to remove most of the additional equipment installed for PURPLE MONARCH and prepare for the autumn programme. The ship sailed for home on 9th July, in company with HMS *Nottingham*, but without the CAG or one-fifth of the Ship's Company embarked so that they could take advantage of early leave to man the ship throughout a busy seven-week period alongside in

Portsmouth.

HMS *Ark Royal* arrived home on 12th July and immediately started the much-needed maintenance period. As usual, she attracted a gamut of visitors over the summer, including numerous organisations, family of the Ship's Company, and some of the ship's affiliates. Most significant of the visitors and in a sign of changing times, the newly appointed Russian Defence Minister, Marshal Pavel Grachev, toured the ship on 21st July. Faced with large scale demobilisation of the former Soviet military machine in the cash-strapped Russia post-*perestroika*, it was not surprising that Grachev appeared particularly interested in the Royal Navy's policies on pay, conditions of service and resettlement. Of more surprise however was his equal interest in ship protection, judging by the impromptu lesson in Response Force duties he gave one member of the Ship's Company whom he met during his tour of the ship.

The ship's engineers took full advantage of the opportunity alongside to make alterations and additions to the ship's fit. For the Weapon Engineering department, the main effort was to remove the additional communications equipment that had been fitted for PURPLE MONARCH and refurbish several systems that were still being trialled or had lain dormant for over a year. At the same time the Marine Engineering department was busy upgrading the safety features to the Liquid Oxygen plant, a task that became a real cliff hanger to achieving the September sailing deadline. A new and experimental machinery surveillance system was also fitted in the Ship's Control Centre but its early failure at sea, leaving the main propulsion system unguarded, caused consternation for the watch-keepers and numerous satellite phone calls back to the design engineers who had failed to provide any adequate documentation to help fix it! The possibility that *Ark Royal*'s faithful auxiliary RFA *Regent*, which had provided afloat support continuously since January 1991, might not accompany the carrier for the autumn deployment caused equal consternation for the ship's Supply Department. Hurried contingency plans were put in place to sustain the ship, which in the end were not needed as *Regent* deployed on time, but the issue nevertheless exposed the potential shortfalls of the CVSG's endurance both in weapons and provisions.

For the fourth year in a row, HMS *Ark Royal* provided the star attraction at Portsmouth Navy Days. As well as the usual static displays of a Sea Harrier from 801 NAS, and Sea King 'J', 'W' and 'A' variants from 820 NAS, 849 'B' and 846 'D' Flights respectively, the Fleet Air Arm Museum helped celebrate the 75th anniversary of the first deck landing on a moving ship by supplying a Sopwith Pup similar to that used by Squadron Commander Edwin Dunning DSC RNAS, in 1917. This time, the Pup made a slightly less majestic arrival, being craned onto the flight deck.

WESTLANT deployments to take advantage of the US Navy's exercise facilities had been a regular feature of HMS *Ark Royal*'s first years in service and what turned out to be the last of the series began in September 1992. She was flagship of Task Group 610.01, again flying Vice Admiral Hill-Norton's flag as Flag Officer Surface Flotilla. Admiral Sir Michael Livesay, the Second Sea Lord, embarked for the ship's departure on 2nd September from Portsmouth, to tour the ship and speak with the Ship's Company, before flying off as the ship sailed west. The *Type-42* destroyer HMS *Exeter* and the auxiliaries, RFA *Olmeda* and RFA *Regent*, accompanied *Ark*. HMS *Triumph*, the Royal

Navy's newly commissioned *Trafalgar*-class attack submarine, also accompanied the task group while en route to the AUTEC range for weapon trials. The CAG re-embarked in the Channel; five Sea Harriers, four SKJs and one SKW arriving to supplement the units already onboard following Navy Days. This reduced air group of only fourteen aircraft reflected the growing pressure on RN airframe availability. The flight deck and air crews worked-up on passage to the Azores, with an intensive programme to blow away the cobwebs of four months without operational flying. The high tempo of flying operations, together with the presence of a specialist team to train damage control and fire fighting techniques, helped familiarise the large number of new Ship's Company to their surroundings. The intensive operations led to a higher maintenance load on the aircraft and with no delivery opportunities for vital spares, cannibalising parts was the only way to keep the required number of aircraft available for flying.

As they had done a year earlier, French ASW assets accompanied TG610.01 for part of the transatlantic crossing, conducting a three-day passing exercise. The nuclear submarine FS *Emeraude* once again provided the target for the SKJs, as well as RAF Nimrod and French Navy Atlantique maritime patrol aircraft. The need to push on after the Azores greatly reduced the opportunities for operational training, but HMS *Triumph* together with US Navy assets provided some benefit, before the submarine had to detach for Florida en-route to AUTEC.

Upon arriving off North Carolina on 11th September, *Ark Royal* took the final briefings for her first major activity of the deployment: participation in the US Navy's FLEETEX 1/93 with USS *John F Kennedy*'s battle group. With primary Command and Control responsibilities retained under American control, *Ark*'s main role was limited to acting as an ASW and ASuW command ship within its allocated sector. 801 Squadron maintained local combat air patrols in quite realistic conditions; the ship being attacked by shore based fighters, mainly US Marine Corps AV-8Bs and USN F-14s, as well as P-3s and other maritime patrol aircraft. Although there was only scant "in contact" time for 820 Squadron, the overall scenario was realistic and provided *Ark*'s command team with useful opportunities to marshal the limited aircraft assets to meet the operational requirements. No real weapons were expended during the exercises nevertheless a careful tally was maintained of 'paper' weapon usage, which revealed that the replenishment stocks carried in RFA *Regent* provided barely for a single outfit reload capability. This shortfall would require significant reworking of the magazines to address properly, exposing the carrier's limited endurance.

In the latter stages of the FLEETEX, HMS *Exeter* was detached to join the US Amphibious Group working inshore where she provided Naval Gunfire Support, AAW and ASuW cover. *Exeter*'s Lynx helicopter, armed with Sea Skua missiles, proved to be particularly effective against the prevailing surface threat. The USN participants in FLEETEX 1/93 operated under national procedures exposing many doctrinal differences between them and their NATO allies. However both sides were keen to explore the common language that separated the two countries and a number of senior exchanges took place. Vice Admiral Hill Norton went on expeditionary visits to the task group ships while *Ark* hosted the Commander US Second Fleet, Vice Admiral William J Flanagan Jr, accompanied by FOSF-designate, Rear Admiral Mike Boyce. Following the exercise, *Ark* put into Norfolk Virginia for a routine visit, accompanied by *Regent* and *Exeter*. Three of 801's Sea Harriers disembarked to the USN Air Station at Oceana, for exercises with the local "aggressor" squadron.

To meet new international marine pollution control regulations, *Ark Royal* had during the previous BAMP received the 'Bromfield fit', a Heath-Robinson arrangement of pumps and flexible hoses designed to allow the ship's sewerage and waste water to be pumped ashore. The fit was greeted with suspicion onboard since it would greatly complicate the process of getting alongside and add to the usual 'harbour hassle'. Norfolk provided the first opportunity to test the system in anger and sadly things did not go smoothly, confirming the Marine Engineering Officer's fears. It was twelve hours before all heads, bathrooms and galleys could be re-opened and then successive failures over the five-day visit of eight of the ten pumps fitted (the system needed seven to work) compounded the problems.

Oblivious to these problems, local press and television crews showed great interest in *Ark*'s "WRNS at sea" and they featured prominently in the US coverage of the visit. The interest was sparked by the growing debate of whether USN female personnel should be allowed to serve at sea in warships. Although women had served in auxiliaries and tenders since 1978 it was not until the US Congress repealed the 'combat exclusion law' in 1993 that the first were assigned to a combatant; six officers and one enlisted sailor joining the aircraft carrier USS *Dwight D Eisenhower* the following year. Senior visitors also showed interest in the carrier, including Vice Admiral Sir Peter Woodhead, NATO's new Deputy Strategic Allied Commander Atlantic, returning to his OUTBACK'88 flagship to host an equipment sales presentation.

Departing Norfolk on 23rd September *Ark* and the other ships rendezvoused with *Olmeda*, which had been visiting Port Canaveral, and then sailed down the Virginia coast to conduct group weapon training. This was due to last until early October but 'rain stopped play'. First, Tropical Storm 'Danielle' swept in forcing the task group south toward Jacksonville, Florida to avoid the worst of the weather. No sooner there, Tropical Storm 'Earl' blew up from the Caribbean sending the group north again. Just as calm weather finally approached, on 30th September the USN ordered its ships and aircraft to 'come in' due to financial restrictions of the Department of the Navy's budget at the end of its financial year.

Frustrated by the failure of the preceding week at sea, *Ark* once again headed south for her next stop at Mayport, arriving on 2nd October. The carrier base in Florida had become *Ark Royal*'s home-from-home in recent years as she made her second visit in less than a year. With many of the Ship's Company who had visited in October 1991 still onboard, there was the usual warm welcome, while families and friends again flew out to exploit the holiday opportunities. The Chief Writer's 'bureau de change' once again did record business, cashing out nearly $2.5 million between the Norfolk and Mayport visits. On the more serious side, *Ark*'s squadrons disembarked to exploit the local facilities for continuation flying training. 820's SKJs practised overland navigation techniques, 849 'B' Flight's SKWs gained valuable insight into the *modus operandi* of several types of air defence aircraft, while 801's Sea Harriers went up against agile long range opponents on the Tactical Air Combat Training Range.

With the Ship's Company rested and recuperated after eleven days alongside in Florida, HMS *Ark Royal* sailed from Mayport to conduct a week of weapon exercises at AUTEC under the auspices of Trial PUNISH '92. The task group was at last brought up to full strength with the addition the diesel-powered submarine HMS *Oracle*, the Type-22 frigate HMS *Coventry* and the West Indies Guard Ship HMS *Cardiff* along with her RFA, *Orangeleaf*. The usual intense ASW activity took place with 820 Squadron in the thick of the action, despite being reduced to only four operational airframes by the discovery of severe cracking of the gearbox frame in the fifth aircraft. Maintaining two available helicopters proved extremely challenging, nevertheless 140 hours of flying were achieved and successful use of the Type-2069 dipping sonar allowed a large number of attacks, sixteen Stingray torpedoes being dropped against *Oracle*. Meanwhile, 849 'B' Flight exercised with *Coventry* and *Triumph* to develop over-the-horizon targeting techniques and practise submarine

periscope detection. 801's Harriers also conducted a few day and night sorties but did not achieve the same tactical success that they had during their detachment at Norfolk and could have been better employed flying from Florida. HMS *Exeter*, fitted with the new Type-2050 hull-mounted sonar also worked hard to gain operator experience and identify tactical improvements for the system's software developers. The Sea King Mk4 from 846 'D' Flight proved invaluable throughout the exercise providing essential logistics support and personnel transport to and from Andros Island. The major casualties of the Andros period were RFA *Olmeda* which suffered condenser failure and had to limp back to Port Everglades and HMS *Oracle* which suffered a major earth on her main battery forcing her to retreat to Port Canaveral for repairs, terminating prematurely her involvement in proceedings. *Olmeda*'s failure had been her second such dose of "condenseritis" in five weeks and demonstrated the fragility of the increasingly aged RFA fleet. Her quick repair nevertheless allowed *Orangeleaf* to proceed with her West Indies Guard Ship programme.

Ark Royal's last stop of the autumn 1992 WESTLANT deployment was Nassau in the Bahamas. The Ship's Company took one final opportunity for 'fun in the sun' despite being low on funds following the excesses of Virginia and Florida. Unusually, both the Governor General of the Bahamas, Sir Clifford Darling, and the Prime Minister, Hubert Ingraham visited the ship, rather than Captain Blackham making calls upon them. This was in recognition of the outstanding services provided by HMS *Cardiff* and latterly HMS *Campbeltown* to the island of Eleuthera in the wake of Hurricane Andrew and set the tone for much improved relations between the island and the United Kingdom.

Overall, the WESTLANT '92 foray was another outstanding success for *Ark*, despite the challenges of operating through the hurricane season. The only significant issues for Captain Blackham were a reoccurrence of a salmonella outbreak onboard, albeit affecting less than half the number of sailors that the same infection had in 1991, and the fragility of both his accompanying RFA and the embarked CAG. He also considered that the nine-week deployment was too short for maximum benefit to military capability; three to four months being the minimum required to allow full consolidation of the tactical lessons learned. Although such deployments were now subject to intense financial scrutiny they still provided enormous value in developing military liaison with the US forces and in many other financially unquantifiable areas, such as relations with the Bahamian authorities. Yet again *Ark*'s Ship's Company behaved impeccably, Captain Blackham attributing this to the improving attitudes in his young crew and the 'civilizing' influence of the WRNS serving at sea.

HMS *Ark Royal* sailed for the UK on 25th October, making a high-speed transit that resulted in the ship burning over fifty percent more than her allocated fuel allowance in order to get home as quickly as possible. The reason for haste was that the ship would host the official dinner held by the Admiralty Board for Her Majesty the Queen to mark the fortieth anniversary of her accession to the throne. Preparations for the Royal Dinner began in early 1991 but detailed planning gathered pace throughout the summer, and *Ark*'s management team would have only ten days from getting alongside to make all of the arrangements necessary and provide a fitting venue. Her Majesty, accompanied by The Duke of York, The Earl of Wessex, HRH Princess Alexandra and Sir Angus Ogilvy were hosted in the hangar by a most distinguished company of officers headed by Admiral Sir Julian Oswald, the First Sea Lord. Every available Flag and Commanding Officer of Her Majesty's Ships, Submarines, Naval Air Squadrons, Royal Marine Commando Units, Royal Fleet Auxiliaries, Royal Naval Reserve Units and shore establishments was there: 197 in all, including a certain Lieutenant John Clink, then in his first sea command in HMS *Archer*, the P2000

patrol boat of Aberdeen Universities Royal Navy Unit. In many ways this was the culmination of the ship's career as a showpiece and flagship during her first period of service. More serious events were in the offing.

HMS *Ark Royal* underwent her usual 'MOT' checks at Portsmouth from 23rd November to 8th January 1993, during which the Ship's Company were given Christmas leave in preparation for the intended early-spring programme of the usual Joint Maritime Conference (JMC 93-1) off Scotland followed by a major amphibious exercise, BATTLE GRIFFIN '93. The DIMHS communications system that had been fitted the previous year for Exercise PURPLE MONARCH was removed to be replaced by the CLX MHS fit and a host of other equipment needed to transform *Ark*'s flag planning suite into an Amphibious Operations Room. A comprehensive maintenance and upgrade package for Sea Dart and installation of the DAMA submarine-satellite communications system completed the weapon engineering work package. Planning the BAMP across a main leave period was by no means ideal, but much hard work by the Ship's Company and Portsmouth engineering staff kept the programme on track. However, *Ark*'s spring programme was thrown into disarray by the escalating hostilities in the civil war raging in the former Yugoslavia.

The Yugoslavia that emerged after the Second World War was a complex federation of six republics: Macedonia, Montenegro, Slovenia, Croatia and Bosnia-Herzegovina, all dominated by Serbia with the federal capital in Belgrade. Built on the Soviet model, the Federal People's Republic of Yugoslavia was home to a diverse population both in ethnic origin and religious belief, which was held together only by the over powering will of its architect and leader, Marshal Josip Broz Tito. Tito gave some autonomy to the disparate republics, but suppressed any nationalist sentiment through his policy of "brotherhood and unity" of the six Yugoslav nations, so that a single Federal Republic could maintain an audible voice on the world stage, wedged as it was between the NATO and Soviet power blocs to west and east. Tito's death in May 1980 gave the opportunity for local power bases in the republics to rise once again and they became increasingly divided along ethnic and secular lines. Regional destabilisation caused by the break-up of the Soviet Union a decade later provided the spark for rekindled nationalist ambitions and the independence agenda dominated the Yugoslav parliamentary elections held in 1990. Systematically, subordinate regions attempted to break from the vestiges of their mother state run from Belgrade.

Slovenia achieved independence virtually unopposed on 25th June 1991. Croatia made a simultaneous declaration but this prompted much greater Serbian opposition and the resulting civil war lasted into early 1992, with sporadic fighting continuing through to 1995. The declarations of independence by Croatia and Slovenia and the warfare that ensued there sparked a crisis in Bosnia. Bosnia's three constituencies, the majority Muslim 'Bosniaks', minority Bosnian Serbs and Bosnian Croats, maintained an uneasy peace but were split on the issue of whether or not to stay with the Federal Republic. The Bosniaks favoured independence, the Croats sought to break from Serbian rule but under a Croatian banner, while only the Serb minority wanted to remain under Federalist control from Belgrade. Both of the minority ambitions were bolstered by political and military support of the leaders of the neighbouring Croatian and Serbian republics, respectively, Franjo Tuđman and Slobodan Milošević.

Bosnia's declaration of sovereignty in October 1991 was followed by a two-stage referendum in February and March 1992. Supported by the Bosniaks and Bosnian Croats, but boycotted by virtually every Bosnian Serb, the result was overwhelming: 99.7% of the turnout voted in favour of independence. On 3rd March 1992, Bosnia-Herzegovina declared independence from Yugoslavia, sparking ethnic violence that quickly escalated into civil war, spreading to the capital,

Sarajevo, a month later. The USA and the European Union both recognised Bosnia-Herzegovina formally as an independent state on 6th April, but this did nothing to quell the fighting which continued throughout the year.

The Bosniaks, the only ethnic group loyal to the Bosnian government, became an easy target for both Serbian and Croatian state-sponsored paramilitary groups, because the Bosnian government forces were poorly equipped and unprepared for the war. Initially, the Serb forces attacked the non-Serb civilian population in eastern Bosnia. Once towns and villages were securely in their hands, the Serb forces – military, police, the paramilitaries and, sometimes, even Serb villagers – applied the same pattern: Bosniak houses and apartments were systematically ransacked or burnt down, Bosniak civilians were rounded up and sometimes beaten or killed in the process. Men and women were then held separately in concentration camps and detention centres where they were then subjected to appalling conditions. In this way Serb control over much of Bosnia was quickly established.

In June 1992, Bosnian Croat forces attempted to gain control of Bosniak strongholds in the centre of the country around the towns of Novi Travnik and Gornji Vakuf, and with further attacks in Prozar during October; any lingering sentiment amongst the moderates for a Bosniak-Croat alliance was killed. Bosniak reprisal attacks led effectively to all-out war between the three sides with atrocities committed against whichever civilian population represented the minority. The area of Central Podrinje had a primary strategic importance to Serbs, as without it there would be no territorial integrity within their new 'Republika Srpska', and throughout 1992 Bosniak villages around the principal town, Srebrenica, were under constant attacks by Serb forces with widespread ethnic cleansing taking place. By the start of 1993, about 70% of the country was controlled by Serbs under their banner of the 'Republika Srpska'.

The international community's engagement

with the war in Yugoslavia grew gradually from September 1991 onward when the United Nations passed Security Council Resolution (UNSCR) 713, declaring an arms embargo against the country. UNSCR 724 signed in December 1991 established the overseeing committee for the sanctions but without an enforcement provision, although it did at least set out a plan for a possible peacekeeping force. The same month the frigate HMS *Minerva* became the first Royal Navy warship to deploy to the Adriatic. A maritime deployment was the most flexible way for John Major's Government to signal Britain's interest in the region following Croatia and Slovenia's secession and concern for deteriorating conditions, without making any overt commitment to the conflict. It also provided a contingency to evacuate British and commonwealth citizens in Yugoslavia if the course of the fighting forced them to leave.

UNSCR 743 passed on 21st February 1992 established the 14,000-strong United Nations Protection Force (UNPROFOR) and UNSCR 749 two months later authorised its deployment. Initially established in Croatia as an interim arrangement to create the conditions of peace and security required for the negotiation of an overall settlement of the Yugoslav crisis, UNPROFOR's mandate was to ensure that the three "United Nations Protected Areas" (UNPAs) in Croatia were demilitarized and to protect the resident populations from fear of attack. In the course of 1992, UNPROFOR's mandate was enlarged both inside Croatia, under UNSCR 762 to include monitoring functions in certain areas designated "pink zones" and under resolution 769 to control immigration and customs at the borders of the UNPAs. As the conflict intensified and extended to Bosnia Herzegovina, UNPROFOR was tasked to ensure the security and functioning of the airport at Sarajevo and the delivery of humanitarian assistance to that city and its environs, through UNSCRs 761 and 770.

By mid-1992, an impending humanitarian disaster loomed in the face of increasingly frequent attacks on civilian aid workers trying to support the displaced Croatian and Muslim people. In response, in September UNPROFOR was further tasked under UNSCR 776 to protect and support efforts by the United Nations High Commissioner for Refugees, to deliver humanitarian aid throughout Bosnia-Herzegovina, and to protect convoys of fleeing civilians if the International Committee of the Red Cross so requested. A 7,000-strong multi-national force deployed the following month; with UNPROFOR's headquarters established at Kisiljak. Eleven hundred French and Portuguese troops based at Bihac controlled the North West sector, while 1,200 Canadian troops controlled Banja Luka further east, supported by half of the 950-strong Dutch contingent. The remaining Dutch forces supported by a 100-strong Belgian Army transport company held Vitez in the centre of the country, leaving 700 Spanish infantry and light armour units to control the Southern sector around Mostar.

The 2,400-strong British Force (BRITFOR) contribution to UNPROFOR deployed under the codename Operation GRAPPLE and was established in theatre from 13th November 1992. Under the command of Brigadier Andrew Cumming (late 17th/21st Lancers) and built around the 1st Battalion, 22nd Cheshire Regiment Battle Group led by Lieutenant Colonel Bob Stewart, BRITFOR was responsible for protecting UNPROFOR's main supply route back to Split on the Adriatic coast. From their bases in Vitez and Gornji Vakuf, BRITFOR patrols quickly started to make a difference, escorting 147 convoys and transporting 11,775 tonnes of aid in the first six weeks alone. But as their presence was felt, they found themselves in an increasingly dangerous and volatile situation, routinely coming under mortar and small-arms attack from paramilitaries. If attacks on BRITFOR units escalated beyond the organic defensive capability of the Warrior Infantry Fighting Vehicles in which they deployed, then they might have to be supported with heavier firepower or even evacuated under fire. This required a secure national base and a source of air support, both fixed and rotary winged, untrammelled by local sensitivities; a classic setting for an aircraft carrier. With the situation ashore deteriorating, deployment of a contingency naval force became imperative

On 4th January 1993, HMS *Ark Royal* received warning orders to deploy for Operation GRAPPLE and completing the BAMP four days later, all departments shifted up a gear to ensure the ship was ready to sail with all dispatch. The Air Department prepared for a reconfigured air group of eight Sea Harriers (two additional aircraft taken from 800 Squadron), three SKWs and eight Sea King Mk4 commando helicopters of 846 Squadron to provide the support helicopter lift required to land reinforcements ashore and/or get the troops out. 820 Squadron would transfer to the accompanying RFA to make room. The ship's stocks of aircraft spares was bolstered by additional holdings released from central warehouses and the commando helicopters came with large amounts of new equipment and a "Fly Away Pack" complete with four-ton truck and trailer. Other stores were also enhanced to near war-stock levels, focussing the minds of the Ship's Company who had to load it that the deployment was not an exercise. Even more communications equipment than had been fitted for PURPLE MONARCH and BATTLE GRIFFIN was also crammed in, giving *Ark* the most sophisticated and comprehensive command and control suite ever deployed in a Royal Navy flagship.

Lance Corporal Wayne Edwards, Royal Welch Fusiliers, was the first British casualty of the Yugoslav war, shot by a sniper while escorting an ambulance in Gornji Vakuf, on 13th January 1993. His death on the eve of *Ark*'s departure, was emotively reported by the British press, crystallising national sentiments with many openly wary of becoming embroiled in a war that could end up a quagmire for the United Kingdom, just as Vietnam had for the United States in the 1970s. On 14th January, Malcolm Rifkind, the Secretary of State for Defence, in his statement to Parliament announcing the decision to deploy reinforcements, rebutted claims from opposition MPs and Conservative back-benchers that Britain was getting sucked in to a conflict that was not their responsibility. Rifkind tried to reassure the House that *"These forces will not be used to intervene in the fighting between the rival factions in Yugoslavia. ... Our position remains that it is not appropriate to intervene in a civil war. ... Our overriding concern, as always is to ensure the safety of our forces. ... We have the right to defend ourselves and the means to do it in a very impressive way."*

The "means to do so" were indeed impressive. Task Force 612, operationally controlled by Commander in Chief Fleet, under the command of Commander in Chief UK Land Forces, consisted of 2,487 Navy, Army and Royal Marines personnel, effectively doubling the UK presence in the Yugoslav theatre. Options were also explored to deploy RAF Tornado F-3 interceptors and Jaguar strike aircraft to Italy. Captain Blackham's task group, TG 612.02, comprised the *Type-22* frigates HMS *Coventry* and HMS *Brilliant*, RFA *Olwen* and RFA *Fort Grange* carrying 820 Squadron, as well as the aviation training ship RFA *Argus*. Acting as an interim LPH, *Argus* carried six 105-mm light guns and the Mortar Locating Troop from 29 Commando Regiment Royal Artillery, as well as two batteries and headquarters elements of 94 Locating Regiment Royal Artillery; 176 vehicles and trailers and 329 military personnel in all. *Ark*'s eight Mk-4 SKAs could deliver all but the heaviest vehicles. The composition of the GRAPPLE task group marked a significant departure from the classic, balanced, blue-water naval task group that the traditional naval concept of operations called for. The mixed CAG in *Ark*, deployment of SKJs to the RFA and a warship-to-RFA ratio of 1:1 were all innovative. The 'mix and match' procedures used to draw together were also new, allowing the TG to be tailored as late as possible to be optimised for the situation in theatre. Captain Blackham's orders were to 'poise' TG 612.02 in the Adriatic within five hours of Split by 26th January, being prepared to land reinforcements from RFA *Argus* in support of British forces ashore. His task group might participate in a withdrawal, enforce the No-fly Zone over the country, and provide air support to troops ashore. *Ark Royal* might operate as an offshore Joint Forces Headquarters, if required.

HMS *Ark Royal* was waved off from Portsmouth by thousands of well-wishers and families of the crew, in scenes not witnessed since the departure of *Ark*'s sister *Invincible* to the Falklands ten years before. From the emotional farewell it was immediately down to business, with embarkation of the air group the following day and an intensive shakedown and work-up by FOST staff off Portland to bring the Ship's Company up to scratch. Upon leaving UK waters, Captain Blackham's immediate tasks were to bring the task group up to standard in the war-fighting disciplines that might be employed in theatre while devoting time to consider the strategic requirements of the mission directive and prepare fully. This was a difficult balancing act, demanding on the one hand close direction of the 'here and now' activity, while on the other being sufficiently detached to conduct estimates, threat reduction and contingency planning for any number of employment options. The balance itself was nothing new, but the compressed timescale in which to achieve it from a standing start was a real challenge. Here again, the flexibility of the CVSG was demonstrated as *Ark*'s experienced and senior operations team could draft, promulgate and then manage the training package for the initial leg to Gibraltar, giving the embarked Battle Staff sufficient breathing space to analyse the mission, write the orders and tailor the training for the second leg from Gibraltar to the Otranto Strait.

As *Ark* transited the South Western Approaches the CAG worked up to combat efficiency with 801 Squadron exercising its air combat skills against Tornados, Buccaneers, Hunters, Falcons and Canberras as well practising using the Sea Harrier's

radar to range ground targets for dive bombing attacks with 1,000-lb bombs. RFA *Fort Grange* with four of 820's SKJs embarked rendezvoused with *Ark* on the 17th, bringing TG 612.02 up to full strength. 846 Squadron used the Sea Harriers to exercise helicopter evasion tactics and once the Gibraltar exercise areas were reached, the landing of the forces embarked in RFA *Argus*. The task group stopped briefly at Gibraltar to take on final stores and fuel. Two Sea Harriers that had suffered mechanical problems during the passage south were sent back to Yeovilton; one was swapped for another, while the second returned after repairs. After the reset at the Rock, on 23rd January *Ark*'s group moved eastwards through the Mediterranean and eventually entered the Adriatic four days later.

Captain Blackham immediately conferred with the ground force commanders in the Flagship. The group's role was to be de-escalatory with no aggressive acts, as it remained "poised" awaiting developments ashore. It is one of the great assets of sea power that it can thus provide decision makers with on the spot options without the dangers of over-commitment or entanglement. This was of especial importance in such a confused situation as Bosnia with everyone fighting everyone else. Over the next few days, *Ark* and her CAG exercised the various actions it might be called upon to carry out while a logistics air head was established at the Italian Air Force base at Bari, with a weekly dedicated Hercules flight from the United Kingdom and a large amount of HDS activity. TG 612.02's battle staff followed the time-honoured tradition of assuming the worst at the outset and configuring appropriately, then carefully reassessing and revising the force's posture as the situation became established. Familiarisation of the local activity levels and behaviour was key to this; looking for patterns of normality and the indicators and warnings (I&W) that might suggest something was afoot.

The local factors were very significant in the confined and almost territorial waters of the Adriatic. While the task group had the theoretical ability to operate with impunity on the high seas, in practice, the logistic demands of sustaining the ships and the political demands of operating inside Italy's sphere of influence required strenuous efforts by Captain Blackham and his staff to keep all of the local nations 'on side'. This led to the early definition of the operating area for the task group, situated strategically to meet the competing demands of the logisticians and the requirements of BRITFOR HQ ashore in Split, while minimising the threat posed by Yugoslav shore-based missiles. The freedom to manoeuvre was constrained by the need to co-operate with and make room for the other maritime operations already underway in the Adriatic; *Ark Royal*'s arrival in theatre being just the latest in a build up of ships operating under national and multinational orders.

Since the United Nations' request for support of its trade sanctions against Yugoslavia imposed under UNSCR 757 on 30th May 1992, both NATO and the Western European Union had deployed naval units to monitor the Adriatic. In July of that year, units of NATO's newly-established Standing Naval Force Mediterranean (SNFM) entered the region under Operation MARITIME MONITOR, taking station off the coast of Montenegro. It was joined in its task by the WEU's Maritime Contingency Force, under Operation SHARP VIGILANCE, which patrolled the choke point between the Ionian Sea and the Adriatic at the Straits of Otranto, between them covering over 9,000 square miles of sea. Both formations quickly realised that achieving greater interoperability would be the key to their success. SNFM, new and relatively inexperienced in sustained operations was replaced temporarily by the far more capable Standing Naval Force Atlantic (SNFL) in September 1992. SNFL had been in permanent existence since 1968 and exercised regularly with coalition partners. As a multinational combined force it had unparalleled experience, endurance and flexibility, which was immediately deployed to develop the modus operandi for the participating units. The pattern of operations was thus quickly

established and progressively enhanced by the time SNFM resumed duties in October, but the force still lacked the clear mandate to enforce the embargo.

UNSCR 787 adopted by the Security Council on 16th November 1992 sought to apply a stranglehold on illegal supplies of weapons and military personnel into Bosnia providing the mandate needed. Emboldened by UNSCR 787, the NATO and WEU maritime roles turned from 'monitoring' to 'enforcement with minimal force', the respective missions redesignated MARITIME GUARD and SHARP FENCE. As part of SNFM, HMS *Gloucester* carried out the first stop and search operation on 26th November under the auspices of MARITIME GUARD, boarding the merchant vessel '*Bore C*' in the Otranto Straits. The Royal Navy was in the vanguard of joint operations, yet again.

The challenges facing the ships in the NATO and WEU groups were two-fold. The first was generating and sustaining an accurate wide-area picture to achieve the level of situational awareness needed to track the myriad of merchant traffic operating in the Adriatic and then choreograph the inspection, boarding and diversion of suspect vessels. The second and more dangerous challenge came from the potential threat of former Yugoslav armed forces against the embargo operations, either to support blockade runners or as part of a general escalation of hostilities against the UN and NATO. This threat was substantial. The naval fleet of the Former Republic of Yugoslavia (FRY) based in Kotor Bay on the Montenegrin coast included four frigates, two corvettes and a flotilla of about twenty fast attack craft, torpedo boats and minelayers. There was also a sub-surface threat posed by five diesel submarines and a small force of midget submarines. The frigates and attack craft were equipped with Styx anti-ship missiles, the most sophisticated variant of which had a range of fifty miles and skimmed the sea during its terminal attack. Three Styx batteries were also stationed along the coast, also protected by 130-mm radar-directed artillery. Embargo picket ships operating just outside the Montenegrin twelve-mile territorial limit might have only sixty seconds warning of an attack. Consequently, ships' companies remained alert, operating in Defence Watches and ready to react, but the tempo of operations was nevertheless relatively low. In contrast, the ships in the Otranto OPAREA maintained a much higher tempo, punctuated by tracking, boarding and diversion operations, with numerous helicopter and seamanship evolutions, but outside the range of FRY forces and with lower risk.

Ark's group was also not the only national task force able to contribute maritime air power over the Adriatic. The United States had taken the precautionary step of deploying the USS *John F Kennedy* battle group from its home port at Norfolk Virginia on 7th October 1992 and she remained in theatre until the following April. Meanwhile, France activated Task Force 470 under Operation BALBUZARD, led by the carrier FS *Clemenceau*, which arrived in theatre the day after the British task group. Accompanying the carrier was the amphibious landing ship FS *Foudre*, protected by the guided missile destroyers FS *La Motte-Picquet* and FS *Georges Leygues* and the frigates FS *Jean Bart* and FS *Suffren*, supported by the tankers *Meuse* and *Marne*.

The operational relationship of *Ark*'s task group with the various national, NATO and WEU task groups ebbed and flowed as the likelihood of operating with or in support of them altered and as the actual command and control relationships changed. Nevertheless, an understanding of each others' missions and requirements was vital at all times and much effort went into keeping the bonds between the TG commands strong. All groups had different tasks and preferred operating areas, driven by different political perspectives, rules of engagement and operational postures. Clearly there was a need to avoid impeding such operations, but there was also much to be gained from exploiting shared assets. Tactical information, including I&W and operational intelligence could be passed to enhance situational awareness; opportunities for aviation, unit, group and weapons training could be capitalised and, crucially, access to precious oilers could be optimised. Captain Blackham understood this intuitively and taking the lead made it his business to create the closest possible co-operation between the forces present while maintaining the national character of his task group. In response, the Americans hosted a meeting onboard "Big John" that agreed a programme of cross training and visits. 801 Squadron took advantage of this for air combat training with both American and French aircraft and simulated Sea Eagle strikes on both groups.

Speculation grew at home by the beginning of February that the entire task group was about to be withdrawn back to the UK, amidst pressure on the government from Tory back benchers. But the possibility of withdrawal was dashed on 5th February 1993 by the US rejection of the first peace plan brokered by David Owen and Cyrus Vance; President Clinton's administration seeking its own unilateral solution. Options among the planners were nevertheless developed to scale down the UK's poised military presence. On 9th February, HMS *Coventry* handed over 'goalkeeper' duties to her sister ship HMS *Brazen* and detached from TG 612.02, bound for escort duties in the Gulf under Operation ARMILLA. By the middle of February, the likelihood of imminent intervention to support BRITFOR seemed less and *Ark*'s task group was stood down to 24 hours notice off Split. The two extra Sea Harriers taken on at Gibraltar returned to the UK. At the end of the month *Ark* earned her first stand-off, visiting Trieste for a run ashore and recuperation period after six weeks continuously at sea.

When HMS *Ark Royal* resumed watch in March the routine of poise and training started once more. Five of 801 Squadron's Sea Harriers disembarked temporarily to hone their bombing skills at RAF Decimomannu and the Capo Frasca range in Sardinia. Their objective was to gradually increase the height at which the pilots could safely and accurately release their 1,000-lb bombs, outside the range of small arms fire and hand held surface-to-air missiles. Meanwhile, *Ark* carried out an encounter exercise with the Italian frigate ITS *Zeffiro* during which 849 'B' Flight's SKWs developed surveillance and probe tactics with 820's SKJs. As the tempo settled and the pattern of FRY operations became established it was possible to make adjustments to the force levels necessary to achieve the mission, continuing the policy of 'mix and match' within the task group. HMS *Brilliant* departed to be relieved by the Dutch frigate HNLMS *Abraham Crijnssen*. On the 11th, 279 personnel were flown home from RFA *Argus* to be kept at 48-hours notice, which relieved pressure on a ship never designed to carry so many people. Eight days later, *Ark* disembarked four SKAs to RFA *Fort Austin* which was transiting back to UK from the Gulf. The arrival of the USS *Theodore Roosevelt* battle group to take over the American contribution from the USS *John F Kennedy* group coincided with a two-week standoff by FS *Clemenceau*, providing a key opportunity for the UK GRAPPLE task group to take stock and reassess its strategy. Rules of engagement and exchange of information problems were solved in another demonstration of the ease with which friendly navies can co-operate together, at least in

relatively low threat environments. *Ark*'s operational tempo was relieved by a welcome standoff at to Piraeus in Greece and the temporary distractions of visits by HRH The Prince of Wales and Rear Admiral Boyce during the month.

HMS *Broadsword* replaced HMS *Brazen* at the beginning of April and all seemed quiet as 801's pilots went back to exercising AAW skills while keeping their hand in for ground support operations by practising dive bombing splash targets. These serials culminated in them dropping fourteen 1,000-lb inert bombs from medium altitude with satisfying accuracy. The maritime situation was quiet enough for a long visit to Naples for self maintenance, beginning on the 13th and lasting nine days.

The landmark event of the visit was a change of command on 21st April. As many had expected, Captain Blackham was promoted to Rear Admiral and returned to Portsmouth as Chief of Staff to Admiral Sir John Kerr, Commander in Chief Naval Home Command.

The new Commanding Officer was Captain Terry Loughran, a former helicopter pilot and an experienced 'MoD warrior' with exactly the right instincts for the challenges the ship would soon have to face.

Rear Admiral T W Loughran CB

(Commanding Officer 1993 – 1994)

The "93 ADRIATIC 94" photograph says it all for me. HMS *Ark Royal* had ended the first decade of her working life fully engaged in the post Cold War pursuit of World order.

The two seven-month operational deployments in support of the United Nations effort to provide Humanitarian Aid to the innocents of Bosnia-Herzegovina and to bring peace to the war-stricken Former Republic of Yugoslavia could not have been further removed from the milk run of the east coast of the United States and the glamour of the ship's earlier deployments. This immensely worthwhile endeavour required sacrifice on the part of our families, but brought its own rewards in terms of personal fulfilment. It brought to the fore two of the Carrier roles, one perhaps in danger of being overlooked in the heyday of ASW; Command of course, but also Power Projection. In the widest sense Operations GRAPPLE and HAMDEN presented the Royal Navy with the opportunity to demonstrate the Political and Diplomatic flexibility afforded by a go anywhere airfield poised in International Waters, beholden to no-one and available at all times as a manifestation of the Nation's will. It brought into focus the enormous communications capability of the CVS, the versatility of her Air Group and the ability of the ship to sustain her operations through her own extensive facilities.

I particularly like the "93 ADRIATIC 94" photograph for another reason: it graphically displays the ship's main armament, her Company, and echoes run through my mind of our modest signature tune throughout my period in command –

in *Ark Royal* tradition – Simply the Best!

It is over fifteen years since the Royal Navy ended operations in the Adriatic. While the UK continues to articulate the case for the new carriers, I am struck by the enduring flexibility *Ark Royal* provided in a world beset by conflict and natural disasters.

Chapter 7

1993 – 1994:
Cleared HOT for Operation HAMDEN

The small town of Srebrenica lies in a mountainous valley in north eastern Bosnia-Herzegovina, not more than ten miles from the Drina River and the Serbian border. The wider part of the bank of the Drina River, where Srebrenica is situated, is commonly referred to as the 'Podrinje' area. During the Roman Empire, Srebrenica was an important source of silver - Srebrenica meaning "silver mine" - but by the 20th Century lead, zinc and iron ore provided the mineral wealth. Nearly three quarters of the 37,000 people living in the Srebrenica municipality were Bosniak Muslim, one quarter Bosnian Serb, with just two percent Bosnian Croatian and other ethnic groups.

Srebrenica became a focal point in the Serb strategy of establishing its 'Republika Srpska' and as the civil war intensified through early 1992, the town was gradually isolated by Serbian military units who set up artillery at all the strategic points and elevations surrounding it, reinforced by regular army units retreating from neighbouring Croatia. By April 1992, Srebrenica had become a ghost town, as the population fled in anticipation of an armed clash between the Bosniak defenders and Serbs attackers. On 18th April the last resistance crumbled and Srebrenica fell to the Serbs. Following their retreat and regroup, the Bosniak forces launched a counter offensive and recaptured Srebrenica by mid May; the retreating Serb forces leaving the devastated town to the Muslim fighters and the civilians that soon followed them. Although the Bosnian Muslims had successfully retaken the town, they remained encircled by Serb forces and cut off. For the next nine months, Srebrenica town and the villages in the area were constantly subjected to Serb military assaults, artillery attacks and sniper fire, as well as occasional bombing from aircraft.

The onslaught was by no means one sided however. Although the Bosnian Serbs enjoyed military superiority, they were greatly outnumbered by Muslim fighters who used the same guerrilla tactics as seen at Srebrenica to retake other villages that had been lost. The Bosniak-held region around Srebrenica actually increased despite the Serb attacks and with the Muslim victory at Kravica in January 1993, the previously isolated pockets of resistance were joined into one contiguous region stretching as far as Žepa to the south and Cerska to the northwest; 350 square miles in all. However, this Bosniak enclave, described as a *"vulnerable island amid Serb-controlled territory"* did not last long. Following significant troop reinforcements over the winter, in early February 1993, Bosnian Serbs launched a major offensive against the Muslim-held territory. Cerska and Kamenica were the first towns to be attacked. Voljevica and Sase in the northeast and Osmače in the southeast of the enclave followed soon after. By March the Serbs had regained all of the Bosniak ground lost the previous summer and the size of the Srebrenica enclave was reduced to less than fifteen miles in diameter, reaching roughly from Potočari in the north to Zeleni Jadar in the south.

Bosnian Muslim refugees fleeing Serb forces had flooded into Srebrenica since its recapture the previous summer, and by March 1993 the influx rose to 80,000 following the latest offensive. Serb forces controlling the access roads stopped international aid from reaching the town and despite the deployment of UNPROFOR to Bosnia in October 1992, only two convoys reached the enclave before Christmas. A humanitarian disaster loomed. Cut off from all supply routes, and without sufficient medicine, food or clean water, the refugees, who usually lived on the streets and without shelter, were left to starve in freezing temperatures. On 28th February 1993 aircraft from the US Air Force's 435th Air Wing based at Rhein Main in Germany, began unilateral operations to supply Srebrenica, conducting night drops of food and medicine near the town. Operation 'PROVIDE PROMISE' as it was named gave some relief to the starving population but for most it was too little and too late.

On 11th March 1993, with the Serb offensive still underway, a delegation headed by the French General Philippe Morillon, UNPROFOR's commander in Bosnia-Herzegovina, arrived in Srebrenica to bring the fighting to a halt and to evacuate the wounded. Spending seventeen days in the town because his departure was initially prevented by the refugees, General Morillon eventually secured terms with the Serbs for a UNHCR convoy to provide humanitarian relief and the evacuation of the most desperate, mainly women and children. Morillon's reports back to the UN uncovered the crisis he had witnessed, but despite strong political pressure from the international community and the efforts by UNPROFOR and UNHCR in the field, the fighting persisted and the humanitarian situation in the area continued to deteriorate. On 16th April 1993, the Security Council, alarmed by the *"rapid deterioration of the situation in Srebrenica and its surrounding areas"* and acting under Chapter VII of the UN Charter, adopted UNSCR 819 in which it demanded that all parties treat Srebrenica and its surroundings as a 'safe area' *"which should be free from any armed attack or any other hostile act."* Following the adoption of the resolution, General Morillon signed an agreement with the commanders of the Serb and Bosnian Muslim forces to demilitarize Srebrenica. Fact-finding missions to the region at the end of April determined that the safe area policy should be extended to other areas; in response, the Security Council adopted UNSCR 824 on 6th May, with safe areas declared in Sarajevo, Tuzla, Zepa, Goražde and Bihac.

The struggle for Srebrenica showed that a harder line amongst the international community would be needed to force a peace in Bosnia, but there was no will to take the necessary military action on the ground, other than to deploy the peacekeepers to the safe areas. Public opinion in Britain and elsewhere was ever more anxious that troops were becoming embroiled in an 'unwinnable' war. More direct action could however be taken in the enforcement of the no-fly zone over Bosnia and the ongoing arms embargo, and Srebrenica also provided the catalyst for these next moves.

UNSCR 781 issued in October 1992 prohibited unauthorised military flights over Bosnia. NATO provided AWACs surveillance aircraft under Operation SKY MONITOR to patrol the no-fly zone, but without any UN-supported mandate to interdict violators. By mid-March, 465 violations of the no-fly zone had been recorded, but the bombing of villages east of Srebrenica by three aircraft on 13th March 1993 was the first violation that resulted in direct combat action, and signalled the Serbian will to flout the resolution. Charges and intransigent denials of responsibility were exchanged at the UN between the Security Council and the Serbian representatives. In a show of strength, the Security Council adopted Resolution 816 on 31st March. UNSCR 816 extended 781 to prohibit not just military but all fixed and rotary-wing flights in Bosnian air space, except for those expressly authorized by the UN Flight Coordination Centre in Zagreb. The resolution also authorized UN member states to "*take all necessary measures...to ensure compliance with the ban on flights*". NATO coordinated the military response to UNSCR 816. On 9th April, the NATO Secretary General, Manfred Wörner, informed his UN counterpart that the "*necessary arrangements*" to ensure compliance had been adopted and that at noon GMT on 12th April 1993 Operation DENY FLIGHT would come into force with aircraft from France, the Netherlands, Turkey, the United Kingdom and the United States offered as enforcers. Initially, DENY FLIGHT was intended only to enforce the no-fly zone; however several NATO members, including the United States, were eager to find ways to end the war and improve the situation of civilians, and hoped that military action could do so. Bill Clinton's platform during the Presidential campaign of 1992 promised a "lift and strike" policy, which included the use of air strikes against the Bosnian Serbs and the US unilateral action under PROVIDE PROMISE was symptomatic of the lobbying for a larger role for NATO airpower in Bosnia. US officials were eager to expand US air operations through DENY FLIGHT, hoping that an aggressive no-fly zone and possible air strikes would end the conflict more quickly. This stance strengthened after the Bosnian Serbs rejected the Vance-Owen Plan on 6th May 1993, Clinton and other US officials openly discussing the possibility of large-scale strikes to coerce the Serbs into acceptance. Ultimately, no such strikes were approved or carried out, but American officials became more open to the idea of using airpower for coercion.

The day after Srebrenica was declared a safe area, the Security Council passed UNSCR 820, strengthening its resolve to enforce a blockade of the Former Yugoslavia already established under UNSCRs 757 and 787. Resolution 820 prohibited imports to, exports from and transshipment of goods through the UNPAs in Croatia and those parts of Bosnia-Herzegovina under the control of Serb forces. It also froze Yugoslav assets abroad and outlawed the provision of business services to Yugoslav companies. Significantly, all maritime traffic was prohibited from entering Yugoslavia's territorial sea, except where expressly authorized.

For HMS *Ark Royal*, Operation DENY FLIGHT and the strengthening of the embargo against the FRY signalled escalation of her involvement in GRAPPLE despite growing misgivings from the politicians at home. Captain Terry Loughran assumed command of HMS *Ark Royal* on 21st April 1993 and rebutting any suggestion of his task group withdrawing from theatre, as had been mooted in the press throughout early spring, he gave it renewed purpose: to support British and UN troops ashore; assist the coalition embargo operations in the Adriatic, and provide assets if required for DENY FLIGHT.

Ark sailed from Naples on 22nd April and the first priority was the support to UNPROFOR and the newly established Canadian force acting as peace keepers in the Srebrenica safe area. The Canadians established a barrier between Bosniak and Serb forces, but tensions rose as they sought to impose General Morillon's directive on the warring factions. Outgunned and exposed, they needed a visible show of resolve. In response, on 23rd April the readiness of TG 612.02 was reduced to 24 hours notice and both factions were made aware that naval and air forces were ready to reinforce UNPROFOR and intervene if required. The following day Captain Loughran declared his Sea Harriers fully capable of delivering the GBU-16 Paveway II laser-guided bomb, adding significantly to the range of 'support' options available.

The flexibility and effectiveness of the Sea Harrier FRS-1 ('FRS' standing for Fighter Reconnaissance Strike) as a weapon-delivery platform had been proven emphatically during the Falklands War. Sea Harriers accounted for over a quarter of all Argentine aircraft lost, with eighty percent of those shot down using the US-supplied AIM-9L Sidewinder missile and the remainder taken out using the trusted twin Aden 30-millimetre cannons. As well as cannons for the ground-attack role, the Sea Harrier could also carry a wide array of munitions for this purpose, including 1000-lb iron bombs, BL755 cluster munitions and rockets. The 800 Squadron aircraft embarked in HMS *Hermes*, famously "counted out" and "counted back" by the BBC journalist Brian Hanrahan on 1st May 1982, attacked Goose Green and the runway at Port Stanley with a mix of air-burst and delayed fuze thousand-pounders as well as cluster bombs. The introduction of the Sea Eagle anti-ship missile in 1985 added greatly to the Sea Harrier's arsenal, giving the aircraft a world-beating long-range maritime attack capability. RAF Harrier GR-3s had been the first jets in the world to use the Paveway II in combat, also during the Falklands War, but it took some years and the willingness of the RAF before the capability would be transferred to the FRS-1. The re-role of the Sea Harrier had taken several months of careful planning and preparation. Bombing runs by 801's Air Warfare Instructor on the Garvie Island range at Cape Wrath proved the aircraft's ability to launch the weapon, with total success achieved during seven attacks. Thirty two Paveway II kits were flown from the Gulf and finally embarked in *Ark* at Naples after convoluted and tedious negotiations with the Italian port authority. The kits needed to be repaired following the weathering and damage they had received in the desert conditions. They were worked on in the air weapons preparation facility in *Ark*'s deep magazine, but this took up two-thirds of the work-space usually reserved for the Sidewinder missiles and Stingray torpedoes. Once repaired the non-explosive components were stored in the already crowded hangar, highlighting once again the inadequacy of the CVSG's ammunitioning facilities. Preparation and loading drills for the new weapon had to be practised, validated then certified, while local modifications to the aircraft's GPS navigation system were required to achieve the reliability needed for targeting laser-guided

bombs. Much work was done with staff from the US battle group to formulate joint tactics and in-flight testing was completed at sea by the 801 Squadron pilots, who flew profiles with USN A-6 and F/A-18s from the carrier USS *Theodore Roosevelt* to prove both laser designation techniques and targeting options. The final step to provide the FRS-1 with a full Close-Air Support (CAS) capability saw a Carrier Borne Ground Liaison Officer embark in *Ark* on 29th April; the first time in twenty years that such an officer had embarked in a UK carrier.

HMS *Ark Royal* reentered the Adriatic on 24th April and Captain Loughran visited the commanders of the BRITFOR ashore, and the American (CTF 60) and French (CTF 470) carrier battle groups operating in the Adriatic over the next week to re-establish links. At the same time UNSCR 820 came into force and both the NATO and WEU task groups stepped up a gear in enforcing the Yugoslav embargo. NATO's Standing Naval Force Mediterranean (TF 432), under the command of Italian Rear Admiral Martinotti, was responsible for the higher risk Montenegro OPAREA, while the WEU Force (TG 621.1) further south patrolled the choke point through the Strait of Otranto. Both Task Force commanders quickly recognised that the Yugoslav naval forces based at Kotor Bay were beginning to adopt a more threatening posture in reaction to UNSCR 820 and greater support was needed for their groups. Rear Admiral Martinotti asked both for Surface Combat Air Patrols (SUCAP) and more ships. CTF 60 in USS *Theodore Roosevelt* delegated TACON of some USN ships to CTF 432 but could not provide a SUCAP during the carrier's declared no-fly period from 7th to 9th May. Captain Loughran, following discussions with Rear Admiral Martinotti and a conference with the commanding officers in his own task groups, received authorization to detach HMS *Broadsword* and for her to operate further east, providing the necessary cover with her two 'Gulf modified' Lynx helicopters armed with Sea Skua missiles. So began a period of close cooperation between TG 612.02 and TF 432 and greater Royal Navy support to the embargo operations. To improve the skills of her boarding party, *Broadsword* embarked training staff from HMS *Cambridge* during the period of her detachment. Meanwhile 820 Squadron and 849 'B' Flight were tasked to conduct surface search in support of the embargo operations, reporting directly to CTF 432.

The composition of TG 612.02 changed during the first half of May. HNLMS *De Ruyter* relieved HNLMS *Abraham Crijnssen* on 4th May, while RFA *Argus* and *Olwen* put alongside on 10th for two-week maintenance periods at Trieste and Soudha Bay in Crete, respectively, tanker duties being taken over temporarily by RFA *Orangeleaf*. The Dutch ship had proven to be a valuable asset to the task group, contributing greatly to the tactical picture working with operations and intelligence staffs to identify the Indicators and Warnings that might suggest increased Yugoslav naval activity. *De Ruyter* quickly established the same strong working relationship with the flagship.

SNFM ships continued to patrol the Montenegro OPAREA and the situation became tense on 13th May when a Yugoslav *Kotor*-class frigate locked up the USS *Kauffman* with its 'Hawk Screech' gun-targetting radar. The incident could easily have escalated given the USN's more bullish stance and robust Rules of Engagement. It was clear that Admiral Martinotti's earlier request for assets needed a greater response to deter the Yugoslav units from further unwise excursions. Accordingly, TG 612.02's Duty Escort was offered and on 17th May HMS *Broadsword* again detached to go under CTF432's TACON, working under NATO Rules of Engagement with air or surface support as required. Thereafter, Yugoslav units mostly confined their activities to within the Montenegrin twelve-mile territorial limit, however the very real possibility that UK naval assets might have to respond immediately in a combat situation prompted the Commander-in-Chief Fleet to increase the 'top cover' in theatre. It had been a

political decision not to send the Commander UK Task Group with *Ark* when she had sailed in February. By May however, with tension increasing ashore and a risk of air strikes, Rear Admiral Brigstocke was directed to take personal command for a temporary period. The admiral arrived in his familiar flagship on the 19th and began a strenuous programme of visits to the CTFs afloat, military commanders ashore and to Her Majesty's Ambassador in Rome to familiarise himself with the situation. On 20th May Lieutenant General Michael Rose, Commander UK Land Forces visited *Ark* to be briefed on the joint maritime operations. From this hectic round of briefings, both General Rose and Admiral Brigstocke gained a clear impression of harmonious relations, mutual confidence and co-operation in theatre, as well as the inherent flexibility offered by the UK task group.

Amidst the operational tempo there was still time for the 'hearts and minds' activity that cemented international relationships between the UK and its Adriatic partners. *Ark Royal* was being supported by regular flights to and from an air head at Bari and on 18th May, Captain Loughran hosted dignitaries on board while at sea, during "Bari-Tonic Day". On 24th May, *Ark* arrived at Corfu for a four-day visit during which Captain Loughran laid a wreath at the grave of the 44 servicemen onboard HMS *Saumarez* and HMS *Volage*, killed when their ships struck Albanian mines laid in the Corfu Channel in October 1946. While *Ark* was alongside, UK Land Forces Headquarters signalled a change to the readiness profile of the task group, requiring it to be within 24 hours of a line 42 degrees north, between 17 degrees and 18 degrees east, with extension to 48 hours notice available on formal request. The significance of this was that it allowed *Ark* to operate further south and to visit Malta for self maintenance.

Another period on patrol was needed before *Ark* could withdraw to Malta and the task group deployed again to support CTF 432. HNLMS *De*

Ruyter relieved *Broadsword* as Duty Escort and assumed the SUCAP duties for SNFM on 28th May. When *Ark* sailed from Corfu the following day, three Sea Harriers were placed at CTF 432's disposal, maintaining Alert 30 status between sunrise and sunset from 30th May until 3rd June. The two aircraft were armed with single 1000-lb bombs and Aden cannons which allowed them to recover to the deck without having to expend ammunition, while the third aircraft was armed with two Sea Eagle missiles. Alert 30 usually included two exercise launches per day and this proved to be a highly successful period for the Sea Harriers with all action launches achieved well within the alert notice, demonstrating the utility of the aircraft. This tempo did not come without a cost however and 801's maintainers needed to work around the clock to keep the reduced number of six aircraft serviceable in the right configuration to meet the full range of possible task orders. This challenge was made all the greater for a period due to poor reliability of the aircrafts' Pegasus engines. All too often, multiple engine changes were needed to keep sufficient aircraft available to support the notice commitment. A late flurry of Yugoslav naval activity tested the responses of TF 432. On 2nd June an Italian fishing vessel allegedly strayed inside the twelve-mile limit and was engaged by a Yugoslav *Mirna*-class patrol boat, killing one fisherman and injuring another. The casualties were handed over to SNFM forces outside the limit. *De Ruyter*'s period as duty escort culminated on 3rd June with a visit to her at sea by the Netherlands Defence Select Committee and she handed back the duty to *Broadsword* the following day. At the same time RFA *Argus* went alongside at Split to offload some specialist vehicles to BRITFOR HQ prior to her departure from the group. The decision had been taken at the end of May to stand down the light gun battery to 48-hours notice to move from the UK, thus allowing *Argus* to return home. She sailed from Split on 4th following a farewell from Admiral Brigstocke and chopped to UK national tactical control as she exited the Adriatic the following day.

HMS *Ark Royal* arrived in Malta for her self maintenance period on 8th June. This was the first time a British carrier had been in Grand Harbour since the previous *Ark Royal* had visited in 1977. An estimated 30,000 people, a tenth of the island's population, turned out to visit the ship which received a rousing and moving welcome and send-off. It was all a wonderful demonstration of the undying affection of the old naval base island for the Royal Navy. Admiral Brigstocke and Captain Loughran called on the Prime Minister, while families and friends were reunited for a few days. Sir Donald Gosling in his new motor yacht *MV Leander* was a welcome and typically generous visitor.

During *Ark*'s stand-off, *De Ruyter* and *Broadsword* once again exchanged Duty Escort duties but this was to be the last chop of the UK task group frigate to CTF 432, as significant changes took place to the structure of the forces carrying out the embargo operations in the Adriatic. The same day as *Ark*'s entry to Valletta, the Councils of NATO and the WEU, at a joint session, reviewed the embargo operations and approved a combined concept of operations for the continued implementation of UNSCR 820. This new concept included a single command and control arrangement for the combined operation "SHARP GUARD" under the authority of the councils of both organisations. By the time *Ark Royal* returned to the Adriatic, the two separate blockade operations, MARITIME GUARD by NATO and SHARP FENCE by the WEU had been united into the new single operation, SHARP GUARD. The ships also combined into a single integrated Task Force 440 under the operational command of NATO's southern naval commander, Vice Admiral Angeli ITN. CTF 440 amalgamated the three former task group commands: NATO's SNFM (Rear Admiral Martinotti CTF440.01) and SNFL (Commodore G R Maddison CDF, CTF440.03), and the WEUMARFOR (Rear Admiral Pellegrino, CTF 440.02).

Ark was back on station on 18th June and the following day Admiral Brigstocke lunched with Rear Admiral Martinotti and Admiral Johnson of the American TF 60. 612.02's commander was rightly anxious to maintain the greatest level of co-ordination possible between these forces despite their reorganization and the changes to operational control that this entailed. He had already sought and gained approval to offer assistance on an *ad hoc* basis to CTF 440, subject to the overriding commitments of national tasking, with the authority granted to make those decisions on the ground.

Admiral Brigstocke's offer of continued support was soon taken up and *Ark* again provided Sea Harriers for SUCAP duties between 20th and 26th June, on alert to support Admiral Martinotti's ships. HMS *Broadsword*, which had detached on 19th to provide equipment to BRITFOR at Split to assist with their recovery of a crashed Spanish armoured personnel carrier, was tasked temporarily to act as Goalkeeper for the Italian tanker ITS *Stromboli* while she replenished CTF440.01 units off the Montenegrin coast. It was then *De Ruyter*'s turn to ride shotgun, for RFA *Fort Grange* on 24th June as she replenished HMS *Birmingham*'s fuel and ammunition stocks at sea. *Birmingham*, as well as her sister ship *Cardiff* and the *Type-22* frigate HMS *Cornwall* formed the Royal Navy contributions to the NATO standing naval groups now amalgamated under CTF 440, but they nevertheless maintained routine national-links with CTG 612.02. Amidst the surface activity, 'A' Flight from 820 Squadron made a welcome return to *Ark* on 22nd June, having been embarked in *Olwen* for five months. The deployment had been slightly frustrating for 820 Squadron, split between the RFAs and with limited opportunities for ASW work, save for a CASEX with USS *Theodore Roosevelt* and USS *Norfolk* in mid-June for the SKJs embarked in *Fort Grange*. The aircraft had nevertheless provided sterling support to 846 Squadron on the task group logistics runs in theatre and to the airhead at Bari, the squadron's

engineering staff having stripped out non-essential kit from the Mk-6 Sea Kings to improve their load capacity. The Bari airhead itself also worked superbly throughout the deployment. The team of three stores accountants on site using 846 and 820 Sea Kings moved four times more cargo than the neighbouring 40-man American team with Sea Stallion heavy lift helicopters at their disposal to supply the US Sixth Fleet. Once again, the Royal Navy had proven, quietly and resolutely, that biggest was not necessarily best.

On 28th June HMS *Ark Royal* sailed south to meet the Italian aircraft carrier ITS *Giuseppe Garibaldi*. The ships had last met at sea five years earlier during *Ark*'s outbound passage through the Mediterranean on her way to OUTBACK '88. Then, the Italian Navy was prevented under national law from operating fixed wing aircraft and the chance to operate 801's aircraft was warmly welcomed. With the legal wrangles finally cleared, the Italians had at last taken delivery of improved AV8-B II+ aircraft, and the opportunity for cross-decking with *Ark* was exploited. Two two-seater TAV8-Bs embarked in *Ark* while two of 801's FRS-1 Sea Harriers landed on *Garibaldi*. With the operational milestone achieved, both ships prepared to host a VIP visit by the Italian Defence Minister and senior Italian naval officers the following day on the 29th. Signor Fabbri and Admiral Venturoni the Italian Chief of Naval Staff obtained an excellent impression of the capabilities they were at last being allowed to obtain for themselves. Admiral Brigstocke, keen to exploit the access to the Italians, emphasized the advantages to the coalition forces in being granted more flexible over-flight and basing arrangements, issues that had not been easily resolved as DENY FLIGHT and SHARP GUARD came into force. *Ark* then made for Soudha Bay, Crete for a five day stand-off.

On 6th July, COMUKTG's staff that had deployed with *Ark* in January and had been at sea almost continuously since May 1992 when they deployed in *Invincible* for ORIENT '92, were finally relieved by FOSF's command team. TG 612.02 reshaped in early July with HNLMS *Jan Van Brakel* relieving *De Ruyter* on 4th July and HMS *Boxer* taking over from *Broadsword* on the 8th, but the most significant change occurred on 13th July when Rear Admiral Mike Gretton took over from John Brigstocke as COMUKTG and commander of TG612.02. A series of high profile visits to *Ark* preceded the handover, including that of Admiral Jeremy Boorda USN, NATO's C-in-C SOUTH who was in overall command of the NATO air and naval efforts, although not TG 612, which remained under strictly national control. Other visitors that day were Brigadier Robin Searby the commander of BRITFOR and Rear Admiral Ian Garnett, Flag Officer Naval Aviation. In summarising his time as the task group's commander, John Brigstocke reflected on the role played by the flagship with which, in one form or another, he had been associated with for over four years: "*Ark Royal has committed herself admirably as a command platform while also remaining ready to contribute to enforcement of the no-fly zone and to conduct air defence of forces at sea, if required. ... I have considered it a privilege to command the* task group *through a busy and interesting period.*"

Despite the change of assets and command of the task group, the core operational work continued with 801's Sea Harriers once again taking SUCAP duties for CTF 440.01 on 13th July. Although *Ark Royal* had declared her Sea Harriers LGB-capable since April there had up until July been no direct involvement in Operation DENY FLIGHT. Land-based CAP, co-coordinated by NATO's Fifth Tactical Air Force (5ATAF) HQ in Vicenza took over the main air-interdiction role. The imposition of the 5ATAF's air limitations had effects on carrier operations, but a liaison team sent to Vicenza in early May worked out the arrangements for the integration of *Ark*'s flying into the overall developing scheme. The scope of DENY FLIGHT would change rapidly though as the situation in Bosnia continued to deteriorate. The Bosnian Serbs

refused to accept the Vance-Owen peace plan, continued to blockade UNHCR missions trying to deliver humanitarian relief and sporadically bombarded Srebrenica and the five other safe areas at Sarajevo, Goražde, Bihac, Tuzla and Zepa established under UNSCR 824. UNPROFOR units in the safe areas lacked the manpower and heavy artillery needed to respond to these attacks and renewed calls, led again by the Americans, demanded that the UN permit the use of air forces to attack the Serb positions. On 4th June, the UN Security Council passed UNSCR 836 giving member states, acting nationally or through regional organizations "*...all necessary measures, through the use of air power, in and around the safe areas ... to support UNPROFOR.*" It was easier for NATO to respond to UNSCR 836 by adding new phases to the existing operation rather than ask the North Atlantic Council to approve a new UN-sponsored mission, and thus DENY FLIGHT became something of a misnomer. General John Shalikashvili, the Supreme Allied Commander in Europe met with Marshal of the RAF Sir Peter Harding, the Chief of Defence Staff, on 5th July to discuss the possible use of UK aircraft for Close-Air Support. Two days later CDS formally offered Jaguars and Sea Harriers. CTG 612.02's staff had already conducted contingency planning for this in response to Operation DISCIPLINE GUARD after the April declaration; these plans now gathered pace in response to the CDS directive. *Ark* was reprogrammed to participate in Exercise CRATER 93-1, 5ATAF's rehearsal of the command and control procedures required for the new phase of DENY FLIGHT, in Italy from 19th to 20th July. From 23rd July, two aircraft onboard *Ark* were put at 30 minutes alert for CAS missions in Bosnia.

This most significant development for the Sea Harrier in Adriatic operations coincided with the end of *Ark Royal*'s first deployment, since she would shortly handover the flagship duty to her sister HMS *Invincible*. The ship entered Palermo harbour for a last Mediterranean port visit and then sailed on the 29th for the handover. The last seven months had been a period of very hard work for the ship, her CAG and her crew. Captain Loughran reflected on *Ark*'s performance, 'poised' in the Adriatic, as the ship left theatre, "*Poise is about living at sea, striking the balance between keeping your military skills at a high level so that you can respond should you have to and yet not staying at such a high level that you become stale. We had to strike a balance between work and play and it is perhaps worth remembering that the work has consisted of eighty per cent of our time at sea and only twenty per cent of our time in harbour. Over one thousand men and women sailed at very short notice in January with great uncertainty as to how long they would be away and what they would be doing. As the months have gone by and the task has become more clear one can only admire the motivation of those on board and the fortitude of the families at home who lent their unstinting support.*"

As HMS *Ark Royal* passed Gibraltar Captain Loughran laid a wreath where the third *Ark* had gone down, and the ship sailed into the Atlantic for the northward leg home. The First Sea Lord, Admiral Sir Benjamin Bathurst, visited en-route to pay a personal 'thank you' to the Ship's Company. Having left one Sea Harrier with *Invincible* to boost 800 Squadron's strength to seven, 801 Squadron flew off to Yeovilton on the 30th July. The helicopters followed on 2nd August. 820 Squadron had reunited its flights on *Ark* the day before handover to *Invincible* and they disembarked together with the 849 'B' SKWs and the remaining 846 SKAs as the ship passed Mounts Bay. *Ark* arrived home on 3rd August 1993, to a sun-lit Portsmouth and an equally warm welcome from families and friends at the dockside. The GRAPPLE deployment had been the longest test yet of *Ark*'s ability to deliver war-fighting capability at reach during which she had consumed 21,000 tonnes of diesel oil and her aircraft 5,500 tonnes of AVCAT. After all this effort *Ark* was home ... for the time being at least.

Back in Portsmouth *Ark Royal* underwent her period of base assisted maintenance. She was back at sea in mid-November for work up, with a reduced air group of three Sea Harriers, three SKJs and SKWs each, the ship participated in two "Thursday Wars" and there was a high level of air activity including exercises with French aircraft. Two Sea Harrier FA-2s now in service with 899 Squadron joined for sea trials, the second time the type had flown from the ship.

Another period alongside allowed a peaceful Christmas leave but the situation in former Yugoslavia meant that a further extended operational deployment to the Adriatic was inevitable. The Government had been considering withdrawal of British forces in the spring but had decided to stick it out for another year. The whole operation in former Yugoslavia had now been re-christened Operation HAMDEN with "GRAPPLE" reserved for the ground forces in Bosnia. The return to the Adriatic necessitated a change of programme for *Ark*. Following 1992's defence cuts under "Options for Change" only two of the CVSGs were normally in active service at any one time with the third placed in extended readiness. With HMS *Illustrious* under refit at Devonport and then completing sea trials and work up until late summer, both *Invincible* and *Ark* would be needed to maintain the roulement in the Adriatic for at least one more deployment each. *Ark*'s planned decommissioning in summer 1994 and period of extended readiness would therefore have to wait until September, after she had completed another seven-month tour off Bosnia.

HMS *Invincible* carried the UK torch in the Adriatic throughout the autumn and winter of 1993/4 and further developed the modus operandi established during *Ark*'s previous deployment, showing the full capability of the CVSG beyond its Cold War role. 5ATAF running DENY FLIGHT soon found the Sea Harrier to be particularly flexible. Uniquely among the aircraft declared, it could do all three roles – air defence, recce and CAS, as well as continuing the SUCAP role for

SHARP GUARD. This meant that any Sea Harrier airborne over Bosnia could easily be redirected to take recce photographs of a developing problem on the ground. Poised in international waters, the carrier also showed its utility, free of over-flight problems, with shorter transit times to targets and the ability to move the 'airfield' away from bad weather. It also offered true '24-7-365' availability, whereas air bases in Italy were still constrained by peacetime operating routines and unable to reliably provide weekend cover.

Probably the most significant event of HMS *Invincible*'s tour of duty was her use as a venue for peace talks in August 1993. In the aftermath of the failure of the Vance-Owen peace plan, the Serb rejection of it responsible for galvanizing the UN Security Council to pass UNSCR 836, David Owen and Vance's successor, Norwegian Foreign Minister Thorvald Stoltenberg, entered a new round of negotiations with the warring factions. These negotiations took place onboard HMS *Invincible* and both mediators cited the advantage of being out of the glare of the world's press, having more intimate conference facilities than had been available at the UN in Geneva and the ability to hold negotiating parties 'captive' for bi-lateral discussions, as important bonuses. Given the pace of territorial division, fragmentation and ethnic cleansing that had occurred during the conflict the new plan acknowledged that Bosnia-Herzegovina could not remain a single country. On 20th August, Stoltenberg and Owen unveiled a map that would partition Bosnia into three ethnic mini-states, in which Bosnian Serbs would be given 52 percent of territory, Muslims would be allotted 30 percent and Bosnian-Croats would receive 18 percent. All parties agreed to the proposals but, in what became a recurring pattern, Alija Izetbegović, the Bosnian President, subsequently renounced the plan and reneged on his earlier agreement to its provisions. While the talks broke new grounds, like those before and after, no lasting settlement was achieved.

Arranging the peace talks onboard at less than 48-hours notice could not have been possible without the new and better command and control equipment that had been installed and proven in *Ark* during her first tour of duty and subsequently exploited in *Invincible*. Direct-dial secure telephones, a real time computer link into a joint intelligence centre, fax machines, rudimentary video tele-conferencing and even local cell phones operating off the Italian telecom system, were all – then – novel facilities for passing and processing information quickly. However, it was symptomatic of the politics and stringent rules of engagement involved that similarly quick decisions could not be taken in the wider chains of command running the NATO and UN operations in the region.

The airborne exclusion role by NATO aircraft within DENY FLIGHT had been relatively successful in preventing fixed-wing aircraft from flying over restricted air space in Bosnia, reducing unauthorized incursions from about twenty per month to only three. Illegal helicopter flights presented a more complicated challenge. All sides in the conflict used helicopters extensively for non-military purposes, and some of these flights were authorized by the UN. NATO fighters were only authorized to shoot down helicopters that committed a hostile act, otherwise they issued orders to "land or exit", in other words, land the aircraft or leave the no-fly zone. Typically, helicopters complied with these orders by landing, but then took off again after NATO forces departed. None of the parties in the conflict respected the ban on helicopter flights, as evidenced when Ratko Mladić responded to a BBC journalist's question about his violation of the ban with the statement, "*The commander of the Bosnian Serb armed forces does not ride on a donkey.*" Deceptive markings on helicopters further complicated matters for NATO pilots and as a result they proved unable to stop most unauthorized helicopter flights. Over 5,700 unauthorized flights were recorded during the Bosnian war.

Providing Close Air Support to UNPROFOR

troops, authorized under UNSCR 836 and enacted through DENY FLIGHT, proved equally difficult as it involved the "dual key" of both UN and NATO approval. UN approval required contact with the United Nations headquarters in New York, making effective coordination nearly impossible given the difference in time zones. The UN approval process was later streamlined when UN Secretary-General Boutros Boutros-Ghali delegated the authority to authorize air strikes to his special representative in Bosnia, Yasushi Akashi. Even after this simplification, however, "dual key" remained a problem as all requests had first to be processed through the UN Air Operations Center in Kiseljak before being passed up the UNPROFOR chain of command to Akashi. After Akashi approved the request, he would make a request to NATO commanders who then had to pass orders back down their chain of command and coordinate with forces on the ground. Unsurprising given the bureaucracy, NATO aircraft did not actually conduct any strike missions during 1993 although a broad plan was constructed to carry out air strikes in August as part of a plan to end the Siege of Sarajevo. After diplomatic intervention, the plan was not executed, but a precedent was established for the possible use of air strikes. This harder line was reiterated in late January 1994 by the new Commander of UN Forces in Bosnia, Lieutenant General Sir Michael Rose, who took over from his previous post as the Commander in Chief UK Land Forces, responsible for GRAPPLE. Rose's predecessor in Bosnia, Belgian Lieutenant General Francis Briquemont had resigned following his criticism of the insufficiency of resources provided to him to effectively execute the UNSCRs in force.

On Friday 28th January, HMS *Ark Royal* sailed for pre-deployment training en route to her operational station. She embarked a more normal air group this time; seven Sea Harrier FRS-1s from 801 Squadron, seven SKJs from 820 and three SKWs from 849 'B' Flight. The group exercised on the way to Gibraltar with 820 Squadron

working with the *Type-22* frigate HMS *Cumberland* on her way in the same direction, but bound for ARMILLA duties in the Gulf. *Ark* also met her sister *Illustrious* while she conducted post-refit sea trials and the two ships sailed together for a time. The Ship's Company enjoyed a new addition to the 'intel' systems fitted having had a satellite television system installed during the maintenance period. This was an enormous morale booster and allowed everyone from the Captain downwards to keep in touch with news at home, but as the ship headed south, the focus naturally turned to monitoring the developing Bosnian situation. With the situation around Sarajevo deteriorating rapidly, there was much talk of possible air strikes in which *Ark*'s aircraft might have to play a part.

On 4th February *Ark Royal* met up with *Invincible* off Gibraltar and after an ENCOUNTEREX in which 800 and 801's Sea Harriers 'attacked' the other squadron's carrier with Sea Eagle missiles, *Invincible* handed back the torch for Operation HAMDEN. 801 Squadron disembarked for bombing practice at RAF Decimomannu while *Ark* went alongside in Gibraltar for a four day visit and Captain Loughran assumed command once again of TG 612.02. The mission directive for HAMDEN was that Captain Loughran's task group should retain in a posture, no more than 96 hours from the Adriatic, to support UK troops ashore, and for the flagship to be in theatre for forty percent of her time in support of DENY FLIGHT. The relaxation of posture from *Ark*'s previous deployment reflected two key factors. First, by December 1993, the degree of confidence that had been established in the known patterns of Yugoslav naval units and the warning provided by the NATO ships, allowed the carriers to move around with the minimum of close escorting, allowing the second escort to revert to 14-days notice in the UK. Over *Ark*'s deployment HMS *Broadsword*, *Beaver* and *Edinburgh* would in turn be on notice for operations. Second, the need to keep war-fighting skills up to speed in areas other than those needed in the Adriatic, such as ASW, had become more and more important. The task group was given the freedom therefore to move around the whole of the Mediterranean subject to the military situation in the Balkans. Training facilities in the Toulon areas were found to be particularly good for keeping skills alive. These arrangements were tested almost immediately after Captain Loughran assumed command of the task group.

On 5th February a single 120mm shell landed on a stall in the packed open-air market square in Sarajevo, killing 68 people and wounding 197 more. In a similar attack by Serb forces the previous day, three mortar rounds had killed ten people queuing for humanitarian aid. The shelling was the worst single atrocity in the 22-month old conflict and came on the day Bosnian Serb, Muslim and Croatian leaders were meeting in the city to discuss its future and were on the verge of agreement. As David Owen put it "*We had reached the point where Bosnian Serbs were ready to take Sarajevo outside an overall peace settlement to try to demilitarise it. I am absolutely determined it is not aborted.*" The mainly Muslim Bosnian Government immediately accused the Serbs of the shelling, but predictably the Bosnia-Serb leader Radovan Karadžić and his Minister for Information Miroslav Toholj, denied the charges and blamed the Muslims, saying, "*Serbs don't kill civilians*". Provisional findings of a UN commission investigating the attack concluded on 13th February that "*there was insufficient evidence to prove that one party or the other had fired the mortar bomb*", nevertheless the massacre had already galvanized the international community into acting to lift the siege of Sarajevo. UN Secretary General Boutros Boutros-Ghali, tempered by General Rose's advice that immediate reprisal attacks were impractical given the failure to identify the culprit and that widespread air strikes might endanger the ongoing peace process, formally asked NATO for confirmation that a future request for air strikes "*against artillery positions in or around Sarajevo*

... responsible for attacks on civilian targets" would immediately be executed under UNSCR 836. In what was described as a "decisive moment" in NATO's history, NATO ambassadors meeting in Brussels on 9th February agreed to Boutros-Ghali's request and issued an ultimatum to the Bosnia Serbs, requiring the removal of heavy weapon from an exclusion zone twenty kilometres around Sarajevo by midnight on 21st February. Failure to comply would result in immediate air strikes.

Ark Royal sailed from Gibraltar on 8th February and cancelling a planned visit to Naples, headed east for the Adriatic in anticipation of developing events. The following morning, 5ATAF requested all available assets move to support operations over Bosnia, vindicating *Ark*'s change of programme, and commenced intensive air operations over Sarajevo in the build up to the NATO deadline. In contrast, the French carrier *Foch* was brought to 24-hours notice but her sailing was stopped by the French President. The intervention reflected the French view that their carrier was a national strategic asset, to be used responsively to events in the national interest. The French reluctance to answer 5ATAF's call was mirrored by Greece and Hungary who were unwilling to commit to the UN request for support.

801 Squadron's training programme at Decimomannu was accelerated so that the aircraft could re-embark early, arriving back at *Ark* on the 10th. That night, CINCSOUTH issued the North Atlantic Council's Execute Order for air strikes around Sarajevo once the deadline had expired, subject only to authorization of the first strike by the UN Secretary General. *Ark* arrived in theatre two days later and 801's pilots were given orientation briefings from 5ATAF and UNPROFOR staff before conducting orientation flights. The 5ATAF brief highlighted that the recce capability of the Sea Harrier was as yet not fully appreciated by the NATO planners, nor was it clear to the pilots why two LGB had been added to their standard weapon inventories apparently

rethinking the preference for dumb bombs. The following day, *Ark*'s Sea Harriers commenced orientation flying for DENY FLIGHT, with four pairs on Exercise CAS (XCAS) duties each armed with a single 1000-lb bomb and one pair assigned for recce duties. Following calls to Admiral Boorda and NATO headquarters staff at Naples, and an update at 5ATAF HQ at Vicenza, Rear Admiral Gretton embarked in *Ark Royal* on Valentine's Day and in anticipation of air strikes commencing, resumed command of the task group two days later. Close liaison was established with Rear Admiral Bill Wright, CTF 60, flying his flag in USS *Saratoga*, and with Rear Admiral Alain Witrand, CTF 470 now at sea in FS *Foch*. A number of attack options were planned to cover the possible range of Bosnian Serb army actions, all multi-national, multi-service and all involving Sea Harrier participation. Captain Loughran also went ashore to liaise with the current COMBRITFOR, Brigadier John Reith in order to better understand the situation on the ground and reassure himself on what he considered to be a diversion of the NATO and UN objectives following 5th February.

NATO's continued escalation appeared at odds with UNPROFOR's efforts on the ground in Sarajevo to broker a lasting peace. It was widely known that Serb forces did not bow to ultimatums, whatever the consequences, and the CNN coverage of the NATO air strike warnings, amplified by intensive flying over the city, as well as apparent tension between the UN and NATO representatives behind the scenes, suggested that a disconnect was growing between the politicians and the military commanders. In fact, the unease surrounded the implicit possibility of blanket air strikes by NATO, rather than the more 'surgical' use of CAS and General Rose was keen to engineer a CAS mission before the deadline expired and for a demonstration air strike on specific targets after 20th February. Rose's "big stick" helped him successfully broker a ceasefire and the large scale removal of Bosnian-Serb heavy weapons from the area surrounding Sarajevo began on 17th February.

In a deal struck by the Russian envoy Vitaly Churkin, Russian troops were to occupy the vacuum left by the departing Bosnian-Serb forces. Despite the Serb failure to fully comply with the NATO ultimatum by 21st February, UN Special Envoy Yasushi Akashi said on the evening of 20th that *"sufficient progress had been made and that there was no need for air strikes."*

Ark Royal's rapid build up to respond to DENY FLIGHT exposed a number of weak areas in her readiness. Persistent connectivity problems with the satellite communications system hampered the ability of the task group staff to process the plethora of information coming to and from 5ATAF and HAMDEN HQ at UK Land Wilton. These were only solved after a terse exchange between Captain Loughran and Fleet HQ that had the satellite link rerouted from Defford through the more reliable ground station at RAF Oakhanger. Stocks of ammunition were also insufficient to support any more than 36-hours bombing and the mix of bomb and fuze types carried was less than optimal. A RAS with *Fort Austin* on 18th February addressed what Captain Loughran described as *"inevitable wrinkles just when you think you have a handle on it all."*

Media interest was also intense, with reporters from SKY, ITN and the BBC witnessing Harrier operations on 13th, Captain Loughran interviewed for Radio 4's "Today" broadcast on 17th and again the following day by South West Television and Angela Rippon for LBC. While the interest was to be expected, the impact of the spotlight on 801's pilots was not anticipated and hasty arrangements were agreed to protect their anonymity and for them to contact their families at home after each mission, to counter any potentially confusing media reports. The pressure on 801's engineering staff was equally intense, with only enough staff to maintain six aircraft but with eight embarked following the arrival of another Harrier on 12th. The GPS kits needed to operate the LGBs were also failing at an alarming rate and threatened to critically affect operations. The front line team also, worryingly, sensed the continuing nervousness among the politicians. Captain Loughran and Lieutenant Commander Mel Robinson, commanding 801 Squadron, attended the Defence Ministers' conference at Aviano on 19th/20th and received personal exhortations from the Secretary of State, Malcolm Rifkind and the Chief of Defence Staff, Sir Peter Harding, for absolute professionalism and "no risk". This perhaps reflected the worries in the MoD at the time, Captain Loughran's network back at his old haunt passing up snippets of turmoil in the corridors of power, with the military wanting to support Rose, the ministers unwilling to commit any more troops and the Treasury refusing any greater capital outlay.

In the first possible use of CAS, on 22nd February a UN convoy was attacked between Tuzla and Sarajevo resulting in the ground forward air controller asking for air support. General Rose supported the request but it was vetoed by Akashi due to the lack of clarity on the ground. *Ark*'s ops team monitored the incident on both the 5ATAF radio net and that of the patrolling E-3 Sentry directing the CAS aircraft but it was difficult to resolve exactly what was happening. *Ark* had just launched a pair of Sea Harriers for XCAS and they were quickly on scene but there was no clear indication whether it was single incident, whether one or two men had been injured (it turned out to be five) and whether or not this was the result of small arms fire or mortar attack. Even a personal intervention on the radio net by Admiral Boorda failed to clarify the picture and the Sea Harriers were eventually called off without engaging any ground targets.

HMS *Coventry*, TG 612.02's accompanying frigate that had been assigned to CTF 440.01 since the beginning of February, chopped OPCON on 22nd February, and her Captain, Chris Stanford, sent a team on board *Ark* to discuss how best to exploit his ship's capabilities. The NATO rules of engagement had routinely allowed *Coventry* inside Albanian and Croatian waters which had greatly enhanced her ability to gather intelligence in support of I&W patrols. National rules did not offer the same flexibility, and without a Fleet Satellite Communication fit, the *Type-22* could not talk with the CTF 60 or the surveillance aircraft flying from USS *Saratoga* that could gather the same information. Captain Stanford was frustrated to find that the kit he needed had been prioritized for HMS *Birmingham* so that she could meet her SNFL duties in the Adriatic for CTF440.03.

A significant breakthrough in the peace efforts came on 23rd February 1994 when the Commander of the Bosnian-Croat Army, General Ante Roso, and his Bosniak counterpart General Rasim Delić, signed a ceasefire agreement in Zagreb. The fighting between Bosniak and Croat forces in central Bosnia broke out in May 1992 following signature of the Graz Agreement by the Bosnian Serb leader Radovan Karadžić and his Bosnian Croat counterpart Mate Boban. The Graz Agreement sought to end Serb-Croat fighting in Bosnia that had broken out the previous November, by partitioning the country between the two sides, allowing each then to concentrate on taking that territory held by the Bosniak majority to achieve the plan. Graz effectively ended the uneasy peace between Croats and Bosniaks. The peace deal signed at Zagreb had taken months of negotiation, spearheaded by a delegation led by US special envoy Charles Redman and US Ambassador to Croatia, Peter Galbraith. Faced with a Bosniak military resurgence in the field, when the US combined incentives for peace with pressure, Croatian President, Franjo Tuđman finally acceded. If Croatia pushed for a Muslim-Croat federation in Bosnia & Herzegovina, Tudjman was told; the US would support Croatia's applications for membership in European institutions, and would mobilize aid for the country, especially for its army. Moreover, the new federation would be able to confederate with Croatia if desired. If, on the other hand, Croatia did not support the US initiative, the US would seek sanctions, reinforced by US Secretary of State,

Madeleine Albright's statement on 6th January that sanctions against Croatia were an inevitable consequence of their involvement in Bosnia. The offer proved sufficiently persuasive, and at the end of February 1994 four days of proximity talks in Washington yielded a "Framework Agreement for the Bosniak-Croat Federation" (The Washington Agreement). The Washington Agreement created a federation of two constituent nations, Croats and Bosniaks and Croatian paramilitary groups would cede control of the area they called "Herceg-Bosnia" (Herzegovina). Croatian paramilitaries would merge with Bosnian army units, and UNPROFOR, which had already undertaken humanitarian aid delivery in Bosnia, would help implement the creation of a unified territory and security force across the federation.

Within days of the Croat-Bosniak peace accord, there was much talk of a new political wind blowing in Bosnia and general recognition of the futility of the loss of lives on all sides. With the hope of peace on the horizon and tensions eased temporarily, on 24th February, Rear Admiral Gretton returned to the UK leaving Captain Loughran once again in charge of the task group. *Ark Royal* stood down from DENY FLIGHT operations the following day and came to anchor in the Gulf of Manfredonia. This rest was cut short by the request from 5ATAF for *Ark* to plug gaps in the DENY FLIGHT weekend programme caused by the absence of the *Saratoga* alongside in Trieste and fog over the Italian air bases preventing RAF sorties. The weekend lull was shattered on the morning of 28th February.

Six Serbian Air Force Soko G-4 Super Galebs had been spotted by an E-3 Sentry while bombing targets in the town of Bugojno. They were warned twice to land or leave the no-fly zone, but both warnings were ignored. Two USAF F-16Cs from the 86th Tactical Fighter Wing/526th Tactical Fighter Squadron patrolling the no-fly zone were then vectored in to intercept the Galebs. Two more warnings were given, both ignored, and the F-16Cs were given clearance to fire. Captain Robert Wright flying the lead Falcon fired a single AIM-120 AMRAAM which dispatched the lead Galeb, and then fired two Sidewinders which destroyed two more Galebs. Captain Scott O'Grady in the second aircraft fired a Sidewinder at the fourth Galeb, but this missile missed. A second flight of F-16Cs was vectored in by the AWACS, and the lead aircraft from this flight destroyed a fourth Galeb. The remaining two Serbian planes managed to escape Bosnian airspace via Croatia. This was the first occasion in its 45-year history that NATO aircraft had committed a hostile act and proved to be the only significant air-to-air combat operation of DENY FLIGHT. Captain O'Grady gained prominence in June the following year when his aircraft was shot down by a Serbian SA-6 missile while patrolling the no-fly zone. His six-day ordeal on the ground in Bosnia and subsequent rescue gave inspiration for the 2001 movie "Behind Enemy Lines" although the film script, subjected to the usual Hollywood embellishments, bore no resemblance to O'Grady's actual story.

The Sea Harriers were airborne immediately after the Galeb incident, rekindling awareness in the pilots, if that was even necessary, of the stakes involved. They were vectored onto a fleeting helicopter contact but it faded before it could be sighted. One further short lived excitement occurred on the evening of 1st March when a large number of MIG-21 Fishbeds and MIG-29 Fulcrums launched from Belgrade. The aircraft remained inside Serbian airspace and the sortie was assessed as a training exercise, but it nevertheless signalled a worrying tendency by the Serb authorities to test the NATO response.

Early March should have seen *Ark Royal* in Toulon, but instead she was at Bari, closer to her operational station with expected events ashore in mind. There she was joined for an overnight visit by Rear Admiral Gretton, hosting members of the House of Commons Defence Committee who were clearly impressed with the ship's vital role. After demonstrating the ship's support for UNPROFOR to the Committee, *Ark* moved south for weapon training in the Ionian Sea before resuming DENY FLIGHT. The air group was reduced by one Sea Harrier sent back to Yeovilton because of pressure on airframe numbers during the FA-2 conversion programme. *Ark* had started DENY FLIGHT with eight aircraft but was now down to only six, with surges to seven or eight only authorized to meet the immediate operational situation. The importance of launching a serviceable pair meant a third aircraft was always briefed and manned putting one half of 801 Squadron on the line for each operational sortie. The engineering staff worked round the clock to achieve this but it was quickly realised that eight aircraft was the minimum number required to declare six available. At least one FRS-1 had to have a complete engine change through this period. In contrast, the RAF Jaguar squadron based at Gioia del Colle in Italy, had the relative luxury of twelve aircraft and fully deployed engineering staff to declare only eight available.

Ark's normal flying programme was to launch five pairs of Sea Harriers per day, the ten sorties split eight XCAS and two reconnaissance. The recce aircraft were kept on alert for battle damage assessment should an attack be carried out but would go out in the afternoons to help improve the general picture of the evolving situation ashore. The Sea Harrier's photo-recce capability had been little used before the operations in the Adriatic but with 5ATAF now fully cognisant of its valuable intelligence, it was now really coming into its own.

On the XCAS missions, the Sea Harriers were assigned surface targets by fighter controllers in American EC-130H Hercules responding to exercise aircraft requests from forward air controllers on the ground. As an alternative to the more normal programme, three-hour Offensive Counter Air (OCA) missions were flown as part of the campaign to prevent breaches of the no-fly zone. During these missions, the Sea Harriers had to in-flight refuel from RAF Tri-Star tankers. 801 Squadron led ably by the quietly determined Lieutenant Commander Mel Robinson, impressed

everyone they worked with. The aircraft, even on recce missions carried a 1,000-lb bomb on the centreline and an AIM-9L Sidewinder missile under each wing, meaning that they were available to deal with threats on the ground or in the air. Because the aircraft normally flew above the effective altitude to use the Aden cannons it was decided not to carry them. This lowered the weight of the aircraft, a critical factor in the warm air of the Adriatic which reduced thrust of the Pegasus engine. Nevertheless, the ship had to go to full speed every time the Harriers launched, with the resulting vibration in the aft end of the ship keeping all awake. By the height of summer, the FRS-1's swing role became almost impossible as the all up weight of the aircraft with bombs, missiles and drop tanks fitted became too high for the available engine performance. Frustratingly slow to respond to the problem, the MoD Safety Authority could not clear use of the US Mk-82 540-lb bomb in time. The US bomb would have delivered two thirds of the hitting power of the UK thousand pounder and allowed simultaneous carriage of Sidewinders.

820 Squadron were also much in demand, largely in the transport role, although the existence of one or two operational Yugoslav submarines advised maintaining skills with the dipping sonar. NATO submarines were present in the Adriatic both to act as a deterrent for the Yugoslav Navy and to gather intelligence information closer to shore than could be achieved by surface units. HMS *Talent*, commanded by Commander Mark Anderson, operated in the Montenegrin area until the end of February, CTF 60 routinely had a *Los Angeles*-class SSN on call and the Dutch SSK HNLMS *Zwaardvis* also operated in the intelligence-gathering role. 820's HDS flown in and out of Split allowed members of the Ship's Company to go ashore to acquaint themselves with conditions there and for Army personnel to visit the ship. For both sides it was a welcome break even if it also involved playing a full part in a day's work both afloat and ashore. Contingency plans

were dusted off in mid March to assist with heavy lift operations supporting the arrival of the Duke of Wellington's Regiment at Split. The BRITFOR reinforcements arrived in theatre onboard the landing ships *Sir Tristram*, *Sir Bedivere* and *Sir Galahad* between 20th and 22nd March. Only the Regiment's advance party could be moved by air; a reminder to all of the necessity of sea lift and the value of the Royal Fleet Auxiliaries.

849 'B' Flight helped out with HDS and VIP taxi work; one of its helicopters was the first to establish HDS connection with Split. The squadron also carried out periodic surface surveillance and navigation training missions. The SKWs were often detached ashore to work both with the RAF and the Italian Navy who were interested in helicopter-borne AEW for their carrier. The main operational AEW work was carried out by high flying E-3 Sentries whose picture was transmitted to Adriatic ships via LINK 11. An American Aegis cruiser based in TF 440's area of operations to the south took over the 'Red Crown' area air warfare coordinator role. The SKW's presence was however reassuring, especially if maverick elements tried surface attacks with fast attack craft. If the conflict escalated ashore, such hostile action by Yugoslav naval units in support could not be ruled out, especially if carrier based air power was involved. A close watch was kept on the Yugoslav and Croatian Navies. The trials aircraft deployed from the UK for *Ark*'s weapon training earlier in the month also remained in theatre to fly simulated missile attack profiles toward the carrier helping the Ship's Company hone their defensive response. The fog of the Adriatic justified the carrier's presence on many occasions but the congestion of other units sometimes made it tricky finding clear areas of sea where the ship could manoeuvre at full speed to operate aircraft. Based on the weather forecast the ship would move, perhaps eighty miles overnight, to find the best operating area expected for the day.

HMS *Ark Royal* was back on station by 14th March for DENY FLIGHT, primarily to support vital humanitarian convoy activity that was in danger of being seriously opposed but also more generally to assert a NATO air presence to persuade the locals of the power available should they push the United Nations too far. It was very gratifying for the Ship's Company to hear from those who had been ashore in Bosnia how much UNPROFOR appreciated the ubiquitous Sea Harriers overhead and the reassuring presence of Britain's Flagship somewhere over the horizon; ready to protect them when threatened and to get them out of harms way if the situation deteriorated. According to the soldiers, the Sea Harriers seemed to possess a remarkable ability to pacify the belligerents whenever their engines were heard overhead. For three days, *Ark*'s Sea Harriers provided air cover to the UNPROFOR Nordic Battalion along the treacherous Route 'MARIO'. The Nordic's objective was to force their way through to Tuzla, first with Leopard main battle tanks, then armoured personnel carriers and finally escorting the soft-skinned UN trucks to bring aid to the town that had been besieged for over eighteen months. In one incident among many, on 25th March, 801's jets arrived on the scene at the Duke of Wellington's Regiment Headquarters at Bugojno just as it was under bombardment from Serbian army. Two British soldiers were wounded but the guns stopped at the sight and sound of the Harriers and before more casualties could be suffered. Overnight, with marginal weather conditions in the Adriatic threatening flying, *Ark* sped northwards to find the optimum weather to make sure her jets could again be over Bugojno at dawn the following day to deter further action. Early the following morning the weather was still on the limits, nevertheless a pair of Sea Harriers launched successfully and did their job as effectively as always.

Ark's presence at sea was especially critical during March 1994 as the task groups under CTF 60 and CTF 470 diverted to undertake their own national tasking. USS *Saratoga* was committed to naval exercises from 10th to 17th March and more significantly from 31st March until 7th April, while *Ark* was due to put alongside in Piraeus. *Foch* left the Adriatic on 18th March, but her relief *Clemenceau* was not due in theatre until 30th March, leaving a twelve-day gap for CTF 470. At the end of *Ark*'s rotation for DENY FLIGHT on 29th March, Rear Admiral Gretton hosted his counterparts from CTF 470 and CTF 440 to a working lunch onboard his flagship. The purpose of the meeting was to discuss TG 612.02's continuing involvement in SHARP GUARD and, more importantly, the long term possibilities of NATO operational control for all maritime forces in the Adriatic. Vice Admiral Prueher, Commander of the US Sixth Fleet and of NATO's Southern Striking Force had made a bid to resurrect the dormant NATO TF 502 at the beginning of March, to bring all maritime air assets under a single NATO-led command. This bid had coincided unhelpfully with the seemingly unrelated request from his superior, Admiral Smith, the Commander of all NATO naval forces in the southern region, for extra ring-fenced air assets to provide SUCAP support specifically for CTF 440. With a guaranteed presence of only six Sea Harriers, Rear Admiral Gretton had to dedicate the aircraft to DENY FLIGHT making SUCAP their secondary duty on an occasional basis or in extreme operational circumstances. On the wider issue of carrier group tasking, Rear Admiral Witrand, CTF 470, pointed out that FS *Clemenceau* was very much a French national strategic asset and it was therefore extremely unlikely that it would be placed under NATO command, echoing his response to 5ATAF six weeks earlier when embarked in FS *Foch*. For the US Navy, the strategic responsibilities of its regional super carrier required it to make regular shows of force further east in the Red Sea, meaning a greater commitment by it to a fixed Adriatic programme was as unlikely as the French. Only the UK committed a CVS at short notice throughout the Adriatic conflict and despite many efforts at ministerial level, shared carrier tasking never came

to fruition, the French proving the least reliable partners. The command team in *Ark* had already realised that they needed to make the most of the coalition assets as, and when, they were available. More by luck than by any coherent multi-national planning, the three carrier groups had achieved seamless cover during *Ark*'s first two months in theatre. All too often however it was the British carrier's programme that expanded and flexed to fill the gaps. *Ark*'s willingness to by-pass port visits and be ready for action won her much respect and admiration, the Italian press dubbing her the "Martini Carrier": Anytime. Any place. Anywhere!

Ark normally operated unescorted, although at least one RFA was usually in the vicinity and RAS operations were regularly conducted to top up with both fuel and a wide range of solid stores and ammunition. The latter replenishments usually took place once a fortnight. As well as jackstay transfers the vertical replenishments by 820's Sea Kings were particularly impressive to watch; their intricately choreographed helicopter movements making the flight deck an even busier place than usual. Up to 120 tons of stores provisions and ammunition were transferred per replenishment. Personnel from every department were involved, at the dumps where the heavy jackstays brought over the pallets, moving pallets across the deck and down into the hangar where they were broken down and finally taken down the internal lifts into the storerooms or magazines. The physical transfer between ships took about two hours with up to a hundred separate loads arriving by jackstay or helicopter. A further four hours were required to strike all the stores below.

It was vital to maintain efficiency that some rest and recreation be given to *Ark*'s hard working Ship's Company and the ship tried to protect its programme of port visits, as operational dynamics allowed. An eleven day visit to Piraeus from 31st March to 11th April allowed the Ship's Company to fly out their loved ones for an all too brief period, but many still took the opportunity to visit some of the nearby Greek islands. Weather throughout the stay was generally good apart from one day when the heavens opened and seemed to remain open all day with torrential downpours. It later transpired that the unseasonably bad weather had been to *Ark*'s advantage. As she sailed from Piraeus with the British Ambassador and head of the Hellenic Navy onboard, it was reported that a Greek terrorist group known as "November 17" had stolen 1944-vintage bazooka rockets and attempted to attack the ship using improvised launchers. The subsequent military police investigation assessed that the terrorists had neither the means to aim the rockets or fire them remotely. It appeared that the rain storm had shorted the timers of the rudimentary launch circuits, preventing the missiles from firing. The whole episode focussed minds and gave a brief foretaste of the severe escalation of hostilities that would mark *Ark*'s most dangerous chapter on her return to the Adriatic.

Following UNPROFOR and NATO's success in holding the truce at Sarajevo and then the Muslim-Croat ceasefire in central Bosnia, the international diplomatic efforts for the rest of Bosnia appeared to be generating real results. In the words of one UN source, the Bosnian Government and Serbs were *"ridiculously close to signing a peace agreement."* In spite of, or because of, this Bosnian Serb forces launched one last offensive against the UN Safe Areas, in a final attempt to gain territory before the prospect of peace might freeze the front line positions. The Serb's greatest prize was Goražde. The town's strategic position along a bend in the River Drina made it important for manufacturing and trade. Its munitions factory once produced most of the explosive caps used in Yugoslavia's armaments industry. Possibly most important of all, the town sat astride the main highway that connected Serbia with the Adriatic and Montenegro. The Serbs have tried to take control of the town almost since the outbreak of the war. However, despite two years of relentless attack, it had held out stubbornly and

remained a blot on the Serb's landscape, an enclave of enemy-held territory which only reminded the Serbs that there was unfinished business in Bosnia-Herzegovina. The bombardment of Goražde began on 28th March and lasted three days, claiming thirty lives and wounding another 132 civilians. General Sir Michael Rose played down the significance of the offensive, expressing confidence on 2nd April that the neither the Bosnian government forces nor the Bosnian Serbs would seek to make *"any major strategic changes"* in the Goražde area, implying neither side had the will nor the means to take the enclave. The following day, US Secretary of Defence William Perry told reporters that the United States would *"not enter the war to stop"* the Serbs from overrunning Goražde, and other senior officials publicly quashed the possibility of using air strikes. Amidst increasingly urgent reports from aid workers of heavy shelling in the area, floods of hysterical refugees and panic in the town, a large number of badly wounded Muslim civilians were evacuated by the helicopters of 845 Squadron based in Split. Several days into the attack a number of UNPROFOR soldiers were injured, and one was killed by Serb fire. Incited to act in defence of his troops, General Rose finally requested retaliatory NATO strikes under the mandate of UNSCR 836. *"With 20/20 hindsight, you can say he was wrong (to delay the action), but we were working with what information we had,"* a source close to the British general said. *"For the last two days we've gone through a series of very fine judgments on where the line lies between peace-keeping, and peace enforcement and war."* Rose's request was approved by UN Special Envoy Akashi and two USAF F-16Cs bombed the designated Serb targets, including a tank and a command post. The Serb bombardment stopped immediately but resumed the next day prompting further *"limited tactical action"*; two USMC F/A-18Cs strafing additional targets in the area.

General Ratko Mladić, the Bosnian Serb

commander, in a tense exchange by telephone with General Rose, threatened the safety of his forces, saying "*one more attack and I will shoot down aircraft - cannot guarantee safety of UNPROFOR and will attack UNPROFOR and your headquarters.*" Making good on his threat, Mladić ordered his forces to surround 150 UNPROFOR peacekeepers, effectively taking them hostage. Mladić again telephoned Rose and told him "*if NATO does not stop its actions, not one UN soldier will leave alive.*" Some of the UNPROFOR hostages were from NATO member states, notably the UK and France, who pushed for an immediate end to the strikes out of fear for the safety of their personnel. In response to the British and French concerns, NATO temporarily recalled its forces, but on 15th April, in response to further Serb attacks, aircraft were again deployed to the area. As Mladić had promised they would, Serb ground units around Goražde attempted to shoot down the NATO aircraft. A French Dassault Étendard IV jet was hit by ground fire while conducting a reconnaissance mission in the area. The jet was damaged, but returned safely to its carrier, FS *Clemenceau*.

Ark Royal sailed from Piraeus on 11th April with tasking to be on station in the Adriatic as early as possible to support the build up of CAS over Goražde. Sea Harriers were soon again over the skies of Bosnia. On the afternoon of 16th April, two jets on patrol flown by Lieutenant Nick Richardson and Lieutenant 'Oz' Phillips were requested to interdict Serbian tanks that were firing into the town, targetting a hospital full of wounded civilians. Special Air Service forward air controllers directed them in to their targets and both aircraft were "Cleared Hot" to engage the tanks, however their attack profile risked too much collateral damage. In order to reduce the possibility of inflicting civilian casualties, the aircraft flew three passes to clearly identify the target. On the first pass Oz Phillips was engaged by a missile believed to be an SA-7 heat seeker, which narrowly missed his aircraft. Despite the danger to themselves, the two aircraft pressed home their attack. On the next pass the lead aircraft, XZ498 flown by Nick Richardson, was hit by a missile and he was forced to eject. Despite the danger, Oz Phillips circled the crash site watching his 'oppo' descend to the ground, acting as the airborne search and rescue coordinator until friendly forces arrived at the scene. Phillips then recovered to *Ark* with only minimum fuel left in his tanks. On the ground, Richardson was lucky to be guided to the SAS team that had called in his aircraft. The SAS unit had been in the area for a while and having suffered one fatality and another serious casualty, was about to pull out as the Serbian enemy closed in. The casualty was being treated at the hospital when it came under attack, prompting the team to call in the Harriers. After rendezvousing with Richardson, the unit remained in the area for a further 24 hours, effectively pinned down by Serb forces, before managing to hike out to meet two French Special Forces Pumas. Under protection of a package of A-6 and E-2C aircraft volunteered by USS *Saratoga*, Richardson was evacuated to Split the following day and returned to *Ark* that evening. He was in good condition apart from a few scratches and was airborne again four days later.

The whole incident had been watched from the ground by a doctor in Goražde hospital, who described it live on Sarajevo radio: "*They have just hit a NATO plane ... flames ... the plane is falling, the Chetniks are shooting.*" Picking up the story, CNN reported the action within ten minutes, prompting Captain Loughran to speak to the press onboard *Ark* with the full story of the pilots' bravery. "*The tank was in a wood, which made it a difficult target. They were on a further manoeuvre to identify it, which they did, when the wing man heard a SAM fired at him. He didn't get any warning until it shot by him and he saw the plume of smoke. They both fired flares to distract any further fire. ... As the UNPROFOR ground controllers were speaking to them and directing them to where the fire was coming from they could actually hear them coming under fire. By any yardstick this was a pretty brave act. They made a second run at the target and this time Lieutenant Richardson's plane was hit. His tail burst into flames and he ejected."*

Recriminations quickly followed for the way the story had been handled onboard, but both Rear Admiral Gretton and Captain Loughran were unmoved. Richardson had been safely recovered uninjured and both pilots had been protected from the media swarm that surrounded them. Most importantly, Nick Richardson had been able to contact his wife almost immediately after landing to allay her fears.

Sea Harrier XZ498 was the first British combat aircraft to be shot down since the Gulf War and was also the first NATO aircraft downed in the Bosnian conflict. After the incident, NATO did not carry out any further strikes around Goražde, and on 17th April, Mladić released most of the hostages he had taken. The effective collapse of Goražde placed a question mark over the credibility of the Western tactics in Bosnia. The seizing of UN civilians and military personnel highlighted the vulnerability of the UN operation as a humanitarian-peacekeeping mission. Over the next few days, the Serbs agreed to, and then broke, several ceasefires in the Goražde area. Controversially, on 20th April Boutros-Ghali approved the use of air strikes to defend safe areas even when UN personnel were not directly threatened, moving outside the scope of UNSCR 836 and this was endorsed by NATO at the subsequent North Atlantic Council meeting. The final ultimatum to Mladić to honour his previous agreements, issued on 22nd April, required for his forces to cease their attacks and withdraw by 27th April, or face additional air strikes. Clearly content with the gains they had made, the Serbs complied with this ultimatum, and withdrew all forces within three kilometers of the town and pulled back their heavy weapons to a twenty kilometer perimeter.

While analysis of the events at Goražde continued, Rear Admiral Gretton met with Rear Admiral Wright and Rear Admiral Witrand to rationalise the next possible moves for their respective carrier groups and consider the short term programme which was due to include a major NATO exercise, DYNAMIC IMPACT, in early May. USS *Saratoga* had been due to stand-off at Palma having completed its DENY FLIGHT phase, but withdrawal now would have sent contradictory message. Instead Wright offered *Saratoga*'s aircraft to support all CAS missions and hoped rationalisation of 5ATAF's command and control procedures would allow greater flexibility in joint operations. Witrand also cancelled *Clemenceau*'s planned port visit, but the ship moved further south to support French troops moved from Krajina to Sarajevo. All three task groups planned and replanned contingencies as the NATO deadline of 27th April approached, and then passed without the threat of strikes being carried through. As the situation appeared to calm, *Ark* opted to pick up her programme and detach to Corfu. *Saratoga* yet hoped to visit Palma, sacrificing the first week of DYNAMIC IMPACT, while *Clemenceau* departed for Toulon.

The short break at Corfu provided a much needed respite for *Ark Royal*'s Ship's Company and allowed the command team to meet up with a number of other ships from the task group. RFA *Olwen* handed over to RFA *Orangeleaf* as the task group tanker on 4th May bringing to an end seventeen months continuously in theatre. Upon leaving Corfu, *Ark* sailed towards Palma to team up with the armada of 93 warships from ten NATO nations that would take part in DYNAMIC IMPACT '94, the largest NATO maritime exercise of its kind since the end of the Cold War. DYMANIC IMPACT was designed to test NATO's ability to protect her sea lines of communication in the Mediterranean and carry out a major amphibious operation, enabling *Ark Royal* to demonstrate the capability and flexibility of an aircraft carrier as a means of power protection. A poorly staffed Operation Order and clear DENY FLIGHT withdrawal symptoms amongst the crew undermined the value of the exercise, as all eyes maintained a close watch on the situation in the Adriatic. Nevertheless some training benefit was gained and new lessons learned to develop the NATO maritime concept. USS *Saratoga* ended the exercise with one last port visit before handing over to USS *George Washington*; the USN's oldest carrier would hand over the flag of CTF 60 to its youngest, before sailing across the Atlantic and into retirement.

For HMS *Ark Royal*, DYNAMIC IMPACT ended with a visit to Palma in Majorca for a much-needed SMP and a visit which most of the Ship's Company considered to be the highlight of the deployment. Ever mindful of events further east, the command continued to monitor the situation so that *Ark* could return at a moment's notice if the situation demanded.

When the *Ark* eventually returned to the Adriatic at the beginning of June, Brigadier Ridgway, the new commander of British forces in Bosnia was able to visit the ship and report a marked improvement in the situation ashore. Peace talks in Geneva had borne some fruit and the American-brokered ceasefire between Bosnian Croats and Muslims had held remarkably well. This led to a formal four-week cessation of hostilities from the 10th June while the UN's Contact Group met to discuss terms for peace. Amidst the hopes of peace, the French hinted at an early withdrawal. In the end they stepped back from this unilateral action but their decision to commit FS *Clemenceau* to the Adriatic for only six weeks in the following six months effectively rang the final death knell for any hopes of joint carrier operations in the region. The programme for USS *George Washington* also appeared to include remarkably little time in the Adriatic as US efforts focussed in the Mediterranean and the Red Sea. Despite the apparent inevitability that the carrier programmes could not be aligned, Vice Admiral Prueher reiterated his pleas for the reestablishment of NATO TF 502, visiting *Ark* on 25th to put the case personally. Having worked tirelessly to 'join up', but witnessed the lack of Franco-American

commitment to the cause, Rear Admiral Gretton's attitude was sanguine. In his view, the UK did not mind coordinating carrier programmes, or coming under command in war time, but they did not wish to subject themselves to the short-notice planning evident in US battle groups, nor jeopardize the sound working relationships established with the French. Admiral Smith, Prueher's boss, visited the ship separately the following day and painted a somewhat different perspective to his deputy. In his view, NATO's withdrawal appeared likely, particularly if the Cessation of Hostilities was breached.

It appeared by the end of June that both sides were ignoring the Cessation of Hostilities. The Muslims, with easier access to arms supplies from Croatia following the unification of the Bosnian and Croat armies and now fighting on one only front, were able to focus their efforts on the Serbs and they pushed them back in a number of areas. However, in most areas the war was reaching its culminating point. The UN forces on the ground tried to take advantage of the ceasefire to try and normalize the situation ashore, re-opening schools, providing essential services and repairing the war-shattered infrastructure. A number of *Ark* personnel were able to get ashore and help with this vital work. In view of the gradually improving situation ashore it was hoped that the same intense level of DENY FLIGHT activity would not now be required.

Despite the sporadic fighting still taking place, both sides gave verbal agreement to Akashi to extend the cessation for another four weeks from 10th July. The outcome of the first round of Contact Group talks was presented in Geneva on 6th July with the warring factions given until the 19th to consider it. The revised map appeared to be based on the "HMS *Invincible*" plan negotiated the previous August onboard *Ark*'s sister by Stoltenberg and Owen. Should the Serbs reject it then it was expected that President Clinton would lift the arms embargo on the Muslims. Conversely, if the Muslims rejected it then sanctions would be

(page 39)
HMS *Ark Royal* operating off Norway during Exercise
TEAM WORK '90.
(Crown Copyright/MoD 1990)

CVS Cold War multi-layered layered air defence – HMS *Ark Royal*'s Sea King AEW,
Sea Harrier CAP, Sea Dart Missile System and Phalanx CIWS.
(Crown Copyright/MoD 1989)

(page 43)
Operation GRANBY task group conducting RAS,
January 1991.
(Crown Copyright/MoD 1991)

(page 45)
GRANBY UK task group enhanced by HMS *Charybdis*, in formation with US 6th Fleet ships USS *Belknap* and USS *Philippine Sea*, February 1991.
(Crown Copyright/MoD 1991)

(page 45)
HMS *Charybdis* breaking away from HMS *Ark Royal*
with USS *Belknap* behind, February 1991.
(Crown Copyright/MoD 1991)

(page 47)
820 NAS Sea King Mk6 carrying Stingray torpedoes
during Trial WOKING at AUTEC, September 1991.
(Crown Copyright/MoD 1991)

(page 47)
HMS *Ark Royal* fires Sea Dart missile during
Trial WOKING, AUTEC, September 1991.
(Crown Copyright/MoD 1991)

(page 56)
WESTLANT '92 task group. HMS *Exeter* leading HMS *Ark Royal*.
RFA *Olmeda* and RFA *Regent*. September 1992.
(Crown Copyright/MoD 1992)

(pages 56-57)
HMS *Ark Royal* exercising with USS *John F Kennedy* during
FLEETEX 1/93, September 1992.
(Crown Copyright/MoD 1992)

(page 57)
HMS *Ark Royal* at Norfolk Naval Base, alongside
USS *John F Kennedy*, 22nd September, 1992.
(Crown Copyright/MoD 1992)

(page 58)
HMS *Exeter* and HMS *Ark Royal* RAS. October 1992.
(Crown Copyright/MoD 1992)

(page 59)
HMS *Ark Royal* hosts Navy Board Dinner to mark
40th Anniversary of HM The Queen's accession.
(Crown Copyright/MoD 1992)

(pages 67-68)
HMS *Ark Royal* – UK flagship for two Adriatic
deployments in 1993-94 under Operation GRAPPLE
and then Operation HAMDEN.
(Crown Copyright/MoD 1994)

(page 74)
HMS *Ark Royal* arrives Grand Harbour,
Malta, 8th June 1993.
(Crown Copyright/MoD 1993)

(page 76)
HMS *Ark Royal* RAS with
HMS *Boxer*, July 1993.
(Crown Copyright/MoD 1993)

(page 77)
820, 846 and 849 NAS Sea Kings fly in formation over HMS *Ark Royal* before departing to RNAS Culdrose, 2nd August 1993.
(Crown Copyright/MoD 1993)

(page 78)
Thorvald Stoltenberg and David Owen, UN special negotiators, flank NATO Secretary General, Manfred Wörner at NATO Headquarters, Brussels, September 1993. (©NATO Photos 1993)

(page 79)
HMS *Ark Royal* (background) resumes HAMDEN duty from HMS *Invincible* off Gibraltar 4th February 1994.
(Crown Copyright/MoD 1994)

(page 81)
Leading the UK contribution to DENY FLIGHT -
HMS *Ark Royal*'s Sea Harrier FRS-1 armed with
AIM-9L Sidewinder missiles, 1994.
(Crown Copyright/MoD 1994)

(page 86)
Carriers in the Adriatic – CTF 470 FS *Clemenceau* (foreground),
CTF 60 USS *Saratoga* (right) and CTG 612 HMS *Ark Royal*
rendezvous, April 1994.   *(Crown Copyright/MoD 1994)*

(page 85)
HMS *Ark Royal* escorts RFA *Sir Tristram*
into theatre.
(Crown Copyright/MoD 1994)

(page 86)
Replenishment at Sea (Ammunition) from RFA *Fort Austin*, 1000-lb bombs moving by heavy jackstay. *(Crown Copyright/MoD 1994)*

(pages 88-89)
Sea Harrier XZ498 flown by Lieutenant Nick Richardson, over Sarajevo April 1994. XZ498 was shot down over Goražde 16th April 1994.
(Crown Copyright/MoD 1994)

(page 90)
HMS *Ark Royal*, SNS *Principe de Asturias* and USS *Saratoga* in company, Exercise DYNAMIC IMPACT, May 1994.
(Crown Copyright/MoD 1994)

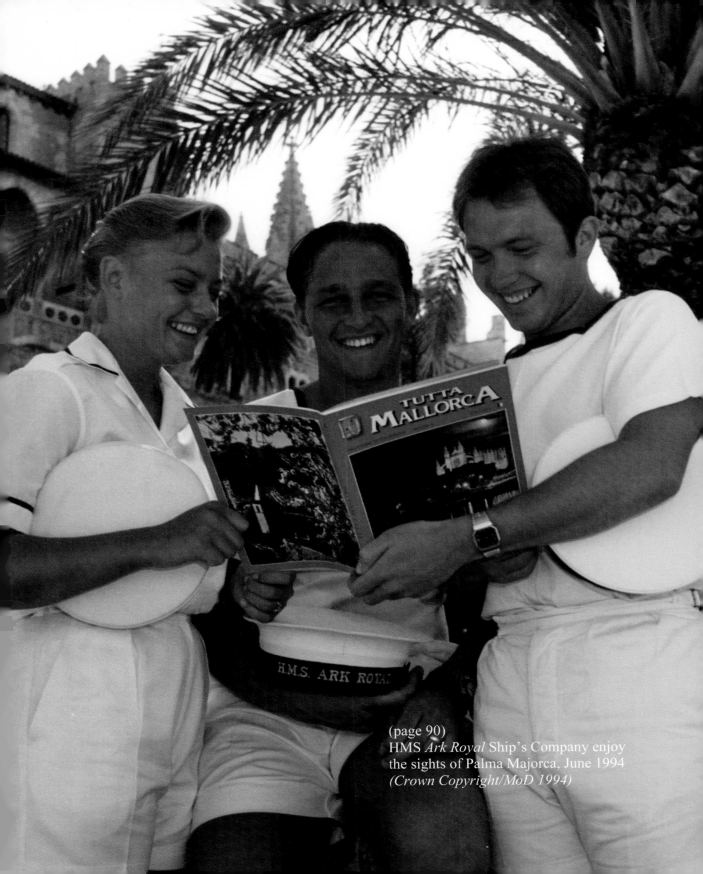

(page 90)
HMS *Ark Royal* Ship's Company enjoy
the sights of Palma Majorca, June 1994
(Crown Copyright/MoD 1994)

(page 91)
HMS *Ark Royal* returns to Malta at the end of her
second HAMDEN deployment, 1st August 1994.
(Crown Copyright/MoD 1994)

(page 92)
HM Queen Elizabeth the Queen Mother visits
HMS *Ark Royal*, September 1994.
(Crown Copyright/MoD 1994)

(page 93)
HMS *Ark Royal* leaves Portsmouth
for Rosyth, 6th May 1999.
(Crown Copyright/MoD 1999)

(page 93)
HMS *Ark Royal* passes under Forth Road Bridge, arriving at Rosyth 11th May 1999.
(© *BRDL 1999*)

(page 100)
Removing HMS *Ark Royal's* forward
aircraft lift platform, 2000.
(© *BRDL 2000*)

(page 98-100)
HMS *Ark Royal* fitting out at Rosyth.
(© *BRDL 2000*)

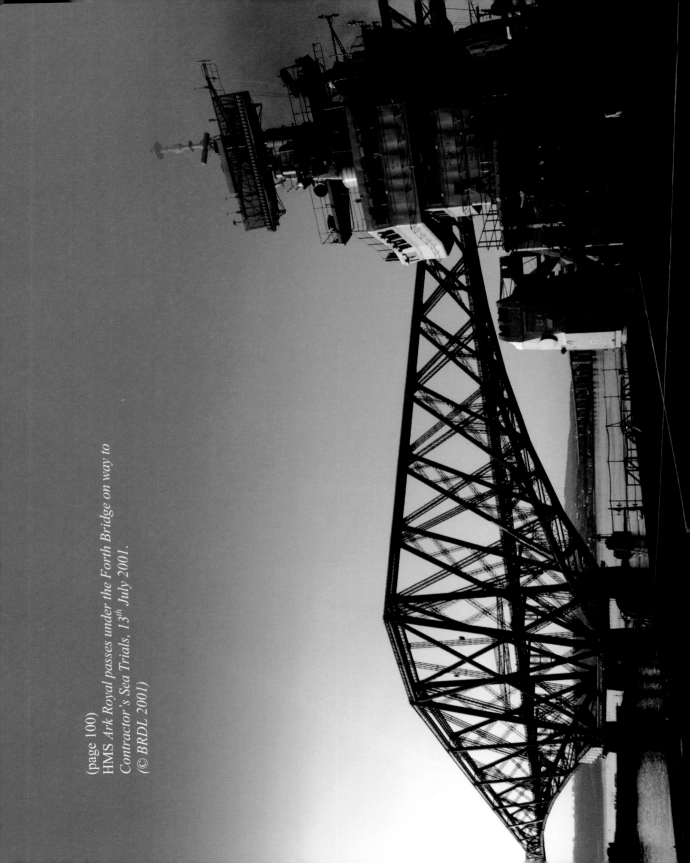

(page 100)
HMS *Ark Royal passes under the Forth Bridge on way to Contractor's Sea Trials, 13th July 2001.*
(© BRDL 2001)

lifted on the Serbs. Signs of a favourable outcome were not good as a chorus of opposing voices raised dissent. The Serbs had everything to gain by the temporary peace arrangements with the lifting of sanctions, but the Muslims had everything to lose by a ceasefire that was not backed up by a lasting settlement. On 19th July the Bosnian/Croat Federation announced that they would accept the proposed terms. The following day the Bosnia Serb Assembly signalled only partial acceptance, subject to ratification of a number of clauses. This partial response was seen by the UK and US as a refusal, however Russia, which had been involved in talks throughout, hoped it merely formed the basis for further negotiations. Four days later, the Bosnian Serbs rejected the map outright. The third Geneva summit at the end of July sought to tighten the sanctions against the Serbs.

As *Ark* entered her last month of HAMDEN operations it was by no means clear whether lasting peace was on the cards. What was equally uncertain was whether or not *Ark*'s planned SMP at Grand Harbour Malta would go ahead due to the intransigence of the Maltese General Workers Union which threatened to blockade the harbour. Last-minute negotiations and direct threats by the British High Commissioner eventually cleared the route and *Ark* went alongside on 1st August with her new escort HMS *Brave* which had relieved *Coventry* at the end of May. As the SMP progressed it was clear that the hopes for peace in Bosnia were unravelling. The intransigence of the Bosnian-Serbs was exhausting all sides, including Slobodan Milošević in Belgrade who severed links with the Assembly on 4th August, foreseeing the continuing US sanctions as an inevitable consequence of their failure to agree peace terms. In response to Milošević's schism, the following day Radovan Karadžić announced his forces would fight on alone, rearmed as they had been after seizing heavy weapons previously surrendered to UNPROFOR. Stoltenberg could not bring the sides together and ten days later fighting broke out once again on the road between Sarajevo and Tuzla.

Meanwhile Bosnian Government forces tried to quell a rebellion by renegade Muslim fighters against their Croat 'partners' in the Bihac region in order to hold the Bosniak-Croat peace accord in place. UNPROFOR soldiers came under attack at Sarajevo on 22nd August.

For *Ark* however, her job was done and she sailed for Palma to prepare to pass on the HAMDEN baton. Between 12th April and 18th August, pilots from 801 Squadron had flown 542 DENY FLIGHT missions without the loss of a single sortie from unserviceability; a truly remarkable feat given only six aircraft were at their disposal for much of the deployment. HMS *Ark Royal* handed over CTG 612.02 to HMS *Invincible* at midday on 28th August 1994. On the same day, the results of the Bosnian Serb referendum showed that ninety percent of the population rejected the terms of the Contact Group peace proposals. To the UNPROFOR troops on the ground and the multinational forces patrolling the Adriatic, Bosnia increasingly began to look like a lost cause.

For Rear Admiral Gretton and Captain Loughran the failure to achieve a lasting peace brought a tinge of sadness, but both were in no doubt of the contribution their flagship had made. HAMDEN had coincided with the start of a very turbulent period in Bosnia, triggered by the shelling of Sarajevo, and consequently was marked by short notice tasking and changes to the programme. All of the task group units had responded to these challenges with the utmost professionalism and done much to enhance the reputation of the Royal Navy. *Ark Royal* in particular had acted with distinction as the command platform, providing a fitting climax to her first ten years in commission.

In September *Ark* paid a last visit to Newcastle, appropriately where both the ship and Captain Loughran were laid down, before coming back to Portsmouth to begin an indeterminate period of Preservation by Operation followed, it was expected, by a major refit. The first phase in the life of the fifth HMS *Ark Royal* was over, a period in which the ship had added still further lustre to an already famous name. She had flown the flag, contributed to the end of the Cold War and then played a central role in establishing operations required to stabilise a disordered world. Her presence had provided Britain with leverage out of all proportion to the investment in her. But as she entered extended readiness, no-one could predict the amount of time she would spend off the world's stage, nor the tumultuous events that would follow her return.

For Bosnia, there was no peace during *Ark*'s exile. The Contact Group peace accord was broken by the end of September 1994 and inevitably the country fell back into war. Fighting between Bosnian and Serbian forces raged for another sixteen months after *Ark* left theatre and a CVS remained in the Adriatic until March 1996, when HMS *Illustrious* completed the final HAMDEN deployment. Srebrenica, which had acted as a catalyst for greater UNPROFOR involvement in Bosnia in March 1993, gained infamy in July 1995 as the scene of a genocide of 8,000 Muslim men and boys by Serbian forces, while Dutch UN forces stood by powerless to intervene. Srebrenica proved the last straw for UNPROFOR and NATO, and the widely talked about but as yet latent campaign of air strikes finally began in August under Operation DELIBERATE FORCE. The massive bombing campaign included land based and carrier-borne aircraft, artillery and Tomahawk missiles fired from the cruiser USS *Normandy*. As they had been from day one of DENY FLIGHT, Sea Harriers – now FA-2 in service - were integral to the UK's military contribution to the campaign. 800 Squadron in HMS *Invincible* opened the account in August 1995 and 801 Squadron in HMS *Illustrious* closed it the following March. Between April 1993 and March 1996, Royal Navy Sea Harriers completed 1,748 operational sorties, fully one third of all UK jet flights in support of Bosnia operations, without a single loss due to unserviceability. Crippled by the aerial and artillery bombardment of DELIBERATE FORCE, Bosnian Serb forces finally surrendered in November 1995. The Dayton peace accords of November and December 1995 laid the foundation for a lasting peace in Bosnia, but enactment of its terms required a massive build up of 80,000 NATO, rather than UN, forces. The NATO Implementation Force (IFOR) and its successor Stabilisation Force (SFOR) remained in Bosnia until 2004.

The Bosnian war cost the lives of 200,000 Bosnian Muslims, Serbs and Croats, including 12,000 children. Over 50,000 women were systematically raped as part of the campaign of ethnic cleansing waged by all sides. More than two million people were displaced from their homes and given refugee status. Slobodan Milošević, Radovan Karadžić and Ratko Mladić were indicted for war crimes by the International Criminal Tribunal for the former Yugoslavia. Milošević committed suicide while in custody. Karadžić remained at large until 2008 and is still under trial at The Hague with a verdict not expected before 2012. Mladić, thought dead for many years was finally captured in 2011.

Chapter 8

1994 – 2001:
Reserve and Refit at Rosyth

For nearly five years HMS *Ark Royal* lay forlornly in mothballs in No.3 Basin of Her Majesty's Naval Base Portsmouth while HMS *Invincible* and HMS *Illustrious* continued to fly the flag for the Royal Navy worldwide, both ships enjoying varied and challenging programmes following their joint HAMDEN duties from 1994 to 1996. HMS *Invincible* led UK forces in the Gulf during the late '90's on Operation SOUTHERN WATCH enforcing another no-fly zone, this time over southern Iraq. The following year she was back in the Adriatic supporting NATO operations in Kosovo. HMS *Illustrious* enjoyed a 'champagne' period in her career, following her 1994 refit, the highlight of which was as the flagship for the worldwide *Ocean* WAVE '97 deployment that included the handover of Hong Kong. She too participated in SOUTHERN WATCH in 1998 and then two years later led the UK task group deployed to Sierra Leone for Operation PALLISER.

Ark's refit was originally scheduled to start in 1997, but with the Ministry of Defence facing an overspend and the Royal Navy unable to afford the running costs of three carriers, *Ark* waited a further year, and then another, as yet more priorities had to be funded first. Despite the obviousness of the 'grey elephant' in everyone's midst, Ministers insisted that it was business as usual and *Ark* was "on schedule". A small team of engineers and logisticians, led by Commander John Wadham, worked diligently to keep *Ark*

alive and to keep *Ark*'s name in the public mind, waiting for the day to move her to the refit yard.

There had always been flux in the programming and extent of the maintenance plans of the three carriers. HMS *Invincible* had been in operational service only six years when she started her first refit in May 1986 at Devonport, but the majority of work focussed on the urgent post-Falklands enhancements that *Ark Royal* had been given in build. HMS *Illustrious* was nine years old when she arrived at Devonport for her first refit in September 1991, emerging in January 1994. In the late 1990s both operational carriers underwent docking periods in Portsmouth to remove their Sea Dart anti-air missile system and extend the flight deck to increase capacity to operate the Harrier GR-7.

When *Ark*'s turn for refit finally came she was nearly fourteen years old and the period in mothballs had taken its toll on the Royal Navy's former flagship. Bereft of engines, weapons, sensors and a host of auxiliary equipment cannibalised to support the operational carriers, it seemed hardly possible that she could be at the 180-days notice claimed. When she had last entered Portsmouth harbour on a bright day in September 1994, with full ceremony and the Ship's Company lining the flight deck, hundreds of well-wishers, friends and families welcomed her home from Bosnia. Now, on 6th May 1999, with her funnels covered, scuttles boarded, paintwork a motley grey patchwork and her flight deck lined only with chacons and the detritus of lay-up, just a handful of dockyard workers watched as *Ark*, under a rain-laden sky, was towed unceremoniously back out to sea.

Ark's departure signalled the first small step on the long road to her recovery and the rest of the journey would take place in Scotland, initially under the charge of Commander Mal Lewis and then Commander Mark Dannatt, before a new Commanding Officer would take the ship back to sea. For the first time a CVS would be refitted at Rosyth, by Babcock Rosyth Dockyard Ltd (BRDL). BRDL had won the contract for future CVS refits following the rationalisation of shipyard capacity between Plymouth, Portsmouth and Rosyth as an outcome of the 1994 Defence Costs Study. In part, the decision was a sweetener for the pill of the closure of the Naval Base at Rosyth with the loss of 700 jobs, announced the same year. BRDL had extensive experience of surface ship and submarine refits, having fulfilled this role for eight decades, while the dockyard was able to handle large ships having been the maintenance home for the Navy's Grand Fleet based at Scapa Flow. Nevertheless, the carrier presented unique challenges.

Strategic planning for the refit began back in January 1997 and BRDL engineers and managers worked closely with the MoD support authorities to draw up the specification of works. *Ark*'s lay-up presented BRDL with unique opportunities as well as some unusual problems. Numerous visits to *Ark* during the lay-up helped quantify the state of the ship, but the planners had the significant drawback of not actually seeing her operational beforehand in order to assess the running state of the systems. Completing the work package in the allotted twenty five months would require close teamwork by the BRDL workforce and the Ship's Company. This got off to a strong start with a joint charity effort by five of the crew and five BRDL employees who joined forces to cycle from Portsmouth to Rosyth, racing against *Ark Royal*'s journey to the Dockyard. The cyclists claimed

victory, arriving at Rosyth first and raising £10,000 in the process for charities. BRDL donated £5,000 to the Children's Hospice Association Scotland (CHAS) and, in recognition of *Ark*'s affiliation with the City of Leeds, the Ship's Company chose to split its £5,000 between a local school for blind children and a cancer charity based in the city.

On 11th May 1999 *Ark Royal* slipped under the Forth Bridges then passed the South Arm of Rosyth dockyard on the final leg of her five-day passage from Portsmouth. *Ark* spent her first night in the Entrance Lock and the following day she was towed to J&K Berth. From there, on 15th June 1999, she was moved into No.1 Dock, where she 'docked down' ten days later, settling into what would become her home for the next eighteen months.

The refit package covered the six main disciplines of the ship, namely: hull, propulsion, power generation and auxiliaries, weapons, aircraft facilities and accommodation services. As well as many sizeable Alteration and Additions, that is, changes to the ship's structure, fabric and facilities, much of the work included update and refurbishment of key systems and recertification of the hull to comply with Lloyd's registration. This required invasive surveys all over the ship, which would reveal the full extent of the work required. Structurally *Ark* appeared to be in a fair condition. Key machinery and parts of her systems had been removed to be used on other vessels or to be returned to MoD stores. The equipment remaining on board had been preserved and the effects of weather and aging minimized by sealing her funnels and sea inlets. Nevertheless the surveys revealed more and more work to do and BRDL had to constantly flex their schedule. Variations to the refit contract and the results of the engineering surveys doubled the original scope of the package from an estimated 853,000 man-hours to 1,600,000; all to be carried out in the original timescale. This demanded much greater resources from BRDL, with an average of 520 workers per week allocated to the project. By comparison, the thirty-month refit of *Invincible* and the 28-month refit of *Illustrious*, both at Devonport, absorbed 370 and 440 workers per week respectively.

The hull work began immediately. As soon as the ship docked down all of her external steelwork was blasted back to bare steel and a holding primer applied while certain structural tasks were carried out. Below the waterline, holes were cut in the outer bottom to allow access to the ship's tanks which carried diesel, aircraft fuel, fresh water and dirty oil, as well as to the watertight compartments and trim tanks. Surveying, blasting and any structural repairs were carried out before the five-month job of renewing paint coatings began.

Significant changes to the ship's structure above the waterline were to occur. The existing catwalks were removed and disposed of and new external walkways were manufactured in the dockyard's workshops, and then hoisted in 32 modules on to the ship before the welders got down to business. Around twelve miles of welding was required on the catwalks alone.

Another major addition was a new Flying Control Position (FlyCo); in effect the ship's airport control tower from where aircraft launches and recoveries were controlled. The old FlyCo, attached to the compass platform, was cut off and a new compartment fabricated in one piece within the dockyard. The new compartment contained an extra row of windows below the existing ones and new skylight windows were fitted in the deckhead which offer improved visibility of the ship's port side and of aircraft as they landed. The superstructure above the starboard waist, known as the 'Alaskan Highway', was extended and raised one deck to accommodate an improved weapon fit and a similar extension was added to the sponson below the flight deck on the port waist.

Towering over the flight deck, between the fore and aft funnels, *Ark Royal*'s main mast supported the R992 medium-range surveillance radar, communication aerials and electronic warfare sensors. For operational and structural reasons the old mast had to be completely replaced. All systems, both on the mast and below deck, were dismantled and the structure cut off at the bottom and then taken away in sections. Meanwhile BRDL constructed a new, sixty-foot high mast. The structure was fabricated on site over ten weeks and then transported to the Syncrolift building where it was assembled into one piece and lifted onto the ship by an enormous crane on the dockside.

Ark Royal's propulsion and steering systems needed a total overhaul. A major survey of the propeller shafts revealed that three sections needed to be renewed. Also replaced were *Ark*'s massive propellers. Designed to propel 20,000 tonnes of ship through the water at over thirty knots, each propeller weighed 26 tonnes and measured around thirteen feet in diameter. Despite their size, they had to be manufactured with precision and then polished to optimize their performance, reducing both their acoustic signature in the water and the level of vibration passed back through the hull. The CVS was renowned for suffering high levels of vibration in the stern when travelling at speed, but following design changes in build this problem was much reduced in *Ark*. Weld repairs were required on both of the rudders while the four hull-mounted hydraulic stabilizers, designed to minimize ship roll in heavy seas, were removed for survey and overhaul.

Even more work took place on the propulsion system inside the ship. A major concern for all was the question of whether or not *Ark Royal*'s gearboxes would need to be replaced, since both *Illustrious* and *Invincible* had suffered gearbox damage in service requiring a complete rebuild during their refits. One shortcoming of the CVS design was that it was extremely difficult to remove a gearbox. The only way to remove them was by cutting a hole in the side of the ship, having first cleared a huge amount of interfering systems, known as 'work in way', including three auxiliary boilers and associated system pipe work, intakes, and exhausts. There was also fuel and steam system pipe work and significant cable removal necessary to clear the access. This had caused a significant headache during both Devonport refits and it was hoped that the same issues would not affect *Ark*. Fortunately they did not and *Ark*'s gearboxes were found to be in reasonably good condition; nevertheless they still took six months to overhaul.

Ark Royal arrived at Rosyth without any main engines and these would need to be refitted. Normally this occurred quite late in a refit programme so that they did not lie dormant for too long; it also provided the MoD with more time to schedule their refurbishment and delivery from Rolls Royce without impacting on the in-service support programme. As soon as *Ark* was returned from dry dock to J&K Berth in January 2001, work began on fitting four refurbished Rolls Royce Olympus gas turbines.

The CVS was designed so that every piece of main machinery, aside from the gearboxes, could be removed from her two engine and two gear rooms using specially designed lifts. In the case of fitting the three-tonne, cylindrical gas turbines, which measured around six feet in diameter and ten feet in length, these were hoisted by a dockside crane down through the aircraft lift apertures and onto the hangar deck. From there, the ship's machinery lifts lowered them to their respective engine rooms where, using a combination of beams, chain blocks and rails, they were deposited into their modules which protected them against fire and provided noise containment. *Ark Royal*'s machinery lifts were used daily to remove and replace equipment and BRDL took on the responsibility for their maintenance.

Elsewhere in the spaces, three of *Ark*'s five auxiliary boilers were renewed with the other two overhauled. Thousands of valves and hundreds of pumps were also removed and overhauled or renewed. Also missing was one of *Ark*'s eight

diesel generators that supplied electricity to the ship. This was replaced and another two rebuilt in situ while the remaining five were given extensive maintenance.

Within the mechanical part of the contract some 30,000 items were removed from the ship and logged under VETS, the Vessel Equipment Tracking System. These items were either returned to the MoD stores, overhauled in BRDL's workshops on site or by sub-contractors remotely. Identifying the serviceability of the mechanical systems proved a major task. Survey after survey revealed that having been laid up for five years, much of the ship's pipe work was defective and associated valves inoperable. These were either repaired or replaced.

A major mechanical change to the vessel was to fit an additional air conditioning plant and to supply extra chilled water to weapons and accommodation areas, which involved fitting miles of new pipe work. Separately, two and a half miles of eight-millimetre pipe was installed so that remote gauges could monitor the ship's fire system pressure and fifty new centre-fed hose reels were fitted throughout the vessel.

For the warfare and weapon engineering departments, the refit would provide a revolution in the fighting capability of the CVS, from a self-reliant ASW escort carrier designed to achieve sea control in the Cold War, to a truly flexible aviation and command platform for the 21st Century able to deliver maritime force projection. *Ark Royal* received a major upgrade of its weapons and sensors as well as its internal and external communications.

ADAWS, the Action Data Automation Weapons System that formed the 'brain' of *Ark*'s combat system, finally received a midlife update under the MoD's £115 million ADAWS Improvement (ADIMP) programme that had begun in 1993. One of the first real-time combat systems, ADAWS was designed around a pair of Ferranti FM-1600E mainframe computers, each with a storage capacity of 128 kilowords and a processor speed of twelve megabits per second, roughly $1/1000^{th}$ the capacity and $1/50^{th}$ the speed of a modern domestic laptop. Nevertheless, these interchangeable computing engines could accept the sensor information from the ship's main radars and sonar, identify multiple contacts and produce a continuous track history for each from which the operators could evaluate threat levels and control the engagement of targets using Sea Dart. In theory, the whole process occurred almost automatically, requiring only oversight and command from the human operator. ADIMPS provided a generation update. Ferranti FM-2420s replaced the FM-1600Es, providing six times the processing power of their predecessor. Moreover, each computer had less to do because radar data was now preprocessed by track extractors for each of the main radars and separately combined to create a recognised air and surface radar picture that the main computer would then interrogate.

A separate dual Combat System Highway (CSH) allowed data to be passed between the sub-systems without necessarily having to be processed centrally, in effect federating the system. The CSH offered greater speed and redundancy, while also providing the interface between the ADAWS computers and a new range of sensors. Twenty two miles of new cabling was wired between the ADAWS Computer Room on 6-deck and the Operations Room above it, which was stripped of all its display equipment for renewal or overhaul. The floating steel rafts, on which the equipment is sited for stability, were removed to the BRDL workshops for modification to suit the new layout of the compartment.

Other additions included a new Electronic Warfare suite based around Outfit UAT, with cutting-edge technology sensors and processing equipment fitted in the newly constructed main mast and a multi-screen control console in the Ops Room. UAT passively detected radar and RF emissions across a wide frequency spectrum with considerable bearing accuracy, and could classify the emitter by analyzing the characteristics of the received pulse against a database of known radars. UAT provided an essential aid for compiling the tactical picture, particularly when the ship operated in EMCON silence and exploited from the principle of 'range advantage' to maximize coverage and gain valuable seconds against a potential enemy attack.

As well as helping to build *Ark Royal*'s tactical picture, Outfit UAT also provided the essential target, ship and environmental information for the improved decoy launcher system, Outfit DLH. Fitted next to the starboard Phalanx and on the newly extended port sponson, DLH could fire chaff and decoys against both infrared and radar seeking missiles, providing the 'soft kill' layer of the ship's defence. The automatic countermeasures controller, Outfit UCB, provided the link between UAT and DLH, optimizing the fire pattern and timing of the DLH decoys in response to the threat presented by UAT and based on the geometry of the missile attack.

Among the internal changes to the ship, BRDL constructed a new Force Operations Room and Flag Main Communications Office, adjacent to the Operations Room, while the Flag Planning Room was redesigned. A capability upgrade in all of these compartments was provided by the installation of the Command Support System (CSS), a near real-time computer network that could communicate through the ship's satellite system with both shore headquarters and other platforms to display intelligence and tactical information.

For the first time *Ark* was also equipped with an office administration network, known as NavyStar, under the MoD's Naval Sector Strategic Architecture programme. NavyStar supported the medium to long-term planning needs of the ship, for example stores, and provided an email interface with shore headquarters and other platforms. Another huge task for BRDL's electricians, around sixteen miles of network cabling alone, as well as new supplies and sockets, was installed to connect and supply the servers, network switches, 140 workstation computers, and printers.

The Special Intelligence Office also received extensive upgrading to carry the latest equipment while the Main Communications Office was stripped and rewired in preparation for a new layout and new equipment. A new automatic message handling system was installed as well as an upgraded SCOT 5 satellite communications system, doubling *Ark*'s data bandwidth to shore. Aerials that had been fitted to the old main mast were relocated on the funnels and the new yardarms on the foremast.

Ark Royal was also fitted to provide a Joint Forces Headquarters (JFHQ) on a 'fit to receive' basis, thereby enabling other compartments to be transformed into planning cells when flag staffs were embarked. The main areas of the JFHQ consisted of the Admiral's Dining Cabin, the Wardroom Ante Room and the guest room, which were fitted with internal communications and computer network connections concealed in the deck heads.

The R992 medium range surveillance radar was replaced by the R996 that was being rolled out across the Fleet, both in the newly built *Type-23* frigates and at refit in the capital ships and *Type-42* destroyers. In theory, the new radar set offered significantly enhanced performance over its predecessor that had been in service, in one form or another, since the 1950s. In practice however, R996 was proving notoriously unreliable due in part to poor design, lack of spares and changes to the operating profiles of the ships that carried it making maintenance difficult. The radar track extractor LFA, a hangover from the 1960s long range R965 and modified for the R996 could not cope with the amount of information passed to it by the extremely sensitive receiver, preventing track data from being issued onto the Combat System Highway. The original design for the masthead antenna and stabilization gear made it virtually impossible to conduct any maintenance at sea, so that if a ship experienced a problem it

needed to return to port to fix it. Insufficient quantities of spare parts compounded the problem of keeping the ships operational. Lastly, ignoring the advice of the radar designers, the MOD accepted that the radar's waveguide, the conduit that passes the high power radio frequency energy from the Travelling Wave Tube Amplifier up the mast to the antenna, could be dried using ship's low pressure air rather than a dedicated and protected supply. However, all too often, ship's air was too wet or its supply unreliable and the resulting arcing inside the waveguide caused catastrophic damage to the system.

Sir Robert Walmsley, then Chief of Defence Procurement, in his cross-examination by the House of Commons Select Committee on Public Accounts in March 2000, assessed the state of the MoD's current procurement projects and was brutally frank in assessing the impact of the failure of the R996 programme. "*The 996 Radar is the most serious problem that affects over thirty ships. £45 million pounds had to be set aside to address technical problems that we should have been able to foresee, at least one of which the contractor told us we were going to be hit fair and square on the chin if we did not take his advice. We did not take his advice and it hit us between the eyes. We have had to put all that right. That is unsatisfactory from the operational point of view and money which we should not have had to spend.*"

Another new radar, the E/F-band R1008, was fitted to meet new Board of Trade regulations for a secondary, independent navigation radar. Sited on the front of the island the R1008 was a singularly unimpressive substitute for the huge R909 tracker that had for the previous fifteen years dominated the view from the Bridge. Two new R1007 radars replaced the old R1006 sets. The forward one mounted atop the foremast provided a high definition surface picture out to around twenty miles, used primarily for navigation by the Bridge watch keepers and in the Ops Room for range clearance during gunnery serials. The aft one fitted atop the pole mast at the rear of the island provided a surface back-up, but was used primarily by the air traffic controllers for aircraft on final approach to the carrier; the radar return from the aircraft amplified by its RRB transponder fitted in the fuselage. A new optical Glide Path Indicator was fitted where the aft R909 had been to assist with helicopter recoveries. The Harrier landing aids, the Microwave Aircraft Digital Guidance Equipment, the Carrier Line-Up Beacon System and the Deck Approach Optical Positioning System, known by their rather less grand acronyms, MADGE, CLUBS and DAOPS, respectively were all removed for overhaul or replacement. A new closed circuit television system was also installed to provide remote surveillance of the flight deck from HQ1 and the Ops Room.

In equipment terms, *Ark Royal*'s principal legacy of the Cold War was the ship's S2016 hull-mounted sonar. *Ark*, like all of the CVSGs could hardly be described as a quiet ship and consequently the passive detection capability of her S2016 sonar set was, at best, limited. Nevertheless, when used in active mode, the powerful transducer offered a reasonable chance of detecting a submarine at close quarters, albeit probably within the striking range of their modern heavyweight torpedoes, or at least acted as a deterrent against them approaching too close to the ship. *Ark*'s ASW strength therefore lay in her role as a platform for anti-submarine helicopters armed with Stingray torpedoes and depth charges and as a command platform controlling a screen of far more capable towed-array frigates; for this she did not need her own sonar set. Although redundant, the decision to remove S2016 was deferred; consequently, *Ark*'s set was given nothing more than routine maintenance and inspection, with some minor modifications completed and the transducer and hull dome inspected and renewed.

The biggest casualty of the refit was the Sea Dart anti-air missile system. Sea Dart had not been fired in combat from any CVS since HMS *Invincible* during the Falklands and aside from infrequent proving firings; no significant upgrades were made to the system during its service.

The accepted wisdom of the late 1990s, backed up by the experiences of Iraq, Bosnia and Kosovo, was that an organic missile-based AAW capability was no longer needed in the capital ships. Her embarked Sea Harriers conducting longer-range combat air patrols, supported by Sea King airborne early warning helicopters, could effectively deal with the airborne threat to a carrier. New over-the-horizon-targeting weapons would increase the range at which attacking aircraft could be engaged.

Improved intelligence gathering techniques, more sophisticated radars and electronic warfare sensors, and link systems capable of passing tactical data between ships in a task group also meant that the carrier's escorts could provide better coordinated layered defence. Attacking aircraft could now be seen and interdicted before they came within missile release range, and if they did manage to launch an attack, 'hard kill' systems like Phalanx and Goalkeeper, backed up by 'soft kill' decoys, would provide adequate, if last-ditch, defence. With the competing priority of more space needed to support a flexible and larger air wing, Sea Dart had to go.

Sea Dart's removal generated around 600 square metres of parking space on the flight deck by transforming the previously unused fo'c'sle area adjacent to the ski ramp. The new starboard hull section, weighing 160 tonnes, created nine compartments: four magazines for aircraft munitions and additional briefing and planning rooms for the increased air group. A weapons lift was also fitted into the newly vacated space and existing magazines were changed to house the latest armaments.

The removal of the R909 tracking radars and transmitters allowed their power rooms to be converted to planning rooms for embarked staff, conveniently situated at the forward and aft ends of the island near the main thoroughfare on two-deck starboard side, used by the air crews in flight preparation.

As well as the flight deck extension, other significant upgrades were completed to *Ark*'s floating runway. Supporting activities on the flight deck were systems and services that operated from the open catwalks which stretched around the ship's stern and up both port and starboard sides. These included fresh and demineralised water supplies; aircraft wash down facilities, fire safety equipment as well as fuelling and defueling systems. Fourteen hundred new securing points on the flight decks, lifts and in the hangar were fitted, to tie down aircraft at sea.

The yearlong job of removing, overhauling and replacing the two aircraft lifts was a major achievement in itself. The size of a tennis court and weighing 28 tonnes, each lift platform was lifted thirty feet from the hangar deck up to the flight deck by sophisticated and temperamental wishbone hydraulic mechanisms. New locking gear and an anti-tilt mechanism were fitted to each lift platform to improve stability and hopefully avoid the sorts of failure that had dogged their early operational life.

Ark's hangar was upgraded to enable better operation of the RAF's GR-7 Harrier aircraft and, for the first time from an aircraft carrier, the ability to fly and accommodate the Merlin HM-1 anti-submarine helicopter. The main power supplies for the GR-7 and Merlin were also updated - a Merlin used just under 1,000 amps alone for starting.

Safety was also a crucial consideration. Even though the hangar covered about the same area as two football pitches placed end-to-end, it could be crowded with aircraft, equipment, live munitions and flammable materials. A fire in this space could very quickly threaten the ship if not isolated and extinguished quickly. To achieve this, the hangar could be quickly divided into three areas by lowering two fire curtains. Each fireproof section was protected by a separate sprinkler

system in the deck head of each space. Renewing and hanging the curtains was a challenge for BRDL and an external contractor was given ten days to complete the task, but needed just seven to get the curtains on board, unroll the heavy-duty material, lay them out and chain block them up and onto a roller.

Several new workshops were constructed and outfitted along with new offices to meet the needs of the GR-7 and Merlin crews. Space for spare parts for the aircraft was extremely tight and BRDL was tasked with fitting new shelving around the hangar, a huge task, which took around a year to complete. Four gantry cranes were also fitted; one fore, two mid and one aft, to lift the heavy spares to and from the shelves, which allowed the GR-7s to be maintained in the aft section of the ship.

Locating the fixed wing aircraft near the aft lift simplified operations on the hangar and flight decks. The hangar and flight decks were made to look like new again thanks to the renewal of the non-skid paint system. Painters got through 4,600 litres of paint to complete the refurbishment which included finishing the intricate multi-coloured flight deck markings.

Since the ship would deploy and operate a greater number of aircraft she needed extra storage for aircraft fuel and so some of the tanks previously used to store diesel oil were converted to carry aviation fuel. Another important addition was the installation of a liquid oxygen making plant to provide the pilots of the fixed wing aircraft with bottled oxygen. Modern aircraft could make oxygen on board, however the Sea Harrier could not and so the ship had to produce it and bottle it instead.

The refit contract included an extensive package of work to bring the ship's office and accommodation areas up to a high standard to meet the needs of the men and women serving in the Royal Navy in the new millennium. BRDL was presented with a huge task but one in which everyone, from project managers to tradesmen, took immense pride. The challenge came in having to complete 463 of the ship's 1228 compartments by the deadline of 30th March 2001, the day 400 of the Ship's Company moved on board. Many of the ship's systems, such as fresh water and air conditioning, had to be up and running for this date and BRDL had to adopt different ways of working to achieve this, while still keeping up to date with refitting the remaining compartments. However, the deadline was met and from this date there was a particularly strong spirit of co-operation between the Ship's Company and BRDL to have all *Ark Royal*'s systems and services completely operational and complete the refit on time and to the highest standards.

The ship was fitted with five new sewage treatment plants, two fore, one mid and two aft; there was a major upgrade of fridges and cool rooms and an additional fridge -storeroom provided. All equipment in the laundry was removed and replaced with up-to-date washing machines, presses and irons. The dental surgery, laboratory and sick bay were also fully upgraded.

Ark had four galleys and a bakery to feed the Ship's Company of 1,100 men and women. The main and wardroom galleys were stripped and corroded sections of the steel decks cut away and renewed before new cabling, linings and equipment was fitted. This included, in the main galley alone: three 80-litre tilting kettles, five combination ovens that could fit ten dishes and five with space for six, two eighty-litre pans, one forty-litre pan, three deep fat fryers, a slicer, a food processor and, for storing the food, two large fridges. A separate preparation area contained a large fridge and a freezer, a food mixer, a cutter/mixer, two potato peeling machines and a garbage disposal unit: everything, including a kitchen sink! The Admiral's galley on four-deck received a similar upgrade so that the Captain's Leading Chef and Steward could entertain up to eighteen guests in style in the Flag Dining Room. The last galley in the Air Crew Refreshment Bar

on two-deck was also overhauled to resemble *Ark*'s very own branch of McDonalds.

All cabins and offices were protected by a state of the art fire detection system. A total of 612 sensors were fitted throughout the ship each feeding back to a central control and monitoring panel in HQ1, allowing a fire location to be pinpointed and dealt with immediately. Extra electrical sockets were fitted to offices and living spaces to allow the use of personal electrical equipment. BRDL called upon the talents of the craftsmen and women in Babcock Joinery to furnish some quarters. Their most impressive achievement was the design of a new Wardroom bar, made from ash wood that stretched the length of the anteroom.

The Ships Staff Move on Board date of 30th March 2001 was a huge milestone for another reason since it coincided with a visit to HMS *Ark Royal* by the Secretary of State for Defence, Geoff Hoon, who witnessed the tremendous teamwork of the Ship's Staff, MoD and BRDL work force to bring the ship up to fleet standard. Nearing the homeward stretch of her two-year refit, *Ark* looked very nearly ready to head back to sea, but it was several more months before she was towed to the entrance lock at Rosyth.

On Friday 13th July 2001 HMS *Ark Royal* sailed out of Rosyth dockyard for sea trials; the first time she had moved under her own power in nearly seven years. *Ark* returned to Rosyth in August to conduct the inclining trial to test her stability and then, while the Ship's Company enjoyed summer leave, the BRDL teams carried out all of the defect repairs and put the final touches to allow her return to full operational service.

BRDL's team had grown attached to *Ark*; Babcock's marketing manager Drew Rance commenting: "*We have 2,500 employees on the site and all of them have taken a great pride in having such a prestigious vessel here. When she sails we will all be losing a friend - she's seen very much as our Ark Royal.*" *Ark*'s refit had cost £147 million and BRDL's performance helped them secure the contracts for all future CVS refits.

Rear Admiral D G Snelson CB

(Commanding Officer 2001 – 2002)

Like many of my predecessors the abiding memory I have of my time in command is the fierce pride of the Ship's Company in their ship.

The extraordinary wartime history of the 3rd *Ark* and then the TV name that the 4th *Ark* made for herself, are now very much history but somehow the name lives on in public consciousness – and immediately engenders pride in all those who walk up the gangway for the first time.

Getting the ship out of refit after seven years of non-running was a major task but the Ship's Company – particularly the engineers – and the

Babcock team in Rosyth worked wonders. She first moved again under her own power exactly as planned in mid July 2001. But that wasn't without its problems; bits of machinery that hadn't been refitted kept failing, the gearboxes gave us nerve wracking moments and the stabiliser unit kept doing funny things!

But the event that really boosted our pride was the visit the ship's sponsor paid us for the ships rededication in November 2001. Her Majesty Queen Elizabeth, The Queen Mother flew onboard by helicopter at the age of 101. She spent many hours onboard meeting with and talking to lots of the ships company. An incredible morale boost for a ship starting out on a new phase of life.

Sadly, of course, the Queen Mother died in March 2002 and a few members of the Ship's Company, including myself, had the extraordinary privilege of taking part in her funeral which was a major state occasion.

But getting ready for operations was what was really important; embarking Merlins for the first time in a Carrier was a real achievement; the Harriers came onboard in good numbers and after BOST we finally set off for the Med to prove our worth. As always with world affairs little did we know that the ship would be landing troops on a hostile coast in the Middle East less than a year later - but that's why the Navy trains for the unexpected.

True to form *Ark* rose to the challenge of another royal occasion when Her Majesty the Queen visited on the occasion of her Golden Jubilee in June 2002 and watched a military display in Portsmouth dockyard.

I left after not much more than a year in command, enormously proud and having been supported by a great Ship's Company. And, as it happens, to command that operation in the Middle East. I couldn't have wished for a better task force flagship!

Chapter 9

2001 – 2002:
A carrier for the 21st Century

HMS *Ark Royal* emerged from refit to rejoin a fleet given renewed optimism and clear purpose to face the challenges of the 21st Century, following nearly a decade of uncertainty and attrition after the end of the Cold War.

The Royal Navy's role after the fall of the Soviet block and disintegration of its primary adversary, the Soviet Navy, had needed a radical review. Aside from the sacrosanct and pivotal role of continuing to deliver the United Kingdom's strategic deterrent, now manifest in the hugely impressive but equally expensive *Vanguard*-class Trident SSBN force, the Navy saw its future doctrine bound in the three core capabilities of amphibious forces, nuclear powered attack submarines and aircraft carriers. Realigning the Navy's role could not be achieved in isolation, particularly in the face of successive defence cuts as the Treasury sought to claim its 'peace dividend', first through "Options for Change" in 1990 and then "Front Line First" four years later. Senior commanders were forced to sacrifice Cold War assets and personnel to protect and invest shrinking resources in the three core capabilities and develop a new doctrine that required them. Between 1st January 1990 and 1st June 1997 the Royal Navy lost a third of its manpower from 62,400 to 41,368. Over the same period, the naval bases at Portland and Rosyth closed; the escort force declined from 45 frigates and destroyers to 35; SSN numbers fell from fifteen to twelve and the entire SSK force was disbanded with the sale

of the four brand new *Upholder*-class boats to Canada, while the number of minesweepers was halved with the loss of the remaining *Ton*-class vessels.

These cuts were in the context of what proved to be in many ways a more unsettled world; the conflict in Bosnia and sanctions enforcement operations against Iraq demonstrating a greater likelihood than for many years of the UK's armed forces being involved in crises around the world, probably in conjunction with the UN, NATO or other allies. Throughout these actions, the Royal Navy had played a central role, demonstrating its ability even within the constraints of sometimes ill-suited capabilities and changing its emphasis from anti-submarine warfare in the Greenland-Iceland-UK Gaps and to operations "out of area", that is outside the North Atlantic.

After being in the political wilderness for seventeen years, the new Labour government that came to office in 1997 was committed to showing that it could be taken seriously on defence matters, and that it had learnt the lessons of its flirtation with unilateralist and anti-European policies during the 1980s. Prime Minister Tony Blair appointed one of Labour's most experienced foreign policy experts, George Robertson, to the post of Secretary of State for Defence. From this position, Robertson presided over a major reappraisal of defence commitments and the coherency of Britain's forces by embarking on the first defence review since 1981. Robertson's Strategic Defence Review claimed to be radical. For the first time, a review would be firmly grounded in the United Kingdom's emerging foreign policy and deal with the geo-political situation following the final collapse of the Soviet Union. It also sought to identify the right tools to equip the Armed Forces to meet the new challenges they would face, and provide them as cost-effectively as possible, rather than simply re-justify or cut existing capabilities. It would not, therefore, be simply a Treasury-led reevaluation of the cost of defence, as opposed to its value, as for the most part both Nott's in 1981 and Healey's in 1966 had been. Robertson's introduction to the resulting White Paper spelt out the extent of his review: "*The review is radical, reflecting a changing world, in which the confrontation of the Cold War had been replaced by a complex mixture of uncertainty and instability. These problems pose a real threat to our security, whether in the Balkans, the Middle East or in some trouble spot yet to ignite. If we are to discharge our international responsibilities in such areas, we must retain the power to act. Our Armed Forces are Britain's insurance against a huge variety of risks.*"

Robertson's vision for the Royal Navy's future role was equally clear with the emphasis shifting from "*large scale open-ocean warfare*" to "*force projection and littoral operations in conjunction with the other two Services, with a premium on versatility and deployability.*" The keyword of the SDR was "joint". At the heart of the review were a series of initiatives across defence to co-ordinate the activities of the three Services more closely, pooling their expertise and maximising their punch, while at the same time eliminating duplication and waste. The most important of these tri-service approaches was the establishment of new Joint Rapid Reaction Forces, which would be the spearhead of Britain's modernised, rapidly deployable and better supported front line.

The Strategic Defence Review spelt out the single service roles in the joint arena and thus the Navy was given its new *raison d'être*: to provide the 'Maritime Contribution to Joint Operations'. Under this concept, maritime forces would play a key role in delivering, supporting and sustaining the joint force. The Navy's inherent mobility and flexibility, together with its ability to deploy early and operate independently of shore support offered a range of options from deterrence to strike with units poised, as they had been in the Adriatic, to respond quickly to escalation. The strike options would include joint combat air power from all three Services using fixed wing aircraft and attack helicopters deployable from carriers, as well as nuclear submarines armed with Tomahawk cruise missiles. When called upon to do so, amphibious forces, reinforced when required by Army tanks, armoured vehicles and helicopters could deploy ashore, having first been delivered to theatre in sealift vessels, themselves protected by submarines, escorts and aircraft. The Navy's MCMV force would clear the mine threat in the littoral environment, while naval fire missions targeted by AEW helicopters in the surface role could protect troops ashore. If required, the maritime component could also support the movement of land and air forces ashore throughout the subsequent campaign and then provide the heavy lift capacity to sustain them in theatre.

"Rapidly deployable" meant new ships for the Royal Navy and significant growth in its amphibious expeditionary capability. The SDR committed to supplement HMS *Ocean* with two new Landing Platform Docks (HMS *Albion* and HMS *Bulwark*), four new Bay-class Landing Ships and improved Roll-on Roll-off ferries taken up from trade. These ships would support a full amphibious brigade as a highly trained and ready force, with better equipment including armoured all terrain vehicles, heavier artillery and weapon locating radar. In this new maritime concept, aircraft carriers had even greater importance and 'would have a wide utility, including deterrence and coercion'. Notwithstanding the messy strategic contexts of that decade, the operational lessons of the 1990s had been well and truly learned. The ability to bring to bear air power from a mobile, national base, not subject to the vagaries of host nation support or the uncertainties of the situation ashore, had been vindicated on numerous occasions. In the Adriatic *Ark Royal* remaining 'poised to protect' UNPROFOR in general and BRITFOR in particular, was a perfect demonstration of the dynamics of post Cold War naval air power. The RAF's long-held claim that air bases in friendly countries for its aircraft made expensive aircraft carriers quite unnecessary had been repeatedly disproved. Indeed, RAF Harriers had regularly operated from *Ark* and her sisters.

Perhaps the most tantalizing indication of future intentions came early in the review process when George Robertson commented in a speech at the Chatham House on 12th March 1998, that the *Invincible*-class might be replaced by a new capital ship. *"Our existing small aircraft carriers have proved useful in post-Cold War crises in tasks for which they were not designed,"* said Robertson. *"We are considering whether, if we do acquire new carriers, they should be larger than the current generation in order to operate a wider range of aircraft in a greater number of roles."* When the review was finally published on 8th July 1998, these plans were confirmed, Robertson proclaiming in his SDR statement to Parliament *"that we plan to replace our current small carriers from around 2012 with two larger, more versatile, carriers ... carrying a more powerful force, including a future carrier-borne aircraft to replace the Harrier."*

Keeping to the promise that the review would be foreign policy led and despite pressure from the Treasury, bottom-line budget cuts were limited to £685 million, with the focus on savings being achieved through "smart" procurement of new equipment, rationalization and efficiencies. Quantity would give way to quality and while the number of Royal Navy units would fall further – from 35 escorts to 32, twelve SSNs to ten and 25 minehunters to about twenty – what would be left would be better equipped, better manned and altogether more capable, and bolstered by new capital ships.

Among the heralded initiatives of the SDR was the historic joint proposal from the First Sea Lord and the Chief of the Air Staff that the Royal Navy and Royal Air Force would build on the success of recent operations in the Gulf and co-operate to develop a new "Joint Force 2000". The core of this initiative would be the establishment of a Joint Force Harrier (JFH), scheduled to stand up on 1st April 2000. The RAF Harriers of No.1, No.3 and No.4 (Fighter) Squadrons and the RN Sea Harriers of 800 and 801 Squadrons would collocate at the RAF stations at Wittering and Cottesmore. JFH, together with the Nimrod maritime patrol aircraft and the RAF's Search and Rescue helicopters, would form 3 Group RAF under the command of a Rear Admiral (formerly Flag Officer Naval Aviation) with a fully joint staff at RAF Strike Command headquarters.

With the emphasis now on maritime power projection, the previous approach of preformed Carrier Air Groups (CAG) attached to each CVS was declared obsolete. Instead, a Tailored Air Group (TAG) of Harriers in both forms, naval helicopters and other assets, would be created for each new operation. The nature of the TAG demanded that the CVS be flexible and capable enough to provide the facilities to support the mission, which was now clearly defined: to deploy JFH and Fleet aircraft in pursuit of national objectives. This mission was broken down into five key roles.

The first role was 'Maritime Strike'; the primary task for the CVS being to conduct of air operations against land targets, while minimising the dependence on host nation support. Missions would include Air Interdiction (AI) of enemy supply routes and lines of communication; Close Air Support (CAS) of deployed friendly ground forces; Defensive Counter Air (DCA) using the Sea Harrier FA-2 to repel enemy air attacks; and Offensive Counter Air (OCA) in order to render the enemy's air assets useless. Increasingly, these missions would require the use of precision and discriminatory weapons delivered by JFH aircraft, supported by the Sea King Mk-7 AEW helicopter.

The CVS's second role was to be 'Littoral Manoeuvre' where it would be able to deploy support helicopters in aid of amphibious or other air manoeuvre operations - not dissimilar to how HMS *Ocean* operated as a Landing Platform Helicopter (LPH). This role was not compatible for a CVS tasked as a MarStrike platform; however, in times of operational need, a strategic decision to re-role a CVS as a second LPH could be taken.

In order to succeed in either the Maritime Strike or Littoral Manoeuvre roles, the CVS needed to operate effectively within the littoral environment (defined as coastal sea areas and that portion of the land, which is susceptible to influence or support from the sea). To achieve this, sea lines of communication between support vessels and the battle area/theatre of operation needed to be protected at all times. This need defined the CVS's third role: 'Optimised Access'. Integrated with other task group units, aircraft, such as the Merlin HM-1 and Sea King Mk-7, would be used to achieve the sea control (or freedom of action to use the sea for our own purpose) necessary to assure littoral access. Optimised Access was thus a concurrent role and the CVS must be capable of supporting this task regardless of other activity.

The fourth role, 'Command and Control', was implicit in all CVS operations as a task group flagship. In circumstances where there was a need to reduce the land footprint of allied forces on allied/hostile territory, the capacity to direct and co-ordinate the battle from onboard the CVS may become a priority. The flexibility of the CVS in supporting Maritime Component Commanders at sea had already been successfully demonstrated, and work to further refine this capability was underway.

The fifth role was designed to catch all other tasks under the euphemistic header, 'Other'. These included Defence Diplomacy; Humanitarian Assistance and Disaster Relief, and Evacuation and Peace Support operations. These tasks would be achieved by adapting the CVS and embarked aircraft capabilities to support the required mission. Although considered to be tertiary roles, any available CVS could be tasked at short notice without specific training, equipment or logistic modification to undertake such a mission.

Almost immediately, George Robertson's analysis of a *"changing world"* proved accurate, with emerging conflicts out of area vindicating the SDR's analysis where carrier capability would once again prove vital. Three operations, BOLTON, ALLIED FORCE and PALLISER, around or immediately following the Defence Review demonstrated the carrier's new global role.

Following the end of the first Gulf War in 1991, UK forces assisted in enforcing the northern and southern no-fly zones established over Iraq and a UN Special Commission (UNSCOM) was put into theatre to verify that Saddam Hussein had destroyed his chemical and biological weapons manufacturing facilities and stockpiles. Iraq's cooperation with UNSCOM was at best sporadic while the regime continually tested the coalition's resolve to enforce the no-fly zones. Violations by Iraqi Air Force jets of the southern no-fly zone in September 1997 intensified coalition patrols and in the UK, plans were drawn up and refined throughout October for a possible coalition response. Saddam's eviction of UNSCOM in mid-November prompted the UK to initiate its response: HMS *Invincible* was ordered to sail from the Caribbean to Gibraltar in preparation for a possible deployment to the Gulf under Operation BOLTON, and duly embarked RAF Harriers. Operation BOLTON formally took over the southern no-fly zone operations previously conducted under Operation JURAL. Despite intense diplomatic activity, from mid-December to mid January 1998, UNSCOM continued to report Iraqi non-compliance with their inspectors. As a result, on 16th January 1998, *Invincible* sailed for the Gulf with No.1 Squadron GR-7s embarked. Although the UN Secretary General appeared to have brokered an agreement in late-February 1998, the UK government ordered its forces to remain poised in the Gulf until it was clearer whether Iraq would actually resume cooperation with UNSCOM. In late March, following improved Iraqi behaviour, UK forces began an incremental re-posturing, withdrawing the aircraft carrier, but deploying Tornado GR-1 aircraft to Kuwait to take over any subsequent strike role.

As tensions in the Gulf eased temporarily, the NATO-enforced peace in the Balkans was shattered in mid-1998 as war erupted in Bosnia's southern neighbour Kosovo. Serbia had applied a political and military stranglehold in Kosovo following its failed attempt to cede in 1990. Kosovo's significant ethnic Albanian population continued to fight for independence and the Kosovo Liberation Army, armed from within Albania itself collapsing, began guerilla operations against the Serbian military in 1996. Fighting escalated to all-out war by 1998. The United Nations, having learned from its experience in Bosnia, recognised that the only effective means of establishing peace would come through the threat of force; subsequently NATO took on this role. When the Rambouillet peace talks collapsed in March 1999, US Ambassador Holbrooke flew to Belgrade, in a final attempt to persuade Serbian President Milošević to stop attacks on the Kosovar Albanians or face imminent NATO air strikes. Milošević refused to comply, and on 23rd March the order was given to commence air strikes under Operation ALLIED FORCE. HMS *Invincible* with seven FA-2s of 801 Squadron led the British maritime contribution, flying 102 DCA missions. Sixteen GR-7s from No.1 Squadron RAF based at Gioia del Colle, flew over 800 AI and OCA missions in support of the 77-day bombing campaign. Significantly, the maritime strike capability of Royal Navy nuclear powered submarines was also demonstrated; HMS SPLENDID launching Tomahawks in anger for the first time.

A year after Kosovo and with HMS *Illustrious*

now the high readiness carrier, it was her turn to answer the call, this time in the former British colony of Sierra Leone. Civil war had raged in the West African country for nearly a decade despite the imposition of UN peacekeepers. By May 2000, rebel forces threatened to overrun the country's capital Freetown, prompting the UK government to deploy the Rapid Reaction Force to reinforce the UN presence, restore order and evacuate UK, EU and commonwealth civilians. Airlifted into theatre via Senegal, the Joint Task Force, under the command of Brigadier David Richards, quickly established military control. HMS *Illustrious* and her task group was diverted from NATO exercises in the Bay of Biscay and arrived in theatre three days later to support the mission. Carrying seven FA-2s, six GR-7s and the usual three Mk-2 AEW Sea Kings from 849 Squadron, she offered a formidable CAS and airborne surveillance capability to ground forces. Three days after Lusty's arrival, *Ocean* with her Amphibious Ready Group embarked arrived off the coast off Freetown to assist in the suppression of rebel activity and the evacuation of non-combatants.

These three, very different operations had vindicated the rationale of the Strategic Defence Review and carriers were once again accepted as the single most important component of Britain's new expeditionary strategy, adding strategic weight by their mere presence.

Shaping the Navy's future role had been 'bread and butter' for Captain David Snelson, HMS *Ark Royal*'s new Commanding Officer, for nearly a decade. Having served as Rear Admiral Gretton's Staff Operations Officer onboard *Ark* during Op HAMDEN, Snelson had been instrumental in developing the CVSG's 'poise' strategy. As the one-star Director of Naval Operations in the MoD during BOLTON and ALLIED FORCE he had transformed the political vision of the SDR into the strategic deployment of naval and joint forces. Most recently, as the Director of the Naval Staff within the MoD, he was charged with formulating, arguing and promoting the Navy's *raison d'être* throughout Government.

Joining HMS *Ark Royal* in May 2001, as the ship emerged from refit, Captain Snelson knew only too well the potential that lay within his new ship and her strategic and political importance. This did not however overcome the challenge of getting her back into service as quickly as possible and he recognised that this would be no small task. The majority of his Ship's Company were new to *Ark* having joined during the final stages of the refit and unfamiliar with how she looked at the beginning, or, indeed, in her previous commission. More of a challenge still, a significant proportion was new to life at sea having only just finished basic training. Much of the equipment was new and the full capability it offered needed to be explored and exploited, while the legacy equipment that had been overhauled and refurbished needed to be test driven to its limits. Captain Snelson's priorities therefore were clear: train the crew to operate the ship safely; prove the ship worked; learn how to operate her new equipment and aircraft, and then bring these three elements together through intensive training and assessment so that HMS *Ark Royal* could resume her rightful role as the Nation's high readiness carrier. The deadline to achieve all of this was a year; *Ark Royal* was scheduled to be declared ready for task on 9th May 2002 following successful completion of her Operational Readiness Inspection.

HMS *Ark Royal*'s sea trials got off to an encouraging start. On Friday 13th July 2001 *Ark* made the first short voyage under her own power for nearly seven years, sailing just across the Firth of Forth from Rosyth to an anchorage position from where preliminary aviation trials could be completed. These were designed to prove the hangar and flight deck facilities with real aircraft before the operational flying serials began in earnest. The following day a single Merlin HM-1 of 814 Squadron landed on, heralding a new era in the ASW capability of the CVS. *Ark* put out to sea the following day and completed the first week of engineering runs unscathed. Her second voyage the following week was more problematic however. During her exit through the Rosyth Channel the ship suffered a total loss of steering and the escorting tugs struggled to gain control in the close confines of the narrows. The line attaching the forward tug parted under the strain and *Ark* just managed to make it into the middle of the river using her engines before coming to a halt on the second tug. A commercial tug came to the rescue but Captain Snelson was somewhat surprised by the tug master's attempt to claim salvage. With the steering gear problem repaired, *Ark* once again carried on with her propulsion trials but this time her two gearboxes started behaving erratically and the ship needed to anchor in Kirkcaldy Bay for three days while repairs were made. *Ark* needed to get underway again for no other reason than on 29th July; HRH The Duke of York was due to visit the ship as part of his farewell tour at the end of his naval career. Repairs made, the ship got back out just in time and the royal visit went ahead without a hitch.

Ark returned to Rosyth in August for her inclining experiment, designed to check the ship's stability, and final defect rectification period before leaving BRDL's care for the last time. On 29th August, HMS *Ark Royal* sailed from Rosyth to return to her homeport in Portsmouth. The Ship's Company had made many friends during what had been a very successful refit and Captain Snelson reflected their mixed emotions as the ship prepared to rejoin the fleet: *"I feel immense pride to be taking Ark Royal to sea following this successful refit. The standard of work of our partners Babcock has been of the highest order and we are all naturally very sad to be leaving Scotland after making it our temporary home for more than two years. We have been moved by the warmth of everyone we have met and with whom we have forged links during that period. Our pride is tinged with sadness at having to leave our friends."*

Over two hundred family members of the Ship's Company sailed with the ship as she left

Scotland to give them a taste of life at sea and during the 42-hour voyage home they witnessed a variety of evolutions. Off the Isle of White, Flag Officer Surface Flotilla, Rear Admiral Ian Forbes, joined the ship to witness her entrance to Portsmouth. Not surprisingly, *Ark*'s return generated huge interest as one of the most evocative names in the Royal Navy came back into the public eye. A fly past of three Sea Harriers, a Merlin and a Sea King greeted her as she entered the Solent and thousands of Portsmouth locals gathered on the sea front to watch her pass through the harbour entrance. With the Ship's Company in Procedure Alpha, a privilege routinely given to the Commanding Officer on his first and last entry to home port, *Ark* paid her tribute as she passed the Round Tower, firing a fifteen gun salute. For Captain Snelson, it was all something of a dream. As a young fighter controller, handling Buccaneers and Phantoms, the then Lieutenant Snelson had stood in Procedure Alpha at the front of the flight deck of the fourth *Ark* - of BBC "Sailor" fame - as she sailed into Devonport on 8th December 1978, on her way to paying off. He could scarcely have imagined then that 23 years later he would be in charge of her successor as she prepared to rejoin the Fleet. "*For me it was a real thrill and a privilege, really quite an emotional moment.*" For Admiral Forbes *Ark*'s return marked a significant increase in his fighting capacity: "*I'm pleased to see her back, and she is coming back in much better shape. Carriers strike a chord with people. They are big bits of merchandise and they make a big military-political statement. As a nation, we are very proud of her.*"

With the ceremony over for now, *Ark Royal*'s next phase of her regeneration was three weeks of aviation and weapons trials in the English Channel during September. For the ship's staff the main effort surrounded testing and proving the Radars, EW sensors, communications and Command System, and firing all of the guns. For the air department, the period marked the first serious return to fixed wing flying operations. 800 Squadron embarked for two periods from 4th to 7th and then 19th to 28th September. Although short, the embarkations were valuable in so much that they allowed a gentle introduction to carrier-borne operations for both the ship and the squadron. The first period focussed on requalification of the 800 Squadron pilots. The second embarked period enabled consolidation of the earlier work and was largely centered on the requirements of the ship, with the pilots conducting general flying practice and some exercise air interdiction sorties. For the ship the period was invaluable in validating the sortie planning and briefing cycle; preparing the aircraft, marshalling them between the hangar and flight deck, and then safely launching and recovering them. The second period was significant for 800 Squadron in that Lieutenant Commander Tim Easthaugh flew off for last time as their Commanding Officer, to take over 899 Squadron on promotion to Commander.

The stand-off between trials periods from 20th to 24th September was to Cherbourg, giving the largely fresh-faced members of the Ship's Company their first foreign run ashore. Sadly, the excitement of the visit overcame too many and the general behaviour was "*not good!*" While Captain Snelson entertained Her Majesty's outgoing ambassador to Paris, Sir Michael Jay, to dinner onboard, the Ship's Company entertained themselves in the local hostelries. For those unlucky enough to be duty over the visit there was a constant stream of miscreants, drunks and partygoers to deal with. As one Duty Chief recalled: "*Cherbourg was closed except for the bars. I copped for duties second night alongside and didn't get a wink of kip; too busy banging them up and putting sentries on the harmless 'mingers' - male and female. One Upper Deck Sentry even decided to go ashore. His first sea-draft and he didn't realise he had to stay onboard when off-watch!*" The cooling off period back at sea allowed heads to clear and the diplomatic fall-out to be dealt with before *Ark* returned to Portsmouth at the end of the month.

Ark remained alongside in Portsmouth conducting self maintenance and defect rectification until 8th October. She then sailed for a short trials period in the North Sea while en route to her next key appointment: reammunitioning at the defence munitions depot at Crombie, just upstream of Rosyth on the Forth of Forth. From Scotland, *Ark* made for her second foreign port, Amsterdam for a routine visit from 20th to 24th October. This time the Ship's Company were "*good as gold*", doubtless inspired by the Warrant Punishment reading for the principal offenders at Cherbourg that had taken place in the hangar on arrival and before leave was piped.

Back in Portsmouth, the focus now turned to preparing *Ark* for two key events, her Ready for Fleet Date Inspection (RFDI) and the ship's rededication, for which everyone onboard hoped that their Sponsor, Her Majesty Queen Elizabeth The Queen Mother, might attend. *Ark*'s links with BRDL were severed on 2nd November by the ship's acceptance off-contract, which placed the ship back in Ministry hands, while the RFDI a week later signalled that she could be handed over to the Commander in Chief Fleet, materially ready for training and operations. Both events went smoothly: *Ark* was now ready for the next major hurdles of Operational Sea Training and then the Aviation Operational Readiness Inspection that would come after Christmas leave. However, before that, all hearts and minds turned to the ceremonial aspects of bringing *Ark Royal* back into service.

Ever faithful to her most famous patronage and to the thrill of the young Ship's Company, the Queen Mother graciously accepted the invitation as the guest of honour at the rededication of HMS *Ark Royal*, at Portsmouth on 22nd November 2001. Her Majesty arrived by royal helicopter on the flight deck of the ship which she had launched twenty years earlier. Accompanied by the Commander in Chief Fleet, Admiral Sir Alan West, the Queen Mother attended the rededication service in front of 1,200 guests, including dignitaries and former

Commanding Officers and then spent several hours meeting members of the crew and their families. It was obvious to all just how proud Her Majesty was to see *Ark Royal* back in service, and the esteem in which she held the new generation of keen and willing men and women making up her Ship's Company. In Her Majesty's address to the assembled sailors she commented, "*I am so happy that I am once again onboard Ark Royal ... you see, I launched her and her predecessor. It is wonderful to feel that now she's going to be at sea and she's guarding our shores just as in the days of yore. She is a wonderful ship and I hope you will all be happy in her.*" Then with the trademark gleam in her eye, she turned to David Snelson and gave him his only order: "*Captain Snelson, splice the main brace!*"

That order would need to be delayed a few days as *Ark*'s final evolution of 2001 was to conduct full power propulsion trials in the South Western Approaches. Operating off Cornwall the opportunity was also taken to embark 814's Merlin HM-1s from Culdrose to complete landing trials. The trials data would inform the aircraft designers and safety experts of the helicopter's operating limits in a CVS. With the trials done and business almost complete for the year, Captain Snelson could now carry out Her Majesty's instruction and the Ship's Company received its rum ration on the way back to Portsmouth. *Ark*'s Ship's Company enjoyed Christmas leave and then spent the first six weeks of 2002 alongside with the ship undergoing maintenance.

Back to sea at the beginning of February, HMS *Ark Royal*'s next milestone would be the most significant in her regeneration since it focussed on her key asset, the Ship's Company who had to prove their ability before the unyielding assessors on the staff of the Flag Officer Sea Training. Since *Ark* was last at sea, FOST had relocated from Portland to Devonport so the ship could expect a warm West Country welcome when it arrived in Plymouth on 23rd February. Shakedown for the first half of February with 800 Squadron embarked brushed off many of the cobwebs and allowed the ship to be cleaned and polished up to the standard expected for Admiral's Rounds, in preparation for FOST's Staff Sea Check. For 800 Squadron the short period at sea allowed its newest pilots, Jim Blackmore, Mike Wilkinson, Matt Whitfield and Paul Tremelling to make their first successful deck landing and takeoffs from the ship, their successes sparking the usual wardroom celebrations! To balance the aviators' fun, the ship's officers ran a series of damage control and fire fighting exercises for the air group to bring them up to speed in preparation for the latter stages of Work Up, although some claimed it was simply a ruse to keep them out of the bar. The aircraft disembarked on the last Friday of shakedown before the ship anchored off Plymouth to complete its final pre-BOST preparations, heading back to base at Yeovilton to take part in Joint Maritime Course 02-1. Operating west of the Hebrides, 800's Sea Harriers provided a standing Combat Air Patrol for orange forces against a steady stream of GR-7s, German Navy Tornadoes, USAF F15-Es and an assortment of Falcon and Hawks; each 4½ hour sortie flying from Yeovilton using VC-10 tanker support in the Irish Sea. *Ark Royal*'s flight deck was left to 820 Squadron as the weekly FOST training serials, each becoming progressively more complicated and challenging, were ticked off by the Ship's Company. Throughout, *Ark*'s team kept on the training curve toward Final Inspection and passing "Satisfactorily" on 21st March 2002.

Back in Portsmouth the crew could enjoy a well-earned Easter leave before the exertions of the summer term started, with both Aviation Operational Readiness Inspection and a Mediterranean deployment to look forward to. But for the Ship's Company the peace of Easter was short-lived, with the tragic news on 30th March 2002 that Her Majesty Queen Elizabeth The Queen Mother had died at Windsor, aged 101. Her Majesty's links with HMS *Ark Royal* had gone back over sixty years, since she launched the previous carrier to bear the name in 1950.

Throughout this period she had maintained a close personal interest in the welfare of the most famous ship in the Navy and the successive generations of men and women that formed her Company. For them, Her Majesty's death marked the end of an era. Like the people of Britain whom she had served equally faithfully for even longer, they had lost their stalwart patron and friend who in her own unique way had done so much to maintain the 'Spirit of the *Ark*'. Diminished by her loss, that spirit would never burn quite so brightly again. A few members of the Ship's Company were privileged to represent the ship at Her Majesty's funeral on 9th April. Captain Snelson's honour was to represent everyone who had served in HMS *Ark Royal*, as a member of the escort for the gun carriage that carried Her Majesty's body in the state procession to Westminster Abbey. Reflecting later on the historic events of April 2002, Captain Snelson tried to sum up the emotions of the Ship's Company. "*All the crew felt a personal loss because she had meant so much to us. She was a wonderful inspiration. She had that special ability to talk to people of all levels. She had a very human touch.*"

HMS *Ark Royal* returned to sea in mid April to complete Aviation Operational Readiness Inspection, the final test that would bestow on her high readiness status and allow her to take over as the Fleet Flagship from HMS *Illustrious*. *Ark*'s nominated Tailored Air Group would include a full set of Sea Harrier FA-2s from 800 Squadron, Harrier GR-7s from No.1 Squadron RAF, Sea King Mk2 AEW from 849 'B' Flight, Merlin HM-1 from 814 Squadron and the venerable Sea King Mk-6 from 820 Squadron for HDS duties. The two fixed wing aircraft offered a set of complementary capabilities that meshed together well to fulfil *Ark*'s varied maritime strike mission. The Sea Harrier FA-2, with its cutting-edge avionics suite exploiting the Blue Vixen radar for beyond visual range engagements and armed with the Advanced Medium Range Air-to-Air Missile (AMRAAM), was still the most advanced fighter in Europe in the air-to-air mode. The introduction into service of the Advanced Short Range Air-to-Air Missile (ASRAAM) to replace the thirty-year old AIM-9L Sidewinder also provided a huge leap in the aircraft's short range offensive capability. The FA-2 could still carry 30-mm Aden cannons, which had a multiplicity of uses. In the attack mode the aircraft could carry 1,000-lb or 540-lb iron bombs. In its reconnaissance role the aircraft was fitted with a simple internal F95 camera, a capability that had proven most useful in numerous operations with the Sea Harrier. For serious air-to-ground work *Ark* would normally embark a squadron of GR-7s. With a more advanced airframe and powerful engine, the GR-7 also had a night ground attack capability. Able to carry the same bombs as the FA-2, the GR-7 could also designate more laser-guided versions, dropped either from itself or other aircraft, and was also equipped with the Maverick television-guided missile for precision attack. *Ark Royal* gave a mix of up to sixteen of these aircraft a secure, mobile base for sustained operations with excellent command and control facilities. It could operate day or night, and high sortie generation rates meant that much could be obtained from a relatively small number of aircraft.

When *Ark* operated a full JFH air group her normal complement of helicopters would reduce to six; four Airborne Early Warning Sea Kings and two Merlin ASW aircraft. *Ark*'s summer deployment would be the final occasion that an 849 flight embarked with the Mk-2 Sea King as the first airframes of the vastly improved Mk-7 variant came on stream. The Mk-7 incorporated the improved Searchwater 2000 surveillance radar with a pulse Doppler mode option that now enabled both surface and airborne targets to be detected and tracked. This, combined with a new Cerberus mission system, communications and data link upgrades, and a new identification-friend-foe interrogator transponder, changed the simple 'AEW' designation to ASAC - Airborne Surveillance and Area Control. The Mk-7 Sea King was now the most sophisticated airborne surveillance aircraft in any naval inventory. The Merlin HM-1 offered a parallel step improvement in capability over the Sea King Mk-6 and could reasonably lay claim to being the most advanced maritime helicopter in the world. Its Blue Kestrel radar, with a sophisticated processing suite, offered an ability to carry out wide area surface surveillance and targeting over the entire littoral. The long range sonar suite, with both sonobuoys and the highly capable AQS 960 dipping array, doubled the capability in the old Sea King ASW fleet, making the life of even the quietest enemy submarine far more hazardous than most submariners would like. The helicopter could carry Stingray homing torpedoes or depth charges if it was appropriate to take on the contact itself, or direct a subordinate Lynx Mk-8 to interdict the target. Both types of helicopter together provided a major new capacity as 'battlespace shapers', providing information to the joint force commander as to the nature of his environment and where he might have to direct his weapons.

Each fixed wing and rotary wing aircraft offered a unique but complementary capability to the carrier. The purpose of the Operational Readiness Inspection was to demonstrate that *Ark Royal* could use these mixed capabilities effectively and safely across a wide range of scenarios to deliver its mission. The squadron ground teams joined *Ark* at Portsmouth on 14th April and the aircraft embarked shortly after the ship sailed the following day. The ship turned left up the Channel and into the North Sea to take station off the east coast exercise areas. ORI got off to a good start in the unusually calm weather. The intensity of operations on the flight deck called for care and coordination, but by the end of first week the ship's and squadron staff had proved their ability to work and socialise together once again. Augmenting the 800 Squadron pilots, Lieutenant Rob Segebath (801 Squadron) joined for training while, Lieutenant Commander 'Jack' London from 899 Squadron, embarked with a BBC team to film en episode for the "999" television documentary series. The piece recreated Jack London's recovery and emergency landing in *Invincible* while on Gulf duty in 1998 after the canopy of his aircraft shattered at 23,000 feet. Jack's heroism in bringing the aircraft back earned him a Queen's Commendation for Bravery in the Air and typified a pilot who was known throughout the Harrier force as a consummate professional. Tragically eight months later, this same bravery was to cost Lieutenant Commander London his life when he delayed ejecting from a twin-seater Harrier T4 after its Pegasus engine exploded to ensure that his student had got out. His death came just a week after the "999" programme aired.

The first week of the ORI concentrated on deck qualifications and then night qualifications for the Harrier pilots, all successfully achieved. By the end of the second week the tempo and complexity of operations had increased significantly with the full range of Harrier missions having been tested, including an ambitious photo reconnaissance sortie covering a significant part of north east England, taking in such strategic sites as the Stadium of Light and the pilot's family home. *Ark Royal* had a temporary respite that weekend, anchoring off Leith and running a boat routine to the port so that the Ship's Company could reacquaint themselves with the delights of Edinburgh. Having weighed anchor on Sunday morning, *Ark* put back out into the North Sea for the final training week ahead of the formal ORI programme. The training continued to build on the previous week's experience with the air crews flying a range of sorties externally generated by Air Tasking Order, ranging from the FA-2s sitting on deck at high alert states, through to fighter escort trips in support of the GR-7s. The more ambitious sorties demanded up to eight fixed wing aircraft launched in a single wave; all achieved in less than two minutes, and the formation of indigenous COMAO packages. Despite the challenges of unserviceable aircraft and the occasional rescrub for the junior pilots, the air group stayed on the training curve, well placed to start the ORI on 5th May. Rather than pulling

into Leith, Captain Snelson elected to berth at the ammunitioning jetty at Crombie, far enough away from civilisation to tempt any members of the crew from stepping ashore. FOST and COMUKTG staff embarked on the Sunday afternoon and the formal three-day assessment began on Tuesday morning, with the air group pitched against a mythical enemy in northern England. Just to add some real excitement to the exercise tension, the first day coincided with a visit to *Ark* by Geoff Hoon, the Secretary of State for Defence.

Hardly had the exercise begun than the weather intervened, fog stopping play temporarily. *Ark Royal* headed south in hope of finding a gap, finally emerging off the coast of Kent. Although a scenic location, the presence of major airports and busy shipping lanes made the area less than ideal surroundings for carrier operations so *Ark* pressed westward into the south coast exercise areas; the mythical enemy being sufficiently cooperative to relocate to Dorset! The hectic flying programme saw the Sea Harriers successfully complete numerous high quality recce missions and take part in several COMAO involving up to nine aircraft, all launched from *Ark*. The assessment staff were well pleased with what they saw, and accordingly issued the signal informing the Commander in Chief Fleet that *Ark Royal* could now be declared at R2 high readiness.

Ark's celebrations did not last long for no sooner had she arrived home at Portsmouth than she was refuelled, reprovisioned and made ready to sail on her first deployment in eight years, for Exercise DYNAMIC MIX '02. NATO's biennial land, maritime, amphibious and air exercise, the DYNAMIC MIX 'battlefield' stretched from the Canary Islands to Turkey. More than 15,000 service personnel; over fifty ships and 150 aircraft from thirteen NATO nations were due to exercise crisis response, humanitarian assistance and collective defence. French forces would join the exercise as part of their normal training relations with the allies. A subset of the main effort, the annual mine-clearance exercise DAMSEL FAIR was added into the MIX, to add value for the participants and optimise use of the NATO planners running the exercises.

HMS *Ark Royal* sailed from Portsmouth on 16th May picking up four 849 'B' Flight Sea Kings including two Mk-7s, two 814 Merlins and eight Sea Harrier FA-2s, this time from 801 Squadron. Escorted by the *Type-22* frigate HMS *Chatham* and *Type-42* destroyer HMS *Cardiff* and supported by the tanker RFA *Orangeleaf*, *Ark* made a sedate passage south enjoying good weather to exercise a flying programme of three waves of up to six aircraft per day. Reaching the Mediterranean five days after sailing, *Ark Royal* met up briefly with the aviation training ship RFA *Argus*, before going alongside at Alicante in Spain for the ship's first foreign run ashore of the year which included the mandatory official reception, as well as optional 'rig-runs' to the local attractions. From Alicante, the first priority for *Ark Royal* was to rendezvous with the other units in her task force: RFA *Argus*, the Italian frigate ITS *Zeffiro*, the American frigate USS *Underwood*, HMS *Cardiff*, and RFA *Orangeleaf*. The force formed up and then conducted manoeuvres through the Straits of Gibraltar, heading east to west before turning around and going back out into the Atlantic, just for good measure. The exercise developed through to the end of May before building up to a freeplay with *Ark* poised just to the west of the Gibraltar straits. The main effort commenced in early June, with eighteen NATO ships from various nations doing battle; *Ark*'s opposing force centred on the Spanish carrier *Principe de Asturias*. The 'enemy' air wing consisted of Spanish F-18s, Mirage and AV8-Bs, and American, Greek and Turkish F-16s. *Ark*'s Sea Harriers played a key role from the start, undertaking a wide variety of missions including CAP, Recce and MarStrike. The crystal clear water in the area also gave the Harrier pilots the unusual role of submarine finder, Lieutenants Parker and Tremelling both spotting dived SSKs operating on the Spanish side. Despite the overwhelming odds against them, 800's pilots gave a good show throughout the battle and the culmination of DYNAMIC MIX was their audacious long range attack with German Tornados against the *Principe de Asturias*. The Anglo-German attack was decisive, but in keeping with NATO's desire to keep all sides happy, the exercise was formally declared a draw. The final event was the essential photo opportunity with all of the units, including the three submarines, formed up.

The reward for the hard work of the Ship's Company during DYNAMIC MIX was a five-day visit to Palma in Majorca. From there *Ark Royal* headed home, disembarking her air group on 18th June before heading up the English Channel. The following day, the ship received an unusual visitor in the form of the rock group Status Quo who had asked to film onboard as part of the public relations campaign for their new album "Heavy Traffic", which would see the group perform a live concert on the flight deck at the end of July. HMS *Ark Royal* arrived at Portsmouth on 19th June and berthed overnight before heading back out into the Solent for a families day, the highlight of which was a four aircraft flypast by 800 Squadron FA-2s. The final event of *Ark*'s summer term was also the finale of her year-long regeneration to become the high readiness strike carrier and Fleet flagship, and it also signalled the end of Captain Snelson's period in command. 2002 marked the fiftieth anniversary of the accession of Her Majesty the Queen and 27th June was selected as the day on which Her Majesty's Armed Forces would show their appreciation. HMS *Ark Royal* was selected to represent the Royal Navy and Her Majesty accompanied by The Duke of Edinburgh visited the ship as part of the day-long celebrations. Their visit could provide no more fitting demonstration that HMS *Ark Royal* was back in business, truly, a carrier for the 21st Century.

Vice Admiral Sir Alan Massey KCB CBE

(Commanding Officer 2002 – 2003)

'There can be no better job in the Royal Navy than to command one of Her Majesty's ships.'

So goes the inspiring folklore that is drip-fed into every Warfare Officer from their very first days at Dartmouth. To which I would simply add that when that ship is an aircraft carrier and the Fleet flagship it simply cannot, possibly, get better.

I was lucky enough to join *Ark Royal* in the summer of 2002, taking over from David Snelson a ship that was straining at the leash to get into her post-refit operational stride. David and his team had done a superb job: *Ark* and her famously proud crew were tight, sparkling, confident and ready.

We had a wonderfully busy programme ahead: fixed wing carrier strike work-ups in the Med before Christmas to achieve high readiness status and then, in 2003, an enticing Far East deployment to support allied naval exercises and defence sales. But one of the Royal Navy's great strengths has always been adaptability: in its ships and equipment, its support mechanisms and- especially – its people. So when the call came to convert *Ark* from carrier strike to amphibious warfare, ready for potential operations against Iraq in early 2003, it was quick, unfussy and effective. And it needed only one adjustment to the ship's complement – a single additional Royal Marines officer – to bring together an epic role-change in no time at all.

This chapter gives all the details of what then transpired. I would merely preface those with a few impressions from my own privileged viewpoint. First, the complexity of bringing all the moving parts of amphibiosity into action, against the clock, and for real. Second, the immensely impressive allied planning and command organisation that put *Ark*, along with *Ocean* and a superb RN/RFA supporting cast, right into the van of the coalition's maritime war effort, just a few miles off the Iraqi coast. And third, the incredible inventiveness, resilience, spirit and courage of a youthful Ship's Company who underwent many weeks of sustained pressure and apprehension, and then the terrible, debilitating shock of losing seven of their own people in one, awful instant. That they endured all this and yet put in a flawless operational performance on the Nation's behalf is, surely, what the name of *Ark Royal* is all about.

Chapter 10

2002 – 2003:
Operation TELIC

Saddam Hussein had represented a destabilizing threat to the Middle East and a persistent thorn in the West's side ever since coming to power in Iraq in 1979.

In 1980 Saddam instigated war against his Persian neighbour Iran that lasted until 1988. Iraq was regarded as a counterbalance to Islamic fundamentalist Iran of the post-revolutionary Ayatollahs, and therefore the West (and specifically the United States) sought to cultivate a constructive, if uncomfortable, relationship with Saddam throughout the 1980s. The Reagan administration provided billions of dollars in aid, nearly all of it on credit to fund Iraq's war and to deter them from forming a strong alliance with the Soviets, becoming "*the third-largest recipient of US assistance*". The political relationship was however ambiguous, reflecting a confused international reaction to the conflict, misaligned to the traditional Cold War power blocs. As former US Secretary of State and elder statesman, Henry Kissinger, famously remarked, "*it's a pity they both can't lose.*"

The end of the war with Iran served to deepen latent tensions between Iraq and its wealthy neighbour Kuwait. Saddam urged the Kuwaitis to forgive Iraq its $30 billion debt, accumulated in the war, but they refused. Kuwait also spearheaded opposition among members of the Organization of Petroleum Exporting Countries (OPEC) to block Saddam's request to raise oil prices by cutting back production. Kuwait was pumping large amounts of oil, and thus keeping prices low, when Iraq needed to sell high-priced oil from its wells to pay off its huge debt. Saddam had always argued that Kuwait was historically an integral part of Iraq, and that it had only emerged as an independent sheikhdom after World War I, when it was given the protection of Britain. This echoed a belief that Iraqi nationalists had voiced for over fifty years and was one of the few areas of common ground in a country rife with sharp social, ethnic, religious, and ideological divides. Kuwait's large oil reserves, discovered in the late 1930s and exploited by the forerunners of British Petroleum (UK) and Chevron (USA), also intensified tensions in the region. Iraq and Kuwait each held roughly ten percent of the world's known oil reserves but Saddam complained that Kuwaiti producers were poaching Iraqi stocks by slant drilling from wells within a disputed region of the border. The apparently conciliatory tones by State Department officials to Saddam's threats to pursue his claims by force led him to believe that the USA would not intervene. This was a serious misjudgment which he would quickly come to regret as his status shifted from sometime partner of the West to its social pariah.

Iraq's invasion of Kuwait in August 1990 dispelled any pretence that Saddam could be contained by his Gulf patrons. Having earlier paid Iraq to prevent the spread of Islamic fundamentalism and provided it with the technology to amass the largest army in the region, the western-backed oil states now found themselves potential victims of Saddam's expansionist ambitions in the name of Arab nationalism and Islam. The invasion was met with universal condemnation, led by the United States and Saudi Arabia. On 2nd August 1990 the United Nations Security Council passed Resolution 660 demanding Iraq's unconditional withdrawal, which was ignored by Saddam, along with ten subsequent UNSCRs between August and November. UNSCR 678 passed on 29th November represented the UN's 'final demand' to him to comply, offered one *"final opportunity, as a pause of goodwill"* while at the same time authorizing member states cooperating with Kuwait to use all necessary means to enforce UNSCR 660 if Iraq did not withdraw on or before 15th January 1991.

The coalition force led by the United States and the United Kingdom won a decisive military victory in evicting Iraqi forces from Kuwait, but its mandate stopped short of pressing home the advantage to take direct action to remove Saddam from power. The peace terms for Iraq were set out by the United Nations in Security Council Resolution 687, adopted on 3rd April 1991. As well as reaffirming thirteen previous resolutions, UNSCR 687 demilitarized the border between Kuwait and Iraq, set out the reparations due by Iraq including the return of property and obligations toward its international debt, and the conditions under which existing sanctions would continue to be enforced.

It had long been known that Iraq had developed weapons of mass destruction and was prepared to use them, not only against another country as they had done during the war against Iran, but also against its own people in suppressing the Kurdish rebellion, where over 5,000 civilians were gassed at Halabjah in 1988. Iraq had also developed the capability to deliver WMD. Its Soviet-sourced SCUD missiles were used extensively during the Iran-Iraq War and its second-generation derivatives, the 'Al Hussein' and 'Al Abbas' with a range up to 800 kilometres, could threaten targets across the Middle East. The Iraqi attacks on Tel Aviv and Haifa, designed to provoke Israel to intervene in the Gulf War and thereby break the Arab-supported coalition demonstrated Hussein's willingness to use indiscriminate tactics to threaten his Gulf neighbours. A central condition of UNSCR 687 therefore required Iraq to meet its international obligations under the Geneva Protocol and the Nuclear Non-Proliferation Treaty to fully declare and immediately desist in all chemical, biological and nuclear weapons programmes, and to destroy all existing stockpiles and ballistic missiles with a range greater than 150 kilometres. A United Nations Special Commission (UNSCOM) was established to conduct inspections of chemical and biological weapons facilities while the International Atomic Energy Authority led the investigation of Iraq's nuclear capability, to ensure its compliance with these requirements. Details of Iraq's biological and chemical weapons programmes surfaced in the wake of UNSCOM investigations. The immediate investigations concluded that there was no evidence the programmes had continued after the war.

While the coalition had no UN mandate to force a regime change in Iraq, the lead elements, particularly in the United States, openly desired such an outcome. Prior to launching the main offensive under Operation DESERT STORM on 16th January 1991, President George H Bush called on the Iraqi people to overthrow Saddam. Within days of the end of the Gulf War on 28th February 1991, Kurdish factions in northern Iraq and opposition Shi'ite Muslims in southern Iraq, emboldened by the regime's defeat and the hope of US support, launched significant rebellions. The Kurdish rebellion in the north gained a foothold, primarily due to the imposition of a no-fly zone across the 36th Parallel established under UNSCR 688 on 5th April 1991, and the deployment of coalition Marine ground forces under the pretence of providing humanitarian assistance. As a result of the allied intervention, Kurdish forces were able to drive Iraqi troops out of much of northern Iraq and create an autonomous zone that subsequently remained largely free of Baghdad's rule. The Shi'ite revolt in southern Iraq reached the suburbs of Baghdad, but the well-trained and loyal Republican Guard forces that had survived the war largely intact, having been withdrawn from battle prior to the start of the ground offensive, suppressed the rebellion by mid-March 1991. Many Shi'ites blamed the United States for not supporting their uprising and standing aside as Saddam's regime retaliated. According to contemporary press reports, President Bush convinced Congress to provide up to $20 million to support the Shi'ite cause in the belief that a coup by elements within the current regime could produce a favourable new government without fragmenting Iraq. Many observers including neighbouring governments, however feared that Shi'ite and Kurdish groups, if they ousted Saddam, would divide Iraq into warring ethnic and tribal groups, opening Iraq to influence from neighbouring Iran, Turkey, and Syria.

Although little overt support was given immediately to the Shias, on 27th August 1992 a southern no-fly zone across the 32nd Parallel was established under the auspices of UNSCR 688 to prevent Iraqi suppression of civilians from the air. The two operations, NORTHERN WATCH above the 36th Parallel and SOUTHERN WATCH below the 32nd Parallel, provided the coalition's capacity to respond to violations, while economic and trade sanctions maintained constant pressure on the Iraqi regime. The established policy toward Saddam was thus one of containment. UNSCOM and IAEA missions continued to investigate Iraq's legacy WMD capability but their efforts were constantly thwarted by non-cooperation by Iraqi authorities.

The Iraqi refusal to cooperate with international observers reflected the regime's wider policy to test the coalition's resolve. Iraqi military helicopters and planes regularly contested the no-fly zones. A thwarted assassination of George H Bush in Kuwait in 1993 prompted newly elected President Clinton to authorise cruise missile strikes on Baghdad. Iraq's repeated breaches of the Security Council Resolutions and refusal to comply with UNSCOM, led the US Congress in October 1998 to pass the Iraq Liberation Act. Prompted by the expulsion of UN weapons inspectors the preceding August after some had been allegedly caught spying for the CIA, the Act sponsored by the Clinton administration effectively made removing the Hussein regime official American foreign policy. $97 million was apportioned for Iraqi "*democratic opposition organizations*" to "*establish a programme to support a transition to democracy in Iraq*." One month after the passage of the Iraq Liberation Act, and in response to Iraq's refusal to readmit UNSCOM, American and British forces launched operation DESERT FOX, a bombardment campaign of Iraq. The campaign's express rationale was to "degrade" Saddam's ability to produce WMD, but US intelligence personnel also hoped it would help weaken Hussein's grip on power. US Secretary of State Madeleine Albright sought to define 'degrade': "*I don't think we're pretending that we can get everything, so this is - I think - we are being very honest about what our ability is. We are lessening, degrading his ability to use this. The weapons of mass destruction are the threat of the future. I think the president explained very clearly to the American people that this is the threat of the 21st century. What it means is that we know we can't get everything, but degrading is the right word.*"

George W Bush's election in 2000 as US President prefaced a more aggressive stance against Iraq. Bush's campaign platform called for "full implementation" of the Iraq Liberation Act including removal of Saddam, while Bush's key advisors, including Vice President Dick Cheney and Secretary of Defense Donald Rumsfeld, were vocal advocates of a more hawkish foreign policy. However there was no international legal basis for such an intervention, notwithstanding that the peace terms under UNSCR 687 demanded Iraq give access to UN and IAEA inspectors to assure that WMD programmes were shut down; such access having been denied since UNSCOM's expulsion in 1998. The cataclysmic terrorist attacks of 11th September 2001 changed all that, setting in train a series of events that would lead to a second Gulf War.

The international political response to 9/11 was decisive and swift. The day after the attacks, the UN Security Council unanimously adopted UNSCR 1368, expressing its determination to combat threats to international peace and security caused by acts of terrorism and recognising the right of individual and collective self-defence. It called on all countries to co-operate in bringing their perpetrators to justice, making it clear that those who supported or harboured them would be held equally accountable. The international community was also called upon to redouble its readiness to take steps to respond to the attacks and combat all forms of terrorism in accordance with the United Nations Charter.

On 20th September, President Bush addressed the joint session of Congress to set out the United States' response to 9/11. *"Tonight, we are a country awakened to danger and called to defend freedom. Our grief has turned to anger and anger to resolution. Whether we bring our enemies to justice or bring justice to our enemies, justice will be done. Our 'war on terror' begins with al Qaeda, but it does not end there. It will not end until every terrorist group of global reach has been found, stopped and defeated."* Singular among the audience of Bush's cabinet secretaries, political appointees, senators and congressmen, was Prime Minister Tony Blair, whose presence Bush acknowledged, *"America has no truer friend than Great Britain. Once again, we are joined together in a great cause. I'm so honoured the British Prime Minister has crossed an ocean to show his unity with America. Thank you for coming, friend."*

Eight days later, the UN Security Council adopted UNSCR 1373, which set out to place barriers on the movement, organization and fund-raising activities of terrorist groups and required states to cooperate on anti-terrorist activity. The UNSCR marked a shift in international law, since it was adopted under Chapter VII of the United Nations Charter and therefore binding on all UN member states. It was widely believed that the USA instigated UNSCR 1373 and illustrative of the universal support being given after the attacks, despite its legal significance, it took only three minutes in session to be passed unanimously by all fifteen Security Council members. UNSCR 1373 gave the legal mandate for the 'Bush Doctrine' of waging preventative war against foreign regimes that represented a potential or perceived terrorist threat to the security of the United States. It was enacted through Operation ENDURING FREEDOM, targetting al Qaeda strongholds first in Afghanistan in October 2001, then the Philippines in January 2002 and the Horn of Africa ten months later.

There was never any substantiated link between Saddam Hussein and al Qaeda nor the 9/11 attacks. Allegations of Iraqi culpability and a connection with al Qaeda were nevertheless implied. In late 2001 for example, Vice President Dick Cheney said it was *"pretty well confirmed"* that attack mastermind Mohamed Atta had met with a senior Iraqi intelligence official. Later, Cheney called Iraq the *"geographic base of the terrorists who had us under assault now for many years, but most especially on 9/11."* Throughout 2002, the Bush administration insisted that removing Saddam from power to restore international peace and security was a major goal, based on the continuing threat posed by his production of WMD and 'known' ties to terrorist organizations, as well as his continued violations of UN Security Council resolutions. This increasingly hostile rhetoric fuelled speculation that the United States might soon act unilaterally against Iraq, however, Bush still sought consensus through the United Nations and in his speech to the General Assembly on 12th September 2002 he pledged to work with the Security Council to meet the "common challenge" posed by Iraq: "*My nation will work with the UN Security Council to meet our common challenge. If Iraq's regime defies us again, the world must move deliberately, decisively to hold Iraq to account. We will work with the UN Security Council for the necessary resolutions. But the purposes of the United States should not be doubted. The Security Council resolutions will be enforced - the just demands of peace and security will be met - or action will be unavoidable. And a regime that has lost its legitimacy will also lose its power.*"

In making its case for confronting Iraq, the Bush Administration characterised the regime of Saddam Hussein as a grave potential threat to the United States and to peace and security in the Middle East region. The administration maintained that the Iraqi regime harboured active WMD programmes that could be used to attain Saddam's long-term goal of dominating the Middle East. These weapons could be used directly against the United States, or they could be transferred to terrorist groups such as Al Qaeda. The United States could not wait until Iraq made further progress on WMD to confront it, since Iraq could then be stronger and the United States might have fewer military and diplomatic options. But Bush's decision to seek a UN umbrella for the confrontation with Iraq led officials to mute their prior declarations that the goal of US policy was to change Iraq's regime. Downplaying this goal may have been to blunt criticism from US allies and other countries that regime change was not required by any UN resolution, but the United States drew little separation between regime change and disarmament: the Administration believed that a friendly or pliable government in Baghdad was required to ensure complete elimination of Iraq's WMD.

US officials continued to gather a consensus for direct action, but the only consistent support came from the United Kingdom. US domestic law was changed on 16th October through House Joint Resolution 114, which authorized the use of military force against Iraq. With the support of large bipartisan majorities, the resolution "*supported*" and "*encouraged*" diplomatic efforts to strictly enforce through the Security Council all relevant UNSCRs regarding Iraq and "*obtain prompt and decisive action by the Security Council to ensure that Iraq abandons its strategy of delay, evasion, and noncompliance*". While acknowledging the role of the UN, and endorsing the President's efforts to act through the Security Council it also authorised George W Bush to use American forces "*as he determines to be necessary and appropriate.*"

On 8th November 2002, the Security Council, acting at US urging, adopted Resolution 1441, giving Iraq a "*final opportunity to comply with the disarmament obligations imposed under previous resolutions.*" UNSCR 1441 was a compromise since Russia, France and China would have vetoed any more belligerent action. It authorised the resumption of weapons inspections and promised "serious consequences" for Iraqi non-compliance. France and Russia insisted that these "consequences" did not include the use of force to overthrow the Iraqi government and both the American and British Ambassadors to the UN, John Negroponte and Jeremy Greenstock, publicly confirmed this reading of the resolution, assuring that it included no "*automaticity*" or "*hidden triggers*" for an invasion without further consultation of the Security Council.

Weapons inspections would be undertaken by the UN Monitoring, Verification and Inspection Commission (UNMOVIC) under the direction of Hans Blix, which had replaced the previously discredited UNSCOM, and the International Atomic Energy Agency (IAEA) led by Mohamed El Baradei. Saddam Hussein accepted the conditions of UNSCR 1441 on 13th November 2002 and inspectors returned to Iraq shortly afterwards. By February 2003, the IAEA "*found no evidence or plausible indication of the revival of a nuclear weapons program in Iraq*". UNMOVIC "*did not find evidence of the continuation or resumption of programmes of weapons of mass destruction*" or significant quantities of prohibited items. UNMOVIC did supervise the destruction of a small number of empty chemical rocket warheads, fifty litres of mustard gas that had been declared by Iraq and sealed by UNSCOM in 1998, and laboratory quantities of a mustard gas precursor. About fifty Al-Samoud missiles of a design that Iraq stated did not exceed the permitted 150 kilometre range, but which had travelled up to 183 kilometres in tests were also destroyed. Blix considered it would take "*months*" to verify Iraqi compliance with Resolution 1441, but that time was not going to be provided by the United States.

The Bush administration became increasingly impatient over Iraq's apparent non-compliance with Security Council disarmament demands and sought to force a solution in the spring of 2003. Based on the military build-up in the Persian Gulf at the start of 2003, analysts speculated that mid to late March seemed a likely time for an attack to be launched, before the extreme heat of summer. The President said on 14th January that "*time is running out*" for Iraq to disarm, adding that he was "*sick and tired*" of its "*games and deceptions*." On 26th January the US Secretary of State Colin Powell told the World Economic Forum meeting in Davos that "*multilateralism cannot be an excuse for inaction*" and that the United States "*continues to reserve our sovereign right to take military action against Iraq alone or in a coalition of the willing.*" The effect of the sustained information campaign by Bush and his advisors was to create a sense amongst the American population that there was some connection between 9/11 and Saddam. An opinion poll for the New York Times and CBS showed that 45% believed Saddam Hussein was "*personally involved*" in the 9/11 atrocities and by January 2003 attitudes had been transformed showing that a similar percentage believed "most" or "some" of the 9/11 hijackers were Iraqi citizens.

In his State of the Union address on 28th January, Bush presented a sweeping condemnation of Iraq. "*With nuclear arms or a full arsenal of chemical and biological weapons,*" the President

warned, "*Saddam Hussein could resume his ambitions of conquest in the Middle East and create deadly havoc in the region,*" and alerted US armed forces that "*some crucial hours may lie ahead.*" Alleging that Iraq "*aids and protects*" al Qaeda, the President also condemned what he saw as its "utter contempt" for the United Nations and the world. In his address to the UN on 5th February, Secretary of State Powell detailed to the Security Council what he described as Iraq's "web of lies" in denying that it had WMD programmes. "*We know that Saddam Hussein is determined to keep his weapons of mass destruction; he's determined to make more. Given Saddam Hussein's history of aggression... given what we know of his terrorist associations and given his determination to exact revenge on those who oppose him, should we take the risk that he will not some day use these weapons at a time and the place and in the manner of his choosing at a time when the world is in a much weaker position to respond? The United States will not and cannot run that risk to the American people. Leaving Saddam Hussein in possession of weapons of mass destruction for a few more months or years is not an option, not in a post-September 11 world.*"

A month later Bush gave another major address on Iraq at the American Enterprise Institute where he said that the end of Hussein's regime would "*deprive terrorist networks of a wealthy patron .... and other regimes will be given a clear warning that support for terror will not be tolerated.*" The President returned to an earlier Administration theme in declaring that post-Saddam Iraq would be turned into a democracy, which would inspire reform in other Middle Eastern states. This latest rhetoric revived American assertions it had made periodically since the 9/11 attacks that the Baghdad regime supported and had ties to al Qaeda and other terrorist groups. Evidence was once again presented that alleged Iraq had provided al Qaeda with technical assistance in the past to help it construct chemical weapons and that a faction based in northern Iraq and believed linked to al

Qaeda, called the Ansar al-Islam, had been in contact with the Iraqi regime. Other 'experts' suggested that there might have been some cooperation when Osama bin Laden was based in Sudan in the mid-1990s. Perhaps unhelpfully, Bin Laden issued a statement of solidarity with the Iraqi people on 12th February, exhorting them to resist any US attack, while also criticising Saddam's Baath Party regime as "socialist" and "infidel."

In attempting to win international support for its policy, the US administration asserted that Iraq was in material breach of seventeen UNSCRs, including Resolution 1441, mandating that Iraq fully declare and eliminate its WMD programs. The British government publicly supported the American stance. In September 2002, Prime Minister Blair in answering a parliamentary question had admitted, "*Regime change in Iraq would be a wonderful thing. That is not the purpose of our action; our purpose is to disarm Iraq of weapons of mass destruction.*" This message was repeated two months later in another parliamentary exchange, when Blair further stated that, "*So far as our objective, it is disarmament, not régime change - that is our objective. Now I happen to believe the regime of Saddam is a very brutal and repressive regime, I think it does enormous damage to the Iraqi people... so I have got no doubt Saddam is very bad for Iraq, but on the other hand I have got no doubt either that the purpose of our challenge from the United Nations is disarmament of weapons of mass destruction, it is not regime change.*"

But the British support was an increasingly lone voice in the international community and among European and NATO partners only José María Aznar of Spain and Silvio Berlusconi of Italy agreed with the Bush-Blair position. A number of allies and Security Council members, including France, Germany, Russia, and China agreed that Iraq did not fully comply with Resolution 1441, but opposed military action, maintaining instead that UN inspections were working to disarm Iraq

and should continue. President Jacques Chirac of France was the leading critic, maintaining that he was not convinced by the evidence presented by Secretary of State Powell. On 10th February, at a press conference in Paris with President Putin of Russia, Chirac said "*nothing today justifies war.*" Speaking of weapons of mass destruction, Chirac added "*I have no evidence that these weapons exist in Iraq.*" France, Germany, and Russia advocated a strengthened inspections regime rather than an early armed conflict with Iraq, and China took a similar position.

On 24th February 2003, the United States, the United Kingdom and Spain (a non-permanent member of the UN Security Council in 2003/4) introduced what was called the "second resolution" at the Security Council, stating that Iraq had failed "*to take the final opportunity afforded to it by Resolution 1441*" to disarm. The proposed resolution was regarded as authorizing the immediate use of force to disarm Iraq. On 10th March, President Chirac said that his government would exercise its right to veto, and Russian officials said that Putin's government would probably follow the same course. Chirac's stance and the lack of success in garnering other support for the second resolution seemed to convince US officials that further diplomatic efforts at the United Nations would prove fruitless. On 16th March 2003, Bush and Blair flew to the Azores for a hastily-arranged meeting with José María Aznar, hosted by his Portuguese counterpart, José Manuel Barroso. The meeting resulted in a pledge by the American, British and Spanish leaders to establish a unified, free and prosperous Iraq under a representative government. At a press conference after the meeting, President Bush stated that "*Tomorrow is the day that we will determine whether or not democracy can work.*" The following day the three governments announced that they were withdrawing the proposed Security Council resolution, and President Bush addressed the American people that evening to declare that unless Saddam Hussein fled Iraq within 48 hours, the result would be *"military conflict, commenced at the time of our own choosing."*

On 18th March 2003, Parliament debated the possibility of Britain going to war in the Gulf. The debate came against a backdrop of unprecedented internal party political division over the issue that echoed deep unrest throughout the country and across Europe. In January, 69% of Britons opposed war without UN support, while 16% opposed war on any grounds. By mid February, just ahead of global anti-war marches and demonstrations, held in 800 cities across the world, the public's position hardened: 91% saw a second UN resolution as crucial and 45% now rejected war even with it. Even though a clear majority of the British public believed that Iraq had WMD (74%), helped international terrorists (59%) and posed a threat to the UK (61%), they still did not support military action. But, as avoidance of conflict appeared less likely through early March following withdrawal of the proposal for the second resolution, it appeared that they were now resigned to the seemingly inevitable course of events unfolding before them. A Guardian/ICM poll of 15th March showed that now 53% opposed military action and 22% under any circumstances.

The political division within the Blair administration was symbolised by the resignation of Robin Cook, former Labour Foreign Secretary and now Leader of the House of Commons. On the eve of the parliamentary debate, Cook in his resignation speech articulated for many the diplomatic and political crisis that he foresaw enveloping Britain by a precipitous move to war:

"The reality is that Britain is being asked to embark on a war without agreement in any of the international bodies of which we are a leading partner - not NATO, not the European Union and, now, not the Security Council. To end up in such diplomatic weakness is a serious reverse. Only a year ago, we and the United States were part of a coalition against terrorism that was wider and more diverse than I would ever have imagined possible. History will be astonished at the diplomatic miscalculations that led so quickly to the disintegration of that powerful coalition. The US can afford to go it alone, but Britain is not a superpower. Our interests are best protected not by unilateral action but by multilateral agreement and a world order governed by rules. Yet tonight the international partnerships most important to us are weakened: the European Union is divided; the Security Council is in stalemate. Those are heavy casualties of a war in which a shot has yet to be fired. What has come to trouble me most over past weeks is the suspicion that if the hanging chads in Florida had gone the other way and Al Gore had been elected, we would not now be about to commit British troops. The longer that I have served in this place, the greater the respect I have for the good sense and collective wisdom of the British people. On Iraq, I believe that the prevailing mood of the British people is sound. They do not doubt that Saddam is a brutal dictator, but they are not persuaded that he is a clear and present danger to Britain. They want inspections to be given a chance, and they suspect that they are being pushed too quickly into conflict by a US Administration with an agenda of its own. Above all, they are uneasy at Britain going out on a limb on a military adventure without a broader international coalition and against the hostility of many of our traditional allies. I intend to join those tomorrow night who will vote against military action now. It is for that reason and for that reason alone, and with a heavy heart, that I resign from the Government."

Fully cognisant of public and political opinion, in moving the Government motion on the Iraq debate the afternoon after Cook's resignation, Prime Minister Blair gave an impassioned speech setting out again his Government's position on the need to *"hold firm to the course that we have set"*, citing France's veto of the second resolution as the final precursor for unilateral action with the USA:

"On Monday night, France said that it would veto a second resolution, whatever the circumstances. Then France denounced the six

tests. Later that day, Iraq rejected them. Still, we continued to negotiate, even at that point. Last Friday, France said that it could not accept any resolution with an ultimatum in it. On Monday, we made final efforts to secure agreement. However, the fact is that France remains utterly opposed to anything that lays down an ultimatum authorising action in the event of non-compliance by Saddam. The tragedy is that had such a resolution ensued and had the UN come together and united - and if other troops had gone there, not just British and American troops - Saddam Hussein might have complied. But the moment we proposed the benchmarks and canvassed support for an ultimatum, there was an immediate recourse to the language of the veto. The choice was not action now or postponement of action; the choice was action or no action at all. In this dilemma, no choice is perfect, no choice is ideal, but on this decision hangs the fate of many things: of whether we summon the strength to recognise the global challenge of the 21st century, and meet it; of the Iraqi people, groaning under years of dictatorship; of our armed forces, brave men and women of whom we can feel proud, and whose morale is high and whose purpose is clear; of the institutions and alliances that will shape our world for years to come. To retreat now, I believe, would put at hazard all that we hold dearest. To turn the United Nations back into a talking shop; to stifle the first steps of progress in the middle east; to leave the Iraqi people to the mercy of events over which we would have relinquished all power to influence for the better; to tell our allies that at the very moment of action, at the very moment when they need our determination, Britain faltered: I will not be party to such a course. This is not the time to falter. This is the time not just for this Government - or, indeed, for this Prime Minister - but for this House to give a lead: to show that we will stand up for what we know to be right; to show that we will confront the tyrannies and dictatorships and terrorists who put our way of life at risk; to show, at the moment of decision, that we have the courage to do the right thing."

Unlike President Bush who required the consent of Congress to take the USA to war, which he had been given by House Joint Resolution 114, Royal Prerogative allowed Prime Minister Blair to commit UK forces. He won the debate by 412 votes to 149, but the 84 Labour members who voted 'no' represented the largest rebellion by Government MPs since the repeal of the Corn Laws in 1846. Twenty four hours after the vote, 200,000 American and British forces, including the Ship's Company, Squadrons and Royal Marines embarked in HMS *Ark Royal*, were committed to battle against Saddam.

Serious planning for operations in the Gulf began in late summer 2002, shortly after Captain Alan Massey took over command of HMS *Ark Royal* from David Snelson. Captain Massey had just paid off HMS *Illustrious* into extended readiness, having commanded her during the bulk of operations in the Arabian Gulf against the Taliban under Operation VERITAS, the UK's contribution to ENDURING FREEDOM. He was therefore ideally placed to understand the role of the CVS both as a Strike Carrier and an interim Landing Platform Helicopter ('Lusty' had a RM detachment onboard throughout VERITAS) and possessed the most up to date operational experience of working with US naval forces in combat. He formed an invaluable partnership with David Snelson who left on promotion to be COMUKMARFOR but would shortly return as the UK Maritime Component Commander in the Gulf operation.

Alongside at Portsmouth through July and August, *Ark* completed her assisted maintenance period at Portsmouth and was due to deploy at the beginning of September as the flagship for ARGONAUT'02, a UK-led multi-national amphibious deployment to the central Mediterranean. Among *Ark*'s many visitors, rock legends Status Quo made a hugely popular return at the end of July to perform a live concert to celebrate the release of their new single "Jam Side

Down", the video for which had been recorded onboard during the return from DYNAMIC MIX in June. Most of the Ship's Company, with an average age of only 22, were born after the group's heyday, but they didn't seem to mind. "*I think they're all right*," enthused eighteen year old weapon engineer Gemma Davies. "*My Mum and Dad have got all their records.*" Another famous visitor was Sir Norman Wisdom. Leading Chef Rick Whittaker had written to Sir Norman asking for a signed photograph to auction for charity, but instead the fifties film star turned up in person to help out and tour the ship.

Ark sailed for ARGONAUT'02 on 2nd September amid widespread speculation of a build up of forces in the Gulf, but Captain Massey was forthright in responding to the media enquiries, while nevertheless conscious of the possible developments: "*I have crystal clear orders – that is to take my ship and her supporting ships down to the Med to conduct pre-planned national and NATO exercises and then bring them safely back home at around the middle of November. But it is now pretty much received wisdom that any part of the UK's Joint Force has to be ready to do anything. I have already warned my crew to be mentally prepared for the possibility of not being home for Christmas, but then I would be doing that irrespective of the climate of the day, simply because we are a high readiness, highly-in-demand unit*".

The aim of ARGONAUT was to demonstrate Britain's ability to deploy, operate and sustain a Maritime task group and its continuing commitment to the security and stability of the region. The Amphibious task group comprising ten British ships with Dutch assault vessel HNLMS *Rotterdam* and the Belgian frigate *Westdiep* was led by the Commander Amphibious Task Group, Commodore Jamie Miller, who flew his pennant in *Ark* during the early stage of the deployment. *Ark*'s escort was the *Type-42* destroyer HMS *Southampton*, with the amphibious elements embarked in the landing ships RFA *Sir Galahad*

and RFA *Sir Bedivere*. A flotilla of four mine hunters, HMS *Blyth*, *Brocklesby*, *Bangor* and *Sandown* formed the UK mine countermeasures group, while task group support was provided by the replenishment ship RFA *Fort Victoria* and tanker RFA *Orangeleaf*.

The deployment started in the Bristol Channel with a period of Force Integration Training for the FA-2 Sea Harriers of 800 Squadron and the GR-7 Harriers of No.1 (F) Squadron RAF. The remainder of the air group comprised the Sea King Mk-6s from 820 Squadron, 814 Squadron with the new Merlin HM-1 embarked in *Fort Victoria*, and 849 Squadron equipped with the recently upgraded ASaC Sea King Mk-7. The technological 'quantum leap' offered by the Mk-7 over the old Mk-2 was profound. As one crew member observed of the old airframe now fitted with cutting edge technology, "*It's like a Morris Minor with Travel Scrabble in the back, now upgraded with a PlayStation 2. One Mk-7 has the computing power of the whole Merlin fleet.*"

From UK waters the task group headed down to the Mediterranean where, after visiting Gibraltar, *Ark* entered Malta's Grand Harbour to contribute to the island's celebration of the sixtieth anniversary of Operation PEDESTAL. PEDESTAL was the name given to a World War II convoy that brought 32,000 tons of supplies to Malta enabling the island to hold out until the siege by Axis forces was lifted. *Ark*'s visit to Malta rekindled a connection for the Ship's Company last enjoyed in 1994 but it was also fitting that the aircraft carrier should represent the Royal Navy for the anniversary of the Santa Marija Convoy. On many occasions during the Second World War, the third *Ark Royal* had ferried aircraft to Malta and covered Malta-bound convoys. While returning to Gibraltar from one such mission, Operation PERPETUAL in 1941, *Ark* was torpedoed by the German submarine U-81. After a struggle against progressive flooding, the carrier capsized and sank. *Ark*'s contribution would later be recognised with her final Battle Honour "Malta Convoys 1941".

At the centre of ARGONAUT '02 were the two NATO amphibious exercises: DESTINED GLORY and ABELIA. Taking place in the littorals of Italy and the south of France they provided the first opportunity for nations involved in the European Amphibious Initiative to develop their operating procedures. During the exercises *Ark* worked with ships and submarines from a number of different nations, including her HAMDEN playmate, USS *George Washington*. The exercises provided the ideal opportunity to work up *Ark*'s amphibious command role and activity onboard was extremely busy with an additional two hundred staff from Commander UK Amphibious Forces and the US Amphibious Group 2 embarked to command and control the exercises. With all training objectives achieved, *Ark* headed for Barcelona for a final run ashore before Christmas, arriving on 28th October. The Ship's Company had five days to enjoy the Catalonian capital before returning to Portsmouth. The ship then underwent a maintenance period and preparations for the main effort of the following spring, as head of the UK Naval Task Group 2003 (NTG 03).

On 29th November 2002, Defence Minister Adam Ingram outlined plans for NTG 03, emphasizing that the deployment was routine and programmed every three years. The main focus of NTG 03 would be Exercise FLYING FISH, a multi-national exercise held under the Five Power Defence Agreement (FDPA) in the Asia Pacific Region. FLYING FISH would be hosted by Malaysia and was scheduled to take place off the Malaysia/Singapore peninsula, starting in June. The task group would also participate in a number of other multinational and bilateral exercises, with Egypt, India and Pakistan and visit over 25 countries pursuing Defence Diplomacy missions, supporting British interests abroad and demonstrating continuing commitment to the security of the Gulf and Asia Pacific regions. Promised visits included the Philippines, Brunei, China, Singapore, Japan and Malaysia, with the plum last leg going to HMS *Marlborough* which would visit Australia and New Zealand. The task group would be commanded by the Commander UK Maritime Forces, Rear Admiral Snelson, onboard *Ark* and would include HMS *Liverpool* as well as *Marlborough*, with support from RFA *Fort Victoria* and *Orangeleaf*. A Fleet submarine would also be assigned.

For *Ark*'s Ship's Company NTG 03 promised the longest and farthest deployment since OUTBACK in 1988 and the sense of anticipation was palpable amongst the young crew. All went on leave hoping against hope that the programme would stick to plan, but behind the scenes planning of another kind had gathered pace for an operation which offered little opportunity for banyans, runs ashore or postcards from tropical destinations. Codenamed "TELIC", those in the know quickly established somewhat wryly that it stood for "Tell Everyone Leave Is Cancelled". Preparations for the Gulf had to be understandably secretive, to protect both operational security and maintain political ambivalence. But this secrecy caused headaches at the tactical level of planning, since it meant excluding many who did not yet 'need to know', resulting, for example, in the refusal of stores depots to issue anything above peacetime stocks of spares.

When the Ship's Company returned from leave on 6th January 2003, it was clear that the following six months would offer a very different future from that envisaged in FLYING FISH. In the few days before sailing, *Ark* was a flurry of activity. Three days of continuous storing brought on dry, fresh and frozen provisions to fill every available nook and cranny onboard. The 'shopping list' included one million cigarettes, 144,000 bars of 'nutty', 2,000 cases of 'goffa' and 1,500 crates of beer. Ground equipment and trucks for the helicopters that would later arrive were brought into the hangar and workshops, as well as other vehicles - including the Captain's official Jaguar XK-12. A large number of weapons chacons also appeared for the use of the Royal Marines embarked military force. Personal, team and wholeship training was completed to hone fighting skills and remember the basics, like making a safe exit from Portsmouth for the Bridge navigation team. Engineering tests and trials proved that the ship, its sensors and weapons were fully operational and at a personal level, every member of the Ship's Company also had to test their respirator, bringing home to many the potential hazards they might yet face.

Amongst the activity there was still time for 'hearts and minds' as Captain Massey hosted a visit by the Lord Mayor of Leeds who had come onboard to wish the ship well and to present a wreath to be laid at the last resting place of *Ark* III. During the 61 years since *Ark* had been lost, it was universally thought that she had sunk 22 miles east of Europa Point, the southernmost tip of Gibraltar, but on 19th December 2002 a marine exploration company working for the BBC found the wreck some eight miles further east. At a depth of about 3,500 feet, *Ark Royal* lay in two sections: twenty metres of the bow had separated from the rest of the ship. A large debris field, which included the remains of the funnel and bridge island, parts of the ship that came loose as the carrier sank, and aircraft from the hangars, was located between the two hull sections. The pictures of the ghost of *Ark* III offered a poignant reminder of the 'perils of the sea'.

On 11th January 2003, *Ark Royal* sailed from Portsmouth, ostensibly still as the flagship of the long-planned NTG 03 headed for the Far East. Her task group had however grown significantly to include HMS *Ocean*, eleven more surface vessels and a Tomahawk-armed attack submarine, to underline the "clear and credible" threat of force that could be diverted to operational status at a moment's notice if Saddam Hussein continued to ignore the demands of the UN. Task force commander, Rear Admiral David Snelson, told the throng of news media on departure that the largest British naval deployment since the Falklands war represented just one part of the "jigsaw" of combat power. *"It is a classic use of maritime power. Having ships like aircraft carriers permits you to deploy considerable combat power on the high seas without necessarily having to bother host nations. There is no doubt that British forces are ready if they are needed."*

While the strategic deception of *Ark*'s routing was entirely justified, such uncertainties touched, not least, the families of those deploying. Flag-waving relatives and well-wishers packed the quayside as the carrier steamed out of harbour, nervously smiling and offering reassurances to one another that their loved ones would return safely. The thoughts of eighteen year old Operator Mechanic Angela Scales summed up what many of the young crew felt, *"I am looking forward to it. Obviously, you are aware of what is going on but no-one knows what is really going to happen and we could be back home in a few months. It is my first time at sea but I am not nervous."* For Leading Hand Chris Kent, the deployment meant he would miss the birth of his first child, *"I am quite gutted to be honest that I will not be there, but I guess that's life."*

Winning the 'hearts and minds' of the Ship's Company was especially important to maintain operational focus and morale. Captain Massey acknowledged that *"it felt odd to deploy for likely war, without any surety that Parliament or the man on the 'Clapham omnibus' would rally in support."* With BBC News 24 beamed relentlessly into every mess deck, and the personal connectivity afforded by the free emails, telephone and newspapers under the ship's Operational Welfare Package, the political context of TELIC was by no means a distant irrelevance for *Ark*'s sailors and Royal Marines, for whom protest marches and associated equivocation at home were significantly disconcerting. As the political conditions for UK's commitment were progressively chipped away to the 'worst-case' with no second UN Resolution and scarce coalition allies, Commanding Officers and Flags found it necessary to reiterate their personal conviction that this indeed was the right thing to be doing. Captain Massey had no doubts at all, but he recognised that some of his people, *"quite reasonably"*, did. Here, the moral courage of the chain of command, right to the very top, had to make the difference but Alan Massey knew he had the right team around him to do so. *"The ship was filled with men and women whose hard-won professional competence was more than matched by unquestioning moral commitment, enthusiasm and – above all – the humanity, humility and humour that most clearly distinguish the really great teams from the merely good. These things were everywhere in evidence: as much so in moments of relaxation, ribaldry and fun as in the long days of hard, repeated training; and eventually in combat itself. The whole team came together with an unshakeable sense of purpose and a determined will to win. And they needed precious little steerage from above."*

Ark's first destination was the Armament Depot at Glen Mallen in Scotland to load up war stocks of ammunition. Still in the strike carrier role but with the decision taken that she would not embark her FA-2s, *Ark*'s ammunitions stocks had to be adjusted to maximise the allowance for the Royal Marine by reducing air weapon holdings to a minimum sustainable level; and then topping up as far as possible with mortars, grenades, bullets and assault munitions. Another example of the restricted information flow which threatened progress was a failure initially to sanction adequate civilian overtime at the munitions facility, potentially delaying *Ark*'s deployment, but this was eventually resolved. On the final day of ammunitioning, on 15th January, COMATG, Commodore Miller embarked along with Delta Company of 40 Commando Royal Marines, 29 Commando Regiment Royal Artillery and the main ground party for 849 Squadron. The mobile sea training teams from FOST also came onboard to oversee an intensive work-up programme. *Ark* sailed from Glen Mallen on 16th January and reached the South West Approaches 24 hours later to conduct test firings of her weapons and decoy launchers, and then embark four Mk-7 ASaCs from

849 'A' Flight. Heading south through Biscay the following day, *Ark Royal* rendezvoused west of Portugal with HMS *Liverpool*, HMS *Ocean* and two more escorts, the *Type-42* destroyer HMS *Edinburgh* and the *Type-23* frigate HMS *Northumberland*. Assault Station training began in earnest once *Ark* was in company with *Ocean*; the two flat tops offering a convenient landing site for each others helicopters to practice the launch and recovery of Royal Marines commando units.

On 20th January HMS *Ark Royal* reached the Straits of Gibraltar and conducted the transit with HMS *Liverpool* in close company. The following morning *Ark* held its remembrance service over the war grave of *Ark* III; the wreath laid by Leading Stores Accountant Lucy Brown whose grand father Marine Thomas Brown was among the survivors of the sinking. That afternoon, five Chinooks from No.18 Squadron RAF embarked and *Ark* met up with another new task group ship, the tanker RFA *Oakleaf* to replenish fuel.

Over the next five days the task group headed east through the Mediterranean with *Ark* conducting familiarisation training for No.18 Squadron and the naval air units while the flag staff conducted contingency planning. Specialist chemical and biological defence training was also completed under the watchful eye of the FOST mobile team, culminating on 25th with a Chemical Exercise to prove that the protection organisation was in place and that the ship's citadel boundaries were intact. Two days later, *Ark* and the task group arrived at Cyprus from where increasingly sophisticated assault training was conducted which built up to a series of WADER exercises where marines were sent ashore.

As the two carriers worked up together off Cyprus, thoughts reasonably turned toward the detailed arrangements for the transition to war phase that would occur after the TELIC ships transited through the Suez Canal. There had been plenty of time for those embarked, particularly those not involved as yet in the planning process, to let thoughts wander to what lay ahead. Many in

3 Commando Brigade were already convinced that war was inevitable while some, many with previous experience of the policy of 'gunboat diplomacy', or 'poise' in modern parlance, were less so. Government denials that the deployment was anything other than a pre-planned exercise failed to impress an increasingly speculative media, some of whom were confident enough to predict the exact nature of future operations in southern Iraq. This façade had already been shattered by the announcement on 20th January by Geoff Hoon, the Secretary of State for Defence, that a major ground force, including the mobilisation of some reservists, centred on 1(UK) Division, equipped with Challenger II main battle tanks, armoured fighting vehicles and self-propelled guns was to be deployed. The force, drawn from units in UK and Germany would eventually total some 28,000 and include 16 (Air Assault) and 7 (Armoured) Brigades. Though diplomacy would continue right up to the commencement of hostilities, there was little doubt among those service personnel moving inexorably towards the Gulf that military operations were now a case of 'when' and not 'if'.

As the task group commanders soon found, there was no standard doctrine for readying for war, not least because one size could simply never fit all scenarios. Generic guidance existed, but much of it was out of date or lacked currency. Thus, Captain Massey and his senior colleagues found themselves with a *"nearly blank sheet of paper"* on which to prepare, but the upside of this - superbly exploited by Commodore Miller in particular - was the impetus to gather the ATG Commanding Officers together into a close-knit 'Band of Brothers'. On several occasions, the commanding officers teased out and talked through the transition-to-war issues, forming a best-practice strategy that had absolute relevance to the circumstances, and universal buy-in. Time was also made for the 'soft' preparations alongside the increasingly intensive combat training and mission rehearsal. These included pre-combat stress briefings; painstaking explanation of chemical and biological antidotes – *"a very tricky area"* given the historical suspicion of Gulf War syndrome; preservation of maximum normality and habitability alongside essential material war preparations; team briefings on the political-strategic context and inculcation of a 'safety-first' mindset. This early preparation meant that despite the pressures of the conflict these carefully considered, deliberate and consistently applied measures helped ensure that every ship was in broadly the same posture - materially, physically and psychologically - as they approached the 'start-line'.

On 31st January, *Ark*'s task group left Cyprus and headed south toward the Port Said waiting area to make the onward transit through the Suez Canal. The transit provided an opportunity for a task group photo opportunity after which *Liverpool* surged ahead to pick up the Naval Attaché to CAIRO and act as a communications relay with the Suez Canal Authority. The American SSN USS *Montpelier* came under the protection of the surface ships to pass into the Red Sea and the task group commenced transit overnight in four distinct groups. All units cleared the Canal by mid afternoon the following day without incident to commence the passage down the Gulf of Suez, with *Liverpool* providing force protection to USS *Montpelier* during her surface transit toward the deeper water she needed in which to dive. The TELIC ships now came under the operational control of the UK Maritime Component Commander, Rear Admiral Snelson, accordingly chopping TACON from TG 342.01 to TG 330.01, with *Ark* designated TU 330.01.01.

Over the next few days the task group units transited south through the Red Sea, some taking on additional tasking to protect UK-flagged merchant shipping, while others had the opportunity to exploit the good weather for rest days and flight deck BBQs. As the ship moved toward the increasing certainty of combat operations, the ship's senior leadership knew how important it was to maintain an atmosphere of normality on board. Yes, the Ship's Company and embarked forces had to prepare seriously for battle, and the threats and risks would be real enough, but the transition-to-war process needed to be measured, carefully balanced and sensibly paced. *Ark*'s department heads took great care to keep familiar routines in place while a varied assortment of 'events', from fitness circuits and aerobics training several times a day, film nights, band concerts, quizzes, quarterdeck church services, to Divisional briefs and meetings were programmed; all designed to break the monotony.

On 4th February *Ark* reached Bab Al-Mandeb, to begin the transit north east through the Gulf of Aden and then northwest through the Gulf of Oman toward the Straits of Hormuz. The waters off Oman provided a useful opportunity for operational training with the pro-Western Sultanate offering ranges and facilities ashore to conduct naval fire support, helicopter landings and amphibious operations. By 9th February all the forward units were in position south east of the Straits of Hormuz to make an overnight transit into the Persian Gulf. The transit did not go entirely smoothly as RFA *Brambleleaf* suffered a propulsion failure requiring HMS *York* to stand off while assistance was given. Further back, RFA *Orangeleaf*, delayed by sand storms at Port Said finally made her way through the Suez Canal, while RFA *Argus* and HMS *Marlborough* stopped at Salalah in Oman.

For the next few days *Ark* operated from the SEAHAWK exercise areas off the United Arab Emirates conducting Offload and Environmental training for the tailored air group, while the escorts practiced boarding operations and established the normal routines for force protection and AAW coverage in the Northern Arabian Gulf (NAG). With most units in theatre by Valentine's Day 2003, the full scale of the achievement in delivering the task group ready to operate became apparent. *Ocean* had been rushed through her docking and work-up. *Ark* had been hastily converted from fixed-wing strike carrier to Landing Platform Helicopter. Seventy five percent of an increasingly fragile RFA flotilla had been mobilised, and just enough escorts and people regenerated from the blight caused by the commitment to cover the fire fighters' dispute during Operation FRESCO to assemble a coherent, mutually supportive and sustainable task group for amphibious combat operations. This achievement could not be underestimated. The task group was ready to go, as ordered, on 15th February, more than five weeks ahead of the eventual assault date. The ATG was the first UK combat formation into theatre; integrating swiftly with other allies and with time to turn generic training into mission-specific, acclimatised combat readiness.

The UK maritime component for Operation TELIC amounted to just over thirty Royal Navy, Royal Fleet Auxiliary, and charter ships, with 45 embarked helicopters. Rear Admiral David Snelson's tasks as the UK Maritime Component Commander ashore included the effective integration, coordination and enabling of these units to form a coherent and efficient task force alongside some sixty US warships and 35 other coalition naval units. This seemed to go extraordinarily well, but the critical success factor was ensuring the Americans were integrated to maintain effective command and control so that planning functions were achieved seamlessly. The Royal Navy had long understood that in modern naval operations the ability to communicate and interoperate with US forces, largely on their terms, was critical to maintain a foothold. This was primarily why UK carriers routinely operated on the eastern seaboard participating in US-led exercises and why they a plethora of US-centric communications and planning systems; each one hard won from the Americans by demonstrating a commitment to cooperate. The TELIC ATG was the most 'network-enabled' UK task group ever, whose real-time access to other nations' communications and information systems was a battle-winning success. Two key revelations were the immensely powerful data LINK 16 network, with its extraordinary speed, accuracy and information content; and the new prevalence of internet-style chat rooms, where coalition Warfare Officers ran the tactical picture and battle, at lightning speed and in complete security. Captain Massey recognised that the speed of this new technology demanded a greater degree of trust in and delegation to the junior officers in his Operations Room and the planning teams, if they were to keep ahead of the bow wave of information that continually washed over the ship. Gone were the days where all signals would be printed and placed on a board by the Yeoman for the Captain to peruse at his leisure. Mission Command, normally a feature of inter task-group units, now became a routine feature of operations within each unit.

For the remainder of February, *Ark* and the other task group units settled into a routine of operational, maintenance and replenishment days while continuing the training build-up. The confined waters of the NAG had to be very carefully managed to avoid conflicts between coalition forces and in particular the American super carriers operating numerous fast jet sorties. The whole area was parcelled up into task-specific boxes or national operating areas between which units transited, while the RFAs maintained a constant resupply shuttle between Jebel Ali, Salalah and the NAG. Toward the end of February the task units anchored off Kuwait within the western area of the Carrier Operating Area-1 to conduct the first large scale amphibious landing exercise, known appropriately as the 'Mother of All Rehearsals'. Reflecting the multinational construct of the force, *Ark* chopped operational control temporarily to come under CTF 51, Rear Admiral Marsh USN, Commander of the Third Amphibious Group, who visited the ship on 28th.

March opened with a visit by the Conservative shadow defence spokesman Ian Duncan-Smith accompanied by the Chief of Defence Staff, Admiral Michael Boyce. For the following two days, *Ark* enjoyed a much-needed stand-down, which included a successful and lively Royal Marine band concert during the first evening. The ship was able to relax its damage control state, from the restrictive '2-Y' to the normal peacetime cruising state '3-X'. This was a subtle but enormously important gesture to a tired Ship's Company whose performance and spirit had been excellent after seven weeks at sea, but which Captain Massey knew he could not afford to take for granted. As *Ark* relaxed slightly, seasonal bad weather in the Gulf, characterised by high winds, poor visibility and choppy seas graphically demonstrated the vulnerability of the amphibious assets to stoppages in their logistic supply line. It seemed that when the weather was poor everything ground to a halt.

The return from the stand-off saw *Ark* once again raise its operational tempo to achieve an appropriate level of capability, readiness and mindset for live operations. Hampered by not having a clear 'D' Day to work toward the key was to maintain a ramp-up of expectations and training levels, but without 'peaking' too early. Useful interaction with US F-18s allowed the engineers to optimise weapon systems and sensors, while everyone sensed that the crew needed to regain the level of operational concentration required for the final rehearsals and preparations for combat operations. Results from the early training serials showed that the relaxed tempo of the stand-off had caused many minds to drift from the imminent second 'Mother of All Rehearsals', final logistic consolidation and maintenance serials. Damage control training was adjusted to refresh basic skills of the Ship's Company as well as identifying a logical sequence of events exercising whole ship responses to major threats and damage. With only a matter of days remaining before the genuine reality of live operations, the emphasis shifted to planning for final weapon system confidence checks and fine-tuning of the Assault Organisation to support the Landing Force tactical movements.

The 6th of March provided a valuable day of

Phalanx and gunnery serials with a simulated air defence exercise against the primary theatre threats, while also exercising unit Mine Threat Warning measures. The tempo could not be maintained however as MOAR2 had to be postponed due to sandstorms while congestion of the RAS corridors - known as the 'Gasoline Alleys' - further complicated the geographical movement of the ship between the rehearsal area and the fall-back position to offload. Concern began to grow that Delta Company had not exercised in their anticipated operational role, having missed both rehearsals. Another headache for the ship's team was how to respond to an edict from MoD requiring all respirators to be retested using new test equipment. Such a directive could only cause alarm to the troops, to the exclusion of things that were operationally far more important and useful as the ship prepared for combat. Similar edicts to make sure every service rifle came with a cleaning manual, and procrastination over the policy on the use of chemical and biological protection measures suggested indecision. Frustrated by the impact of these policies on the ground, Captain Massey reflected tersely that it was *"difficult to stop your people from panic, when your upper echelons are apparently paralysed by it."*

The second MOAR serial eventually took place on 8th March but, as feared, Delta Company received little benefit from it and time was running out to programme another opportunity to integrate them fully. In a clear signal that events were about to escalate, the first activation of communications restrictions under the 'River City State' policy came into force overnight on 8th and 9th by all units. River City State restrictions cut off email and personal telephone communications for the Ship's Company at critical operational points so that the release of sensitive information could be controlled. It was never popular to invoke, but nevertheless necessary to ensure operational security.

As the flagship, HMS *Ark Royal* was the perennial attraction for the panoply of media outlets aiming to find the scoop story among the task group. *Ark* hosted three categories: a TV documentary team for eleven weeks; embedded journalists for about four weeks; and the usual mixed bag that would 'parachute in' for one-off media events. They all played a part in the ship's preparations for war, and specifically in shaping the moral battlespace. The Ship's Company and command teams, unused to such intrusion, were reticent to recognise the 'opportunity' provided by the media amidst the perceived 'threat' and many treated them with suspicion and even hostility. More and better media training was needed if this important outlet was to be understood at all levels. Invariably the 24 hour 'parachutists' seeking the fast headline caused the greatest mischief, if sometimes inadvertently. The main event of 13th March was undoubtedly the Press Conference held onboard during the morning, where the stage management was essential to shape the impression gained by the members or the media as well as the overt messages passed. At the last minute, *Ark* could not afford to show any sign of indecision or ill-preparedness, given the potential impact edited and re-edited short news clips might have where context could easily be lost. The presence of the embedded BBC/ITN News teams gave the ship a sense of immediate impact back to the UK. Being able to see BBC News 24 live reports onboard was an example of how issues could be instantly conveyed, helping to provide positive feedback to the Ship's Company on how they were being perceived at home.

By the middle of March almost every aspect of *Ark*'s military capability had been tested, developed, retested and honed, but none more so than the airborne surveillance and control capability provided by 849 'A' Flight's Mk-7 Sea Kings. The air crews had worked tirelessly to develop their LINK 16 capability, well beyond its designed limits, into a true joint asset with users ashore enthusiastically embracing the enhanced situational awareness that it provided. It was entirely in 849's nature: even the newest, youngest members of the Squadron were instantly imbued with the same desire for that winning professional edge. To Captain Massey, it was exciting to see how, with almost every new sortie from *Ark*'s deck, the 849 crews worked innovatively to push the boundaries of what the Mk-7 could bring to the ship and the wider task group. Pride in their achievement was palpable, and widely shared; *"even 'Wings', an anti-submarine helicopter observer, seemed just about willing to admit that 849 were onto something very special with their swiftly evolving warfare capability."*

HMS *Ark Royal* by this time was also now committed to a final configuration of material state and training preparations, and in Captain Massey's assessment his Ship's Company was fully ready for combat operations. A regime of 'tripwire' 36 hour readiness checks, top-up briefings for NBCD and the developing geo-political and tactical situations would be maintained, but the emphasis now was firmly on maintaining the ships present state and continuing logistic consolidation with training on-the-watch. The Ship's Company would not have long to wait.

The Heads of State meeting in the Azores on 16th March 2003 and the subsequent rhetoric from President Bush gave a clear sign that combat operations were imminent. Captain Massey ordered a Clear Lower Deck of his Ship's Company to establish a common baseline of awareness of the evening's events in the Azores, beamed live via TV, and to focus collective minds on the task ahead. There was now a tangible sense of imminent activity amongst Massey's crew, and he was impressed by the manner in which all ranks were well informed, hungry for information and paid attention to the readily available news coverage. They watched almost in real time as the pace of events suddenly quickened in response to the collapse of the diplomatic process and the withdrawal of the draft second UN resolution the following day.

All elements of 3 Commando Brigade were now as equally prepared as the ATG ships and the majority of units moved ashore to Assembly Areas close to the Iraqi border. The decision not to launch from the amphibious ships because of a significant inshore mine and coastal radar threat was a disappointment, not least because the sortie times to the Al Faw from the Kuwaiti Assembly Areas were much longer than those from the ships. Only Delta Company 40 Commando embarked in *Ark* would launch direct from sea to objective; as Captain Massey had told the Ship's Company upon arriving in theatre, *"my ship is now a weapons delivery platform and Delta Company is the weapon."* For the Officer Commanding Delta Company, Major Matt Pierson, he understood the value of the relationship that his men had formed with the ship. *"The Ark gave us as much as she could and accepted our need to train as a land force, not an embarked military force during ship's defence exercises. Space and facilities were fiercely competed for, but the willingness to help was never in doubt. What we needed, in expertise or kit, she gave...although the Buffer is probably still not aware of her 'generosity'. When we flew into Al Faw we were absolutely ready and the Ark had much to be thanked for."*

With all the Commando units now in their assembly areas and final confirmatory orders passed, there appeared to be a pause around 18th March while the final momentous decisions were taken in Washington and London. To the men of 3 Commando Brigade, whether sat on their equipment in the Kuwait desert, or lying on their bunk onboard *Ark*, quietly reflecting on what lay ahead, there was a sense of surreal inevitability. The odd joke was cracked to relieve tension but, in the main, most people kept their own counsel and pondered what the next twenty four hours would bring.

The maritime battle staff had astutely 'booked' *Ark*'s and *Ocean*'s operating areas far in advance, with the ATG 'heavies' in shallow water screened by the escorts, with the assault lanes reaching only a few miles off shore. This would be their operating position for a considerable period after the first shots were fired, requiring the Merlins of 814 Squadron in RFA *Fort Victoria*, supported by tireless searching and probing by Lynx helicopters from the escorts, to maintain a continuous and accurate surface picture to guard against attack. Saddam attempted some form of pre-emptive action on the evening of 18th March when a mass of 58 dhows were driven forcibly southward out of the Khor Abd Allah waterway. This swarm absorbed the full attention of the escorts in the northern area, including *Marlborough* and *Chatham*, while a lone Iraqi tug slipped away out of continuous tracking, somewhere across the launch lanes. Subsequent search operations by the British minehunters verified that no mines had been sown; nevertheless the incident provided a salutary lesson on the overarching need to maintain situational awareness and force protection measures.

The task group's Notice to Execute was reduced to four hours on 18th March and *Ark*'s Chinooks moved ashore in anticipation of action. Captain Massey addressed the Ship's Company, during Action Stations, of the imminence of conflict. Although a few expressed surprise, the overall mood remained very positive; the majority sweeping along the remainder in their sense of focus and purpose. At 21:00 local time on 19th March HMS *Ark Royal* chopped tactical control to come under the US commander, adopting agreed TELIC rules of engagement to activate OPLAN 1003V. Captain Massey recorded in his personal diary, *"So this is it – and we are ready for anything."*

The coalition military campaign began in the early hours of 20th March 2003, some ninety minutes after the expiry of a US ultimatum for Saddam Hussein to leave Iraq. Following intelligence about the location of senior members of the Iraqi leadership, US aircraft and cruise missiles struck regime targets around Baghdad. *Ark*'s crew witnessed the missiles launch from adjacent American cruisers and woke up to the reality that their participation would very shortly be called upon. Iraqi forces responded the following afternoon by launching a barrage of Theatre Ballistic Missiles against targets in Kuwait, forcing coalition troops and Kuwaiti civilians to don protective clothing as a precaution. *Ark* came to Action Stations and the rapid, efficient and thoroughly focussed response of the Ship's Company re-stated the confidence of Captain Massey in their war-fighting attitude. The start of operations had been eerily quiet for the ship but the Iraqi response provided the impetus to get adrenalin and concentration properly flowing. *Ark*'s orders arrived just as the Ship's Company was stood down. The assault mission onto the Al Faw peninsula was to start late evening, with Delta Company due to land approximately three hours after zero-hour. The crew therefore had time to rest, eat and focus on the forthcoming night's events. Amid the pause, a message was received from Her Majesty The Queen that was passed immediately to the mess decks: *"At this difficult moment in our nation's history, I would like to express my pride in you, the British service and civilian personnel deployed in the Gulf and in the vital supporting roles in this country and further afield. I have every confidence in your professionalism and commitment as you face the challenges before you. Especially for those of you now waiting to go into action, may your mission be swift and decisive, your courage steady and true and your conduct in the highest traditions of the service both in waging war and bringing peace. My thoughts are with you all and with your families and friends who wait at home for news and pray for your safe return."*

At 22:00 (local) on 20th March 2003, the shore elements of 3 Commando Brigade commenced the assault of the Al Faw peninsula in southern Iraq. Three Brigade's landing marked the first opposed helicopter assault by British forces since the Suez Crisis of 1956, and theirs were the first conventional coalition boots on Iraq's territory. Intelligence reports indicated that the pre-planned positions were occupied with a company-strength of Iraqi forces supported by some armoured vehicles. This offered some concern to the Marines landing but there was a good degree of confidence that the pre-assault fire missions would neutralise much of the threat and enable them to close quickly with any remaining defenders. The fires were provided by a four-ship gun line comprising HMS *Chatham*, HMS *Marlborough*, HMS *Richmond* and HMAS *Anzac*, in the first naval fire support mission since the Falklands conflict, and combined UK/US shore artillery from the Offensive Support Group (OSG) on Bubiyan Island off the coast of Kuwait. The witheringly effective Naval Fire Support kept Iraqi heads down while the Marines got ashore. The threat of anti-aircraft artillery and surface to air systems understandably focussed the attention of the 845 and No.18 Squadron helicopter pilots. Their Sea Kings and Chinooks were extremely heavily laden and cumbersome, and conditions for takeoff from the assembly areas and much of the run in to the objectives were appalling. Nevertheless with the lead elements already on their objectives, sorties would have to be flown throughout the night to ensure initial gains were consolidated. Through the outstanding skill of the pilots, and not a little luck, every sortie achieved its objective and safely extracted. This first conventional action had strategic significance; given the importance of establishing early ascendancy over the enemy and, critically, in preventing a potential environmental disaster were the Iraqis to destroy the oil pipelines and refinery equipment.

Despite the fire support and pre-emptive insertion of Special Forces to secure and mark the Landing Zones (LZs), they remained "hot" and it was vital that units reached and secured their specific points before the enemy could react and threaten the helicopters as they came in to land. Marines fanned out from each LZ as they orientated themselves and began to move towards their objectives. Most sank ankle-deep into mud due to the weight of their 100-lb bergens as they tried to move ashore, while facing sporadic small arms fire from numerous directions. Each commando troop located the source of the enemy fire and then mounted assaults against them. Contact reports began to come in thick and fast to the Commando Tactical HQ and a number of indirect fire and close air support missions were called in to neutralise in-depth defensive positions. The first prisoners of war appeared almost immediately adding to the early confusion. The speed and violence of the commando assault had had the desired effect, shattering the enemy's cohesion, command structure and will to fight. Despite a number of the oil installations having been prepared for demolition, all were taken intact.

At one minute after midnight on 21st March 2003, HMS *Ark Royal* raised her battle ensign and came to Action Stations to begin combat operations against Iraq. A rolling delay to the launch time of Delta Company came into force as the ship awaited confirmation of progress ashore, but finally clearance was received to begin the operation. The assault organisation worked seamlessly to offload the marines throughout the night. Several delays were encountered due to unsuitability of the landing site and variable progress ashore, which protracted the offload, but by 06:00 the embarked forces had been cleared ashore and *Ark* was able to revert to defence watches. Captain Massey's unintended yet aggressive policy of 'Train hard, Fight Easy' had been unequivocally proved; the team pushing through the night to get Delta Company ashore while maintaining the maritime surface picture. The principal worry for *Ark* was the integrity and effectiveness of the 'Ring of Steel' to her northern flank, since placed so close to the shore, she was under constant threat from mines, fast attack craft and shore bombardment. The Australian amphibious command ship HMAS *Kanimbla* took on the primary role of force protection, carrying out Maritime Interdiction Operations, launching round-the-clock multinational boarding parties against suspect Iraqi vessels in the Khor Abd Allah

[page 111]
HMS *Ark Royal* enters Portsmouth
following her refit, 31st August 2001.
(Crown Copyright/MoD 2001)

(page 111)
814 NAS embark with Merlin HM-1s in HMS *Ark Royal* for aviation trials. 800 NAS with Sea Harrier FA-2s are already embarked.
(Crown Copyright/MoD 2001)

(page 112)
HM Queen Elizabeth the Queen Mother attends the
Rededication of HMS Ark Royal, 22nd November 2001.
Her Majesty is escorted by Captain David Snelson and
Lieutenant Commander Jerry Kyd
(Crown Copyright/MoD 2001)

(page 113)
Captain David Snelson forms part of the escort procession at state funeral of HM The Queen Mother, 9th April 2002. (Crown Copyright/MoD 2002)

(page 115)
COMAO Package of No.1 Squadron Harrier GR-7 and 800 NAS Sea Harrier
FA-2 aircraft refuel in-flight from an RAF VC-10 tanker.
(Crown Copyright/MoD 2002)

(page 116)
HMS *Ark Royal* in the Straits of Gibraltar, May 2002.
(Crown Copyright/MoD 2002)

(page 116)
HMS *Ark Royal*, with 801 and 814 NAS embarked, in close company with
USS *Underwood* during DYNAMIC MIX '02, May 2002.
ITS *Zeffiro*, HMS *Cardiff* and HMS *Chatham* are on the horizon
(Crown Copyright/MoD 2002)

(page 116)
HMS *Ark Royal* escorted by
HMS *Chatham* during
DYNAMIC MIX '02, May 2002.
(Crown Copyright/MoD 2002)

814 NAS Merlin HM-1 helicopters operating from HMS *Ark Royal* 2002. *(Crown Copyright/MoD 2002)*

(page 116)
800 NAS flypast during Families Day
onboard HMS *Ark Royal*, 20th June 2002.
(Crown Copyright/MoD 2002)

(page 116)
The Queen and the Duke of Edinburgh onboard
HMS *Ark Royal* to celebrate Her Majesty's
Golden Jubilee 27th June 2002.
(*Crown Copyright/MoD 2002*)

(page 129)
HMS *Ark Royal* in company with HNLMS *Rotterdam* (back) and FS *Foudre* (middle) during Exercise ABELIA, October 2002.

(Crown Copyright/MoD 2002)

(page 131)
HMS *Ark Royal* sails from Glen Mallen having
loaded war stocks of ammunition in preparation for
Operation TELIC, 16th January 2003.
(Crown Copyright/MoD 2003)

(page 116)
Four 849 'A' Fight Sea King ASaC embark in HMS *Ark Royal* in the South West Approaches, 17th January 2003.
(Crown Copyright/MoD 2003)

(page 131)
No.18 Squadron Chinook and 845 NAS Sea King Mk4 conduct familiarization training onboard HMS *Ark Royal* during passage through eastern Mediterranean, 23rd January 2003.
(Crown Copyright/MoD 2003)

(page 131)
Marines from Delta Company 40 Commando
Royal Marines conduct weapons training
onboard HMS *Ark Royal* during Mediterranean
passage, January 2003.
(Crown Copyright/MoD 2003)

(page 132)
HMS *Ark Royal* transits the Suez Canal,
2nd February 2003.
(Crown Copyright/MoD 2003)

(page 135)
HMS *Ark Royal*, carrying weather-beaten Chinooks of
No.18 Squadron, in company with HMS *Ocean* in the
Northern Arabian Gulf, March 2003.
(Crown Copyright/MoD 2003)

(page 138)
Delta Company 40 Commando Royal Marines load into
Sea Kings from 845 NAS to begin the night assault on
the Al Faw Peninsula 21st March 2003.
(Crown Copyright/MoD 2003)

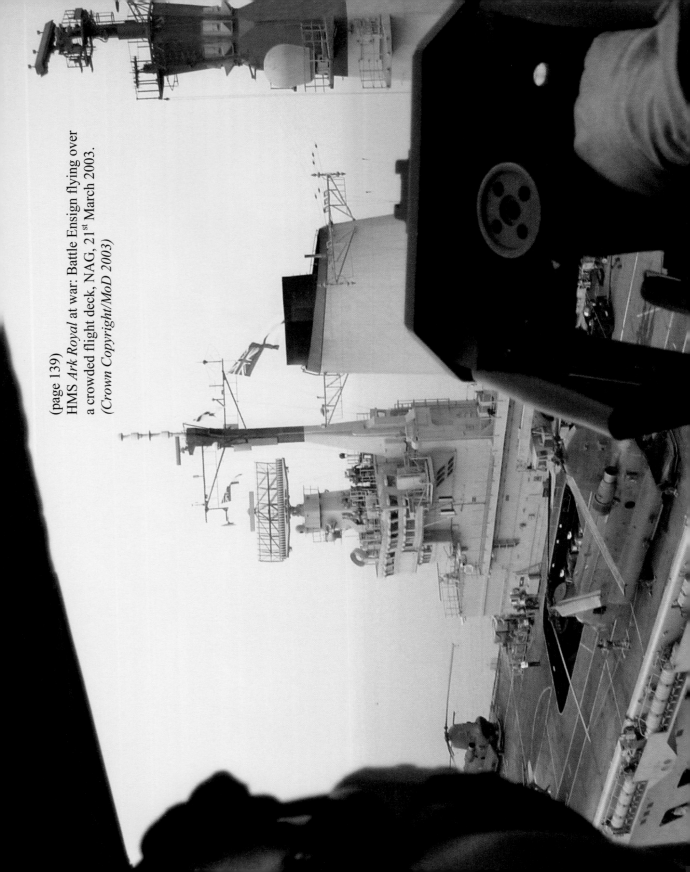

(page 139)
HMS *Ark Royal* at war: Battle Ensign flying over
a crowded flight deck, NAG, 21st March 2003.
(Crown Copyright/MoD 2003)

(page 139)
Royal Marines of 3 Commando Brigade establish a foothold on the Al Faw Peninsular 21st/22nd March 2003.
(Crown Copyright/MoD 2003)

(page 140)
The eyes of the task group: Sea King ASaC XV672 of 849 'A'
Flight patrolling the NAG: HMS *Richmond* in the background.
(Crown Copyright/MoD 2003)

(page 142)
820 NAS conducting Vertrep between
HMS *Ark Royal* and RFA *Fort Austin*,
while *Ark* continued to support 3 Cdo
Bde ashore, April 2003.
(Crown Copyright/MoD 2003)

(page 142)
HMS *Ark Royal* with 820 NAS embarked from RFA *Fort Austin* transits west through the Mediterranean having been released from TELIC duties, 11th April 2003.
(Crown Copyright/MoD 2003)

(page 142)
800 NAS, left in UK during TELIC, rejoin HMS *Ark Royal* at Palma Majorca on the journey home, 5th May 2003.
(Crown Copyright/MoD 2003)

(page 142)
HMS *Ark Royal*'s triumphant homecoming to Portsmouth, 17th May 2003.
(Crown Copyright/MoD 2003)

(page 153)
HMS *Ark Royal* arrives at Amsterdam, 15th November 2004 having been delayed in the North Sea by gales.
(Crown Copyright/MoD 2004)

(page 153)
HMS *Ark Royal* Ship's Company exercising the
Freedom of the City of Leeds, 21st November 2004.
(Crown Copyright/MoD 2004)

(page 155)
Harrier GR-9 aviation trials, February 2004.
(Crown Copyright/MoD 2004)

(page 155)
HMS *Ark Royal* berthed at Hamburg,
11th-15th March 2004.
(Crown Copyright/MoD 2004)

(page 155)
Last launch of a Sea Harrier from HMS *Ark Royal*,
flown by Lt Cdr Phil Mould RN 800 NAS,
17th March 2004.
(Crown Copyright/MoD 2004)

(page 156)
Out in style – ZD613 in unique
livery to mark the disbandment of
800 NAS, goes vertical flown by the
Squadron CO, Cdr Paul Stone RN.
(Crown Copyright/MoD 2004)

waterway. The mine threat was very real: two boats from *Kanimbla* intercepted and boarded two Iraqi mine laying vessels which were found to be carrying both World War I vintage drift mines and state-of-the-art Italian Manta acoustic mines. The detection of a possible mine by *Fort Victoria* on the evening of the landings added to the feeling of exposure amongst the mission essential units, especially with the escorts committed to NFS duties in the far northern NAG, depriving the task group of their sensor and weapon capabilities for force protection.

Five hours after 40 Commando's insertion they were secure on the Al Faw with, remarkably, no serious casualties, even from unexpected small arms fire encountered from across the Shatt-Al-Arab waterway in Iran. The Marines now dug in and set up anti-armour weapons in preparation for the expected counter attack coming south from Basrah. Meanwhile, a few miles away, things were not going to plan for 42 Commando. Having waited in the assembly area they had embarked in USMC helicopters to deploy to the north of 40 Commando and establish a blocking position to prevent the expected move south of Iraqi armour and reinforcements. Flying conditions were marginal. Tragically, shortly after take-off, a USMC Sea Knight helicopter crashed killing the four-man crew and eight members of the Brigade Recce Force. The insertion was immediately aborted while 42 Commando regrouped. 40 Commando appeared increasingly isolated. Within a few hours, 42 Commando was reloaded and flying forward, poignantly over the still smouldering crash site en route to the Al Faw. The sight provided a grim reminder, if any were needed, of the reality of war.

42 Commando landed and immediately spread out to re-designated positions to prevent the infiltration of Iraqi forces. The marines were immediately in contact with Iraqi forces encountering some spirited but thankfully ineffective resistance as they moved forward. Professionalism, sound battle discipline, a willingness to close with the enemy and a good degree of luck prevented any friendly casualties. Extremely accurate artillery fire from Iraqi positions threatened the advance but the nature of the terrain meant its location could be quickly established and the guns neutralized with counter-battery fire from the OSG and US Close Air Support. Even given the massive weight of coalition air power, and the fantastically comprehensive daily Air Tasking Order, Captain Massey reflected later that UK forces *"really could have done with some of our own embarked Harriers for responsive, close air support on the Al-Faw - and even the Sea Harrier FA-2 would have more than adequately met the need. A UK CVS in direct support of the ATG would have made a big difference."*

As 42 Commando established itself, the main US Marine force, the 15th Marine Expeditionary Unit crossed the Kuwait-Iraq border and move around the town of Umm Qasr. Their objective was to secure this critical port area to enable the flow of humanitarian aid to begin as early as possible through the deep-water port facility. Resistance was fairly light. Though minor gun fire and some harassing artillery continued throughout the day, the Al Faw was now relatively secure and one of the strategic aims of the coalition, the protection of the vital oil infrastructure, had been achieved. By the late evening of 21st March, less than 24 hours after launching, the Brigade had established a significant footprint inside southern Iraq.

Aside from landing Delta Company, *Ark Royal*'s other key battle-winning role was to build an accurate joint land picture, using 849's ASaCs and it wasn't widely understood at the time just how important their contribution was. The ASaC's major and unique task at the critical early stages of the assault was to maintain a continuous airborne radar watch for enemy movements towards the Marines, in order both to provide advance warning to the Land Headquarters ashore and to direct other British attack forces to cut the enemy off. The

"Red Rats" did this with stunning and unprecedented success, the crews pushing the aircraft's mission system to its newly-defined limits while flying round the clock in sometimes tricky conditions and congested airspace. They had a single, unswerving aim: to look after their comrades on the ground. It was while conducting this vital task that tragedy struck.

At 04:22 on 22nd March, Sea King XV650 call-sign "Red Rat 35" launched from *Ark*'s deck to take over the airborne surveillance duty from Sea King XV704 call sign "Red Rat 34". The aircraft were flying three hour sorties which included a thirty minute handover window, with the handover normally taking place inside the operational area to ensure seamless surveillance was maintained. However, XV650's launch was delayed due to a technical problem on *Ark*'s deck and XV704 had already withdrawn to begin her return to 'mother'. Operational airspace management required both aircraft to transit west to a safe area to deconflict with other coalition airborne activity. At approximately 04:24 both aircraft called 'visual' in response to air traffic control instructions from Homer in *Ark*'s Operations Room, confirming that each aircraft could see the other. However, ninety seconds later approximately five miles from *Ark*, "Red Rat 34" and "Red Rat 35" collided head-on. Rescue boats were launched immediately and within seven minutes a Merlin from 814 Squadron was on scene, but it was clear that there could be no survivors. Lieutenants Andy Wilson, Phil West and Marc Lawrence in XV650, and Lieutenants Philip Green, Antony King, James Williams and Tom Adams USN in XV704 lost their lives in the collision.

The crash came as a "*shattering, unimaginably awful blow*", Captain Massey recalled. "*At a stroke, we lost seven of our finest, most dedicated young airmen, causing a shock wave which – although we perhaps even underestimated its effect at the time – reverberated through every ship of the task group, and indeed through the whole of the deployed British contingent in the area. My own crew in Ark will never forget the personal impact of that moment, and the effect it had on us in the hours and days that followed. The sudden loss of close colleagues and friends is not something for which you can readily prepare or train in advance: there is no 'right' formula, and I suspect it will always come down to individual strength of character, spirit and heart. But this was a very, very tough time for the ship. And we could not even begin to imagine what it must have been like for the families: they were constantly in our minds, but frustratingly and painfully beyond our practical reach.*"

In the end, focus on the mission became "*a kind of all-consuming therapy, with an intensely personal edge*" as everyone onboard pushed on to complete the task. 849 Squadron insisted on getting their remaining aircraft back into the air as quickly as possible and theirs became the primary mission as *Ark* moved from the assault phase to sustainment. The "Red Rats" were reactively tasked on 25th March to fix the position of enemy armour moving south from Basrah, which was then subsequently engaged with Lynx helicopters armed with TOW missiles, flown from HMS *Ocean*. This combination of surveillance and firepower lifted the atmosphere onboard *Ark*, reinforcing that there was still work to do.

Following the disembarkation of 40 Commando, *Ark*'s priority moved to support the troops ashore but discussion quickly turned to her withdrawal from theatre. Having already landed its Chinooks, No.18 Squadron offloaded their remaining equipment and personnel from 23rd March to set up an operating base at Ali al Salem. The squadron had been onboard *Ark* for over sixty days and the ship was sad to see it go. With helicopter assets at a premium, the offload was completed by sea using the ship's crane to transfer equipment and stores to the MV *Passat* which rafted up alongside for two days.

Draft proposals from Rear Admiral Snelson on 26th March considered extracting the Amphibious Task Group and both the immediate and medium term implications were staffed over the next few days, with the specialist teams in both *Ark Royal* and *Ocean* taking the lead in the deliberations. Some of the finer details of the disengagement included considering the continued viability of stationing the 'flat tops' so far up-threat; how best to continue supporting 849 'A' Flight operations; the role of the helicopters still embarked in *Ocean* as the land campaign moved quickly northward away from the coast, and the transfer of the ground force's bulk ammunition still onboard *Ark* and *Ocean*, either to ashore or more likely to the RFAs. The residual combat mission for both ships was largely reactive, such as 849's tasking in Basrah supporting anti-armour sorties. The joint view from sea was that the residue of the helicopters from 845 and 847 Squadrons embarked in *Ocean* should swiftly move ashore and that onboard stocks of Landing Force ammunition and stores should be released. The four-star commands back in UK could then determine how and when both ships should be withdrawn from theatre to regenerate their core roles. *Ocean* would resume her part in the Amphibious Ready Group, while *Ark* reconfigured back to the high readiness strike carrier role and either continued east to pick up her NTG 03 programme, or headed west to home. The timing of these decisions was particularly sensitive; too early while bitter fighting was still going on could undermine the maritime contribution and its credibility among the 'joint' community, while waiting too long would diminish the operational effectiveness of both units.

The early gains on the Al Faw peninsula and in the Rumaylah oilfields by UK and US forces were pressed home. Within four days of landing, UK forces had taken Basrah's airport, despite encountering significant resistance and begun expanding their area of control in the surrounding region. After several days of raids, British troops entered the town of As Zubayr, southwest of Basrah and on 6th April 2003, British Commanders judged that conditions were right to enter Basrah itself in strength. Elements of 3 Commando, 16 (Air Assault) and 7 (Armoured) Brigades launched assaults from three directions, encountering only patchy resistance and stormed the Ba'ath Party headquarters. Careful timing minimised casualties on both sides and the UK forces were welcomed by the local people.

With the eastern flank secured to prevent any Iraqi counter attack of the supply routes north, US forces could push forward to Baghdad. The speed of advance was remarkable: by the fourth day the US Army was at An Najaf, less than sixty miles from Baghdad, while US Marines were pressing north along a different route towards Al Kut. After several days of consolidating their position while attacking Iraqi forces with artillery and aircraft, US forces engaged the Republican Guard divisions around Baghdad. By 4th April they had seized the city outskirts, including the International Airport, and began to make successful forays within the city boundaries. Four days later they secured the city approaches and took up positions in central Baghdad overnight for the first time. On 9th April 2003 crowds gathered in the centre of the city to welcome coalition forces and destroy symbols of the old regime. By now the west and north of Iraq had largely been secured, and a few days later the northern cities of Tikrit, Mosul and Kirkuk fell to coalition troops.

As the ground forces pushed north and Saddam's resistance crumbled, the plan for *Ark* crystallised. By 1st April it was decided she would go no further east and instead of regenerating carrier strike at Diego Garcia in the Indian Ocean, she would do so on the passage home to UK. *Ark's* dream of 'eastern promise' evaporated, but the overriding hope for her Ship's Company was to see the completion of the 849 Squadron salvage operation and recovery of the aircrew before having to leave theatre. Extremely brave and selfless efforts by teams from HMS *Grimsby*, HMS *Brocklesby*, RFA *Diligence* and the USS *Catawba* who spent day after day in the dangerously exposed waters of the crash site successfully recovered six of the seven airmen. In moving ceremonies onboard *Ark* the Ship's Company were able to pay final tribute to their fallen comrades. The last casualty, Lieutenant Marc Lawrence, was eventually recovered by a team from HMS *Ramsey* in June 2003.

It would be another ten days before all of the logistics arrangements were in place, including moving elements of 820 Squadron from RFA *Fort Austin* and transferring *Ark*'s war stock of ammunition to her. On 11th April 2003, HMS *Ark Royal* accompanied by HMS *York* and RFA *Fort Victoria* were released from TELIC duties and began the passage home. As *Ark* left the Persian Gulf 800 Squadron, which had been left in the UK during the operation, began preparations to meet her in the Mediterranean. The ground crew joined on 4th May at Palma Majorca and the aircraft embarked three days later, sixty miles southeast of Ibiza. The jets were due to remain onboard for only a week, leaving on 13th May to the Spanish Air Force base at Torrejan. Sadly, two days of flying were lost due to unfavourable wind conditions but the flying programme was adjusted and useful training achieved. What particularly struck 800 NAS's pilots was how welcome they were made to feel by *Ark*'s Ship's Company despite their obvious fatigue and desire to get home.

HMS *Ark Royal* returned home to Portsmouth on 17th May 2003, after 126 gruelling days away. The reception given to *Ark*'s Ship's Company was overwhelming with over 4,000 family and well-wishers providing a welcome not seen in Portsmouth since the Falklands War twenty one years earlier. *"It was a tremendous occasion – marvellous to see so many welcoming crowds. We wanted and needed this moment, though nobody forgot our losses"* recalled Admiral Snelson.

In reflecting on the achievement of his ship and the contribution she had made to the early coalition effort Captain Massey recognised that his Ship's Company, with an average age of just 25, had made the pivotal difference. *"If there is one overwhelming conclusion I would draw, it is that our people and their training were what finally made the biggest difference, and ensured that this indeed demanding scenario was got pretty much right. There was much uncertainty, and considerable stress; a need to work up to focussed combat readiness, and then to sustain it; a demand for innovation, skill and stamina; and a call for substantial physical courage in the face of real risks and threats. The training we injected, once deployed, was aimed wherever possible at the specifics of the Gulf setting; but it could never have succeeded without the in-bred core of skills and self-confidence that come, from the ethos of 'train hard, fight easy'. It really worked. Moreover, the real battle winners - the people - demonstrated once again their enormous reserves of character, resilience, determination and spirit; and that intelligent leadership, thoughtful handling and constant, honest communication are the minor but vital cogs in the gearbox of irresistible moral strength. Our system and style delivered, in spades."*

Alan Massey's young team would forever be remembered by a new Battle Honour for HMS *Ark Royal*: "Al Faw 2003".

Of course, it would be many more years before the early campaign successes and removal of Saddam's regime resulted in the lasting peace and stability to justify George W Bush's premature belief in May 2003 that it was "mission accomplished" in Iraq. Coalition forces remained embroiled in an increasingly violent civil war within the country for a further seven years. Control of post-Saddam Iraq rested with the Coalition Provisional Authority under the leadership of Paul Bremer until July 2004 when sovereignty was handed over to an Iraqi interim government. The following January, Iraqis elected a transitional government to draft a Constitution which was ratified in October of that year and paved the way for the election of Iraq's first democratic National Assembly in December 2005.

Saddam Hussein escaped from Baghdad and remained at large until he was captured by US forces at Tikrit on 13th December 2003. Tried of crimes against humanity and convicted by an Iraqi court, Saddam was hanged on 30th December 2006. The US Congress 'Iraq Study Group Report' published the same month as Saddam's execution concluded that "*the situation in Iraq is grave and deteriorating*" and "*US forces seem to be caught in a mission that has no foreseeable end.*"

The appointment of US General David Petraeus as the military commander in Iraq in February 2007 sought to arrest this deterioration and heralded a surge in US force levels designed to suppress rebel activity and accelerate training of the Iraqi forces to deal with the insurgency. Over the following eighteen months the surge tactics had a marked effect on reducing the insurgency and the number of Iraqi civilian and coalition military casualties. Iraqi-led offensives in the north and south of the country throughout 2008 strengthened the government's position and established a framework for the gradual withdrawal of coalition forces. The 'US-Iraq Status of Forces Agreement' of December 2008 set out that US Forces would withdraw from Iraqi cities by mid-2009 and all forces would withdraw by the end of 2011.

On 30th April 2009, UK forces formally ended combat operations in Iraq and handed over control of the multinational division to US forces. Secretary of State for Defence John Hutton assessed the British contribution: "*I think when the history is written of this campaign, they will say of the British military 'we did a superb job'.*" During the six-year conflict, Britain lost 179 servicemen and women, of which 136 were killed in action. In comparison, US casualties to September 2010 were 4,421 of which 3,492 were killed in action.

Two months after the British withdrawal, Prime Minister Gordon Brown announced a public inquiry on Iraq to be led by Sir John Chilcot, which would consider "*the UK's involvement in Iraq, including the way decisions were made and actions taken, to establish, as accurately as possible, what happened and to identify the lessons that can be learned.*" Former Prime Minister Tony Blair appeared before the enquiry first on 29th

January 2010 and then again on 21st January 2011 to clarify his earlier testimony. The boundaries of the authority under UNSCR 1441 given to Bush and Blair remain the subject of much legal debate. On the specific issue of Iraq's ability to develop WMD, subsequent evidence released to the enquiry showed that the Joint Intelligence Committee in March 2002 reported that "*Intelligence on Iraq's WMD and ballistic missile programmes is sporadic and patchy. From the evidence available to us, we believe Iraq retains some production equipment, and some small stocks of chemical weapon agent precursors, and may have hidden small quantities of agents and weapons,*" while a classified Cabinet Office report concluded "*Saddam has not succeeded in seriously threatening his neighbours.*"

Publication of Lord Chilcot's final report is expected before the end of 2011. Whatever the wider issues and doubts surrounding the Iraq War in the supposed clarity of hindsight, for the 1,080 men and women who sailed from Portsmouth on 11th January 2003 onboard HMS *Ark Royal* there could be little doubt of the perils they would face. Nor too was there any doubt of the fortitude, courage and determination they showed while doing their duty during the darkest days of Operation TELIC. For seven, that duty would demand the ultimate sacrifice.

The last words on the most momentous events in the life of *Ark Royal* deservedly go to Alan Massey, who wrote in 2007, "*Four years on, the Iraq war has become deeply immersed in controversy, and plenty of popular wisdom-after-the-event. But this should never be allowed in the slightest to demean or diminish the quality and value of all that was achieved at sea, on the ground and in the air during that perilous period. These things deserve to remain a source of the utmost professional pride and satisfaction, in which everyone connected with Ark Royal and her task group, can justifiably share. One dares to hope that the same will also, always, apply to the memory of the 849 boys who gave everything for our cause, and our people. Their commitment, and the unique part they played in the vibrant lives of their Squadron and ship, will never be forgotten."*

Commodore A R Nance OBE Royal Navy

(Commanding Officer 2003 – 2004)

The HMS *Ark Royal* I joined was fresh from distinguished service in the Iraq War. Commanding her was a privilege unalloyed, despite the short period and taking her into refit; it was a pleasure to be amidst such able and motivated people.

It was a busy nine months, but perhaps undemanding compared to some. First we handed over the role of Fleet Flagship to HMS *Invincible* and then said goodbye to the war veterans going on draft. Amidst it all we paid tribute to those of 849 Squadron who had died in combat. We gave honour to them and their families, families grieving because of the 'dangers of the sea and air'. It was poignant. We stand on the shoulders of giants. It was a stimulating autumn, hosting the staffs entrusted with buying the new carriers. The command team also shaped the *Ark Royal* we so keenly wanted to emerge from refit. It seemed to have some effect.

Many of the Ship's Company were destined to be transferred to HMS *Illustrious*. Knowing that HMS *Invincible* would go into preservation, we were building the Navy's inheritance, creating skills for the country's newest, and soon to be only, strike carrier; not just waiting for a refit. So our time in the North Sea brought us 800 Squadron's FA-2 Sea Harriers and sea trials for the new Harrier GR-9 and a range of helicopters to rebuild the Executive, Air, Logistics and Engineering Departments' inputs to carrier capability. The Warrant Officers and Senior Ratings were key and it was a thrill to see. It was also my thrill to see the whole ship's team thrive. I am sure that all carrier Commanding Officers feel the same: the privilege of their trust and of leadership, and the thrill of their development. My team was special to me and one of my great tasks was to delegate, building skills and confidence and reinforcing the respect of the new Ship's Company for their seniors.

Our Taranto Night was as spectacular as ever. But amongst its thrills there was sadness too. We said goodbye to the first Sea Harrier Squadron when 800 Squadron disembarked for the last time, to be swept into Joint Force Harrier. As the Navigating Officer of HMS *Sheffield* in 1982 I was so grateful for the umbrella the FRS-1 gave us all. They changed the battle and were 'a precious few' despite the ship and aircraft losses. Thank you.

The new Ship's Company enjoyed the port visits: Amsterdam had not lost its attractions; Hamburg was welcoming despite the impact of the third *Ark Royal* on the *Bismarck*, manned from there; Newcastle was as open hearted as ever a Tyne-built ship enjoyed. All received us with dignity and delight. The plum was London and Princess Anne's re-launching the Sea Cadet Corps, influencing a new generation of naval people. Others have done more, but we did our bit. Finally, we had an amazing Ship's Company Dance in Portsmouth. A bevy of tuxedos and ball dresses, with pink champagne and entertainment from our benefactor; it was so impressive. Those people are our legacy.

That says it all. Care over ones command is a given, exploiting one of the Navy's prime assets to achieve long term strategic impact was the task. The Departmental Heads and I worked hard to hold high the torch of *Ark Royal* during my tenure, a torch made brilliant by our predecessors and by naval service that saved the country in 1588 and inspired her again in the 1940s. That torch was handed over.

I write in the wake of the decision to decommission her prematurely. Her light will burn on, in her people and in the civilians who have valued her contribution to their future:

BZ *Ark Royal*.

Chapter 11

2003 – 2004:
Swansong of the Sea Harrier

By the time HMS *Ark Royal* returned from the Gulf, it appeared to casual observers that the wheels were coming off the SDR-heralded Joint Force Harrier (JFH) and the 'joint' part of JFH was *"being undermined as part of a conspiracy theory for the RAF to take over embarked fixed wing aviation from the Fleet Air Arm."* The organisation stood up on 1st April 2000 under the command of Rear Admiral Iain Henderson as Flag Officer Maritime Aviation and AOC 3 Group Strike Command lasted just over three years. On 1st October 2003, 3 Group, now commanded by Rear Admiral Scott Lidbetter was subsumed into 1 Group, under the RAF's "Project Future Strike", bringing all fast jet types under the unitary command of Air Vice Marshal Chris Moran. The reorganisation within the RAF higher command came hot on the heels of the MoD's decision to withdraw the Sea Harrier from service by April 2006, leaving only RAF GR-typed aircraft for an RN-RAF force that while integrated at the tactical level would henceforth be driven solely by 'light blue' policy decisions.

Central to both the original creation of JFH and the decision to withdraw the FA-2 was Air Chief Marshal Sir Jock Stirrup. As the Assistant Chief of the Air Staff from 1998 to 2000, Stirrup coordinated the RAF's contribution to the 1998 Strategic Defence Review and then saw through its implementation, the most heralded initiative of which was the amalgamation of RN and RAF Harrier units within JFH. Stirrup had come to the

MoD from command of 1 Group and went back to the RAF as Deputy C-in-C Strike Command. His instinct for adapting the RAF to strengthen its position was well-honed, as he reflected in cross examination by the Defence Select Committee in 2002: *"I think that the Air Force, by and large, has done pretty well in the past at reinventing itself. It is always a challenge and it is always difficult, but it is a question of seizing the future and shaping it rather than reacting to it and being forced by it."*

In 2002, Stirrup took over from Vice Admiral Sir Jeremy Blackham (*Ark*'s former Captain) as the Deputy Chief of Defence Staff (Equipment Capability), with overall responsibility for delivering the capability requirements of all three services. In describing his role to the Select Committee, Stirrup was clear of his priorities. *"We have three key parameters when dealing with our projects: time, cost and performance and we consider them all,"* Stirrup argued. He went to explain, *"Obviously, we are always alive to the possibility of trade-offs between them. If somebody comes along to us and says, "Look, we cannot deliver this capability but we can deliver eighty per cent of it for half the cost", then we would take a very close look at it. If delivering eighty per cent of the capability meant that you could not win, we would not be interested. If it meant that you could, perhaps you might have to do something else with another system, perhaps you might have to change your processes a little but you could alter things and deliver the necessary outcome for fifty per cent of the cost, then of course that is what we would wish to do. We need to use the money as wisely as possible. We have a responsibility to the taxpayer, but also of course I have a much closer interest which is squeezing as much capability out of the resources available as I possibly can."*

The "conspiracy theory" of an RAF take-over of the Harrier force and the possibility of a single mastermind at work suited the dramatists, but there were compelling arguments for both the integration of 3 Group and the rationalisation of the Harriers types. Rear Admiral Lidbetter, who retired in 2003 having handed over 3 Group, argued in the Naval review that *"the reorganisation of Strike Command is a sensible initiative to reduce overheads and increase war fighting effectiveness in the same way as the Navy has done in 'Fleet First'. The RN personnel within JFH are probably best placed to judge whether the changes spell terminal meltdown for embarked fast jet aviation or a paradigm shift to catalyse a strike focus for the RN ahead of the Joint Combat Aircraft and CV(F)."* Having worked closely with the RAF Lidbetter was no fawning proponent of their methods and recognised when a *"naive and transparent attempt to forward the interests of the RAF"* was attempted some years later by the then Chief of the Air Staff, Air Chief Marshal Sir Glenn Torpy RAF. Writing to the Daily Telegraph on 14th June 2009, Lidbetter suggested, bluntly, a different approach: *"He [Torpy] is soon to be put out to grass and I hope that his successor will take a more balanced view. Absorbing the roles of the RAF, its aircraft, and the people required to fly and service them, into the Royal Navy and the Army would bring huge cost-savings while offering much improved co-operation and integration."*

The development programmes for the RAF and Royal Navy variants of the Harrier were both based on the original GR-1 design, but diverged widely from that which first entered service in 1969. The RAF's first iteration of the GR-1 was the GR-3, which became operational in the mid 1970s. The Sea Harrier FRS-1 was essentially an air defence version of the all-metal GR-3. Fitted with the Pegasus 11 engine, the Navy's version featured a raised cockpit and a 'bubble' canopy for greater visibility and an extended fuselage to accommodate the Ferranti Blue Fox radar, made from corrosion-resistant alloys or coated to protect it against the marine environment.

By the time the FRS-1 entered service in 1980, the RAF was already in the advanced stages of bringing into service its second generation aircraft that would make the GR-3 obsolete. A joint development begun in 1973 between Hawker Siddeley (latterly British Aerospace) and McDonnell Douglas in the USA gave rise to the Harrier II, an extensively modified form of the GR-3/AV-8A. The original aluminium alloy fuselage was replaced by one which made extensive use of composites, reducing its weight to offer greater payload capacity or aircraft range. An all-new one-piece wing provided around fourteen per cent greater surface area and increased thickness for greater lift in flight. The first new prototype flew in 1981 with the American production aircraft, the AV-8B, flying in 1983. The GR-5 was the RAF's version of the Harrier II, fitted with the more powerful Pegasus 11-21 Mk.105 engine. The BAE-built development GR-5 flew for the first time on 30th April 1985 and the aircraft entered service in July 1987.

As the GR-5 came on stream, approval was given for the Royal Navy to upgrade the Sea Harrier to FRS-2, latterly called FA-2, standard that would incorporate changes derived from the operational experience of the FRS-1 in the Falklands. The FA-2 design included the world-beating Blue Vixen radar, a larger air-to-air weapons load, increased range, improved cockpit displays and an electronic countermeasures suite to provide a defence against radar-homing anti-air missiles. These features, combined with the introduction of the advanced AIM-120 medium-range and AIM-132 short-range missiles, put the FA-2 among the top rank of air-to-air combat aircraft in the world.

First flight of the FA-2 prototype took place in September 1988 and a contract was signed for 29 upgraded aircraft in December that year. In 1990 the Navy ordered eighteen new-build FA-2s, at a unit cost of around £12 million and four further upgraded aircraft were ordered in 1994. The first aircraft was delivered on 2nd April 1993 and early sea trials took place on *Ark Royal* in 1993 and 1994. Both the GR-5 and FA-2 shared similar versions of the Pegasus 11-21 engine, providing around 21,500 lb-ft of thrust.

But even as the first FA-2 entered service the role of the carrier-borne fixed wing aircraft was changing. At the time of the attrition order for the last FA-2s, the aircraft's primary role centred on supporting large naval task groups operating in the North Atlantic. Following the 1998 Strategic Defence Review the operational focus of the Royal Navy's Invincible-class carriers shifted to power projection in the littoral. In parallel with the development of the FA-2, the RAF developed the GR-7, mechanically almost indistinguishable from the GR-5 but with a greatly upgraded avionics package which included a forward-looking infra-red (FLIR) system and night vision goggles for the pilot, giving the aircraft true day/night and all weather capability for the first time. Together with new weapon systems such as the Maverick AGM-65 stand-off missile and Paveway II laser-guided bomb, the GR-7 provided a significantly greater power projection capability than the FA-2. The offensive capability provided by the GR-7 thus became the principal military output required from the UK's embarked fixed wing aircraft. This, and the small size of the CVS, with its attendant inability to embark very large numbers of fixed wing aircraft and retain the necessary helicopters, provided the impetus for a Balance of Investment study across the Joint Force Harrier.

It had emerged by 2001 that both the FA-2 and the GR-7 would require significant upgrades to allow them to remain effective until the single replacement Joint Combat Aircraft was expected to enter service in 2012 and take over both aircraft roles. Both types needed expensive structural work. Early Sea Harrier airframes were approaching 25 years old and because of its poor serviceability, despite the Herculean efforts of ground crews, the Sea Harrier could not provide adequate Air Defence cover unless a minimum number of aircraft were embarked, making it impossible to embark sufficient GR-7s for offensive support operations and the minimum number of helicopters needed for AEW, ASW and HDS duties. The GR-7 needed a replacement tail section of its fuselage to combat accelerated fatigue, but this was already included in the GR-9 upgrade programme. Aside from the fuselage issue, the principal limitation in both aircraft types was the limited performance of the Pegasus 11-21 engine in 'hot and high' conditions. In cool northern European and Atlantic conditions the engine provided adequate power to enable a fully loaded aircraft to launch from the deck of a CVS, but as already had been shown in the Adriatic by the FRS-1s and in the Gulf by land-based GR-7s, it could not cope year round with ambient conditions out of area. Engine limitations meant the aircraft had to sacrifice either endurance by taking less fuel, or offensive payload by carrying fewer munitions. The more modern GR-7, already aerodynamically superior to the GR-3/FA-2 airframe, was also designed from the outset to accept a more powerful engine; the Pegasus 11-61E Mark 107 giving around 3,000-lbft more thrust than the 11-21. To remain effective, the FA-2 would require the same engine, but it was not designed to accept it, while the upgrades required to address radar obsolescence and its limited electronic countermeasures suite were more expensive and carried greater risk than those needed to bring the GR-7 up to GR-9 standard. Without these upgrades, the aircraft would become rapidly obsolescent from around the middle of the decade.

Taking all of these factors into consideration, the Balance of Investment study concluded, in light of the increased emphasis on embarked offensive capability, that the GR-7 should be upgraded to GR-9 and that the FA-2 should be withdrawn from service by 2006 before it passed its 'sell-by' date. This assessment was shared by Rear Admiral Lidbetter; *"the bottom line is that no argument was sufficiently telling to justify the very large amounts of money required to equip just eight FA-2s with the more powerful engine"*. By the time of its withdrawal, the Sea Harrier would have been in service for over 25 years and the migration strategy for Joint Force Harrier announced in February 2002 provided a robust carrier-based offensive strike capability based on an all Harrier GR-9 force. This met the requirement recognised within the SDR and confirmed by the emerging conclusions of the MoD's post 9/11 SDR "New Chapter" published the same year.

On 28th February 2002 the Armed Forces Minister, Adam Ingram, announced the strategy to take forward Joint Force Harrier (JFH) into the era of the replacement carriers and joint combat aircraft. In announcing the plan he said: *"Recent commitments to the next phase of the Joint Strike Fighter programme, confirmation of the order for a further three Type-45 air defence destroyers, and the entry into service of new smart weapons have given renewed impetus to the offensive role of Joint Force Harrier. These have allowed us to plan with greater certainty its way ahead, taking it into the era of the Future Joint Combat Aircraft and the future carriers. We have concluded that Joint Force Harrier should migrate to an all Harrier GR force maximising investment in one aircraft type. It is further planned to upgrade the GR-7 to GR-9 to ensure a credible expeditionary offensive capability is maintained until the aircraft leaves service."* In responding to questions off the back of Ingram's announcement, a MoD spokesman was quoted in The Daily Mail as saying *"These days we don't fight the kind of wars where our ships need defending from enemy warplanes far out at sea. Aircraft Carriers are now mostly supporting shore operations by flying strike missions and it makes far better sense to spend our money on Harriers which can do that best. If necessary, we can rely on coalition forces to provide the outer air defence for surface ships."* It seemed that defence thinking had, in two respects at least, gone full circle in the fifty years since the Sandys and Healey Defence Reviews. Air defence for the high seas fleet would once again be provided by missile-based destroyers, and land-based or coalition sourced carrier aircraft would provide anti-air cover in the littoral, rather than organic sea-based forces.

Ingram's announcement signalled the end for the venerable Sea Harrier, causing public consternation and disquiet in Parliament, not least since it highlighted an apparent disconnect in the planning process within the MoD. The Defence Select Committee noted in its 2002 Annual report: *"Whatever the rationale for withdrawing the Sea Harriers early, it is regrettable that the MoD was taking delivery of new Sea Harriers only a few years before making that decision. At the very least, we are presented with a poor impression of long term planning in the MoD."*

The disquiet was caused by the perceived loss of a critical layer of the Royal Navy's air defence capability that the withdrawal of the Sea Harrier would cause. It was acknowledged that the Navy's air-defence layers, whether carrier-borne aircraft or destroyer-borne missiles, had weaknesses, particularly in tackling sea-skimming missiles. The layered defence was being strengthened, with improvements to the combined capability to detect, identify and track these threats, and in wider "situational awareness". Some of these had already been introduced, such as the upgraded Sea King Mk-7 ASaC that had operated with huge effect from HMS *Ark Royal* during Operation TELIC. Others represented mid-life updates for principal sensors, including the still troublesome R996 radar and the by now venerable R1022, both fitted in *Ark*. ADAWS was also being upgraded and the newly incorporated colour screens, ability to track aircraft using automatic Identification Friend or Foe, and LINK 16 connectivity would greatly improve the functionality of the system. In addition, the Command Support System had already been fitted in every major warship, giving wide-area, near real-time, connectivity for intelligence gathering and force planning.

These improvements would provide the enhanced situational awareness necessary to counter modern missiles in high density threat environments and give improved warning of attack. Actual engagement ('hard kill') or distraction and seduction ('soft kill') by decoys of the threat would then be conducted through several layers of the air defence envelope. The Sea Harrier provided the outer most layer against enemy aircraft (it had no capability to shoot down missiles) with a combat radius of around 200 miles. Sea Dart Mod 2 in the *Type-42* destroyers provided area defence to an effective range in excess of fifty miles and was now fitted with a new infra-red fuze triggered by the attacking missile's heat signature giving it a capability for the first time against sea skimmers. The 'soft kill' layer was improved by the defensive decoy system DLH, already fitted in *Ark* and to be fitted to all major warships, incorporating the radar-frequency active decoy round (ADR). The ADR complemented the passive chaff rounds in defeating anti-ship radar-guided missiles, while the flare-grenade infrared decoy was designed to seduce heat seeking missiles. The final hard-kill layer for the capital ships was provided by either the Signaal Goalkeeper or Vulcan Phalanx close-in weapon system, while the frigates had their own protection and could offer short range cover with Sea Wolf.

Aside from these improvements, the principal arguments put forward to mitigate removing Sea Harrier from the order of battle was the supposed imminent introduction of two new, key enablers for integrated area air defence: the *Type-45* destroyer fitted with the Principal Anti Air Missile System (PAAMS) and a task force data fusion system known as the Co-Operative Engagement Capability (CEC). The *Type-45* was due to enter operational service by 2007 and its combination of

Sampson radar and Principal Anti-Air Missile System (PAAMS), offered far greater capability than the R996/909s and Sea Dart offered in the *Type-42*s. Therefore theoretically, fewer ships were required to provide the same coverage. Using a mix of ASTER-30 and ASTER-15 missiles, PAAMS could intercept aircraft at ranges of up to forty miles from the ship and provide a multi layer defence against sea skimming missiles. The ships would typically be deployed well ahead of the high-value units being protected. CEC provided a similarly revolutionary, but as yet theoretical, advance in air and missile defence over ADAWS by combining and distributing sensor measurement data from units within the same task group, thereby providing an integrated, netted, air defence system. Such a system, if it could be made to work, would greatly enhance detection, tracking and identification of air targets, as well as providing engagement co-ordination.

It was accepted that the *Type-45* did not fully replicate the capabilities provided by the Sea Harrier, indeed the FA-2s and the anti-air destroyers were not envisaged so much as substitutes, but as different layers of air defence for the fleet. Sir Jock Stirrup acknowledged that the substitution was less than ideal and in other circumstance would have preferred to retain the Sea Harrier until the joint combat aircraft entered service. "*If you were to say to me, would I prefer to continue to have the kind of capability that the Sea Harrier produces up until 2012, my answer would be "of course", but not at any cost given the opportunities in other areas that we would have to forego if we were to make the necessary investment and that is the fundamental point,*" argued Stirrup. The rationale for not upgrading the FA-2 was thus accepted, but with the caveat that all of the planned improvements in air defence, including a commitment to procure all twelve *Type-45*s, should be fulfilled on time and to specification.

The decision to cancel the Sea Harrier and upgrade the GR-7 to GR-9 would shape the final nine months of HMS *Ark Royal*'s fleet time before she herself paid off for her second period of extended readiness. *Ark*'s new Commanding Officer, Adrian Nance was expert in the doctrine and concepts of the fleet's air defence and had seen every layer of it in action. As a young officer he had served in the Falklands War and witnessed the battle-winning effect of the FRS-1s. He knew Sea Dart intimately having commanded two *Type-42s*, including HMS *Cardiff* during the first Gulf War, and then seen the point defence capability of Sea Wolf as Captain F6 in the *Type-23* HMS *Montrose*. Latterly he had held two warfare-related posts as a Captain, first as the Director of the Maritime Warfare Centre and then as Director of Joint Warfare in the MoD. But these somewhat esoteric and academic matters paled against the more fundamentally important job of maintaining the 'Spirit of the *Ark*' among the members of his Ship's Company as they sensed their dispersal while the ship slipped gracefully into upkeep.

While *Ark* rested alongside, her normal squadrons regrouped and prepared for change. 800 Squadron deployed for a short period in Malaysia for Exercise FLYING FISH and then to Nellis Air Base in the USA. A short hop from the bright lights of Las Vegas, over the deserts of Nevada, the FA-2s made their debut in the twelve-day Exercise RED FLAG, one of the most exacting tests of air power with over 100 jet aircraft from four nations tangled in the skies. 800's pilots joined colleagues from the Israeli and German air forces and American F-16s from the 'Aggressor Squadron' to act as former Eastern Bloc attackers. Outnumbered four to one throughout the exercise, the Sea Harriers were denied full use of their radar and advanced missiles, or their legendary manoeuvrability, instead made to mimic the tactics and capability of their former Soviet foes. Despite these handicaps 800 Squadron put in a good show with its reputation held high and important lessons learned. For the Squadron's staff officer, Lieutenant Ian Peattie, the visit to Nellis was especially memorable since he tied the knot to his fiancée Anita, at a unique Las Vegas style ceremony, witnessed by the squadron officers in mess dress, Senior Rates dressed as Elvis and the staff officers dressed as cowboys. Three FA-2s remained in the United States to take part in another series of exercises under the codename HIGH RIDER, at the China Lake Air Base in California, to test their bombing and weaponry skills.

Meanwhile *Ark*'s oldest companion, 820 Squadron, stood down on 11th July 2003 ending thirteen years service with the Sea King Mk-6, to stand up again on 1st September equipped with the Merlin HM-1. Their first task was to embark in HMS *Invincible* during September for Exercise NORTHERN LIGHT. *Invincible* had followed *Ark* into refit at Rosyth in September 2001 and now come through her year-long regeneration process. The culmination of that process was the major NATO exercise with *Ark*'s former CO, Rear Admiral David Snelson, embarked in his role as the Commander UK Maritime Forces, to certify *Invincible* and her Harriers from 801 Squadron ready to assume high readiness duties. *Invincible* passed her test and took the baton from *Ark* at the end of September. Later in the year, 820's Merlins conducted shallow water ASW training in Kiel where the focus was on developing tactics against diesel submarines. The squadron formed a strong bond with the German U-boat U25, who was their playmate for the exercises.

Relinquishing high readiness operational status was the trigger for many of *Ark*'s Ship's Company to move on to new jobs and a significant proportion of those that had taken *Ark* from refit and then to war left the ship through the autumn. For the new joiners that replaced them, the challenge was completely different since they had to learn the ropes and gain as much sea experience as possible since many of them would eventually move to HMS *Illustrious* as she emerged from refit in mid-2004.

HMS *Ark Royal*'s autumn 2003 programme was confined to the North Sea with aircraft refresher training and a major visit to her birthplace, North Shields on the Tyne. First stop however was Amsterdam and despite bad weather delaying the ship's arrival until 15th November, the Ship's Company made the most of the foreshortened visit to this most cosmopolitan city. From the Netherlands, it was a short trip back to the UK and up to North Shields, with *Ark* arriving on 19th November. As ever, the Tyneside community came out in their thousands to see their most famous ship come home. Ship Open to Visitors attracted the largest crowd on *Ark* since 1988, with queues stretching hundreds of yards back from the entrance of the commercial dock. The breadth of *Ark Royal*'s popularity was demonstrated by visits from three very different VIPs while she was alongside.

Ark's most distinguished visitor was Captain Alan 'Alfie' Sutton CBE, one of the most illustrious and decorated naval aviators of the Second World War who was awarded a DSC and bar. Sutton was the last survivor of the 42 young naval airmen who on 11th November 1940 attacked the Italian fleet at Taranto, southern Italy, causing devastation that altered the balance of power in the Mediterranean and changed the nature of naval warfare. Sutton, an observer, and his pilot "Tiffy" Torrens-Spence, led the second wave of twelve Swordfish from HMS *Illustrious* against the heavily defended Italian naval base.

Ark's most popular visitor was Nell McAndrew; glamour model, pin-up and Forces sweetheart. The star of ITV's first "I'm a Celebrity Get Me Out of Here!" came onboard to present the NAAFI Dividend cheque to the Ship's Welfare Fund. The astonishing donation of £17,965 reflected the enormous amount of business done by the ship's canteen in beer and 'nutty' sales during the 2002/3 year which included those to boost morale during Operation TELIC. Having presented the cheque, Miss McAndrew then spread her own brand of morale by touring the ship, signing copies of her calendar and posing with sailors for photographs.

Ark's most famous guest of the trip was Sir Jimmy Savile, an old friend of *Ark* IV and a strong supporter of the Navy, who made a goodwill stop and was treated to a tour of the ship. Sir Jimmy met old acquaintances and did not disappoint with his trademark combination of cigars, jewellery and catchphrases. *"Many of the crew remember him from his 'Jim'll Fix It' days – some even admitted having sent letters to him all those years ago,"* recalled Lieutenant Vicky Whale, who had been given the tricky job of escorting the Sir Jimmy during the visit. In deference to the unique place he held in the TV memories of most of the crew Sir Jimmy was given a unique memento by them – an *"Ark Royal* FIXED IT FOR JIM" badge.

Sir Jimmy Savile was also a famous son of *Ark*'s affiliated city, Leeds, and he accompanied 200 of the Ship's Company when they travelled on 21st November to exercise the Freedom of the City. During World War II various government-sponsored campaigns were mounted to encourage people to raise money for the war effort. One of these was Warship Week and in Leeds it was to be held on 30th January to 7th February 1942. As an additional incentive for the week, in November 1941 Leeds decided to adopt HMS *Ark Royal* III, so famous was she, having helped sink the German battleship *Bismarck* and then dodged numerous German and Italian attacks during her service in the Mediterranean and running the Malta convoys,. Just days later, *Ark* was torpedoed and sunk in the Mediterranean. The Admiralty immediately assigned her name to a new carrier that began building in 1942 and the people of Leeds seized the initiative for what they renamed "Ark Royal Week" by changing their target of £3.5 million for a replacement hull and some refitting to over £5 million for a replacement ship. A huge march took place down The Headrow in the city centre, led by the Navy and followed by military vehicles and personnel. The grand total raised was £9,301,293 (equivalent to over £350 million in 2009) collected from pocket-money contributions sent by children to buy nuts and bolts, to individual sums for £250,000 from businesses to purchase Fulmar naval fighter planes, which cost £5,000 each.

HMS *Ark Royal* was granted the Freedom of the City of Leeds in October 1973 and Captain Nance led the Ship's Company to celebrate the thirtieth anniversary of this honour and also to thank locals for their support to the ship during the Gulf War. The Ship's Company formed up in front of Leeds Civic Hall for inspection by the Lord Mayor, Councillor Neil Taggart and was then watched by thousands of citizens who braved the brisk weather as it marched through the City with Bayonets fixed, Colours Flying and Drums beating, for the first time in nine years. A Royal Marines band, a platoon of Sea Cadets from TS *Ark Royal* and members of the Royal Naval Association and Royal British Legion formed the rest of the procession. "*It was an auspicious occasion and the freedom parade is a tradition to be treasured and maintained. The visit to Leeds provided Ark Royal with a perfect opportunity to show the people of Leeds how highly we prize our relationship with them,*" reflected Captain Nance.

With the ceremonies over *Ark* prepared for eight days of aircraft operations in the North Sea with the FA-2s of 800 Squadron. Ground staff embarked at North Shields on 24th November and the aircraft joined two days later after the ship had sailed. The weather for much of the initial period of flying from ship was described as "*interesting*". Driving rain and high seas characteristic of north Scotland in November added significantly to the complexities of flight deck operations, but did little to dampen ambitious range of sorties including dusk and night flying. Five live 1000-lb bombs were dropped on the north east ranges on Sunday 30th with additional aircraft dropping three kilogram dummy bombs against a towed splash target. The sorties provided a rare opportunity to prove the ship's weapon supply routines that had not been much tested since returning from Iraq, and to operate live ordnance. The sorties were made all the more challenging coming the day after the Wardroom 'Saturday Night at Sea', held to celebrate Taranto night. Flying operations

continued into December with *Ark* doing nothing more than exotic than a lazy circuit between Aberdeen and the Wash; the proximity of east coast airfields giving opportunities for 800 Squadron to fly affiliation sorties with RAF Tornado F-3s and Jaguars. The weather continued to be a challenge but did at least abate enough for a limited number of dusk and some night flying trips. With training over for the year, the jets disembarked to Yeovilton on 4th December and *Ark* arrived at Portsmouth the following day. Her arrival marked the end of the most momentous year in the life of the fifth HMS *Ark Royal* and for her Ship's Company signalled a well-deserved Christmas leave.

Ark's New Year was spent at Portsmouth undergoing maintenance before she sailed at the start of February for what would be an emotional final farewell to her Sea Harriers of 800 Squadron. The weather gods again failed to recognize the significance of the event and *Ark* was delayed sailing from Portsmouth due to bad weather, but the squadron finally embarked eight FA-2s on 5th February, minus their senior pilot who was delayed at Yeovilton by an unserviceable aircraft; he eventually caught up on 7th February. 849 Squadron also provided two Sea King Mk-7s and 771 Squadron a Sea King Mk-6 for the multinational exercises. The exercises off the east coast of England and Scotland, involving a total of forty aircraft with four RAF Tornados acting as the enemy, provided a varied and interesting flying programme to enable the pilots to achieve their training objectives. Lieutenant Commander Mark Whitfield achieved Full Night Qualification, while Day Certificate of Competence was given to 800's new pilots Lieutenants Compain and Flatman, and Captain Fenwick RM. During the evolution Fenwick in aircraft ZD581 diverted to RAF Leuchars with hydraulic failure. The aircraft subsequently developed a fuel leak and was broken down and road transported back to Yeovilton; Fenwick gaining the dubious honour of scrapping the first of 800 Squadron's FA-2s. As the Sea

Harriers pounded *Ark*'s deck on operations, another important aircraft embarked for several days for sea trials, giving 800's pilots a glimpse of their future: the Harrier GR-9. Flown by BAE test pilots, two GR-9s arrived on 11th February and remained onboard for three days to prove the landing aids and new avionics and to conduct integration testing with the ship.

During a stand-off from the flying, *Ark* revisited Rosyth for the first time since the 2001 refit. *Ark*'s visit naturally generated media interest, with Captain Nance confirming that the crew was "*delighted*" to be back in Scottish waters, adding that "*the exercise went excellently. We had an impartial group of assessors on board and we got a high score.*" Berthing alongside Rosyth for Valentine's weekend gave the Ship's Company a chance to reacquaint themselves with the Scottish capital while 800's ground crews reset the FA-2s for the next phase of operations.

Back at sea on 16th February the flying programme continued, with the air group now reduced to seven aircraft as ZD613 flew off early back to Yeovilton to get a special paint job for the memorial flight planned to coincide with the disbandment of 800 Squadron at the end of March. Amongst the flying programme, *Ark* had two important visits to make during her final period at sea. The first was to London from 25th to 29th February, with the obligatory and nerve wracking passage through the Thames Barrier. High crosswinds at the barrier made the transit especially tricky; Captain Nance providing a calming influence to the two Port of London pilots who had turned white as a sheet at the realisation of how narrow the gap between the ship and the pontoons was. The purpose of the visit was to help launch a two-year recruitment campaign for the Sea Cadets Corps, to improve their facilities and broaden the opportunities open to its 15,000 cadets. The Royal Navy provided assistance through the provision of support and training for the Sea Cadets units known as Training Ships, many of which were based in inner city areas. With

400 TS units nationwide, the Sea Cadets represented the Royal Navy's "footprints in the community" by providing worthwhile activities for young people who otherwise might not have the opportunity to develop their skills and become valuable and able members of society whatever their chosen career. *Ark Royal*, berthed off the Royal Naval College at Greenwich, provided a spectacular venue to launch the campaign. The Princess Royal was the guest of honour at the inaugural reception aboard, where Her Royal Highness was met by the First Sea Lord, Admiral Sir Alan West and chairman of the Sea Cadets, Vice Admiral Sir Jonathan Todd.

The second important visit was *Ark Royal*'s final foreign visit of the commission, to one of her favourite haunts - Hamburg. Arriving on 11th March for a four day visit the Ship's Company was treated to an exceptional run ashore courtesy of Sir Donald Gosling. Sir Don had celebrated his 75th Birthday onboard *Ark* during her visit to London and in return he flew out to Hamburg and arranged with various local establishments to provide entertainment and hospitality for the crew as his final farewell before they dispersed to their new ships.

Leaving Hamburg on 15th March, the thoughts of the Ship's Company turned to the future as their ship was shortly due to pay off into extended readiness prior to another refit at Rosyth. Some were destined to join HMS *Illustrious* as she emerged from refit later in the year and so would continue to experience Sea Harrier operations from the deck of a CVS. However, for most, the return of *Ark* to Portsmouth marked the end of an era and it was a time to reflect on the contribution that the Sea Harrier had made to the Royal Navy's history. For Captain Nance it brought back memories of the Falklands War during which he served as the Navigating Officer in HMS *Sheffield*, "*I was so grateful for the umbrella the FRS-1 gave us all. They changed the battle and were 'a precious few' despite the ship and aircraft losses.*" Captain Nance had more to reflect on as he was followed for *Ark*'s final day at sea by a TV crew from BBC's "So What Do You Do All Day?" presented by Adrian Chiles. Chiles witnessed the last Sea Harriers leaving the flight deck, having bid farewell with tea and cakes in the Air Crew Refreshment Bar. Later, over dinner on the bridge, Captain Nance shared some of his memories from his career with the presenter.

The final act for 800 Squadron should have been a fly past over Portsmouth Naval Base as the squadron's 'mother ship', HMS *Ark Royal*, entered harbour. But, yet again, weather played against the ship and the fly past had to be cancelled as the fog descended, bringing a low-key end to 24 years of service with the squadron by the Sea Harrier in its two guises, the FRS-1 and FA-2. The seven remaining FA-2s led by 800's Commanding Officer, Commander Paul Stone, launched for the last time on 17th March 2004 and the honour of the final aircraft launch was given to the squadron's senior pilot Lieutenant Commander Phil Mould. 800 Squadron disbanded on 31st March 2004 and would reform two years later as a Harrier GR-7 Squadron based at RAF Cottesmore, part of the Naval Strike Wing of Joint Force Harrier. For HMS *Ark Royal* however, it would be much longer before she once again saw Harriers in number on her flight deck. As the curtain fell on her second, short commission in April 2004 it had already been agreed that she would emerge from refit two years later as a Commando Carrier, operating helicopters with the Royal Marines.

Chapter 12

2004 – 2006:
Return to Rosyth

HMS *Ark Royal* completed her last tour of operational duty in April 2004 and entered a second period of Extended Readiness, first at Portsmouth and then, from July 2005, at Rosyth. Following decommissioning, the crew quickly dwindled from the peak level of 1,300 down to only 58 engineers and logisticians, led by Commander Steve Thomas, charged with looking after the ship before she became operational again. As before, many of *Ark*'s systems were put into long term preservation, but, to reduce the cost of getting the ship running again, many were also maintained as normal, in what was termed a 'keep-alive' state. During the extended readiness a package of work was developed to return the ship to sea by September 2006. This work was shared between the time alongside and the nine-month Docking Period in Rosyth.

The restorative Docking Period commenced at Rosyth in October 2005 and combined hull maintenance, major system maintenance and a separate package of enhancements, targeted mainly at improving *Ark Royal*'s amphibious capability. The reasoning for this was that *Ark Royal* was selected to be the natural substitute for the Navy's bespoke amphibious carrier, HMS *Ocean*, which was shortly due to start her first major refit at Devonport. Babcock, now subtly retitled Babcock Surface Ship Ltd (BSSL), again undertook the contract for *Ark*'s refit and having only been out of Scottish hands for four years, like an old friend, the ship was welcomed back into the

fold with open arms. BSSL was by now also very well used to the particular challenges of refitting aircraft carriers; the company in its various guises having been in continuous possession of at least one CVS for all but two months since *Ark*'s last arrival in June 1999.

The work planned for *Ark Royal*'s docking period was relatively small; the estimated cost totalling £18 million, or roughly one third of *Ark*'s full refit budget four years earlier. It was bid for very competitively by BSSL, but also meant that all sides – contractor, Ministry and Ship's Staff – had to work tremendously hard to achieve the required work, for four reasons. First, much of the work package was aimed at additions to the ship's already considerable capability. Second, unusually but reflecting changing times, the Ship's Company would actually do much of the refit and maintenance work. Third, the programme was very tight and assumed a great deal from the 'keep alive' policy that refurbishment work would be light. Because of this, the fourth challenge was that the project came with a considerable amount of risk that had to be managed dynamically to complete the package without incurring significant overspends or delaying the ship's return to operational service. The Navy could not afford to gap the LPH capability so *Ocean* could not enter dock for her much needed refit until *Ark* had worked up and taken on the high readiness amphibious role. HMS *Ark Royal* had operated in the Gulf War as an LPH and many lessons had been learned from this experience, which needed to be embedded into the ship's capability. There were also upgrades to be completed that would exploit new technology and add real innovation to the twenty-year old ship.

The most obvious change was a brand new advanced-technology mizzen mast sited on the aft end of the island. QinetiQ, the British defence technology company formed in 2001 from the greater part of the former Government-owned Defence Evaluation and Research Agency won the contract in December 2003 to design the technology for such a mast. BSSL's subsidiary, Babcock Design & Technology (BD&T) was given the task of completing the detailed design and manufacturing, to deliver the mast by September 2005. Looking something like a giant chess pawn, the four-storey mast consisted of a steel and composite frame onto which was fixed an outer skin made in panels from frequency selective or 'tuned' composites. These panels allowed the radar and communications equipment fitted inside the mast to 'see out'. Whereas traditionally this sort of equipment was mounted on conventional steel masts and fully exposed to the weather, on the Advanced Technology Mast it could be enclosed within the structure, thus totally protected from the elements, reducing significantly the amount of maintenance needed and through-life replacement costs. The mast itself was also designed to be virtually maintenance free; lighter and stealthier than conventional masts, as well as inherently corrosion resistant, long-term costs would be substantially reduced. Despite the sophistication of the covering skins they could be manufactured using existing and well-established shipyard techniques.

The upper half of the mast housed three key systems. At the top was a brand new commercial satellite television receiver, appropriately called Outfit CNN, which provided a significant bandwidth increase for the ship and enabled her to receive a media feed into the ship to gather real-time 'open-source intelligence'. It had been recognised since Operation HAMDEN that the dissemination of information by commercial news outlets was always quicker than through military channels and so it was essential to track the output in order to be able to influence or respond to it.

The aft Radar 1007 radar was installed on the deck below CNN, having been moved from the external pole mast, which was removed. The purpose of the aft facing 1007 radar remained to assist with control and recovery of aircraft, but now the ship's capability in this respect was significantly enhanced with the installation of two new systems: the SPN-720 Precision Approach Radar (PAR) fitted in the mizzen mast below the aft 1007 radar, and a Tactical Air Navigation (TACAN) transponder fitted on top of the aerial stack on the foremast.

Providing assistance to aircraft so that they could recover to 'mother' at night and in all weathers was essential not only for flight safety but also to deliver the military task successfully. Air traffic controllers could use three methods to guide aircraft onto the deck of an aircraft carrier, depending on the technology fitted to the ship and the aircraft. Mode I was fully automatic, providing a hands-off landing for the pilot, but had only been used in American carriers fitted with the automatic landing system, JPALS. Not surprisingly, pilots did not use it often, preferring not to hand off much of the aircraft's controls to a computer, but it was important nevertheless for the controller to be able to take control when all other systems failed, or the pilot was unconscious. The second type of approach, Mode II, provided line up information to the aircraft so that the pilot could control his approach. This information usually fed a crosshair display, or "needles", pilots lining up their approach and getting confirmation of their readings from an onboard computer. The third type of approach, Mode III, involved a controller tracking the approaching aircraft by radar, radio or transponder returns and "talking down" the pilot, providing him with precise instructions for a safe landing. The challenge for a pilot was to find a small, moving target in the middle of an ocean through cloud, rain and fog, then get close enough to it to line up accurately and make a safe hover approach across the deck to the designated landing spot. Add to this that the aircraft had to be light enough to land while still carrying live ordnance, then excess fuel from already limited reserves had to be ditched before committing to the final approach. After this point, a significant delay or diversion would almost mean having to ditch. An Incident Signal filed by Lieutenant Commander Tim Easthaugh, the senior pilot of 801 Squadron in September 1999, described the perennial problem of ship recoveries. Easthaugh wrote: *"Four Sea Harrier FA-2 (callsign "Vixen") launched from Yeovilton at 1330A for routine recovery to HMS Illustrious (R06). Weather conditions from Illustrious prior to launch were Blue CAVOK* [good for aircraft recovery]. *At launch, weather conditions at all suitable diversions within fifty nautical miles of R06 were Colour Amber or Worse* [risky]. *Intention was to hold diversion fuel for Yeovilton until RO6 Command was satisfied with conditions, then dump fuel to achieve hover weight. On arrival on Homer frequency* [contact with the ship] *the weather was passed as greater than ten kilometres and nil significant cloud. Clearance to dump below diversion fuel was given and Vixen were marshalled in two pairs for CASE II recoveries separated by three minutes. Vixen 1 Section was vectored onto the centreline at six miles and given descent to 600 feet for the slot; but was unable to gain visual contact with the ship since it had steamed under 8/8 stratus estimated base 150 feet approximately two minutes earlier.*

Vixen 1 declared a PAN [emergency] *and initiated a four-ship diversion to St Mawgan. All aircraft landed safely but Vixen 1 and 2 landed below Minimum Landing Allowance with 450-lb and 400-lb fuel remaining."*

Tim Easthaugh later revealed Vixen 1 and Vixen 2 had less than two minutes flying time left before they would have had to ditch. 'Several lessons were learnt' from the incident, however

some argued the Flight Safety adage that 'there are no new lessons, just old lessons and new people to learn them!'

As an all-weather carrier, the CVS was fitted with a suite of landing aids to assist with aircraft recovery, but this had not always been the case. *Ark*'s predecessor had been fitted with a gyro-stabilised precision approach radar, the SPN-35, but no similar technology was initially provided for the CVS, presumably because it was not felt to be needed for slower flying helicopters and the STOVL Sea Harriers. As Lieutenant Commander Chris Morris recalled, when he joined HMS *Invincible* in build at Barrow as her first air traffic controller: *"she was fitted with the very latest Radar Recovery Aid – my chinagraph. I did not even have a Centreline until we physically refitted one of the Radar heads so that the Ships Head Marker pointed astern."* The radar in question was the Kelvin Hughes R1006, designed for ship navigation, which operated in the India band (three centimetre wavelength). Aircraft returns did not show up well at this wavelength, so to overcome this significant disadvantage naval aircraft were fitted with a transponder (Outfit RRB), which enhanced their radar response. To help pilots land vertically on the correct spot on deck a marvellously simply devise was designed and bolted onto the ship's main mast. Known as 'The Bedford Christmas Tree', it comprised nothing more than a few lights clamped bolted onto two pieces of metal joined in a 'T shape'. By aligning the single red light on the Tree with the others, and comparing his position over the flight deck centerline, a pilot could make a precise landing on four-spot, the normal landing point located amidships.

It took some years to develop a precision approach system, and the Royal Navy's preference was the pilot interpreted Microwave Aircraft Digital Guidance Equipment (MADGE), first fitted in *Ark* in 1986. There were advantages to using MADGE as it could be used under the strictest emission control (EMCON) conditions and it provided navigation information to the pilot out to thirty miles from the ship. At fifteen miles range the pilot would receive landing guidance information similar to a land based Instrument Landing System (ILS). The major drawback with MADGE was that it was not adopted globally; therefore aircraft from other forces, including the RAF, were not able to use this to recover to British carriers. The RAF did not carry MADGE or I-Band transponders so had no reliable means of recovery onboard in bad weather conditions. MADGE was therefore removed after the FA-2 left service and a new system had to be developed that would be compatible with the GR-7/9. The solution was the SPN-720 precision approach radar.

The SPN-720 offered Mode III landing, manual approach, during which the radar controller relayed continuous updates to the pilot on his position and direction via a secure VHF radio channel. The SPN-720 employed an I-band Doppler radar with an operating range of about twelve nautical miles. Using Low Probability of Interception technology ensured that the radar radiated minimal power to reduce the possibility of counter detection. The antenna fitted on a stabilised gimbal automatically locked onto the landing aircraft but could provide simultaneous control of two jets. The American AN/TRN26(M) TACAN system was installed at the same time as a fallback for PAR. RAF GR-7/9s already had a TACAN transponder but up until now the CVS did not carry the equipment to use them. The antenna was located at the highest point of the ship, on top of the antenna stack on the foremast. This gave the transponder the greatest possible range over the horizon.

The final equipment to be fitted in the mizzen mast was the BOWMAN HF and VHF communications fit designed to operate with land forces. BOWMAN was a £2.4 billion programme to replace the Army's ageing Clansman radios and equip the Army and Royal Marines with a new radio system. BOWMAN was designed to bring digital communications to the battlefield but it was, like most other complex equipment projects, plagued with problems. Soldiers complained the radios were too heavy to carry while the sets were too complex for battlefield use and their lack of capacity made sending messages slow. "Better Off With Map And Nokia" was how some British soldiers described the expensive and cumbersome new kit. Nevertheless, if *Ark*'s battle staff wanted to talk with the troops they deployed ashore then BOWMAN, for better or worse, was the only means to do so. The compartment at the base of the mast housed the transmitter equipment and radio sets while the Chelton loop and monopole whip aerials were fitted on the weather deck around the mast.

Following several years of effective dormancy, *Ark Royal*'s S2016 mainframe sonar was finally removed leaving the ship with no organic anti-submarine capability. It had long been accepted that the most effective anti-submarine weapon was in fact another submarine and that the SSN (and even more so, the SSBN) had won the passive sonar battle against surface hunters. The surface ASW fleet was moving away from traditional passive back to active detection methods, but using active towed arrays rather than hull-mounted arrays. S2016 was thus a legacy that had little or no practical application. Instead, *Ark* would rely on its hugely capable Merlin HM-1 helicopters carrying passive and active sonobuoys, dipping sonar and Stingray torpedoes to prosecute submarines, and be fitted with the Surface Ship Torpedo Defence System (SSTD) for self protection. SSTD was designed to combat acoustic passive search/active homing torpedoes, using two elements: deception of the torpedo and optimized evasion by the ship. Acoustic torpedoes detect a target passively but then home and attack the target in active mode. SSTD combated this using the S2170 passive towed array to detect the torpedo's active transmissions, with a processor to calculate the geometry of the attack and then advise the optimum evasion technique for the ship. At the crucial moment of the attack the system would automatically launch acoustic countermeasures to distract or jam the torpedo's homing head, while the ship evaded. These measures would be ineffective against a much simpler wake-homing torpedo. A wake-homer worked simply by detecting variations in the water pressure generated by the ship's propellers and then weaving across and up the wake until it passed under the ship, at which point a magnetic or acoustic fuze detonated the warhead. SSTD attached a non-acoustic decoy on the tow cable designed to instigate premature operation of the torpedo fuze, causing the warhead to detonate before the torpedo came within range of the ship.

Inside *Ark*, the command system ADAWS received another mid-life upgrade, this time focusing on the quality of the man-machine interface, replacing the old monochrome console displays and the 32-inch horizontal three position tactical displays with colour flat panel monitors. Each new console had its own graphics engine, radar scan convertor, advanced function keyboard and tracker ball, greatly enhancing the user operability and simplifying track management. The core computers, the Ferranti FM-2420s remained largely unchanged, with only minor modifications done to compensate for removal of the 2016 sonar from the system. The other most significant ADAWS upgrade was to provide a target data extraction capability for the Interrogator Friend or Foe (IFF) system and improved Link 16 functionality. For the first time the IFF data was integrated with the ADAWS combat management system, giving an IFF tracking capability. The IFF tracks would be combined with tracks from the air and surface surveillance radars and tracks reported by the data link, giving significantly enhanced situational awareness by supplying improved track position, velocity and identity information to the operator. The additional Link 16 functionality built on the Data Link interface in the existing ADAWS system to provide the ship's Command Team with Anti-Air Warfare Control and Aircraft Direction

capabilities via the Data Link.

The main radars and communications that should have been kept alive proved extremely temperamental when it came to recommission them. Radar R996 suffered from poor air quality to its waveguide, requiring both a new antenna and section of the waveguide to be replaced. The R1022 long range radar, while more robust than the R996, still suffered considerable teething troubles in its transmitter sub-system that were to plague the ship for over a year after return to service. Even the normally reliable R1007 navigation radars suffered defects, which did not help the removal and reinstallation of the aft set. The external communications infrastructure within the ship was already virtually obsolescent by the time *Ark* entered the docking period, but there was no programme of upgrades planned leaving the maintainers to nurture the systems back to life and then fix each defect as it appeared.

The marine engineering work of the docking period focussed largely on maintaining the material state of *Ark*'s hull and domestic systems to overcome obsolescence improve habitability and meet safety and environmental legislation. Recertification of the hull and associated systems and preservation of the structure were essential. Some upgrades were also put in. New environmentally less-unfriendly incinerators were installed, as were additional plants for making fresh water. A Marinark Rapid Evacuation System (MRES) was fitted on the starboard waist just aft of the aircraft recovery crane. The MRES allowed the Ship's Company to abandon ship without having to jump straight into the sea from the flight deck or boat bays, some forty to fifty feet above the water. Changes to the air conditioning and chilled water systems aimed to make new accommodation spaces habitable. These new mess decks were needed to accommodate up to two companies of fully kitted and armed marines; 137 extra bunks in all with sufficient spare room for each marine to store his Bergen.

The ships planning facilities also needed to be

converted to enable the amphibious battle staff to plan the raids and prepare the troops before disembarkation. *Ark*'s planning rooms, previously optimized for strike operations, were reconfigured for amphibious operations with BOWMAN communications and additional planning aids fitted. The whole organisation of the Ship's Staff onboard was critically reassessed so that it could become the most efficient possible 'marine processing' facility. A small team of Royal Marines, led by a Lieutenant Colonel, joined as the ship's amphibious liaison staff, providing an intelligent interface between the dark blue hosts and khaki guests. Members of the Ship's Company were trained as Assault Guides whose job was to escort disembarking marines from their mess deck deep in the bowels of the ship to the hangar where they prepared to move up to the flight deck. The air engineers, had to prepare the hangar and flight deck for a much wider range of possible aircraft types as well as the core UK aircraft. Sea King Mk-4, Apache AH-64, CH-47 Chinook, CH-56 Sea Knights and VM-22 Ospreys could all be expected to be recovered, serviced and readied for launch. This required aircraft starting systems to be upgraded, new stowages found for aircraft equipment including Harrier drop tanks and the workshops overhauled. The Weapon Supply Party normally used to supplying prepared weapons for aircraft now made sure that the ship's magazines and weapon lifts could accommodate the ammunition needed by a Commando unit, including mortars, small arms, anti-tank missiles, demolition charges and a host of other beach-clearing explosives. They took responsibility for everything from providing small arms ammunition to each individual marine, to delivering palletized 105 millimetre artillery shells to the flight deck for under slung flight by Chinook to the beach.

Despite the initial assessment that the total work package was relatively light, the programme very quickly fell behind schedule, due to delays in delivery and installation of the new upgrades, supply shortfalls for replacement Ministry-supplied items needed to refurbish equipment, and significant growth in the amount of refurbishment work needed. The programme had to be compressed and other savings identified as too many delays cut into the limited risk reserve quickly depleting it. Undocking was delayed with a knock-on effect to Marine Engineering system commissioning which started eight weeks late. The biggest impact however was on the date for Ships Staff Move On Board (SSMOB). This process needed to be very carefully managed since it was accompanied by a surge in the crew size without having accommodation facilities available ashore to house them. The drafts and appointment dates of the individuals had been worked out months in advance and these people could not be held back without significantly clogging up the training pipelines that had prepared them for sea. SSMOB thus took place with *Ark* still in dock.

The latter stages of the docking period focussed on recovering the programme, with hard fought negotiations between BSSL, the MoD and the ship resulting in a two-week delay to *Ark*'s Ready For Sea Date. Harbour Acceptance Trials were conducted through July 2006 and the ship was ready by the end of September to go back to sea. The RFSD inspection passed, but only just, and *Ark* sailed from Rosyth on 29th September 2006 for post upkeep trials and sea safety training. *Ark* was nearly back in Fleet hands, but the programme through the winter would expose teething troubles that Ship's Staff would have to fix before it would attain full operational status.

The docking period had highlighted the challenges of compressing the maintenance of a capital ship and expecting it to still be in a high material state after 22 years in service. Many lessons were identified that would be applied to future CVS dockings and in particular to develop a radical departure from the norm for *Ark Royal*'s final docking, planned at Portsmouth for 2009.

Commodore M P Mansergh CBE Royal Navy

(Commanding Officer 2006 – 2008)

Breathing life back into *Ark Royal*, after a number of dormant years in Portsmouth and Rosyth, was both a challenge and a great honour. For some, this marked a return to their favourite Aircraft Carrier; for the majority, the ship's first departure from Rosyth on 29th September 2006, marked the start of two wonderful and, for me, very privileged and active years in the Fleet Flagship.

Equipped as the high readiness LPH, the versatility of *Ark*'s capability and the flexibility and willingness of all on board, ensured the successful embarkation of forces, ranging from 40 Commando ahead of their deployment to Afghanistan, the NATO Battle Staff of Rear Admiral Morisetti during a Baltic deployment, Special Forces, 42 Cdo, 1 Rifles and the US Marine Corps, as well as supporting CHF, ASW, ASaC, Lynx and US Marine Corps Air Squadrons, for exercises from Lisbon to Norway and the Baltic to WESTLANT.

My lasting memories are encapsulated in three areas: firstly the magnificent support given by all *Ark Royal*'s affiliates, whose encouragement enthused the ship at every level, no more so than in the very special and most generous assistance given to the Ship's Company by Sir Donald Gosling, to whom I am indebted. Secondly, in a programme affording the ship many opportunities to visit UK ports, our faith in the loyalty and immense pride in the Royal Navy of the British public manifested itself in every way, as we returned to *Ark*'s birth place on the Tyne, to London for the 25th Commemoration of the Falklands and to the Mersey during Liverpool's year as the City of Culture. Finally, I shall never forget the willingness, determination and dedication of a truly exceptional Ship's Company, who rose to every challenge, deeply proud to be associated with their very special ship.

Chapter 13

2006 – 2008:
An *Ark* for the Royals

Captain Mike Mansergh assumed command of HMS *Ark Royal* on 11th July 2006, with the ship in the final stages of her refit at Rosyth. By now, the ship was once again afloat and her Ship's Company had been living onboard for nearly six weeks. Commissioning of the ship's systems was in full swing but it was clear that delays in the programme would impact on the time available to complete formal harbour trials and make sure the ship was not only ready to return to sea, but also capable of meeting what was going to be an extremely demanding operational programme. Harbour Acceptance Trials which started on the day Captain Mansergh arrived were noticeably compressed. The marine engineering trials were already eight weeks late, while concern was growing that the mizzen mast and its associated Precision Approach Radar and BOWMAN radio systems would not be completed in time. The ship also needed to be restored, which took several days of uninterrupted effort that seemed impossible to fit into the shrinking programme. The knock-on of these delays was that the sea trials phase would also have to be compressed in order get to Portsmouth on time. All sides worked extremely hard to make the progress and some time was clawed back; nevertheless the Ready For Sea Date was put back two weeks to the end of September.

Admiral Sir Jonathon Band, the First Sea Lord, visited the *Ark* on 11th September to see final progress and he was impressed by what he saw.

Despite the delays, there was a clear plan to get the ship out of the contractor's hands. Just over two weeks later, *Ark* slipped from Rosyth to conduct the first set of a series of trials in the Firth of Forth and North Sea. As usual, the trials focussed initially on propulsion and marine engineering, but did not set a good omen as the port inner Olympus gas turbine failed within only a few days of operation and needed to be changed. Repairs complete, the ship continued on with her programme through October. The first aircraft serials were completed that month; passing the formal rotary wing Sea Acceptance Trial (SAT) allowed the further operational and type familiarisation to begin. Perhaps in a sign of the new joint environment, *Ark*'s first visitor was an RAF Search and Rescue Sea King from RAF Boulmer on a routine sortie. Completing full ammunitioning at the defence munitions depot at Crombie, *Ark* left Scottish waters for the last time on 26th October, to return to Portsmouth and complete her trials from her base port.

Ark's men and women were returning to a fleet manning structure reshaped following the implementation of the Navy Board's Personnel Change Programme (NBPCP). For the warfare and weapon engineering departments, NBPCP ended the Warfare Branch that had been introduced in 1993. The rationale then had been that with the increased reliability of modern equipment and prevalence of 'repair by replacement', dedicated junior rating mechanics were no longer needed;

instead, cross-trained 'Operator Mechanics' would operate and help maintain their equipment. While the concept was supposed to provide better trained ratings, in practice it turned them into jacks of all trades, but masters of none. The deep specialist warfare skills now lay with the Petty Officers and above who had grown up through the old regime, while the weight of the most mundane maintenance tasks fell to the over-skilled engineering Artificers. Only a relatively small band of Weapon Engineering Mechanics remained who clung to their old branch structure under preserved conditions of service. The Warfare Branch was dealt a weakening blow from the outset, since in the mid-1990s the recruiting taps were turned off in response to "Front Line First". The failure to recruit created a 'black hole' in the manning profile which tracked first through Leading Hand and then by the mid-00s to Petty Officer. Artificer numbers were also short and because of their promotion to Senior Rating level by qualification, rather than by time served and selection, the shape of the branch had slewed to the right, producing too many Chiefs and making it unsustainable. Similar issues existed with the marine engineering specialisation that had retained its mechanics. NBPCP introduced wide ranging changes designed to alleviate these problems. Warfare and seaman ratings returned to operating their kit. Engineering Technicians replaced both Artificers and Mechanics giving a balanced, structured and sustainable single career structure from Ordinary-rate to Warrant Officer first-class. Other changes sought to harmonise the ratio between sea time and shore time for personnel and transfer the powers for managing ratings' careers down to the ships and waterfront organisations that employed them. For the first time in over a decade, department heads and their coordinators finally felt empowered to employ and flex their personnel as they saw fit to meet the needs of the ship, the service and so far as possible, the aspirations of the individual. With these new structures in place, despite short-term gaps in some key areas in the Warfare and ME departments; *Ark* was now better manned than ever to meet the challenges ahead.

Alongside in Portsmouth the priority was to prepare *Ark* for her next series of trials to test her weapon systems and aviation facilities. The mizzen mast was finally completed and PAR set to work while the TACAN antenna, too high to be fitted at Rosyth since it would have collided with the spans of the Forth Bridges as the ship passed underneath, was also installed. *Ark* was ready for trials by mid November and set out into the English and Bristol Channels for a three-week battering in atrocious weather. Two Harrier GR-9s from the Boscombe Down trials unit embarked to conduct the PAR trials, calibrate the other landing aids including TACAN, and complete the fixed wing SAT, while two Chinooks from No.18 Squadron RAF joined for a week to prove the flight deck facilities. Neither PAR nor TACAN worked successfully but since these were designed for fixed wing aircraft operations and the Boscombe Down GR-9s would be the only Harriers embarked for the foreseeable future, the priority focussed on getting the ship ready for Fleet Date Inspection and the always welcome eight-week 'holiday' in the West Country courtesy of Flag Officer Sea Training. For now, *Ark*'s sister HMS *Illustrious* in the strike carrier role would have to take on the mantle of bringing PAR and TACAN fully into service.

With Fleet Date Inspection achieved on 8th December, there was time before Christmas to complete the sea trials programme and conduct more intensive shake-down operations ahead of BOST. Squeezing every available day out of the programme, *Ark Royal* remained at sea until Friday 22nd December and was the last Portsmouth ship to come back alongside before the Christmas shutdown. Back from a well-earned leave, the Ship's Company was soon back at sea for a week of weapons training before arriving at Devonport and BOST. The format of BOST had changed since *Ark* was last put through its mill. The Staff Sea Check and Shakedown was now replaced by a

Material and Safety Check and then BOST Phase 1, involving a week alongside and then a relatively gentle escalation of damage control training and assessment. By the end of the sixth week in FOST's capable hands, *Ark*'s young crew had been trained and assessed in all of the core disciplines of war fighting and damage control, while sustaining the ship at sea. The next phase of training would see a departure from the normal carrier regeneration process. In the strike role, *Ark* would have completed three weeks of aviation training working up to Aviation Operational Readiness Inspection. However, as an LPH she needed a fundamentally different assessment to prove that she could operate as a command amphibious platform, working with other ships and a variety of helicopter types to land a company-sized marine force ashore and then maintain effective command and control. *Ark*'s assessment therefore came in the shape of Exercise SOUTH WEST MARINES, where she became Commander of the Amphibious task group, with Alpha and Charlie Companies from 40 Commando and a tailored air group of three Sea King Mk-4s, one Mk-6, two Chinooks and three Mk-7 Lynx helicopters embarked. To add to the mix, two of the Navy's newest amphibious assets, the landing platform dock HMS *Albion* and the landing ship RFA *Largs Bay*, were put under *Ark*'s task group command. The exercise went smoothly and its successful completion allowed the Commander in Chief Fleet to declare *Ark Royal* at 'R2', high readiness status. HMS *Ocean* could now be released to pay off into refit.

Having achieved R2, the Ship's Company was finally rewarded with a foreign run ashore and there could be no better place to let off steam than Amsterdam, last visited in 2004. Everyone enjoyed the five-day visit making the most of the facilities this most cosmopolitan city had to offer. Back at Portsmouth on 15th March, the last major event before Easter was the ship's Rededication Ceremony. The First Sea Lord officiated at the ceremony, accompanied by the ship's Friend,

Commodore Sir Donald Gosling RNR. Following the death of the Queen Mother the decision had been taken not to ask for a new sponsor for the ship and thus 'Sir Don', as he was known to everyone, became an even more central father figure for the Ship's Company. Admiral Band rightly reflected that they were the greatest contributor to the success of *Ark Royal*'s regeneration, *"the men and women who live and work in the ship have my last vote of thanks; without them there might be a ship, but there would be no heart or capability, and it is because of their hard work, dedication and professional approach that Ark Royal stands ready to begin her operational tasking."*

After two weeks' Easter leave, HMS *Ark Royal* sailed for the CARINA deployment. CARINA started with the ship participating in Exercise COCKFIGHT between 20th and 23rd April. COCKFIGHT was the final phase of the combined UK and Netherlands Submarine Commanding Officers' Qualifying Course which evaluated each student's ability to command his submarine independently through multiple scenarios with little respite between each. For good reason, the course was nicknamed "Perisher"; the pass rate was only about 60% and invariably, unsuccessful candidates faced banishment from the submarine service in any capacity. *Ark*'s role was to provide both a high value unit to be attacked and a command platform to give tasking to the participating submarines during their shallow water phase.

After COCKFIGHT, *Ark* went straight into the biannual Joint Maritime Conference, now known as Exercise NEPTUNE WARRIOR, since the exercise control staff was based at HMS *Neptune* at Faslane. *Ark*'s task group came under the tactical command of the Commander Amphibious Task Group, Commodore Philip Jones, who had last served onboard as Admiral Brigstocke's staff officer in 1993 during Operation GRAPPLE. Three squadrons embarked for CARINA; 824 Squadron for operational flying training, elements of 848

Squadron for a short period of Operational Conversion Phase (OCP) training, and 847 Squadron Lynx Mk-7s providing the amphibious task group support squadron role. NEPTUNE WARRIOR 07-1 provided the opportunity to work up the one-star battle group organisation and refresh the amphibious training achieved during BOST. The training went smoothly as *Ark* exercised off the west cost of Scotland and the final evaluation confirmed she was ready to move to the next level as a two-star command platform. On completion of the exercise, 824 Squadron disembarked at Faslane and *Ark* proceeded to Copenhagen for an informal visit from 6th to 9th May, before heading up the Kattegat to Gothenburg.

During the four day stop at Sweden's second city the maritime battle staff of Rear Admiral Neil Morisetti, COMUKMARFOR, embarked to prepare his flagship for Exercise NOBLE MARINER, the main effort of the CARINA deployment. NOBLE MARINER along with two simultaneous exercises, NOBLE AWARD and KINDRED SWORD, was the major test of the combat readiness of NATO's high readiness military force, designated NATO Response Force 9 (NRF9), which included full Maritime, Land and Air Component Commands. Taking place between 14th and 25th May 2007 the exercises were designed to test a range of operations including humanitarian relief, provision of a security assistance force to stabilise a regional crisis, and escalation of the crisis response requiring the full spectrum of military force. The three exercises took place simultaneously in the North Sea, Kattegat, Danish Straits and in the Southern Baltic Sea including adjacent Danish, German, Swedish and Polish waters, airspace and land. The fictitious scenario required NATO forces to deploy the NRF9 to a Joint Operations Area (JOA) off the coast of Poland, in response to an escalating conflict inside a divided country. Operating under a UN mandate, exercise participants had to respond to a range of situations, including terrorist acts by extremist groups, a dispute over oil and gas reserves, smuggling of weapons including possible chemical weapons, refugees and displaced persons as well as instances of religious and ethnic cleansing. The exercises would culminate in an amphibious assault to conduct Non-combatant Evacuation Operations (NEO) and establish the conditions ashore to restore regional stability and security. This would then allow Non-Government Organisations (NGOs) and humanitarian relief efforts to re-enter and assist those caught up in the conflict.

The Maritime Component of NOBLE MARINER, under Admiral Morisetti's command, consisted of over forty units from thirteen different countries, ranging from mine countermeasures vessels and maritime patrol aircraft up to the Amphibious and Carrier Strike Groups. Ahead of assuming the mantle as NRF9 the capabilities and readiness of these task groups would be evaluated by the UKMARFOR battle staff, reporting to NATO Commander in the Eastern Atlantic, Commander in Chief Fleet, Admiral Sir James Burnell Nugent. The battle staff's job was to refine their command and campaign planning skills within the Effects Based Approach to Operations framework using assets from Standing NATO Maritime Group 1 (SNMG 1), Standing NATO Maritime Mine Countermeasures Group 1 (SNMMCG 1) and supported by elements from Strike Force NATO.

As the exercises began the NRF9 Task Force split, the high readiness forces (SNMG 1, SNMCMG 1) proceeding into the southern Baltic to provide an early NATO presence, while *Ark*'s amphibious group and the strike group led by HMS *Illustrious* and HMS *Manchester* proceeded west of Denmark to complete Force Integration Training. Thereafter the forces regrouped to demonstrate NATO's resolve to stabilize the situation in the self proclaimed state within the scenario. The finale of the exercise saw *Ark*, HMS *Albion* and the Landing Ships, RFA *Mounts Bay* and RFA *Largs Bay*, conduct amphibious rehearsals onto the Danish island of Bornholm, ahead of a main commando assault at Ustka on 21ˢᵗ May.

The assaults proceeded without a hitch and as the exercise played to its finale, Admiral Morisetti was satisfied to declare HMS *Ark Royal* capable of acting as his two-star command platform, allowing her on 25ᵗʰ May 2007 to take over the Fleet Flagship duty from HMS *Illustrious*. *Ark* made two more stops before heading back to Portsmouth at the end of the CARINA deployment. First she visited Gdynia in Poland to help strengthen Britain's relations with her new NATO partner. Poland's participation in NOBLE MARINER along with forces from the former Soviet states of Estonia and Latvia, and the NATO Scandinavian countries, demonstrated the strategic shift in the political situation around the Baltic and the Alliance's composition following the fall of the Berlin Wall. From Gdynia, *Ark* then enjoyed three days in her old German haunt of Hamburg, before heading home to Portsmouth for a few days of maintenance.

One of the enduring connections that successive generations in HMS *Ark Royal* had maintained was with the ship's affiliates. These affiliations promoted not only *Ark Royal* but the Royal Navy as a whole to a wider audience that might not otherwise see Britain's maritime forces in their normal day to day lives. *Ark*'s principal link was with the people of the City of Leeds, who had joined forces during World War II to raise the money to fund the replacement for the third HMS *Ark Royal*. With the connection to Leeds there followed a number of affiliations in Yorkshire, including Leeds United Football Club. Other affiliations were made with schools' Combined Cadet Forces and Sea Cadet units across the country, as well as local and national charities, including the RNLI. The ship also fostered inter-service links with the Army and RAF. *Ark*'s Army link was with the Queen's Royal Lancers, formed in 1993 following the amalgamation of *Ark*'s old regiment, the 17ᵗʰ/21ˢᵗ Lancers, with the 16ᵗʰ/5ᵗʰ

Queens Royal Lancers. No.1 (F) Squadron RAF and the Red Arrows provided *Ark*'s links with the RAF. The ship also maintained close links with industry and the City of London, through Jaguar Cars and the Worshipful Company of Shipwrights. It was important to maintain the links with these organisations and as well as sending members of the Ship's Company on expeditionary visits, every opportunity was taken to host visitors at sea to show off *Ark Royal* in action. Such an opportunity came on *Ark*'s next short passage on 11ᵗʰ June from Portsmouth up to London, with a range of guests onboard to see *Ark* go through her paces as a helicopter carrier. The visit to London coincided with the national commemoration of the 25ᵗʰ anniversary of the Falklands War. Moored at Greenwich, *Ark* provided the backdrop for the formal Royal Navy commemorative activities in the capital.

HMS *Ark Royal* returned to Portsmouth on 19ᵗʰ June for a well-earned maintenance period and summer leave, enjoying a families day on 22ⁿᵈ before the dockyard teams and ships staff got down to the business at hand. Back at sea on 17ᵗʰ September 2007, *Ark* continued a continuous tempo of amphibious exercises, befitting her high readiness status as COMUKMARFOR's NRF9 flagship. Next on the agenda was Exercise GREY HERON in the Solent and South Coast Exercise Areas and *Ark* was again joined by *Albion* and the two *Bay*s, and elements of 3 Commando Brigade HQ. The two-week training package was designed to bring the main landing force, 45 Commando Group embarked in *Mounts Bay*, up to the readiness level required to take over as the lead commando unit in late October. All aspects of amphibious operations, including boat and helicopter drills, assault station routines and ship to objective manoeuvre (STOM), were practiced. 45 Commando were given exposure to their new 'landing chariot', in the shape of the Offshore Raiding Craft, as well as being brought back up to speed in the inflatable raiders and landing craft carried by the RFA. Familiarization on both the

Sea King Mk-4 and Chinook CH-47 airframes was also given, which allowed for cross-decking of troops between *Ark* and *Albion*. Once all training was complete, the initial phase of the exercise culminated with Company-level assaults onto Scraesdon and Tregantle Forts. On the way back to Portsmouth, *Ark* picked up unusual companions in the shape of the 5,800-ton *Luyang*-class guided missile destroyer *Guangzhou* and the 20,500-ton auxiliary *Wei Shanhu*. The Chinese warships had just made a rare four day goodwill visit to Portsmouth Naval Base, bringing almost 500 Chinese naval personnel from the People's Republic of China.

One essential element of *Ark Royal*'s amphibious role that has thus far not been tested was her ability to land and support UK Special Forces (UKSF). The next two exercises in *Ark*'s programme, CHAMELEON in the Irish Sea and Bristol Channel in October and then KOMODO DRAGON off the south coast in early November provided the opportunities to do so. KOMODO DRAGON in particular proved *Ark*'s ability to embark and host a Joint Task Force HQ; the staff flown on by No.7 Squadron RAF and the exercise witnessed by the Director Special Forces, Major General Adrian Bradshaw and the Commander Joint Force Operations, Brigadier Ed Butler RM. Concurrent with the UKSF exercise, 848 Squadron embarked to support amphibious operations, while 702 Squadron embarked to conduct operational conversion training of their new pilots. On 9th November with the UKSF elements of training completed, *Ark* headed south toward the Iberian Peninsula in company with RFA *Fort George*. Reflecting the fact that Royal Navy warships no longer simply 'transited' or 'made passage', *Ark* conducted maritime security operations south through the Bay of Biscay under the codename Operation HOUND. Both she and *Fort George* monitored civilian and military shipping in the area with electronic warfare surveillance teams in both ships. At the same time 702 Squadron carried on with an increasingly challenging flying

programme. *Ark*'s destination was Lisbon, and she arrived at the Portuguese capital on 14th November, having first completed air defence exercises with five Portuguese Air Force F-16s. While alongside, as a demonstration of the UK's commitment to coordinate anti-narcotics operations, through activities like Operation HOUND, *Ark Royal* hosted a conference for the Maritime Analysis and Operations Centre – Narcotics (MAOC-N). The MAOC-N, based in Lisbon, was an international agency set up to coordinate anti-drug trafficking action by several European Union states, using shared intelligence on drug smuggling operations, by air or sea, to apply the most suitable military and/or law enforcement teams to respond to situations that arose. The MAOC-N's area of operations stretched from the Cape of Good Hope to the Norwegian Sea, with the UK contribution focusing around northern Africa, the Bay of Biscay, the Channel and the North Sea. Other highlights of the visit to Lisbon included a well-attended official reception which included HM Ambassador Alex Ellis, the Portuguese Secretary of State for Defence, Dr Joao Mira Gomes, Commander of the Portuguese Navy, Vice Admiral Vargas de Matos and Commander of the US Sixth Fleet, Vice Admiral James Winnefeld.

HMS *Ark Royal* sailed from Lisbon on 17th November and 702 Squadron once again got airborne to continue their pilot training, while the ship's operations and intelligence teams resumed Operation HOUND. Back in UK waters, *Ark* hosted Nicky Campbell and his BBC Radio 5 Live production team who broadcast their show from sea, including an interview with the First Sea Lord, Admiral Sir Jonathon Band. After a weekend alongside in Portsmouth, *Ark* was back at sea on 26th November for Amphibious Air Assault training with Charlie Company of 1st Battalion the Rifles and Lima Company 42 Commando embarked, and 848 Squadron's Sea King Mk-4s. Initial familiarisation and conversion practice at sea culminated in air assaults on 29th November, with the Commando Training School at Lympstone and Scraesdon Fort nominated as the targets.

Ark's final week at sea in 2007 was used to complete scheduled maintenance calibration firings and towed target shoots on her three Phalanx mounts, assisted by a maintainer loaned from HMS *Liverpool*, and to conduct further operational conversion training, this time for 845 Squadron. The single 845 Sea King embarked achieved only limited training, having suffered an engine malfunction on approach, recovering with a priority landing. The defect was successfully repaired and aircraft disembarked as *Ark* transitted to participate in FOST's 'Thursday War' off Plymouth, before returning to Portsmouth on 7th December. Pre Christmas events included the first visit on 17th December by the new Commander in Chief Fleet, Admiral Sir Mark Stanhope, during which he met a cross section of the Ship's Company over lunch. The following day the Court of *Ark*'s affiliated livery company, the Worshipful Company of Shipwrights, held an extraordinary meeting on board, to swear in Sir Donald Gosling as an Honorary Freeman of the Company. The Shipwrights also generously awarded laptop computers to three members of the Ship's Company noted for their outstanding contributions to innovation and efficiency in the previous twelve months.

HMS *Ark Royal* started 2008 as she had finished 2007; in maintenance alongside at Portsmouth, hosting a variety of VIPs and interested visitors to the Fleet Flagship. These included Quentin Davies MP who was leading the team charged by Prime Minister Gordon Brown with looking at ways to improve national recognition of the Armed Forces. Another was a dinner for Fleet Commanding and Executive Officers, hosted by Chief of Staff Capability, Rear Admiral Philip Willcocks with principal guest, General Sir Timothy Granville-Chapman, the Vice Chief of the Defence Staff. *Ark* also hosted the Annual Sponsor's Dinner for the Royal Navy Football Union, attended by Vice Admiral Sir Tim McClement, in addition to several lower profile but

important visits from both MoD and industrial partners. Following on from the NBPCP enacted in 2006, the Navy Board's next directed personnel study was 'Project Fisher' to look at ways of manning the future fleet once the *Type*-45 destroyer, *Queen Elizabeth*-class carrier and the future frigate came into service. *Ark*'s Air and Air Engineering departments had already been guinea pigs for minor manning trials, but the Fisher team came onboard to canvass wider views of the Ship's Company to inform their studies.

Ark Royal's first planned outing of the year was to conduct operational conversion for the Merlin HM-1s of 824 NAS. However the training called for a hunter-killer submarine to provide a decent target and as the only one available, HMS *Talent*, had already been committed for operations up north, *Ark*'s programme changed to rendezvous with her off Norway. The shift of exercise areas made it worthwhile for *Ark* to participate in the NATO multi-national Exercise ARMATURA BOREALIS. This and other short-notice changes to *Ark*'s programme promised the Ship's Company a varied and exciting year, with the main focus looking toward two transatlantic deployments, first for Exercise CONSTANT ALLIANCE in April, followed by a UK/US Joint Task Force Exercise in July. It had been over fifteen years since *Ark Royal* had last visited the United States and everyone was determined to make the most of the promised opportunities.

Ark Royal sailed from Portsmouth on 5th February and after routine trials following the maintenance period, she turned east and then north into the North Sea. Two 849 Squadron Sea King Mk-7 ASAC embarked for familiarisation and air defence exercise tasking the following morning. The ship then spent 36 hours conducting gunnery serials, deck landing training and fighter control working with USAF F-15E/Cs from the 492nd and 493rd Fighter Squadrons based at RAF Lakenheath, Tornado F-3s of No.43 Squadron from RAF Leuchars, and Typhoons undergoing evaluation with No.17 Squadron from Coningsby. In between serials and overnight, *Ark* conducted high power propulsion trials en route to her birth place, North Shields. Arriving on Tyneside on the evening of 8th February, the ship hosted a well attended reception for reservists and local businesses, under the MoD's "SaBRE" marketing and communications campaign, Supporting Britain's Reservists and Employers. Ship Open to Visitors the following day attracted in excess of 6,500 locals, with many having to be turned away, proving once again the deep affection for and abiding interest in Tyneside's carrier.

With 83 affiliates embarking on the afternoon of 11th February, *Ark Royal* left North Shields to make a fast transit to Poole harbour, the headquarters of the Royal National Lifeboat Institute. There, early in the morning of 13th, she rendezvoused with a number of inshore RNLI boats to promote their "Train one, Save many" campaign. Back in Portsmouth, 824 Squadron ground staff embarked over the 14th and 15th, while the Naval Base Commander, Commodore David Steel launched "Meet the Navy 2008" onboard and Admiral Stanhope held his inaugural conference for serving Commanding and Executive Officers, and dinner in the evening.

Ark sailed four days later for the start of Exercise ARMATURA BOREALIS, with four Merlin HM-1s of 824 Squadron embarking south of the Isle of Wight, before routing through the Dover straits. After holding off the north east coast for two days in relative shelter while the helicopters conducted landing patterns, *Ark* departed UK waters on 20th February for transit to Bergen in Norway. The forward R1007 radar antenna broke down during the North Sea passage and given that it was essential for safe navigation needed to be replaced as soon as possible. The radar maintainer conducted the precarious evolution in sub-zero temperatures and disconcertingly high winds while the ship refuelled during its eight hour stop at Bergen. Amidst this excitement, the Norwegian naval base commander and also Commanding Officer of HNoMS *Fridtjof*

Nansen lunched on board with Captain Mansergh, facilitating a face to face opportunity to discuss the forthcoming exercise.

ARMATURA BOREALIS was NATO's major maritime exercise of the first half of 2008, designed to test its capability to land a Brigade sized amphibious force in hostile conditions against a live enemy. Four nations, Spain, Germany, Belgium and the Netherlands would participate with the United Kingdom and the host country Norway with over 3,000 personnel committed in 25 ships and submarines. Of these 3 Commando Brigade contributed around 1,500 men, learning skills in the harsh Arctic climate of northern Norway that they would then use when they deployed to Afghanistan. Norway's coast provides challenging terrain coupled with an incredibly testing climate. Overcoming operational and tactical problems here was demanding and the Marines had trained in Norway for decades, refining skills and honing talents to get it right. "*If you can fight and survive in Norway then you can do it anywhere,*" was the Corps' accepted wisdom. Major General Garry Robison RM, Commander UK Amphibious Forces acting as CTG 445, led the main naval force centred on HMS *Albion* and HMS *Bulwark*; the former ship having handed over the baton of the high readiness role to her younger sister just before the start of the exercise. RFA *Mounts Bay* again formed a key part of the group. *Ark* provided a second command platform and acted as ASW Force Commander, with 824's Merlins working up and the *Type-22* towed array frigate HMS *Cornwall* providing escort duties.

Chopping operational control to CTG 445 on 25th February, *Ark* arrived off Andoya Island and Captain Mansergh transferred to *Albion* for initial briefings. *Ark* would first be under the tactical command of CTG 445.08 led by the Norwegian Commodore Haakon Tronstad, conducting ASW suppression ahead of the amphibious assaults. With 824's main training focused on conducting active anti-submarine warfare, inclement weather and fragility of the aircrafts' dipping sonar sets frustrated their early progress toward achieving their training standard. Looking for cover, *Ark* relocated south into Vestfjorden, where some ASW training with HMS *Talent* was achieved, despite poor conditions and later some excellent anti-surface warfare training with 824 Squadron operating against Norwegian inshore fast patrol boats. Operating throughout the exercise in Defence Watches, *Ark* would retreat into the protected waters of the Ofotfjorden to anchor and refuel from the Norwegian tanker HNoMS *Valkyrien*. At the beginning of March *Ark* chopped to the UK Amphibious Task Group 445.01 under Commodore Paul Hudson, as it relocated from Harstad to prepare for the entry into theatre and the amphibious assault. 824's training continued despite the poor conditions, but their focus on achieving this mission caused some disquiet among the other participants that they were not more readily available to support the wider exercise.

Late in the afternoon of 2nd March two Sea King Mk-4s landed on *Ark* in a snow storm for fuel, and disembarked three press reporters and one military escort. With further snow forecast, after the press acquaint on *Ark* finished it was thought safer to transfer the reporters via boat to the mainland for their onward journey from Bardufoss airport, rather than fly them out. With *Ark* at anchor following a second RAS with the *Valkyrien*, the boat transfer set off at 0300 on 4th March, to the Norwegian base at Ramsund about five miles up an inlet from the Ofotfjorden. The transfer did not go smoothly. In the darkness the boat coxswain misjudged the approach to shore and being too far to port of the safe track ran the Pacific-22 aground while heading at twenty knots for the narrow inlet. One journalist was injured and the boat suffered substantial damage to its hull. The crew and the passengers were subsequently rescued by *Ark*'s second boat, with the damaged hull eventually recovered at high water the following morning. Not surprisingly, given that the passengers were a photographer for the Mail on

Sunday, the editor of an aviation magazine and a Press Association reporter, the story quickly became public knowledge.

While the boat maintainer worried about how to get the damaged Pacific-22 to *Ark*, the ship's air engineering effort was directed at preparing 824's Merlins to support Royal Flight tasking on 5th March so that they could transport His Majesty King Harald V of Norway to the task group. For the remaining three days in theatre, 824's focus was on completing their ASuW syllabus and tackling active and passive ASW training with HMS *Talent*, the finale of which included four successful depth charge drops from the Merlins. *Ark* departed Norwegian waters on 8th March en route to Faslane, where 824 Squadron disembarked to HMS *Gannet*, the Royal Naval Air Station at Prestwick.

The maritime exercise area for ARMATURA BOREALIS retraced historic ground for the Royal Navy. At the head of the Ofotfjorden lay the port of Narvik; which on 10th and 13th April 1940 was the scene of the earliest and among the most intense naval battles between the Royal Navy and the Kriegsmarine during World War II.

Following Hitler's order to invade Norway, in early April 1940 six Kriegsmarine groups broke out from their bases in Germany to sieze all of the key ports along the Norwegian coast. Intelligence reports soon reached the Admiralty that German destroyers were off Narvik, and the 2nd Destroyer Flotilla under the command of Captain Bernard Warburton-Lee, was ordered to go in pursuit. Leaving HMS *Hotspur* and HMS *Hostile* to guard the entrance to the fjord, at 04:30 on 10th April 1940, Captain Warburton-Lee in HMS *Hardy*, accompanied by HMS *Hunter* and HMS *Havock*, crept in to Narvik harbour under cover of darkness and thick snow to find five German destroyers and a host of tankers and merchantmen lying at anchor. The warships were part of the ten-strong Destroyer Group Two charged with landing 1,900 Austrian mountain troops and taking control of the surrounding fjords. Warburton-Lee's ships made three passes on the enemy, being joined after the first pass by *Hotspur* and *Hostile*. The H-class destroyers sank two of the German warships, disabled one more and destroyed six merchantmen before withdrawing almost untouched. The British force was making its way back to the Vestfjorden when at 06:00 three German destroyers emerged from the Herjangsfjord to give chase. Minutes later two more German destroyers came out of Ballangen Bay to block the British exit from the Ofotfjorden. HMS *Hardy* was the first British ship to be hit and Warburton-Lee was mortally wounded in the attack. Crippled and with her bridge destroyed, *Hardy* was subsequently beached. *Hunter* was the next ship put out of commission, coming to a dead halt in the water after several hits. *Hotspur* was then hit and received damage to her steering system, causing her to crash into *Hunter*. Several more hits were registered on the pair until *Hotspur* was able to reverse out of the wreckage. *Hostile* and *Havock* meanwhile had raced ahead, but turned about and came back to aid the retreat of *Hotspur*. The German ships having received a few hits and, more importantly, being critically short of fuel, were not able to pursue. HMS *Hunter* sank in the middle of the Ofotfjorden with the loss of 110 of her 145-man crew.

There HMS *Hunter* lay, undiscovered, for nearly seventy years until, on 5th March 2008, the Norwegian mine hunter HNoMS *Tyr*, while conducting mine clearance exercises as part of ARMATURA BOREALIS, detected the wreck on her side-scan sonar trace. Three days later the ships of the British task group led by Major General Robison in HMS *Albion* sailed in line over the wreck site laying wreaths in tribute to those who had lost their lives, closing the chapter on one of the most remarkable Royal Navy battles of World War II. Following her Norwegian adventure, HMS *Ark Royal* was due to spend 48 hours alongside in Faslane to replenish and refuel before heading west to Norfolk Virginia. It seemed that the Fates were still not smiling on *Ark* as she came alongside at

the Scottish submarine base and berthed at the old Polaris jetty. The berth had not been designed for such large ships and storm force conditions during the evening *Ark* was pushed onto shore by the high winds, crushing the jetty side. Tugs were needed to hold the ship off throughout the night, leaving over half of the Ship's Company stranded ashore on a wet and windy Wednesday night in Helensburgh. Hasty arrangements were set up in HMS *Neptune* to house the waifs and strays and the Senior Rates' Mess ended up looking more like air raid shelter with bodies, blankets and bedding adorning the public rooms. Having first lost a boat and now suffered damage the ship's hull and Captain Mansergh was understandably keen to get back to sea as soon as possible, fearing that '*bad luck comes in threes*'. After clearing the Irish Sea and receiving a final top up of fuel from RFA *Orangeleaf* in the South West Approaches on 15th March, *Ark* turned west for the Atlantic crossing. Sure enough, *Ark*'s third spell of bad luck struck as she struggled through particularly rough weather for an all-too slow transit to Norfolk. Without the benefit of tanker support to increase her line of advance Captain Mansergh could do little to minimize the discomfort for his Ship's Company. After nine days of storm-tossed seas, *Ark* finally came in range of the US coast and rendezvoused with the US tanker USNS *Laramie* on 24th March for fuel, before heading into Norfolk.

The introduction and integration of the British and American teams for Exercise CONSTANT ALLIANCE started immediately. *Ark*'s American tailored air group was made up of three CH-46E Sea Knights from the Marine Medium Helicopter Squadron 774 (HMM774), known as the "Wild Goose", and two MH-60S Knighthawks of the Helicopter Sea Combat Squadron 26 (HSC26), known as the "Chargers". They would carry *Ark*'s Embarked Military Force of 138 marines provided by India Company from the 3rd Battalion, 8th Marine Regiment based at Camp Lejeune.

Ark Royal began CONSTANT ALLIANCE on April Fool's Day, with the marines embarking and quickly settling in to life onboard a British warship, while their helicopters worked up to achieve deck qualifications. Two USN warships were assigned to escort the carrier; the cruiser USS *Normandy* and the destroyer USS *Mitscher*. Both ships were fitted with the Aegis air defence system which incorporated the immensely powerful SPY-1D phased radar, which caused some technical issues for the British ship if they operated too near to each other. *Ark*'s own radars were still dogged by teething problems and poor reliability since leaving Rosyth, and the interference from the Aegis ships only added to the headache.

Once the helicopters had achieved their deck qualifications, the force was able to move on to more advanced training off the Cherry Point exercise areas. As CTG, *Ark* gained maximum benefit from multiple training serials as the initial phase progressed, although towed target shoots were lost due to a failure of the tow aircraft. Remotely controlled surface targets were employed in the second week as the scenario developed allowing for live fire exercises against a realistic Fast Inshore Attack Craft (FIAC) threat. The exercise game play was modeled on the well-trodden "Treasure Coast" scenario that *Ark* would come to know and love during her subsequent visits to the USA. As is always the case with these scenarios, 'peaceful negotiations' had broken down requiring the marines to invade. The culmination of the exercise thus saw a full company assault into the Camp Lejeune area, witnessed by Brigadier General David Berger USMC, the former CO of 3/8 Marines and now the Assistant Commander of their division, the 2nd Marines. *Ark* withdrew on completion of the landing having recovered the full air group, before steaming north into thick fog for a replenishment with USNS *Laramie* and USS *Normandy* off Cape Hatteras. The following morning *Ark* was back in Norfolk with the USMC helicopters still embarked as the fog had not lifted to allow their safe departure 24 hours earlier. The helicopters finally left that afternoon, allowing the Ship's Company to enjoy a weekend alongside

before *Ark* set sail for home. Without tanker support, following a last top up from *Laramie* on the 15th, *Ark* was again forced to make a 'leisurely' passage home, arriving in the UK nine days later.

Back in home waters and after a weekend alongside, *Ark* hosted a Defence Industry Day at sea with 151 guests invited from industry, equipment project teams and the wider MoD. During the day, a Lynx from 702 Squadron, a Sea King from 771 Squadron and a Merlin from 820 Squadron embarked and then conducted routine training serials to give the assembled audience a taste of life in a helicopter carrier. Alongside again in Portsmouth on 28th April, *Ark* immediately entered a Fleet Time Support Period (FTSP), scheduled to complete a month later. The highlight for many of the Ship's Company during the period alongside was the chance on 17th May 2008 to support Portsmouth Football Club as they took on Cardiff City in the FA Cup Final at Wembley. The team had been invited onboard in the week before the final and the ship enjoyed her association with the club. Inspired by the presence of greatness in their midst, Pompey won the match 1-0!

Ark's next period at sea in June 2008 offered both an opportunity for 702 and 771 squadrons to conduct more training and for the Ship's Company to build on the affiliations rekindled at the start of the year. The port visit to Liverpool was the undisputed highlight of the short trip. *Ark* had always attracted a large number of recruits from the north west of England, and for the ship's 'scousers', the four-day visit provided the opportunity to show off both the ship to friends and families, and the city to shipmates. Berthed at the cruise liner terminal adjacent to the Liver Building, the ship hosted a formal evening reception and dinner on 6th June, for civil and military dignitaries from the region. A highly successful SOTV event the following day attracted 5,000 people, presenting the usual security and safety challenges for the ship's Officer of the Day. A wag amongst his Duty Watch happily reassured him that suitable preparations were in place,

"Don't worry Sir, I've bolted down the brass work and there are metal detectors on the jetty just in case!" Two hundred and fifty of the Ship's Company, led by Leeds-local Warrant Officer Mark Fisher, travelled across the Pennines on the 8th to exercise the Freedom of the City and while public turnout was disappointingly low, close ties were once again established with *Ark*'s affiliates in the area. Another opportunity for regional engagement was exploited as *Ark* departed Liverpool on 9th June, with Vice Admiral Sir Paul Haddacks, Lieutenant Governor of the Isle of Man and five members of the Tynwald embarked. To add to the departure, the Mersey Marine Fire Unit provided simulated Opposing Forces to conduct a Force Protection exercise in the Mersey channel with 702's aircraft launched from alongside. Next stop was the Isle of Man, with *Ark* arriving at Douglas Bay later that evening to land the Manx residents before proceeding north and west of Ireland for further 702 Squadron training. A team from the Portsmouth Flotilla had also embarked at Liverpool to conduct the annual engineering advisory visit; a routine inspection designed to ensure *Ark* maintained her high standards between formal training periods at FOST. Happy with what they saw, and eager to get off, the PORFLOT staff disembarked by helicopter to the Scillies on 13th June while *Ark* transited slowly east to anchor off St Ives the following day and dress ship overall for the official birthday of HM The Queen. The operational pause conserved fuel, permitted some low level 'R-and-R' and maintenance before 702's training moved into its final tactical phase. 702 Squadron conducted a range of maritime and overland tactical serials before *Ark* positioned in the South Coast Exercise Areas on 18th June for a RAS with RFA *Orangeleaf*. The opportunity was taken for *Ark*'s new CO-designate, Captain John Clink, to join the ship and witness the evolution as part of his platform endorsement prior to taking command. *Ark* got close enough to *Orangeleaf* to pass the guidelines but with winds in excess of fifty knots conditions on the RFA's deck were too

dangerous to RAS, and the ships conducted an emergency break-away. The final 702 flights were conducted at Portland overnight on 19th and 20th June while the ship sailed around in circles to calibrate her electronic warfare sensors off the QinetiQ range. With the checks complete and *Ark*'s sensors back 'in date' for another year she berthed at Portsmouth on 20th June.

Ark's short self maintenance period focused on preparations for the second US visit of 2008. The weapon engineers in particular battled to get the American and NATO command and control systems, CENTRIX, SIPRNET and NSWAN fitted and working so that the ship would be able to operate effectively within the USS *Bataan* amphibious battle group. As the Fleet flagship she again played host to a number of visitors through June, including a follow-up session with the Project Fisher team and a delegation from Thales involved with the design of the future carrier. Portsmouth FC, with FA cup in hand, made a triumphal return to the ship on 25th June and the following day Admiral Sir Mark Stanhope returned onboard to star in a video production for the Navy's internal communications programme "Two-Six". Jeff Stultiens, the latest of a long string of artists to work onboard *Ark*, visited the ship on 30th June. He had been given access by Admiral Burnell-Nugent to the Fleet to produce a series of images and portraits, including one of the admiral, which would visually encapsulate the wide variety of tasks that the modern navy was required to undertake. Among others of Stultiens' subjects was Lieutenant Colonel Mark Searight RM, the ship's amphibious operations officer. Somewhat less auspicious and less romantic, but nevertheless vital to keep *Ark* at sea; the last visitors of June were a dockyard team to conduct the ship's Sanitation Inspection while the ship was 'wound' port-side to, so that her hull could be painted.

Captain Mansergh's final month in command of HMS *Ark Royal* was due to be spent at sea, with the ship's second visit to America for a Joint Task Force Exercise (JTFEX), codenamed Operation

BRIMSTONE. The Ship's Company was naturally enthusiastic about the short visit across the Atlantic but what the ship really needed was a longer operational deployment with dedicated UK forces embarked to hone her amphibious skills and consolidate the lessons already learned. It had been fifteen months since *Ark* was last at BOST and concern was raised that with a paucity of airborne and expeditionary assets to operate with, due to ongoing commitments in Afghanistan, her fighting edge may have blunted. A combined inspection team from Fleet HQ, FOST, Portsmouth Flotilla and the 'trappers' of Naval Flying Standards Flight, under the command of Commodore Nick Lambert, was thus assembled and arranged to assess the ship as she was put through her paces with the US Marine Corps embarked.

Ark was due to leave on 2nd July, but her departure was delayed by 36 hours so that she could be the venue for the signing of the Production Contract for the *Queen Elizabeth*-class carrier, by Baroness Taylor, the Minister for Defence Equipment and Support, Alan Johnson, the Chief Executive of Babcock VT and Ian King, the Chief Operating Officer of BAE Systems. The First Sea Lord, Admiral Sir Jonathon Band, and Deputy Commander in Chief RAF Air Command, Air Marshal Ian McNicoll, witnessed the signing on behalf of the two services that would, in theory at least, benefit most from the historic contract.

With the formalities completed, *Ark* sailed from Portsmouth to commence transit to Norfolk. After a brief replenishment from RFA *Bayleaf*, early on 4th July *Ark* headed out for the unsupported transatlantic crossing. Weapons and sensors were tested against Falcon aircraft in the South West Approaches following the RAS and once out in deeper water *Ark* deployed her S2170 towed array to conduct a long-overdue Sea Acceptance Trial of the Surface Ship Torpedo Defence System. Rapidly deteriorating weather precluded the planned Maritime Surveillance missions as *Ark* tracked south toward Gibraltar overnight. The severe conditions lasted for two days but the

restrictions of operations at least gave the Ship's Company some sporadic rest before defence watch training began in earnest. New assault guides and wardens were trained in the procedures for non-combatant evacuation, prisoner handling and mass casualty reception. As more data from the BRIMSTONE scenario became available, routines were refined and reviewed to ensure *Ark* was ready for all eventualities. This included training the Ship's Company at Actions Stations with simulated battle damage requiring both the Operations Room and the Bridge team to relocate to their secondary command positions. Poor weather continued throughout the week, limiting opportunities to conduct maintenance and also impacting on 854 Squadron planned flying programme. Despite best efforts, a mismatch of equipment and damage to one of the aircraft regrettably prevented the anticipated rate of flying being achieved.

Nearing the eastern seaboard, *Ark* was met by USNS *Lewis and Clark* for a RAS before putting into Norfolk. 854 Squadron detached to Chambers Field just ahead of *Ark*'s arrival so that the crews could link up with advance ground teams and commence flying operations with host squadrons the following day. The liaison with US forces started immediately; a USMC communications team established the radio networks for the exercise while the returning ground teams from HMM774 and HSC26 set up the facilities to recover in due course their Sea Knights and Nighthawk helicopters. The embarked force for BRIMSTONE was provided by the 3rd Battalion of the 9th Marine Regiment based at Camp Lejeune. The task group flagship USS *Bataan* and *Ark*'s escort for the initial phase of the exercise, USS *Mason*, also made early contact with their British counterparts, while Vice Admiral Chanik, the Commander of the US Second Fleet hosted an informal reception for *Ark*'s officers. The 38-man Fleet Operational Assurance Visit team under Commodore Lambert arrived in theatre on 20th July and witnessed the Marine and aviation ground staff embarkations and attended the pre-deployment conference. Everything was thus set for BRIMSTONE to start the following day.

One regrettable incident of the Norfolk visit was the collapse of the aft brow from its supporting platform, which injured three Petty Officers who were on the gangway at the time. Two were taken for hospital treatment but returned to the ship within eight hours; but a leg injury to the third necessitated his repatriation to UK.

HMS *Ark Royal* sailed from Norfolk on 21st July, at Action Stations in anticipation of simulated attacks by fast inshore craft. The posture also allowed the ship to quickly settle into the Defence Watch routine that had been practiced during the crossing and would remain in force for most of the ten-day exercise. The ship transited from the Virginia Capes areas overnight 21st/22nd toward the assigned Joint Operating Area further south, with a transit through a simulated 'choke point' against surface and submarine opposition providing another excuse for Action Stations. *Ark* took station in the sea echelon areas off Camp Lejeune late on 22nd July to conduct further training and assault preparations. The next morning, following replenishment from USNS *Leroy Grumman*, the ship was brought to Action Stations once again to support the flyaway of her entire landing force. Having achieved these final serials under the approving gaze of the Deputy Commander Strike Force NATO, Rear Admiral Chris Snow and the Fleet OAV team, *Ark* was able to declare herself ready for Operation BRIMSTONE just before midnight on 23rd July. The inspectors disembarked to Cherry Point the following morning leaving *Ark* to conduct three days of free-play exercises responding to orders from the task group commander in USS *Bataan*. On 24th *Ark*'s US Marines completed an 'on order' Joint Personnel Recovery serial and prepared for landings on 26th. The order came late on 25th and at 0615 the following morning 3/9 USMC Quick Response Force were put ashore by helicopter to engage the enemy. Back 'home', or at least onboard, for tea

and medals in the afternoon, the Marines regrouped once again to launch a deliberate raid on 27th, with 98 marines remaining ashore on completion. The final administrative offloads were completed the following day to New River before *Ark* detached to Mayport.

Mayport had been *Ark*'s home from home during the first seven years of service, but few onboard could now remember the carrier's enduring affection for the Florida base, since her last visit in 1992. The Ship's Company set about acquainting themselves with this most picturesque naval base but did not have long to enjoy it. A change of command beckoned meaning *Ark* had to look pristine and she was then due to sail for home the following day.

On 31st July 2008, Captain Mansergh handed over command of the Fleet flagship to Captain John Clink OBE. During his period in command, Captain Mansergh had led *Ark* from the depths of refit to assume the status of the high readiness commando carrier, taking her from the arctic conditions of Norway to the tropical conditions of Florida along the way. Despite a lack of assets to build up the durability and sustainability that comes with operating a permanently assigned embarked force and aircraft, *Ark* nevertheless demonstrated to all who visited her that she was Able, Ready and Keen, to coin her informal motto throughout Mansergh's command. Captain Mansergh was certain where the praise for this achievement lay, "*I have been deeply impressed throughout the past two years by the continuous good humour, willingness, professionalism and dedication of my Ship's Company during Ark's regeneration from extended readiness and operation as the R2 LPH. Ark lives up to her reputation as the Fleet Flagship and I am confident I leave my relief in very good hands.*"

Sailing from Mayport on 1st August 2008, under the new command of John Clink, HMS *Ark Royal* would continue to live up to this reputation as new challenges awaited, including her regeneration to Carrier Strike.

Commodore J R H Clink OBE Royal Navy

(Commanding Officer 2008 – 2010)

It has been the greatest honour to command *Ark Royal*, the Fleet Flagship, and to experience from a most privileged position the 'Spirit of the *Ark*'. There is something very special about this great ship and, most of all, her wonderful people. On joining, one is struck immediately by the friendliness and understated professionalism of everyone onboard – all who wear an *Ark Royal* cap tally are caught up by the passion and pride that has endured through the last twenty-five years.

Every chapter in the Ship's life has its moments. Sir Don Gosling's 80th Birthday Party was a welcome opportunity for us all to thank him for his generosity over many years. Then I think of four months in dry dock for a 'super' MOT and 'go faster' paint on the hull. This was followed by the enduring challenge of BOST in an extraordinarily windy autumn. Cracking visits to Liverpool and Newcastle (twice!) preceded the first jet flying for over six years as *Ark Royal* became the Nation's Strike Carrier again. Our AURIGA Deployment began with a Joint Warrior Exercise where you can expect surprises but perhaps not a volcanic ash cloud curtailing flying or our fast passage south to become a ferry for stranded passengers – quickly cancelled but closely followed by the discovery of cracks in our fuel tanks and then the remarkable turnaround of an emergency docking. We then raced across the Atlantic to catch up with the AURIGA task group and take our place as COMUKCSG's Flagship. The runs ashore in Norfolk, Mayport and Port Canaveral were welcome breaks between exercises. At sea, the buzz of having twelve US Marine Corps Harriers pounding the decks and the progress made by our own Joint Force Harriers and helicopter squadrons marked a great step forward in moving on with Carrier Strike. In Halifax, with the First Sea Lord embarked, we had the honour of participating in the Canadian Navy's Centennial Fleet Review by Her Majesty the Queen as well as welcoming David Cameron onboard for his first Prime Ministerial visit to the Royal Navy.

I made my watchwords 'Lead-Live-Laugh' and at the end of my time I am very proud to say that we led the Fleet with style, lived up to our enviable reputation and found lots of time to laugh and enjoy ourselves.

Chapter 14

2008 – 2010:
The *Ark* strikes back!

With her American exploits over for another year, HMS *Ark Royal* sailed for home on 1st August 2008. USNS *Lewis and Clark* refilled *Ark*'s tanks two days out from Mayport, but from there she would make the transatlantic crossing unsupported and so pushed east at a very sedate eleven knots; the passage made uncomfortable by surprisingly windy conditions. The relative calm of the return voyage was shattered, briefly, on 8th August. At just after 11:00 a flood alarm from one of *Ark*'s deep magazines activated in HQ1. Simultaneously, the Minerva fire alarm activated in the same area. The emergency response team was immediately on the scene. Fortunately, there was no fire, but the spray system had operated and flooded the magazine, which was full of artillery and mortar rounds, to a depth of three feet before the system was isolated. What ammunition could be saved was moved to other stowages while expert advice was sought from shore on how to handle the remaining stock.

In keeping with the new Navy directive to 'patrol' rather than just 'transit', *Ark* was tasked to conduct Maritime Security Patrol duties once she crossed the meridian at twelve degrees west. 854 Squadron's ASaC Mk-7s that had worked so well through the JTFEX were now suffering tedious defects which, with worsening weather, thwarted the squadron's daily flying programme, or the hopes of some of the Ship's Company in getting a birds eye view of their ship. Instead, airframes were consolidated to ensure enough were available to support the maritime security tasking scheduled for 11th and 12th August. In the event, very little merchant traffic was observed and with sea states building through SS6 and winds increasing, flying was restricted to daytime only on the 11th. 854's last duty before departing to Culdrose was to fly on the weapons experts on 12th August to look at the flood damaged munitions. The surveys by the inspectors revealed that the ammunition had actually faired pretty well; nevertheless as a precaution it would be off-loaded and replaced at the earliest opportunity.

HMS *Ark Royal* returned to Portsmouth on 14th August 2008 and following the precedent set for her previous Commanding Officers, John Clink was given the honour of a full ceremonial arrival with the Ship's Company arranged in Procedure Alpha on the flight deck. There should have been another special welcome for *Ark*, in the shape of a fly past by a single Harrier flown by John Clink's younger brother, Adam. Coming in the wake of a recent controversy surrounding 'inappropriate' use of military assets, the response from Fleet Headquarters was, unequivocally, 'no', *"Daily Mail readers would have a field day."* The rebuke gave *Ark*'s media team a valuable lesson in how best to portray the Fleet Flagship in these seemingly politically correct and cash-strapped times. Henceforth *Ark* would be 'green', 'efficient' and 'cost-effective'. Style and a sense of humour would have to be reserved for those who came to see her in person and in this respect

Captain Clink had no doubt that his Ship's Company could, and would, perform well. "*I have been from the lowest deck to the top towers and I can see the industry going on,*" he reported. "*You shouldn't be in these jobs if you don't have a passion for it and I have already seen 650 people committed to making Ark Royal a success.*"

The main effort of August and September alongside in Portsmouth was to complete the ship's routine maintenance and allow the Ship's Company to take summer leave before the busy autumn programme got underway. Taking advantage of the warmer weather, the focus for the work was ship's husbandry and preservation of the upper decks. When the majority of the crew returned from leave at the start of September the ship looked more like a giant marquee, with most of the flight deck shrouded in tarpaulin covers, and smelling of fresh paint. Major store ship evolutions throughout September brought the fridges and provision stores back up to deployment levels, while elements of the Ship's Company were similarly refreshed in damage control and fire fighting training at HMS *Phoenix*. Leaving the deputy heads of department in charge of the maintenance package, *Ark*'s commanders visited Belgium for a tour of the site of Wellington's famous victory at Waterloo and liaison visits to NATO HQ in Brussels. As the Fleet Flagship *Ark* attracted visitors of her own through the month, playing host to the Surface Warfare Officers' Association for a cocktail party on 18th September, and the Navigation and Direction Officers' Association dinner the following week. Nick Clegg also visited as part of a broader Navy acquaint for the leader of the Liberal Democrats.

In the face of shrinking budgets, it had become almost the norm for defence purse holders during the third quarter of each financial year to seek savings that would avoid any embarrassing overspend by the following March. The 2008 financial "difficulties" saw *Ark*'s fuel allocation for October being reduced by £500,000 with a proposal that the ship should conduct the forthcoming JOINT WARRIOR at anchor in the Firth of Clyde. Given the major impact this would have both on ship's operational capability and her credibility should news leak, robust negotiations with fleet planners sought to withdraw *Ark* from a later commitment to Staff College Sea Days at the end of October and instead use the fuel judiciously for the biannual war games off Scotland. The ship eventually won the battle, but the suggested in-year savings came off the back of a tough spending review which potentially had far graver consequences for *Ark* as a range of options were considered on whether or not, and then how to, regenerate her to Carrier Strike. "*The uncertainty and information leaks from various sources led to the inevitable rumours which in turn had a destabilising influence across the ship as a whole,*" reflected Captain Clink as he tried to bring focus to what had appeared to be a muddled and messy process. One encouragement throughout this period of uncertainty was a collective visit by the aviation community in Fleet Headquarters and the Strike Group battle staff to *Ark* to flesh out more detail of the ship's transition plan from LPH back to CVS. "*Ark's open and welcoming nature will assure a strong and enduring relationship. The ship has a positive eagerness to assume the UK's Carrier Strike role as soon as it can,*" reported her new Captain.

With her fuel allowance restored, HMS *Ark Royal* sailed from Portsmouth for JOINT WARRIOR on 2nd October. Delayed by 24 hours due to high winds and an unserviceable tug *Ark*'s hastily redrawn programme still allowed for calibration firings of her three Phalanx and two 20-mm cannons south of the Isle of Wight, but she had to miss the fun of a FOST 'Thursday War' off Devonport so that she could maintain her appointment at Faslane. Two days later, *Ark* anchored off the Tail O' the Bank, allowing the battle staff and 854's ASaC helicopters to embark from Prestwick. At the adjacent anchorage to *Ark* was FS *Tonnerre* the brand new and highly capable, if somewhat ugly, *Mistral*-class French LPH. *Ark*'s battle staff came from the US Navy COMDESRON 24 organisation and it was vital that they should quickly understand the capabilities of the ship and get to know her command team, since they would be the prime movers in exploiting joint US/UK training opportunities in the future. Huge amounts were learned by both teams and the visit of Rear Admiral Quinn USN (Commander Strike Force Training Atlantic) served to further cement *Ark*'s relationships with the Mayport and Norfolk training commands for the proposed deployment the following year.

From anchor, *Ark*'s Scottish exercise started with an exit through a mine-swept channel and then the unwelcome attention of a swarm attack from armed rigid inflatable boats. The first week of the exercise was designed to develop *Ark*'s Combat Enhancement and Force Integration Training. This so called CET-FIT phase proved most demanding due to conflicts between 854's need to fly and the wider requirements of the exercise. The explanation for this was quite simple: the wind was blowing from the wrong direction. *Ark* had constantly to reverse course to head into the prevailing wind in order to launch and recover aircraft, preventing her making any sensible headway toward the next JOINT WARRIOR serial. Programming refuelling and replenishment opportunities was equally challenging since only one tanker was provided for the force that was split between the east and west coasts of Scotland. To make matters worse, the weather deteriorated significantly and while the ships in the Minch were able to find some shelter, the *Type-23* frigate HMS *Argyll*, acting as an anti-submarine screen unit, took a beating in high seas to the north. Consequently, the ASW-orientated theatre entry phase was cancelled and *Ark*, along with the remaining forces, remained in the lee of the Minch until the final assault into Loch Ewe overnight on 15th October. Having successfully landed HMS *Albion*'s Royal Marines, the amphibious task group conducted a 'choke point' exit through the

Sound of Mull, HMS *Gloucester* and HMS *Somerset* escorting HMS *Ark Royal* and HMS *Albion*. With fuel constraints impacting on the programme and *Ark* extracted from Staff College Sea Days, the ship returned to Portsmouth on 19th October. JOINT WARRIOR had provided a useful 'top up' of the ship's amphibious operational capability. Her next spell at sea would provide a similar refresher of her anti-submarine skills.

At the end of October, *Ark Royal* sailed for ASWEX 08-2. Loitering briefly in the south coast exercise areas to embark three Merlin HM-1s from 820 Squadron, conduct towed target gunnery and sensor alignment trials with JSATO Falcons, she turned her bows south on Halloween and headed for Gibraltar. Northerly winds through Biscay again hampered *Ark*'s attempts to make ground and at the same time work up her Merlins. The focus was therefore on deck work while the marine engineers exploited the deep water and lack of flying to conduct main engine 'tune and balance' followed by propulsion trials. Guy Fawkes day was celebrated with gunnery practice against a towed Larne target, with concurrent 820 flying serials and an air defence exercise controlling Portuguese Air Force F-16s. *Ark* transited through the Gibraltar Strait on 7th November and made one emotional stop before going alongside. With the ship taking station some thirty miles off the Rock, the Ship's Company held a Service of Remembrance and laid a wreath over the last resting place of *Ark* III. At Gibraltar the ship was opened to visitors with around 10,000 locals coming onboard over two days. The SOTV proved very successful despite a debacle surrounding the unserviceability of a newly procured set of ladders designed to allow visitors to ascend from the hangar to the flight deck in large numbers. Infuriated by the apparent incompetence, Captain Clink demanded answers, highlighting in his monthly report that *"these ladders have been an ongoing issue since August 2007!"*

As *Ark* departed from Gibraltar on 10th

November, news reached the ship that her ASWEX playmate HMS *Trafalgar* had been delayed at Devonport and would not be able to make the intended rendezvous off southern Spain. In the absence of higher guidance, *Ark* requested the rendezvous be moved further north to the South West Approaches to allow *Trafalgar* to recover her programme. The Ship's Company would lose their planned visit to Lisbon, but the priority had to be achieving the ASW training. With approval from the submarine operations staff at Northwood the Notice of Intent to conduct submarine exercises was re-established and all assets redirected to rendezvous on 13th November. The Naval Flying Standards Flight that was scheduled to join via Lisbon to assess 820 Squadron were redirected and collected by helicopter from Culdrose. Exceptional efforts by 820's engineers enabled the squadron to have two aircraft simultaneously available for a significant period and all three aircraft on 17th, despite two engine changes and a potentially crippling cracked windscreen replacement. Two aircraft continued the hunt the SSN while the third was tasked to support the landing of one of the Ship's Company on compassionate grounds. The squadron received a 'Good' assessment from the Trappers. With the exercise successfully completed, *Ark* proceeded east toward Mounts Bay where the 820 Squadron aircraft disembarked on 20th. The annual hassle of testing the citadel and prewet systems to prove *Ark*'s ability to operate in a chemical or biological environment was undertaken as the ship sailed up the Channel. With just enough time to complete an air defence exercise and Phalanx towed target shoot on 21st en route, *Ark* came alongside for Christmas early the following day. In Portsmouth, the ship was at 24-hours notice for Operation ADANA, National Quick Reaction Alert against Russian intruders flying into UK airspace and other possible airborne incidents post 9/11.

The command priority at the end of 2008 was to finalise and agree the programme for 2009 since there was still considerable uncertainty as to how, and exactly when, *Ark* might regenerate as the R2 Strike Carrier. She would need at least a six-month work package and docking to recertify the hull and carry out essential maintenance. Traditionally a ship came out of fleet time and handed over to a shipyard with Ministry oversight for this; indeed just as *Ark* had done in 2005/6 at Rosyth. The disadvantage of that process was that most of the Ship's Company departed, making the operational regeneration when a new crew joined far more challenging. The preference then was to complete the docking period as quickly as possible, allowing the crew to remain with their ship. This of course introduced problems of its own; not least having over 400 personnel living on the ship while it was in dock put pressure on the hotel services and would mean that major work package items such as galley refurbishment and hull blasting, could only be completed during leave periods to minimize disruption. The programme proposed by the ship looked taut, with a ready for sea date in September and BOST before Christmas, but this was the only way to guarantee achieving Carrier Strike by the required date of 10th March 2010. Fleet Headquarters and the authorities in Defence Equipment and Support (DE&S) were nervous that these timescales were unachievable, based on previous experience with overruns on maintenance periods and emerging defects, but after much dialogue agreement was finally reached on 9th December. The plan would have *Ark* deammunition in January, hand over Fleet Flagship to HMS *Illustrious* and R2 LPH to HMS *Albion* on 13th February; start maintenance immediately; dock down from March until July, and then start sea trials in September. BOST would start in November and complete before Christmas 2009, allowing a further maintenance period and Aviation Operational Readiness Inspection to be completed by mid-March 2010, in time for *Ark* to participate in the first JOINT WARRIOR of that year. It all looked simple; the challenge now was to deliver it!

Ark Royal's Ship's Company returned from

Christmas leave to be given the news of the programme for the next twelve months. The first priority was at Glen Mallen in Scotland to deammunition, which would allow for one round Britain trip and offer visits to Liverpool, Orkney and Newcastle, and a chance to take families to sea for a two-day transit back to Portsmouth. Sadly, giving them the news proved problematic as technical problems hit the ship's NavyStar computer network wiping it out for five days. It subsequently transpired that a virus had infected NavyStar and with systems now connected globally via intranet and Internet systems it had also attacked large parts of the defence computer infrastructure. While it had no impact on operational equipment or weapon systems, the global shutdown nevertheless exposed the Ministry of Defence's dependence on Information Technology and its vulnerability to cyber attack.

Ark sailed on 12th January for a three day passage to Liverpool. As well as the usual crew, she took with her four members of the Worshipful Company of Shipwrights, six university students, seventeen members of the 1st Mechanised Brigade HQ staff, and 120 Sea Cadets. The plan was to show *Ark*'s visitors the varied roles she carried out at sea, including equipment trials, weapon firings, helicopter sorties and boat operations. Unfortunately severe weather put paid to most of the fun with gunnery serials cancelled and many of the cadets spending a significant portion of the trip in sickbay or their bunks. Arriving at Liverpool on 15th January, *Ark* swapped her passengers for local visitors eager to see the ship again. Over 10,000 people crossed the ship's gangways during the three days alongside, making good use of the reworked SOTV ladders that were finally received before sailing, thanks to the Captain's intervention at Gibraltar.

Next stop was Glen Mallen, with another group of university students and two charity prize winners onboard for the overnight voyage. As the ship headed north, ammunition was transferred from the deep magazines into the hangar using the two main weapon lifts, prepositioning it for offload the following day. This preparation paid dividends as the whole evolution took only two days leaving the Ship's Company two spare days to enjoy the sights of Argyll and Bute in January. Leaving Glen Mallen on 26th, *Ark* made her way through the Sound of Mull, the Hebridean Sea and the Minch to anchor in Scapa Flow the following morning. A team was landed to Lyness to visit the local school and another landed on Flotta Island for a leadership exercise to recover a 'downed pilot', while Her Majesty's Lord Lieutenant of Orkney and the Chief Executive of the Island Council embarked, via the Orkney Lifeboat and pilot boat, for lunch with the Captain. The ship stayed at anchor overnight and then made a high speed departure through the narrow Hoxa Sound to test the navigation skills of the Officers of the Watch. Successfully avoiding the rocks, *Ark* made it safely to open waters and headed south to North Shields. The Tyne pilot embarked on the afternoon of the 29th to take *Ark* alongside at Corporation Quay, North Shields. Reaffirming *Ark*'s popularity with the northeast and Newcastle's popularity with the Ship's Company, 6,000 visitors came onboard despite the biting cold weather while the crew thoroughly enjoyed the city and its hospitality. The visit coincided with the Premier League derby at St James's Park between Newcastle United and Sunderland. Supporters of both clubs from among the Ship's Company were privileged to visit their home stadiums, meet the teams and then attend the match. The game ended one-all, allowing both sides to save face.

Ark remained alongside on 2nd February to embark affiliates and families for the transit to Portsmouth. Most were late getting to Newcastle due to nationwide snow and ice snarling the transport networks and so sailing was delayed by 24 hours to get everyone onboard. With over 200 guests braving the cold on the flight deck to witness the departure, *Ark* sailed on the evening of the 3rd bound for Portsmouth. *Ark* encountered two of Britain's newest and most expensive anti-air defence capabilities on the trip south. During exercises in the North Sea on 4th, the ship controlled American F-15Es of the 494th Squadron based at RAF Lakenheath against RAF Typhoons from No.11 Squadron, as well as Tornado F-3s from No.43 and Hawks from No.100 Squadrons. The Typhoons, each with a 'ticket price' of £138 million, provided a spectacular close range display. The following morning, Ark rendezvoused with HMS Daring, the first of class of the Royal Navy's six £1 billion Type-45 destroyers, as she conducted sea trials, before arriving at Portsmouth. The Ship's Company could now concentrate on the docking period that would start immediately, or so they thought.

The mini-refit was due to last from February until September. To apportion costs to the correct MoD support budget, the first month of the refit would form a standard Fleet Time Support Period (FTSP) with the remaining seven months termed a Contractor Support Period (CSP). The take-on meetings for both were due to take place on 6th and then 9th February, but with contract wrangles still ongoing; these had to be put off. The FTSP thus started without an agreed way ahead for the CSP. Much of the early work was consequently carried out 'on risk' and preparations proceeded slowly while the contractual difficulties were resolved. The ship hosted one very special guest before docking down. The 5th March marked the 80th Birthday of Sir Donald Gosling and a lavish party was held onboard, hosted by the Navy Board in recognition of the decades of support that Sir Don had given to the Royal Navy. The evening culminated in a Ceremonial Sunset with the Band of Her Majesty's Royal Marines Beating Retreat and a firework extravaganza set to music, the likes of which had not been seen in Portsmouth since the millennium.

Ark entered dry dock on 9th March and it looked most likely that she would flood up on 19th August, although dates varied from plus or minus two weeks. With the ship docked down the

engineers could start in earnest with the job of refurbishing and recertifying the ship's systems. Progress through March remained painfully slow however and it appeared that the Babcock VT staff had other priorities, with Ark eerily quiet for a ship supposedly swarming with dockyard workers. For the marine engineers the main package involved the usual hull maintenance and surveys, blasting of the hull and painting, as well as overhaul of the auxiliary systems. The weapon engineering package was particularly light. Aside from the installation of a fibre-optic network for NavyStar's successor, DII, the main effort concentrated on reconfiguring Ark's afloat planning facilities from their amphibious role to support carrier strike, which included installation of specialized command, control, communications, and intelligence systems. Having learned the painful lessons of allowing the sensors and weapon systems to lie dormant through the refit in 2001 and the docking in 2006, it was essential that they be kept alive if they stood any chance of regenerating when the ship returned to sea. A complicated plan was thus hatched to provide all of the life support systems, including power, chilled water and dry air to allow the equipment to be operated, if not transmitted given the limitations in dock.

For the warfare teams, aside from supporting the engineering effort, the priority was to maintain the war fighting skills as much as possible throughout the docking. This included Command Team Training at HMS DRYAD at the end of March, secondment of officers and ratings to HMS Illustrious during their exercises in May, and completion of essential refresher training. On a broader front a huge investment was put into developing the Command, Leadership and Management of the Ship's Company. The initiative was launched by the Second Sea Lord, Sir Alan Massey, returning to his old ship on 20th March, and included organized development training onboard, sport and adventurous training expeditions and battlefield tours. A team from Ark

(page 158)
HMS *Ark Royal*'s most obvious update of the 2006/7 refit – the advanced technology mizzen mast being fitted at Rosyth.
(©BRDL 2006)

(page 162)
HMS *Ark Royal* sails from Rosyth on completion of her refit,
29th September 2006.
(*Crown Copyright/MoD 2006*)

(page 166)
Harrier GR-9s from Boscombe Down embark for
aviation trials of PAR and TACAN, November 2006.
(Crown Copyright/MoD 2006)

(page 169)
HMS *Ark Royal*, HMS *Albion*, RFA *Mounts Bay* and
RFA *Largs Bay* take part in Exercise GREY
HERON, in the Channel, September 2007.
(Crown Copyright/MoD 2007)

(page 170)
HMS *Ark Royal*, in company
with the PLA(N) destroyer
Guangzhou in the Channel,
September 2007.
(Crown Copyright/MoD 2007)

(page 172)
Aurora Borealis during ARMATURA BOREALIS –
HMS *Ark Royal* operating near the Arctic Circle,
February 2008.
(Crown Copyright/MoD 2008)

(page 172)
HMS *Ark Royal* in Arctic conditions during
ARMATURA BOREALIS, Norway, February 2008.
(Crown Copyright/MoD 2008)

(page 173)
HMS *Ark Royal* conducts ASW training with HMS *Talent*
and 824 NAS, in the Vestfjorden, Norway, February 2008.
(Crown Copyright/MoD 2008)

(page 174)
"Gotcha!" - HMS *Ark Royal* seen through the attack
periscope of HMS *Talent*, Vestfjorden, February 2008.
(Crown Copyright/MoD 2008)

(page 174)
US Marines of 3/8 USMC embark in HMM-774 Sea
Knight helicopters operating from HMS *Ark Royal* during
Exercise CONSTANT ALLIANCE, April 2008.
(Crown Copyright/MoD 2008)

(page 182)
HMS *Ark Royal* at anchor astern of the French LPH,
FS *Tonnerre*, off the Tail O' the Bank during JOINT
WARRIOR, October 2008.
(Crown Copyright/MoD 2008)

(page 183)
HMS *Ark Royal* leads HMS *Albion*, HMS *Gloucester*
and HMS *Somerset* through the Sound of Mull,
16th October 2008.
(Crown Copyright/MoD 2008)

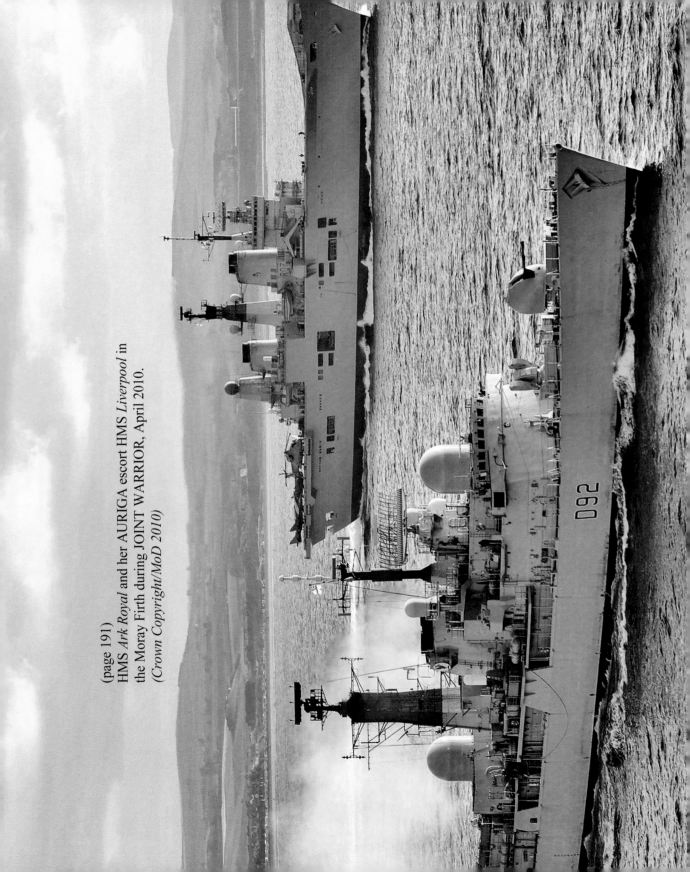

(page 191)
HMS *Ark Royal* and her AURIGA escort HMS *Liverpool* in the Moray Firth during JOINT WARRIOR, April 2010.
(Crown Copyright/MoD 2010)

(pages 192-3)
HMS Ark Royal with US Marine Air Group 14 embarked during Exercise CAPELLA STRIKE, off Norfolk Virginia, June 2010.
(Crown Copyright/MoD 2010)

The pilot's eye view from a RAF Harrier GR-9 waiting to launch from HMS *Ark Royal's* flight deck.
(Crown Copyright/MoD 2010)

(page 194)
HMS *Ark Royal* Ship's Company mark the ship's
25th birthday in style.
(Crown Copyright/MoD 2010)

(page 194)
Prime Minister David Cameron addresses the Ship's Company of
HMS *Ark Royal*, at Halifax Nova Scotia, 23rd June 2010.
(Crown Copyright/MoD 2010)

(page 195)
USS *Barry* leads HMS *Ark Royal*
and RFA *Largs Bay* during
COMPTUEX, July 2010.
(Crown Copyright/MoD 2010)

(page 195)
USMC MV-22 Osprey lands on HMS *Ark Royal*
during COMPTUEX, July 2010. No.1 Squadron
RAF Harrier GR-9 in foreground.
(Crown Copyright/MoD 2010)

(page 196)
No.1 Squadron disembarks at the end of AURIGA to fly back
to UK via Bermuda, 1st August 2010. HMS *Ark Royal* arrives
home twelve days later.
(Crown Copyright/MoD 2010)

(page 206)
Apache AH-64 attack helicopter
in HMS Ark Royal's hangar
during JOINT WARRIOR,
September 2010.
(Crown Copyright/MoD 2010)

(page 210)
HMS *Ark Royal*'s 'twelve good men and true' at their reunion dinner 1st November 2010, with Sir Don Gosling (seated right) as guest of honour.
(l-r standing) Alan Massey, John Brigstocke, Adrian Nance, Mike Mansergh, Terry Loughran.
(l-r seated) Jerry Kyd, James Weatherall, Mike Harris, Neil Rankin, John Clink, Jeremy Blackham, David Snelson.
(Crown Copyright/MoD 2010)

(page 210)
Her Majesty The Queen visits HMS Ark Royal, 5th
November 2010. Her Majesty is wearing the *Ark Royal*
broach originally given to the Queen Mother at the
launch of *Ark Royal IV* in 1950.
(Crown Copyright/MoD 2010)

(page 211)
HMS *Ark Royal*, on passage from Glen Mallen to North Shields
meets HMS *Dragon* on Contractor's Sea Trials in the Scottish
exercise areas, 16th November 2010.
(Crown Copyright/MoD 2010)

(page 211)
Over 10,000 Tynesiders pay one last visit to HMS *Ark Royal* during her final port visit to North Shields, November 2010.
(Crown Copyright/MoD 2010)

(page 211)
Hundreds of Tynesiders bid farewell to their ship as she leaves North Shields for the last time, 24th November 2010.
(Crown Copyright/MoD 2010)

(page 211)
Harrier GR-9 ZG508 launches for the final time from HMS *Ark Royal*, 24th November 2010. The four-ship launch from *Ark* marked the end of the 48-year Harrier era, which began with the first landing on HMS *Ark Royal* IV in February 1963.
(Crown Copyright/MoD 2010)

(page 212)
HMS *Ark Royal's* final run ashore –
Hamburg, November 2010.
(Crown Copyright/MoD 2010)

(page 212)
"I can't feel my hands!" - clearing snow from
HMS *Ark Royal's* flight deck December 2010.
(Crown Copyright/MoD 2010)

(page 213)
The ghostly image of HMS *Ark Royal* emerges from the mist as she makes her final entry to Portsmouth, 3rd December 2010.
(Crown Copyright/MoD 2010)

(page 214)
Sir Donald Gosling is presented with HMS *Ark Royal*'s white ensign at the Decommissioning Ceremony, 11th March 2011.
(Crown Copyright/MoD 2011)

(page 215)
HMS Ark Royal - Zeal Does Not Rest - 1981-2011.
(image Crown Copyright/MoD 2008)

also competed in the prestigious Royal Navy Field Gun Competition in June; the first ship's crew to do so in over a decade. Showing a great effort, the team only narrowly missed out on reaching the final and in doing so beat many teams from much larger shore establishments.

Ark also worked hard to get on the front foot in preparing to regenerate for Carrier Strike. To ensure full interoperability a joint MoD and USN party visited on 30th April, with the US delegation led by Rear Admiral Mike McMahon USN, Program Executive Officer US Aircraft Carriers. Discussions covered elements of the respective Aircraft Carrier projects including aviation integration, build strategy, programme and project management, and mission and combat systems. The first planning conference for the 2010 Carrier Strike deployment took place during Easter leave.

The ships hull was blasted during Easter leave to reduce as far as possible the pain and grief to the Ship's Company. For those on duty however, the experience was almost unbearable; the constant, teeth-rattling noise of the windy hammers replaced by the gut-wrenching smell of the primer paint applied to seal the hull. To add to their despair, the main galley and significant parts of the water and sewage systems were shut down to allow essential maintenance. True to the *Ark* spirit, the Ship's Company put up with the harbour hassle and looked forward to getting back to sea, with a new 'buzzword' to focus on: "AURIGA". The NAAFI queue gossip from the output of the carrier strike planning conference was that *Ark*'s deployment, called AURIGA, would take her to the USA and Canada, including - "gen dit" - a return to New York for the first time in twenty years.

Work progressed through late spring and early summer. The pace eventually increased but with it came worrying growth in the package as defects emerged and schedules had to flex to accommodate this. On the positive side, the rudders that should have been dropped would now not be, but whether or not the main shaft bearings could be replaced depended on finding a replacement set; known to exist but somehow lost in the stores system. Work on the starboard inner main engine grew as it became clear that the power turbine required replacing, while the extent of corrosion of the engine and diesel generator exhaust stacks meant that whole sections needed to be refurbished, made all the more complicated by the widespread existence of asbestos in the funnels. The greatest risk to undocking came however from the work package to refurbish the sea chests and tubes. All of the propulsion and auxiliary machinery in the engine and gear rooms relied on sea water for cooling; this water entered the ship through grated openings in the bottom of the hull known as chests, and was fed to fresh water heat exchangers through the sea tubes. Everywhere needed to be surveyed and remedial work undertaken as necessary, but the balance to be struck was the extent of the work to be undertaken. Wholesale replacement was unaffordable, but missed work might have significant consequences for the downstream programme, since this was intended to be *Ark*'s last ever docking.

The keep alive services for the WE equipment were eventually commissioned by May and a basic routine of harbour trials developed, supported by subject-matter expert visits from MoD agencies and industry. The air engineering work to support embarkation of the GR-9 progressed slowly as, despite constant pressure from Ship's Staff, with test gear, starting equipment, stowage facilities and workshops all needing updated but seemingly little focus being applied to achieve it. Resurfacing of the flight deck went well, right up to the point that the line painters misjudged the reference point with the result that all of the markings on the aft of the flight deck were two feet out of place. Various options were considered to fix the mistake but in the end the only option was to blast it off and start again.

Several significant Carrier Strike events took

place marking the centenary of the Naval Aviation celebrated under the "Fly Navy 100" banner. *Ark* personnel also attended the Future Air Space War Game at the Defence Academy at Shrivenham in mid-May designed to investigate future air capability requirements. On 12th May Captain Clink hosted the newly appointed Commander UK Carrier Strike Group, Commodore Simon Ancona, who would lead the AURIGA task group, while away teams visited RAF Cottesmore to begin detailed planning with Joint Force Harrier for the arrival in early 2010 of the GR-9s. Sensing early that a Defence Review may be in the offing and keen to promote the continued utility of carriers, at the request of the Assistant Chief of the Naval Staff, *Ark* hosted a visit by Cabinet Office Senior Civil Servants for them to hold a series of meetings and to expand their knowledge of the Royal Navy.

In June and July, *Ark* handled a punishing schedule of visits and acquaints; visitors and planners arranging almost daily visits, seemingly oblivious to the fact that the ship was deep in maintenance. Some of these, such as a visit by the Senior Management Team from King's College School, Wimbledon on 9th June, helped strengthen links with the ship's affiliates. Others, such the annual Base Logistics Inspection, were necessary for *Ark*'s regeneration and included routine inspections, audits and advisory visits. Others again, such as a visit by the Director of Training at Britannia Royal Naval College to give an update on the training syllabus for young officers helped shape *Ark*'s understanding of her future role in the wider Naval sense. Some visits, such as that by the Association for Christian Conferences and Teaching Military Ministries International on 4th June simply offered an opportunity for those not familiar with the Royal Navy to gain some insight and wider understanding of the role of the UK's maritime forces. Probably the most significant visitor throughout the summer was the new Commander in Chief Fleet, Admiral Sir Trevor Soar who visited *Ark* on 19th June to meet a selection of Portsmouth Flotilla Commanding Officers over breakfast and then some of the Ship's Company. Admiral Soar's message to *Ark*'s officers and senior ratings was blunt and unequivocal: "*make sure you achieve Carrier Strike on time and to standard.*" The Royal Navy's last two deployments, TAURUS in 2009 and ORION in 2008 had been beset by problems, with ships and submarines not regenerating in time either through technical delays or training shortfalls. In the year of a possible defence review it was vital that the Navy could be presented as cost effective, efficient and able to deliver; thus AURIGA was critical not only to the Navy's credibility but also to supporting its argument for developing carrier strike further.

Suitably energized, *Ark Royal*'s Company redoubled their efforts to get the ship out of dock on time. The hull work was completed and an innovative 'Intersleek' paint scheme applied during early summer leave. Setting to work of the weapons and sensors was also completed and only needed the ship to get back to sea to prove everything still worked. Formal visits by FOST staff commenced in mid July with the first phase of the Safety Assessment and Readiness Check to ensure the watch keeping and safety organisation was in place to manage the ship at alongside in harbour. Departmental FOST administration visits also started to assure the ship's preparations were firmly on track for BOST in November.

Ark's Contractor Support Period continued throughout August. The programmed flood-up was achieved on 4th August along with the ship's cold move out of 'D' Lock to a tidal berth on the North West Wall, six days later. The engineering trials work started apace now the ship was out of dock, only hampered by safety restrictions which prevented operating the ship's main radars in harbour. Nevertheless, by the end of the month, everything seemed to be 'on track', if only just. To mark *Ark*'s return to sea, on 4th September the Ship's Company conducted full Ceremonial Divisions on the Flight Deck in front of Vice

Admiral Sir Alan Massey and then held a Families Day. The highlight of the day was a display by one of *Ark*'s RAF affiliates, the Red Arrows.

More FOST checks, drills and inspections continued through the first three weeks of September as the final trials were completed. The main effort was the second phase of SARC, from 21st to 24th September to satisfy FOST that *Ark*'s crew was safe and competent to operate the ship in a peacetime environment at sea. On the final day of SARC 2, the Ship's Company also successfully presented the ship Ready for Sea to Commodore Ancona. *Ark* was ready to go back to sea.

Following seven months in deep maintenance, HMS *Ark Royal* sailed, as scheduled on 25th September for shakedown and sea trials. The ship's Standing Sea Emergency Party, drilled and tested through the second phase of the SARC process, was given an early run out for real as the ship headed for Portland. The port inner gas generator (PIGG) suffered a minor fire that was very swiftly dealt with by the watch keepers in the space. The incident highlighted the value of and need for the FOST training and focussed everyone to ensure that proper standards were maintained. FOST Initial Sea Safety Training followed over the next two days, concurrent with the Sea Acceptance Trial (Air), so that *Ark* could be declared safe to operate rotary wing aircraft. With this milestone achieved, the engineering sea trials began in earnest on 29th and continued until 9th October. Just to mark the end of the trials period, PIGG burst into flames for a second time just as *Ark* returned to Portsmouth and the engine was changed while alongside. Repairs and further testing at sea proved unsuccessful and the engine was eventually changed during the defect rectification period from 19th to 22nd October. The formal closure to the docking period came on 23rd October when final inspections confirmed the work package was more or less complete, save a few significant items that would be carried over until the next maintenance period in January 2010.

The end of October saw *Ark* back at sea for a short shake down prior to arriving at Devonport on 5th November to start BOST. Propulsion trials proved the new port engine and during full power trials *Ark* achieved 31.7 knots; thanks in part to her new Intersleek low friction paint scheme. The usual six-week extravaganza courtesy of *Ark*'s friends in the West Country then followed, with the Ship's Company staying on or ahead of the training curve and the complexity of the damage control and warfare scenarios increased. A paucity of aviation assets hindered full development of the air group. Nevertheless a welcome short embarkation from 24th to 26th November by the Maritime Counter Terrorism Air Group, with one CH-47, two Sea King Mk 4s, one Sea King Mk 5 and two Lynx helicopters for day and night deck qualifications and air assault training helped break the monotony for the flight deck teams. High winds also hampered training but as the final week approached the crew rose to the occasion, putting in a decent show at the final inspection, demonstrating their ability to sustain a war fighting posture whilst reacting to and recovering from sustained battle damage. With a credible "Satisfactory" assessment *Ark* returned to base port to commence a maintenance period and enjoy some well earned leave ready for the next phase of training in the continued build up to becoming the UK's High Readiness Strike Carrier.

January 2010 started slowly for HMS *Ark Royal*. Severe wintry conditions in the first week of January put paid to starting the maintenance period on time and hampered efforts to address the material weaknesses exposed through BOST. Key ME work included refurbishment of the port shaft train, including replacement of the port outer clutch, and thrust block seal, as well as replacing the aft aircraft lift seal and one of *Ark*'s eight diesel generators. The priority for the weapon engineers was to recommission the port and starboard weapon lifts. Unique to the carriers, these lifts were obsolescent and difficult to maintain. Most of *Ark*'s lift motor parts had gone to *Illustrious* to keep her operational at the start of the CSP and it took months to get refurbished replacements back onboard. On 25th January *Ark* resumed the role of Fleet Flagship and took over the duties of the UK's High Readiness Strike Carrier four days later to allow *Illustrious* to pay-off into non fleet time and refit. Declaration at this point was somewhat academic since *Ark* had not completed the final phase of regeneration, namely Aviation fixed wing Safe to Operate and Operational Readiness Inspection (STO/ORI), nor had she reammunitioned. Whether she was actually at five days notice for operations was therefore a moot point, but it rightly signalled her intent to be so.

Back at sea on 8th February, *Ark*'s weapon engineers completed the necessary trials and annual checks on TACAN, PAR and R996 to support embarkation of the air wing. Marine engineering trials and warfare serials were then completed en route to Glen Mallen where from 15th to 17th, *Ark* on-loaded the requisite Carrier Strike ammunition. More trials in the vicinity of Faslane followed prior to embarking eighty family and friends for a short passage to Newcastle along with two Lynx from 815 NAS. *Ark* arrived at North Shields on 24th February, just over a year after her last visit. The welcome was just as warm; it seemed that Tyneside never got bored of seeing its ship come home. While *Ark* was alongside 857 Squadron conducted a pre-embarkation meeting ahead of the deployment; elements from No.1 (F) Squadron RAF visited to understand the challenges they would face if they were to embark, and members of an independent television production team to establish the baseline conditions and identify opportunities for filming during AURIGA. The footage would eventually air on the Discovery Channel as "HMS *Ark Royal*". The obligatory Ship Open to Visitors attracted 5,270 members of the public on 27th February and the following day, the ground staff from Naval Strike Wing and 814 Squadron personnel embarked ready to sail for STO/ORI.

The 1st of March 2010 marked a momentous day for HMS *Ark Royal*. Six Harrier GR-9s from Naval Strike Wing accompanied by two Merlin HM-1s from 814 Squadron landed on ready for three weeks of fixed and rotary wing operations that would culminate in the Aviation Operational Readiness Inspection. It was the first time in six years that Harriers had operated en masse from *Ark*'s deck. For very many of *Ark*'s crew they had either never experienced fixed wing operations or could hardly remember what a Harrier looked like: STO/ORI was going to be a challenge worth savouring!

The first week of STO started at a walking pace with discrete flying activities. Harrier operations progressed from pairs to fours then built up to four aircraft semi-operational sorties. *Ark*'s serials included surface and air defence exercises supported by various airborne assets and developing procedures for concurrent fixed, rotary and ship activity in week two. During the second week the complexity of operations increased overlaying air defence serials with fixed wing flying and operations at Action Stations. The end of this phase was a refuelling at sea with RFA *Wave Knight* while 814 Squadron conducted vertical replenishment using one Merlin onto the stern of the ship, while a wave of Harrier launches took place from the bow ramp. The photographs taken by 814's second Merlin were dispatched to Ministry of Defence and Royal Navy headquarters, providing unequivocal proof that *Ark* was ready for ORI.

Ark hosted a number of influential visitors throughout STO/ORI including Dr Julian Lewis MP, Shadow Minister for Defence with specific responsibility for the RN, Lord Myners, Financial Services Secretary to the Treasury, four members of the Air Squadron, as well as the Scottish print and TV media. The need to maintain the positive message regarding the utility and flexibility of carrier strike ahead of the General Election and Defence Review was not lost on the Ship's Company who played their part to the full, keeping the bargain they had made with C-in-C Fleet nine months earlier. The final week of STO added the final polish to the previous two weeks training and developed a scenario culminating in a Non-combatant Evacuation Operation that would be used during later exercises to demonstrate *Ark*'s readiness. Rear Admiral Simon Charlier, Chief of Staff Aviation embarked on 15ᵗʰ March for the final inspection. *Ark* successfully rose to the occasion and delivered a very creditable performance demonstrating the ability to conduct Theatre Entry, Strike and NEO operations.

With the final phase of training completed, HMS *Ark Royal* was certified at high readiness status for contingent Carrier Strike Operations. She returned alongside Portsmouth on 18ᵗʰ March for final maintenance and storing prior to deploying for AURIGA. An emergent defect on the port propeller needed *Ark* to move to a non-tidal berth in 'C' Lock while divers inspected the damage and effected repairs on the cone assembly. Work completed, *Ark* returned to Sheer Jetty on 31ˢᵗ March ready to host Commodore Ancona's pre-sailing conference. *Ark* was ready to sail for AURIGA, on time and at the required standard, just as everybody had expected her to. The *Ark* Spirit was alive and well.

On 6ᵗʰ April 2010 HMS *Ark Royal*, flying the broad pennant of the Commander UK Carrier Strike Group, sailed in Procedure Alpha for the first leg of AURIGA, Exercise JOINT WARRIOR off the coast of Scotland. The tailored air group comprising seven GR-9s of 800 Squadron, two Sea King Mk-7 ASaCs of 849 Squadron, two Merlins HM-1s from 814 Squadron and two Lynx of 212 Flight embarked in the Solent and *Ark* proceeded to meet up with her task group escorts USS BARRY, HMS *Sutherland* and HMS *Liverpool*. The four ships conducted task group manoeuvres and pre-exercise work up while transitting to Faslane. Thereafter *Liverpool* escorted *Ark* to the Moray Firth and then the carrier conducted varied fixed and rotary wing sorties in response to CTG tasking. Visitors during the first few days of the exercise included Vice Admiral Andy Matthews,

Chief of Material (Fleet) and Tony Graham, head of the DE&S project team for the new carriers. The scenario progressed to the Live Exercise phase on 16ᵗʰ April; however, along with the rest of the UK, the massive eruption of the Icelandic volcano Eyjafjallajökull impacted flying operations. To maximise availability of air assets, and underlining the inherent flexibility of a moving airfield, *Ark* repositioned to the north of Ireland to continue flying operations. Closely monitoring the movement of the 'red line' of the ash cloud inside which the Civil Aviation Authority had prohibited flying, *Ark* was able to maintain a programme of fixed wing and helicopter sorties. The volcanic ash cloud continued to move south but fixed wing flying continued until 17ᵗʰ April when, without consultation, the RAF higher command within 1 Group ordered 800 Squadron to disembark its GR-9s to RNAS Prestwick. The entire RAF fleet based in UK had already been grounded by the cloud and it seemed to those onboard that inter-service rivalry and politics were once again getting in the way. Presumably, with a defence review just around the corner, *Ark* provided an unhelpful and untimely reminder of the flexibility and adaptability of maritime based aircraft and carrier power. AOC 1 Group's decision certainly raised significant questions over the command and control arrangements for the embarked fixed wing assets within the carrier strike group. With aviation restricted, the remainder of JOINT WARRIOR for *Ark* focussed on her command role, and on 17ᵗʰ a specialist medical team embarked via boat from Oban to trial the newly embarked high-volume Surgical Module. *Ark*'s last evolution was to provide command and control for a naval fire support mission by her escorts on to the ranges at Cape Wrath, but as this completed *Ark* received immediate tasking in response to real world events further south.

With the ash cloud spreading, civil airspace over Europe and the eastern Atlantic was closed, leaving over 200,000 Britons stranded on the continent. The political imperative to pacify British travellers frustrated by the lack of air travel saw Prime Minister Gordon Brown announce on 20th April that as well as increasing commercial sealift and cross-channel capacity, the Royal Navy was being dispatched to assist. Brown's announcement came somewhat out of the blue since no formal tasking had yet been received from the Foreign Office or the MoD, nevertheless *Ark* detached from JOINT WARRIOR and headed at speed southwards. Orders eventually came through under Operation CUNNINGHAM. *Ark Royal*, still off northern Scotland was ordered to make a high-speed transit to the western Channel to wait for further tasking. Needing to replenish fuel and transfer Commodore Ancona's staff to another platform since JOINT WARRIOR was still underway *Ark* conducted a RAS with RFA *Fort George* before sprinting south. The RAS appeared to have gone smoothly, but during engineering rounds afterwards it was discovered that *Ark* had started taking on water in the bilge of the aft engine room. Subsequent investigations revealed that a split had opened in the vicinity of one of the sea chests and while the bilge pumps could easily cope with the ingress of water, investigations would be needed to understand the extent of the failure.

Ark arrived in the Channel on the morning of the 21st April with plans set to turn her into an ark of a different sort. All of the officers' and senior ratings' accommodation would be offered up to civilian families trying to get home, with the hangar used for single and more able-bodied passengers; enough room for 1,450 extra guests on each trip. It was expected that *Ark* would carry out return journeys to and from the northern French ferry ports into Portsmouth, but in the end she and the other Royal Navy ships were stood down. Now unexpectedly near Portsmouth, the decision was taken to reset alongside, allowing an opportunity to investigate the leak in the engine room. The investigation revealed that *Ark* had suffered a catastrophic failure within the structure of the sea chest in a diesel fuel tank; the same location where

Captain Weatherall had in 1986 reported "*confidence reducing*" cracks that required the ship to dock. With a tight deadline to meet, *Ark* could little afford an emergency docking but in-water repairs would at best be only temporary and her high readiness status and transatlantic deployment demanded the opportunity be taken now to fix the problem. Consequently, *Ark* was cold moved to 'D' Lock on 27th April and docked down that evening. AURIGA was due to continue immediately after JOINT WARRIOR with *Ark Royal* conducting anti-submarine exercises with *Sutherland* on the transatlantic voyage. This phase could if necessary be absorbed, but it was imperative that *Ark* arrived in Norfolk by 15th May in time to embark the USMC personnel and AV-8Bs that would form her air group for the first multinational exercise CAPELLA STRIKE. If *Ark* did not arrive on time then it would cause major embarrassment to the Navy and undermine all of the hard work achieved by the Ship's Company in regenerating her on time. The marine engineering hull team led by Warrant Officer Bob Crozier and dockyard staff therefore set a punishing schedule to complete the repair package and at the same time change the starboard inner main engine that had proven temperamental since leaving Portsmouth.

The repairs were finished by the evening of 5th May, the dock flooded overnight and *Ark* cold moved to Sheer Jetty the following morning. *Ark* needed at least 24 hours to refuel, so 212 Flight and 857 Squadron embarked with the ship alongside. Following a successful basin trial the ship departed at high tide on the evening of 7th May to rejoin the AURIGA deployment. With only seven days to make the crossing, *Ark* needed to achieve a twenty knot average speed and therefore needed as much fuel as possible. The duty FOST tanker thus deployed 400 miles west of the Isles of Scilly to rendezvous with *Ark* and give her a final top-up before she pushed on to the States. The AURIGA programme for *Ark* would include visits to Norfolk in Virginia, Mayport and Port

Canaveral in Florida, and Halifax in Nova Scotia. Although some of the AURIGA ships would enjoy more 'eye-catching' destinations, sadly for *Ark*'s Ship's Company, the glittering prize of New York became an early casualty of the cost-savings demanded by Fleet Headquarters. Berthing in the Big Apple was now "*too expensive*" and the single opportunity to do so would go to HMS *Albion* who was due to join up with *Ark* for the latter stages of AURIGA in July.

Six days after leaving Portsmouth, *Ark* reached the US continental shelf and met up with the USNS *Wally Schirra* to replenish her fuel tanks, drained very nearly to their reserve limits by the four thirsty Olympus gas turbines. With all the hard work nearly complete, *Ark*'s Ship's Company enjoyed a sports afternoon on the flight deck under the American sunshine before the ship arrived at Naval Station Norfolk, Virginia, on 14th May. COMUKCSG and his staff re-embarked after the brows were on, followed over the next three days by 150 USMC personnel and equipment from Marine Air Group 14. With local introductions, formalities and inductions, HMS *Ark Royal* sailed, exactly on time, on 18th May 2010 for Exercise CAPELLA STRIKE. Poor weather at the USMC air station at Cherry Point delayed the arrival of the jets by 24 hours, but from the 19th twelve USMC AV-8Bs landed on; representing the largest number of Harriers to operate from a British CVS since the withdrawal of the FA-2 in 2006.

With so many aircraft embarked *Ark*'s flight deck was busy, made doubly so by the much faster paced deck qualification (DQ) process employed by the Americans. The American pilots were keen to exploit a deck provided almost entirely for their own use. The *modus operandi* on US amphibious carriers was that the Harriers played second fiddle to the helicopters and therefore had only limited opportunities to fly; thus nine days of dedicated flying was a gift, which they made the most of. If the Joint Force Harrier deck qualification process during ORI had resembled touring car testing at Les Mans, then the USMC approach during

CAPELLA STRIKE looked and felt more like stock car racing. Each qualification involved multiple landings per sortie, engine running refuels and hot handovers between pilots; the aircraft kept alive on auxiliary power as one jumped down and the other strapped in. Tactical flying covered the complete gamut of core maritime warfare areas including recce, close air support, strike, offensive and defensive counter air sorties. The Marine Air Group's embarkation proved the full capability of the CVS in the carrier strike role and firmly cemented relationships between the two prime users of STOVL jets. As the jets disembarked on 27th May, *Ark*'s Ship's Company could reflect that they were back in the van of carrier operations.

Following CAPELLA STRIKE, HMS *Ark Royal* arrived in Mayport for an operational standoff. The official reception, for 145 guests including community and council leaders, Navy League and senior US military personnel, was held on the first night alongside allowing the remaining four days to be dedicated to relaxation. A major success of the visit was a sports day and BBQ exploiting the full facilities of the US naval base, followed by a Ship's Company live concert in the evening. On 2nd June the ground staff for No.1 (F) Squadron RAF arrived to conduct their induction training and prepare for the arrival of *Ark*'s third fixed wing air group of the year which would accompany the carrier for the remainder of the AURIGA deployment. The next exercise, SEASWITI (South Eastern Anti-Submarine Warfare Integrated Training Initiative) run by COMDESRON 24 would provide the main opportunity for HMS *Sutherland* fitted with S2087 sonar and 814's HM-1 helicopters from *Ark* to demonstrate that the Royal Navy still led the world in anti-submarine warfare. *Ark* sailed on 4th June and waited for her jets to arrive while *Sutherland*, USS *Barry* and the Merlins got to work with the red force submarines. Weather delayed the start of the tanker trail for the UK GR-9s coming across the Atlantic, but six aircraft finally arrived 24 hours after *Ark* had left Mayport. Amongst the 814

Merlin sorties, *Ark*'s deck teams concentrated on supporting deck qualifications for the RAF pilots, but in comparison with the USMC activity during CAPELLA STRIKE, progress through SEASWITI seemed, frankly, pedestrian; the six British jets taking five days to complete what the twelve US jets had done in only three. Proactive management by *Ark*'s command team enabled the ship to achieve key serials through the exercise alongside the fixed wing flying. However, far more could have been achieved had the Harrier element already been deck-current, highlighting the readiness mismatch between the CVS strike carrier and her air group. This mismatch had been a product of the dissolution of the FA-2 squadrons and the five-year commitment of the JFH squadrons to Afghanistan from 2004 to 2009, which resulted in each air group effectively having to start from scratch each time they embarked at sea. This could have been alleviated by allocating the 800 Squadron aircraft that had worked up in *Ark* during STO/ORI as they had no urgent operational tasking during the AURIGA deployment to prevent their accompanying the carrier. To *Ark*'s team, on the very cusp of achieving real fluidity and a level of confidence that could only come from sustained operations, it seemed that they had been 'short-changed'.

SEASWITI came to and end on 10th June and *Ark* returned to Norfolk for a short weekend alongside. Vice Admiral Bob Cooling, Chief of Staff to the Supreme Allied Command Transformation, used *Ark* as the venue for the annual UK-NATO Flag raising event in the Norfolk area. The following day, *Ark* hosted the pre-sailing conference for the next phase of AURIGA, the Canadian led Exercise HALCYON RENDEZVOUS that would take place between Norfolk and Halifax, Nova Scotia. The first day out was a VIP sea day for sixteen senior US Navy, US Marines and senior Department of Defence civilians; one Merlin embarking half the guests from Andrews Air Force Base with the remainder flying out from Norfolk. The day proffered a valuable show-case opportunity to demonstrate the benefit to all parties of the continued ability for the UK and, more importantly, the USA, to train alongside its allies. One of the more challenging serials of the exercise was a pan-task group damage control scenario requiring away teams from *Ark* to recover the stricken *Sutherland* and *Barry* and which culminated in a towing exercise between the carrier and *Liverpool*. A simulated straits transit serial incorporating live firings against remote controlled targets also proved highly beneficial, giving a rare opportunity to conduct realistic Force Protection training. Tactical training opportunities were also provided for No.1 Squadron, with strike missions using practice bombs, Paveway II and Paveway IV laser guided bombs. Once in the vicinity of Nova Scotia the GR-9s participated in COMAO operations and fighter affiliation training with Canadian F-18s; despite persistent fog in the area all bar two waves were achieved.

On 23rd June, *Ark Royal* arrived alongside at Halifax, in conditions eerily similar to her last visit almost exactly twenty years earlier: pea soup fog with visibility below fifty yards. *Ark*'s visit coincided with the International Fleet Review for the Centennial of the Canadian Navy. Her Majesty The Queen would take the salute at the IFR as part of her official tour of Canada. The IFR coincided with Canada hosting the G8 summit at Huntsville Ontario, which provided the UK's new Prime Minister, David Cameron, with his first foreign visit. *Ark* provided an ideal venue for the Prime Minister to make an early commitment to the UK's Armed Forces, ahead of the national Armed Forces Day, and to present himself as the newest statesman among the world's heavy weight powers. The Prime Minister toured *Ark*, met selected personnel and addressed the Ship's Company.

In his speech, Cameron urged the country to get behind Britain's Armed Forces in what was widely received as a moving tribute to the men and women of all three services. "*I want our military, once again, to be front and centre in our national life. I want us to be proud of you.*" Committing the government to rewrite its Military Covenant, which gave personnel guarantees about health care, family support and schooling, Cameron said "*I want it renewed and refreshed and written into the law of the land.*" The Prime Minister also sought to calm fears about the planned Strategic Defence Review, pointing out that there had not been a review since before 9/11 and the wars in Iraq and Afghanistan, but reiterating the Navy's core role in delivering that new security. "*I also wanted to say something about the Strategic Defence Review that we are undertaking, that I know of course causes huge concern and worry right across our armed services. It is right that we have one. We have not asked the fundamental questions about the defence of our country, about our role in the world, since 1998. I know that whatever the outcome of this review, whatever the changes we will have to make, we should make them together and recognise that the Royal Navy is going to have a huge role to play in our future, in our defence, and in our security.*" For *Ark*'s assembled company there seemed to be no higher recognition for the work they had done during the previous twelve months, or greater validation of their place in the Government's strategic defence plans.

After the Prime Minister's visit, the First Sea Lord, Admiral Sir Mark Stanhope, hosted an official reception onboard for 500 guests and the following morning held tri-lateral talks with his US and Canadian opposite numbers, USN Chief of Naval Operations, Admiral Gary Roughead; and Canadian Chief of Maritime Staff, Vice Admiral Dean McFadden. June closed with the Canadian International Fleet Review by Her Majesty The Queen. The Ship's Company lined the flight and weather decks, with the ship dressed overall while Her Majesty and the Duke of Edinburgh sailed past onboard HMCS *St Johns*.

Ark Royal sailed from Halifax on 30th June, under another blanket of fog, to head back toward Norfolk for the final exercise of AURIGA, the Composite Training Unit Exercise (COMPTUEX) for the amphibious carrier USS *Kearsarge*. 849 Squadron rejoined the ship at Halifax bringing the air group up to full strength although a roulement of No.1 Squadron personnel put the fixed wing training back several steps. Bringing the new pilots up to speed was hampered as the GR-9s started to break down. The first aircraft diverted on 1st July due to a malfunction while flying in the vicinity of Halifax. An engineering team was sent ashore and the aircraft was later recovered. Five days later a second GR-9 diverted to the Naval Air Station at Oceana and the team again successfully repaired the aircraft and got it back to mother.

COMPTUEX was the UK's major task group exercise for 2010, with not only *Ark*'s task group taking part, but also the UK Amphibious Task Group, led by HMS *Ocean*. The two groups rendezvoused off Norfolk on 7th July for an intra-task group conference before conducting a simulated straits transit. The "Treasure Coast" scenario was again played out, providing the framework to plan and execute Carrier Strike Operations. During the first six days of COMPTUEX, *Ark* provided fixed and rotary wing assets to support the strike group's 'Insight, Shape and Prepare' operations while the amphibious group conducted 'wader' training for their amphibious landing. 849 and 814 Squadrons conducted core AAW, ASuW and ASW training. Joint intelligence gathering and surveillance missions were included in this package; 849's helicopters conducting target indication sorties against ground targets using their Searchwater radars, with 814's Merlins and the GR-9s providing visual recce and assessment. The Harriers also conducted range operations and further live weapon sorties in the Virginia Capes areas while additional missions were flown to develop procedures for the use of GR-9 and LGB in the maritime environment. Given the weight of the exercise, *Ark* and *Ocean* attracted a number of senior visitors throughout the exercise. From 12th to 14th July, COMUKMARFOR, Rear Admiral

Peter Hudson, visited, followed by Rear Admiral Tom Cunningham, Chief of Staff (Aviation), and Air Vice Marshal Greg Bagwell RAF, Air Officer Commanding 1 Group. On 18th, Admiral Soar accompanied by his Chief of Staff (Capability) Major General Garry Robison RM, toured *Ark* as part of a wider visit to the AURIGA task groups.

In the midst of the string of VIPs, the amphibious group conducted a beach assault on 15th and maintained tactical operations ashore for the next four days with the strike elements from *Ark* once again providing recce, close air support and surveillance assets. Following an engine defect in HMS *Ocean* which limited her speed and ability to conduct flying operations, on 18th two Sea King Mk-4s and one Lynx Mk-7 diverted to *Ark*. Additional crews were later transferred from *Ocean* to keep the aircraft operational while 814's Merlin provided spares from RFA *Fort George* to assist with the defect rectification. The latter stages of COMPTUEX from 21st to 24th July saw *Ark*'s carrier strike group join forces with USS *Kearsarge* and the 26th Marine Expeditionary Unit to form an Expeditionary Strike Force led by Commodore Ancona, for the final assault phase of the exercise.

Ark completed participation in COMPTUEX on 24th July and was due to return to the UK. HMS *Ocean* was tasked to head south toward the Falklands so the AURIGA air groups were redistributed to ensure each ship was optimally configured for their follow-on programme. 212 Flight transferred to *Ocean* while *Ark* took four Sea King Mk-4s and one Lynx Mk-7. With the shuffle complete, *Ark*'s ships dispersed to ports along the eastern seaboard for a final run ashore before heading back to the UK. For *Ark*, this offered the unusual destination of Port Canaveral, a major ammunitioning facility for USN assets and normally a stop for British SSNs en route to AUTEC in the Bahamas. Five days in the Florida sunshine gave the Ship's Company a last chance to work on suntans, stock up on 'gizzits' and visit local tourist attractions including the Kennedy Space Centre. Thoughts quickly turned to home however and the promise of a well-deserved summer leave.

HMS *Ark Royal* sailed from Port Canaveral on 1st August 2010 and made an altogether more leisurely passage home, accompanied by her faithful escort HMS *Liverpool*, arriving at Portsmouth twelve days later. For Captain Clink, nearing the end of his two-year period in command, *Ark*'s return to UK marked a point to reflect on the scale of the achievement of his Ship's Company in bringing the ship from the depths of not one but two dockings to the height as the UK's high readiness strike carrier. *"Flying from the sea is complex, exciting, and takes a great deal of teamwork and effort. I think we can be justifiably proud of a job well done. Ark's had a successful deployment and it's thanks to the hard work of the Ship's Company that we have achieved so much. It's all very fitting for a ship which is celebrating her silver jubilee this year."* Moreover, the Ship's Company had lived up to their Captain's watchwords spelled out when they had first met at Mayport in July 2008: *"Lead"*, *"Live"*, *"Laugh"*.

After leave, *Ark* would undertake the second JOINT WARRIOR of the year and then look toward a string of celebrations to mark her twenty fifth year in commission. The outstanding performance she had given in the run up to and during AURIGA suggested that she and carrier strike had a busy future, with the Harriers now back from Afghanistan, replaced by Tornado GR-4s and therefore available for deployed maritime operations. Everyone hoped that the tempo in *Ark Royal* would continue and she would deploy as the flagship for the next task group deployment, to the Indian Ocean in spring the following year, for COUGAR '11. For John Clink, however the autumn promised a new start elsewhere as he was due to hand over the keys to *Ark*'s twelfth Commanding Officer, Captain Jerry Kyd.

Captain Jerry Kyd Royal Navy

(Commanding Officer 2010 – 2011)

In reading the preceding chapters in the history of the fifth HMS *Ark Royal*, I am struck by the enormous honour afforded to me to be one of the 'twelve good men and true' entrusted with command of the Royal Navy's most famous warship. For me, it is a return to a favourite sea-going home. In 1985, as a very proud eighteen year old, I nervously opened my very first Appointment letter and read with glee that I was one of the lucky Midshipmen to be going to the then brand-new HMS *Ark Royal* for my Fleet training, under the command of James Weatherall. The ship gave me a superb introduction to life in a vibrant, busy and

fun Wardroom and I remember with fondness the superb training opportunities afforded by so many Departments. The size also helped us to remain hidden when the Commander was on the prowl! It was not all work and I remember particularly well the enormous 'training' value of eight days alongside Manhattan, New York as a young and naïve junior officer in June 1986 for the unveiling of the refurbished Statue of Liberty! Slightly older and wiser, sixteen years later I returned in 2001, as David Snelson's Navigating Officer. The ship was emerging from several years in mothballs and the subsequent refit in Rosyth to re-activate her was difficult and challenging, but we made all the milestones on time and soon Harriers, Sea Kings and the new Merlin were once again pounding her decks in the North Sea. We quickly brought her machinery and systems back up to full operational capability, although I do remember, with a shudder, the stress of losing all steering as we exited the Rosyth Channel one evening, in very tight navigational waters, and then we lost the forward tug as her line parted too! Miraculously, we staggered into safer water in the middle of the river, stopped engines, dusted ourselves down and took a helpful line from a tug, which then promptly claimed salvage! The following year, I left the ship with a heavy heart whilst alongside in Palma, just before she deployed east for the Iraq invasion in 2003.

Another eight years passed and I was thrilled to be appointed as the Commanding Officer in 2010. Of course, much has changed in the fabric of the ship over the intervening years but the enduring passion, fierce pride and unstoppable 'can-do' attitude of her Ship's Company remain as strong today as they have ever been. This 'Ark Spirit' is tangible and palpable to anyone who serves or visits her – she is truly a unique warship. Although some of the detail in the stories told may have lost clarity with the passage of time, still crystal clear were the memories of the challenges overcome, the hard work achieved and most of all, the enormous sense of fun shown by everyone who served in her.

HMS *Ark Royal*'s Silver Jubilee in 2010 gave many former shipmates the chance to revisit their ship. I was delighted to welcome onboard my eleven predecessors for a dinner on 1st November 2010. Sir Donald Gosling, a special friend of the *Ark Royal*, also attended. He has been such a passionate supporter of the ship over the quarter century and although various Commanding Officers have come and gone, Sir Don has perhaps been the *Ark Royal*'s true sentinel, mentor and father-figure. In him, the ship has been most fortunate and many thousands of her sailors have benefited from his legendary hospitality,

generosity and friendship. We were also hugely honoured to be visited by Her Majesty the Queen on 5th November at Victory Jetty for Divisions and lunch to celebrate the ship's 25th Birthday. It underlined the historic connection with The Queen Mother and a truly memorable day was had by all, not least the Ship's Company and their families, who saw at first-hand the esteem in which they and the ship are held by the Her Majesty.

But all good things come to an end. Having paid visits to the River Tyne and Hamburg and launched the last Harriers in the North Sea, I brought the ship into Portsmouth for the final time on Friday, 3rd December in thick fog and bitingly cold air. We passed the Round Tower at 09:40 and we could just about see and hear the cheers from the crowds on the shoreline and we replied by playing 'Sailing' by Rod Stewart over the tannoy. We rang off her engines for the last time and there were plenty of lumps in throats and a few tears as the lines and ropes tightened her to the jetty, never to go to sea again. A glass of champagne for the Ship's Company and their families in the hangar and that was it. Surreal, sad and hugely emotional.

As the Nation's High Readiness Strike Carrier and the Royal Navy's Fleet Flagship, HMS *Ark Royal* has been at the heart of the United Kingdom's defence capability. Over 25 years, she weathered controversy, adapted to meet changing priorities, proved emphatically her ability to deliver wide-ranging capabilities, and upheld the finest traditions of her name and the service. Still at the cutting-edge, it was with sadness but with huge pride that *Ark Royal* de-commissioned on 11th March 2011, a tragic consequence of the 2010 Strategic Defence and Security Review. But I know that right up until I rang off her engines for the last time, she and her amazing crew, whom I have had the privilege to command, have answered every call of the Nation, wherever and whenever they were needed. She is iconic, the best of British, the legend of the Royal Navy. But it is her crew that must take the final bow; after all, the 'Spirit of the *Ark*' shines in all of them.

Chapter 15

2010 – 2011:
"In my beginning is my end"

"We will accordingly decommission HMS Ark Royal immediately."
Strategic Defence and Security Review, 19th October 2010

Even in black and white it seemed hardly believable. HMS *Ark Royal*, the Fleet Flagship, that had just been refitted, regenerated as the Nation's High Readiness Strike Carrier and demonstrated emphatically its versatility and strategic value through the AURIGA deployment, was going to be scrapped as part of the coalition Government's Strategic Defence and Security Review.

The whispers began over the weekend preceding the announcement. A rearguard action was being fought by the "Tornado mafia" and conspiracies were afoot. Last minute private lobbying of Prime Minister David Cameron by the Chief of the Defence Staff, Sir Jock Stirrup, and the Chief of the Air Staff, Sir Stephen Dalton had convinced him that the Tornados were best for Afghanistan and the Harriers should go, despite the huge expense this would reintroduce to the defence budget. The additional cost could be offset slightly; since, without the Harriers, savings could be made by scrapping their carriers early. Alerted of the change of plan, Admiral Sir Mark Stanhope, the First Sea Lord, had allegedly told Mr Cameron bluntly that he *"could not endorse as his military advice"* the decision to axe the Harriers and considered it a *"political, not military decision."* The logical outcomes of the SDSR reached through proper consultation and endorsed by the

National Security Council were being changed, despite their transparent validity by any sensible measure of capability or cost. The Royal Navy was being ambushed, yet again, by the Royal Air Force.

The full extent of the behind-the-scenes machinations that delivered the final version of the 2010 Strategic Defence and Security Review might never be known but the constant stream of leaks and back briefs to the media provided ample ammunition for the conspiracy theorists and entrenched diehards to believe that war had broken out between the services.

There was no disguising the fact that the SDSR was driven by the overriding requirement not only to cut immediate spending but also to eradicate the 'black hole' in the defence budget that had been allowed to grow over the previous decade. All three services faced cuts potentially on a scale not seen since the 1966 Healey Review, with not just ships, battalions or squadrons at stake, but entire capabilities that could undermine their long term viability as independent forces. It is little wonder then that every ploy was used to win the arguments, however desperate or divisive.

The defence cuts needed to be seen in the context of the national spending crisis that faced the coalition government when it took power in May 2010. In 2009, the forecast public sector net borrowing was the largest in Britain's peacetime history and set to get even bigger. The forecast for 2010 was a record £704 billion, or 48% of the country's Gross Domestic Product, while income amounted to only 37% of GDP. According to the International Monetary Fund, Britain's 11% budget deficit was the highest of any country in the G7 or G20 and if spending was left unchecked, the public sector debt would double by 2015, to around 90% of GDP. Over the same period, the average growth in GDP was forecast to be only 2.4% per annum. Increased debt also increased the cost of that debt as financial institutions set higher interest rates that reflected Britain's weaker status. Britain was already paying, at a rate of £120 million a day, £43 billion a year in debt interest; in other words, more than the entire defence budget for the same year. By 2015 that could rise to £70 billion, enough to afford the country's education budget.

Reducing the budget deficit was the most urgent issue facing Britain. The new government committed to an immediate Comprehensive Spending Review, the first to be conducted since 2007 because of the uncertain economic outlook following the global crash of 2008. Aside from protecting the budgets for health and international development, all government departments would face average real term cuts of 25% over the four years of the CSR, with some facing cuts of up to 40%. The Ministry of Defence would be spared the full reduction; subject to the outcome of the SDSR, but could still expect at least a ten percent cut in real terms by 2014. But the challenge for the Ministry of Defence planners was not just to achieve in-year savings. Their entire budget was bust.

Over the previous ten years, defence planners had adopted a 'commit now and pay later' policy to meet the demands generated by new interventions despite being provided with only limited increases in their core budget. A quadrupling of additional income from the Treasury Reserve to help fund the additional costs of operations in Afghanistan, Kosovo and Iraq,

meant the MoD just about remained in the black from 2004 to 2008, but this could not ameliorate the strains on the budget caused by an exploding equipment bill. The rapidly evolving character of warfare since 2003 had generated demands for a wide range of new capabilities that were not envisaged by the previous SDR; many did not even exist in 1998. The department continued to invest a large part of its resources in legacy programmes such as Typhoon rather than target it to emerging requirements, such as more helicopters to support troops in Afghanistan, often because it had no choice but to do so. Prohibitive and binding contracts tied the money down. With Typhoon, for example, the Government was committed to buy a third tranche of 86 aircraft it neither needed nor could afford because contractually it was obliged to do so, and attempts with the international partners to reduce the UK order ran aground. The preferred solution to this dilemma was to delay costs by pushing programmes to the right. While this strategy realised temporary savings, it inevitably increased the final total costs. The effect of this policy was to generate a 'black hole' in defence funding amounting to £36 billion between 2010 and 2020. The assessment by the Public Accounts Committee of the MoD's financial performance was scathing, reporting that it had "*failed to match its future plans to a realistic assessment of the resources available*", showing that "*a consistent pattern of planned overspend demonstrates serious organisational failings and a dangerous culture of optimism.*" Worryingly, the Navy's future carrier project merited particularly damning comment, "*The Accounting Officer has not discharged his responsibility to ensure that planned and committed expenditure across the defence budget represents value for money. For example, in 2008 the Department signed a contract to buy new carriers which was unaffordable, without having identified compensating savings. Because these savings were not subsequently found, it was necessary within a year to delay the project, resulting in an enormous cost increase and poor value for money."*

Calls for a new strategic defence review and a re-evaluation of the MOD's spending plans had been high on the political agenda for three years before the eventual review took place. In 2008 the Conservative opposition joined the calls emanating from within the British media and the political establishment and subsequently stated that it would hold a defence review after the General Election, should the party take office. In July 2009 the Labour Government announced its intention to conduct a new Strategic Defence Review early in the next Parliament. Set within the context of the National Security Strategy, the review would *"be designed to ensure that we develop and maintain armed forces appropriate to the challenges we face and the aims we set ourselves as a nation"*. Among the issues to be considered in a preliminary Green Paper, were the strategic context for defence, including the lessons learnt from recent operations and the changing nature of conflict. The experience of working in partnership with other arms of Government and a review of the contribution defence could make to the projection of soft power, including conflict prevention would also form a strand of its thinking. Most urgent, given the technological advances and increasing cost of defence equipment, the scope for more effective processes in defence, in particular procurement would also be considered. Lastly, the Green Paper would consider the modern day requirements on, and aspirations of, the UK's armed forces personnel.

Prior to the publication of the Green Paper however, the MoD announced in December 2009 its intention to re-balance the future defence programme in order to support personnel on operations in Afghanistan, a priority consistently stated by the Government. In his Statement to the House on 15th December the Secretary of State for Defence, Bob Ainsworth, committed *"£900 million over the next three years, and reductions elsewhere to make these enhancements affordable and to match our expenditure against available resources."* As part of that re-balancing exercise equipment enhancements for Afghanistan would, for the first time, be funded out of the MOD's core budget, as opposed to the Treasury reserve. This included a better dismounted close combat equipment package; more tactical radios and additional communications facilities for Special Forces; increased funding for intelligence, surveillance, target acquisition and reconnaissance capabilities and a doubling of the Reaper unmanned airborne surveillance capability. There would also be improvements in counter-IED capabilities, an additional C-17 aircraft and defensive improvements for the ageing C-130J in order to maximise its deployability, and a further 22 new Chinook helicopters to enter service by 2013. In order to fund those enhancements reductions would subsequently be made in *"lower priority"* areas. Ainsworth spelled out that the RAF would bear much of the burden of the reductions, *"We will reduce now the size of our Harrier fast jet force by one Squadron, close RAF Cottesmore and consolidate the Harrier force at RAF Wittering. We plan to reduce our Tornado and Harrier force by a further one or two Squadrons; decisions on the make-up of our future force will be taken in the defence review."*

The MoD aspired to reduce the RAF to two fast jet platforms: the Typhoon and the Joint Strike Fighter, pursuing the second phase of the Typhoon future capability programme to introduce a ground-attack role so that it could take over from the Tornado GR-4. The Nimrod MR-2 would also be withdrawn from service by March 2010 and the introduction of the Nimrod MR-4A slowed. For the Royal Navy one survey ship and one mine hunter would be withdrawn from service early; while the planned reduction of some of the older maritime Lynx and Merlin HM-1s would be brought forward. Service personnel numbers would be reduced by 2,500 through the slowing down of recruitment and preventing extensions to service, rather than through redundancies.

Responding to that announcement the shadow

defence spokesman, Dr Liam Fox commented that the Government *"by their own definition, are trying to fight wars on a peacetime budget. Our defences are being cut not as a response to a diminished threat – if anything, the threat is going up out there – or a reassessment of our strategic needs, or in order to reshape our armed forces. A Government who has had four Defence Secretaries in four years, one of whom was part-time and no defence review for eleven years is now cutting the capability because of their own catastrophic economic management."*

Fox gave a more detailed analysis in a speech to the Royal United Services Institute, two days after the publication of the Green Paper. While predictably full of political rhetoric it nevertheless gave a clear indication of the Conservative's intent when or if they formed the Government in the next Parliament. *"It is a dangerous world - you don't need me to tell you that. The MoD needs a new vision and new life that only a new Government has the energy to provide. The next SDSR will have to be a step change and full overhaul of the status quo, not a minor tinkering to the system. It will be carried out ruthlessly and without sentiment. Tough decisions will be made and there will be winners and losers at the end of the process but Britain will be safe and our interests secure.*

The 'battle lines' between the three services started to be drawn when the first signs of a defence review were imminent. In normal years, each service always held in reserve options on how to save money in the event that the overall defence budget looked by being breached. For the Navy, these options ranged from cuts to the operational budgets, such as fuel and ammunition allowances for ships and canceling deployments; making minor 'tweaks' to the existing equipment programmes, delaying a capability here or an enhancement there, to offering more extreme measures, such as the withdrawal from service of ships and submarines. Since 2008, these 'normal business' discussions had become increasingly tense as the extent of the 'black hole' became clear

and the savings required each year reached the order of £2 billion. In a review year, more fundamental answers were needed on not just the cost of defence, but the shape, structures, capability and size of the forces charged with delivering it. Afghanistan was recognised as a key 'shaper' for defence thinking, not only in capability terms which all three services would be scored against, but also its financial impact on the budget.

The Chiefs of Staff sought to influence the public debate through broad capability-based statements of need, usually through tightly controlled interviews with the media or carefully staffed speeches to defence institutes. The Afghanistan campaign appeared to give the Army the upper hand in the debate; their argument being that large numbers of troops were required to maintain the roulement tempo with simpler and therefore *cheaper*, but more plentiful battlefield support, in the form of helicopters, lightweight aircraft capable of CAS and armoured vehicles. Both the RAF and the Navy recognised that while Afghanistan needed to be acknowledged, and the tri-service as opposed to Army contribution therefore highlighted, its significance for future planning must be downplayed. Unless clear cases could be made by both services the increasingly expensive equipment programmes needed to sustain them may be seen as irrelevant to Britain's future defence needs.

The First Sea Lord's pitch, made in the classically doctrinal language of the old Admiralty, was given in a speech to The Chatham House on 27th November 2009. In it, Sir Mark Stanhope argued that *"appropriately structured, trained and resourced"* maritime forces could *"afford the Government a highly cost-effective, military means by which political and diplomatic influence can be leveraged to prevent conflict. When necessary, they can also apply decisive combat force in support of national objectives. The ships and submarines that guarantee the freedom of the seas also exploit those freedoms for strategic and operational effect, free from the constraints of host nation support or the need for access, basing and over-flight permissions from other countries. Warships are incredibly versatile and can deploy for many months with a small logistic foot-print and very controllable political overheads. A single ship can do everything from diplomatic engagement, the delivery of humanitarian aid, capacity-building by training other forces, containment and coercion through embargo operations and the delivery of decisive combat power onto the land. A balanced maritime force can deliver amphibious forces, Carrier Strike, Naval Gun Fire and submarine-launched Tomahawk cruise missiles. That last bit – the ability to strike with precision – really matters. The case for conflict prevention activity is strong, but there can be no guarantees that it will be successful in every case.*

The First Sea Lord's speech reminded commentators that a third of the 'Army' commitment in Afghanistan had actually been provided by Naval forces, in the shape of 3 Commando Brigade Royal Marines and the Naval Strike Wing element of JFH. Stanhope also argued the case that the MoD's current prioritisation on the fight in Afghanistan should not *"lead to UK Armed Forces structured predominantly for a relatively narrow spectrum of land-locked, counter-insurgency operations and which lack the ability to conduct high-end war-fighting or indeed any of the vast array of operations in which the country's Armed Forces may be engaged in the future."* Two wider messages could also be inferred from Stanhope's speech. First, amongst the broad range of Naval capabilities, the pivotal and enduring role of the escort remained paramount. The Navy's credibility relied not just on capital ships and submarines, but on having a decent number of frigates and destroyers. These numbers had dropped steadily and a critical mass needed to be sustained. While an argument could be levied that the new *Type-45* destroyers offered such a capability improvement over the *Type-42*s that significantly fewer were needed to provide the

same level of air defence for a task force, the same could not be said for the general purpose frigate that would eventually replace the *Type-23*. Single-ship operations demanded at least like-for-like replacement and therefore safeguarding the *Type-26* Global Combat Ship programme was essential. Very subtly, Stanhope also distanced the Navy from being seen as the single-service champion of a successor for Trident. His only statement, *"while the UK remains nationally committed to retaining a Continuous At Sea Deterrent, the Royal Navy will continue to deliver it,"* neither advocated replacing it, nor accepted that the enormous cost to do so should come from the Navy's portion of the defence budget.

With the two jet-type model already set out for the RAF, its priority was to preserve the fast jet fleet as efficiently as possible and achieve autonomy of fixed wing operations in the limbo period before the full introduction of Typhoon at FGR-4 standard and the F-35 Lightning JSF. This required rationalisation of the three legacy fast jet types, the twin-seat Tornado F-3 and Tornado GR-4 aircraft and the single-seat Harrier GR-9, but under RAF terms. Those terms had already been clearly set out. As early as December 2008, the Chief of the Air Staff, Sir Glenn Torpy, relit the old rivalry with the Navy to control all aviation by offering to disband the Harriers by 2013, under the unofficial slogan "one nation, one air force". Torpy's successor Sir Stephen Dalton continued this theme when he made the RAF's SDSR pitch on 15th February 2010, in a speech at the International Institute for Strategic Studies entitled "Dominant Air Power in the Information Age."

"Afghanistan must serve as a prism to view the future, not as a prison for our thinking," said Dalton, echoing the First Sea Lord's appeal to look beyond the immediate land-locked desert campaign. He then made an impassioned case for the RAF and land-basing. *"One of the most vivid direct threats to national security is a 9/11-style event ... but with the 2012 Olympics approaching, it is not the only one,"* Dalton surmised, justifying

continuance of the RAF's most important and enduring duty – the control of the air above the UK; his assertion ironically apposite given in the 70th anniversary year of the Battle of Britain, the last occasion the RAF had been called upon in this role. Dalton's analysis that *"the disaster at Bluff Cove in the Falklands War, with the subsequent loss of* Sir Galahad, *is a stark reminder of the consequences of the failure to gain control of the air,"* rightly recognised the risks to expeditionary forces in attempting an opposed amphibious landing. But he failed to acknowledge that the RAF in 1982 could not provide such cover, a task thus vested entirely in the Sea Harriers in HMS *Invincible* and HMS *Hermes*. On the issue of the need for aircraft carriers in the future, Dalton saw them as a means to an end, rather than an organic air platform in themselves. *"Carrier-strike obviously offers one such capability and, in principle, I support it as one of the clubs in the golf-bag of options available to us. Yes the opportunity cost may be high, but if this country wants to have the ability to demonstrate its will and capability to engage on a global-scale, then it is entirely arguable that we should have such force elements. Whilst the nature of carrier operations means that the effective range, payload and weight of effort of carrier-based aircraft is markedly reduced in comparison to land-based contemporaries, carrier aviation can be useful in key scenarios and it would give us options. Nevertheless, in our joint operational concept, Carrier Strike aircraft would be deployed to operating bases on land as soon as practicable, to maximise capabilities and minimise costs, in accordance with the principle enshrined in current defence policy that land-basing aircraft is preferable."*

The Chief of the Air Staff extolled the virtues of the Tornado as a central pillar of the RAF's inventory, making no fewer than seventeen references to the aircraft, citing its "key role" during high-intensity, top-end war fighting in Kosovo and Iraq. In comparison, Dalton mentioned

the Typhoon just three times and the JSF only twice. Tellingly, he completely ignored the Harrier and the MoD's analysis from Kosovo, nor gave any acknowledgement that Britain's efforts in the Adriatic had been a truly joint affair. The facts told a somewhat different story. RAF aircraft flew 1,008 strike missions during Operation ALLIED FORCE, approximately 10% of all NATO missions over Kosovo. Of these, over 60% were flown by sixteen Harrier GR-7s based at Gioia del Colle in Italy, with the remaining 40% completed by twenty Tornado GR-1s based in Germany and Corsica. Land-based and immovable, weather conditions either at the aircrafts' bases or their target locations precluded strike operations on 57 days of the campaign and when the aircraft did fly, only sixty fixed and 75 tactical targets were hit. Success of the Paveway II and III LGBs dropped from both aircraft types was 65% and 53% respectively. The only British aircraft over Kosovo to achieve 100% mission availability was the Sea Harrier; seven FA-2s flying 102 sorties from HMS *Invincible* and frequently taking on the GR-7's tasking. A single UK SSN, HMS SPLENDID, operated in the Adriatic with impunity unhindered by poor weather conditions, firing one in ten of all NATO Tomahawk strikes. All of SPLENDID's missiles hit their designated targets.

The RAF had thus set out its stall and it should have surprised no one that the Harrier would be its target to be axed. Both the Navy and the RAF had another target in their sights, however: the Army's manpower bill. While the cost of the future equipment programme publicly caused the most angst, the largest single cost was in personnel, with the uniformed element accounting for £8.9 billion per year. Between 1993 and 2008, the RN and RAF had lost 39% and 49% of their manpower, respectively, while the Army over the same period had shrunk by only 24%. The operational tempo for all services had increased since the end of the Cold War, but contrary to the public's perception that the Army was being hardest hit, relative to their size the Royal Navy and Royal Marines bore the lion's share. The Armed Forces Pay Review Body reported that between 2007 and 2009 the proportion of RN personnel deployed on operations and undertaking other military tasks peaked at 22%; the RAF peak was 14% and the Army's 20%. Harmony – the ratio between the time a serviceperson spends on operations and the time they are home – was the other factor used to determine 'stretch'. The Army estimated that 5% of its trained strength breached its harmony guidelines (individual 415 days in thirty months and unit tour interval 24 months); particularly in niche trades where there were manning shortfalls. The RAF reported breaches of its guidelines (less than 2.5% of individuals complete 140 days separated service in one year, with unit tour interval 16 months) between 3.2% and 7.7%, dependent upon rank. The RN, despite having the toughest harmony rules (individual 660 days in a rolling 36 month period and unit deployed for 60% of the time) and the highest tempo, managed to curb harmony breaches at 1.2% through proactive policies to meet its targets.

The Secretary of State in outlining the scope of the SDSR, in his speech "The Need for Defence Reform" to the Royal Institute of Chartered Surveyors on 13th August 2010 acknowledged these manning pressures, "It has been widely commented upon that it takes our Armed Forces of over 180,000 to sustain a combat force of under 10,000 in Afghanistan. We need to challenge some of the fundamental assumptions which drive force generation, such as tour lengths and intervals, taking into account the varying pressures on our personnel resulting from widely varying missions to see if we can update our practices and produce greater efficiency while implementing the military covenant." It was widely anticipated therefore that the Army might face losing up to 20,000 troops, but it was the incoming Chief of the Defence Staff, General Sir David Richards, who won the first round in the SDSR by safeguarding the Army's strength in a direct appeal to the Prime Minister. Cameron accepted that it would be politically

damaging to slash the Army and the decision was seen as a victory for Richards, who had "outmanoeuvred" Ministry of Defence officials. "This deal is a realisation that we can only succeed in Afghanistan if we back the army to the hilt and concentrate resources where they are needed," reflected one senior army officer. To the reported fury of the other service chiefs, the Royal Navy and the RAF would therefore bear the brunt of the cuts again, each having to save £1.5 billion a year, and cut 10,000 posts. There would be further savings of £2 billion a year from canceling procurement projects, closing military bases and making 10,000 civil servants redundant. The fight between the services was about to intensify and unattributed quotes came thick and fast from "senior Navy commanders", "Army sources" and "MoD insiders", to fuel the public debate.

For the Ship's Company of HMS Ark Royal however this debate came a long way down the list of their priorities as they sought to regenerate the ship and prepare for a busy autumn programme following the AURIGA deployment. With the majority of the Ship's Company on leave through August the advanced leave party, enhanced with engineering support from the dockyard, completed the necessary preparations for an inclining experiment to test Ark's stability. The experiment required detailed surveys to be carried out to calculate where all of the weight lay in Ark and determine her centre of gravity, then accurate measurement of the reaction of the ship to being listed to port and starboard. Ark was cold moved from Victory Jetty in to 'D' Lock on 2nd September and with final adjustments made the following day, the incline experiment itself was successfully conducted on the 4th. Ark was cold moved back to Victory Jetty on 6th September, just in time for the majority of the Ship's Company to return from summer leave.

The main effort in the first week back was to make the final preparations the Commanding Officer's handover. Captain John Clink, Ark's longest serving Commanding Officer would hand over to Captain Jerry Kyd on 14th September. John Clink and Jerry Kyd were among the first generation of officers who had formally served in the carriers and were now returning as Captain in command. John Clink had been James Burnell-Nugent's navigating officer in *Invincible* in the late 1990's. For Jerry Kyd, returning to his own old ship for the second time was like coming home. He had completed his Fleet Time under James Weatherall in 1986, and then navigated *Ark* under David Snelson's command fourteen years later. Some of the fabric of the ship had changed in the intervening ten years, but the *Ark* spirit was still the same and very much alive.

From 15th to 23rd September *Ark*'s Company continued to make provision for the forthcoming Recovery and Trials Period (RTP), embarkation for the first time since 2008 of the two-star UK Maritime Battle Staff and then Exercise JOINT WARRIOR 10-2. Although she retained the Carrier Strike mantle there were no immediate plans to embark Harriers through the autumn and instead, *Ark*'s primary role would be as the command platform for the exercise. Nevertheless, her time at sea would be exploited to refresh the crew in handling the Apache AH-64 and provide qualification training for its pilots. The formidable firepower and target-tracking capability of the Apache had already been demonstrated to impressive effect on the battlefields of Afghanistan. Over the course of their time onboard *Ark Royal*, the Army Air Corps detachment would explore how these capabilities might be further extended by operating from a seaborne platform. On 24th September, three Apache aircraft from 656 Squadron, 4 Regiment AAC embarked alongside Victory Jetty and two days later *Ark* sailed from Portsmouth for the RTP en route to Faslane. The following day the Apache crews commenced initial deck qualifications while overnight the ship conducted a partial calibration of her Electronic Warfare suite, Outfit UAT, going around in circles half a mile off Portland Bill.

The EW calibration was just one of a series of routine 'health checks' of *Ark*'s weapons and sensors that the ship needed to complete to remain in date for operations and the weapon engineers had managed to cram in an intensive trials package on the way to Scotland. The annual check of the Precision Approach Radar was conducted off Plymouth on 28th September, while the ship participated in FOST-supported air defence exercises. The following day, *Ark*'s Phalanx mounts were put through their paces conducting live firing tests against towed targets flown by JSATO aircraft from Bournemouth. In anticipation of the forthcoming FOST Directed Continuation Training (DCT) ordered for November, the Ship's Company exercised their response to aircraft emergencies including crash on deck and fire in the hangar as part of ship's self-generated work-up preparations. In the midst of this, the AAC pilots completed day deck qualifications and moved on to night training. Sadly, bad weather in the Irish Sea prevented all crews achieving the 'tick in the box' and the residual training was programmed for the early stages of JOINT WARRIOR 10-2.

Ark Royal arrived alongside HM Naval Base Faslane on 1st October and Rear Admiral Paul Hudson, Commander UK Maritime Force, embarked along with the remaining battle staff augmentees. With the pre-exercise briefings, fuelling and storing completed, *Ark* sailed from Faslane on 4th. As promised, *Ark*'s early operations focussed on completing the night qualifications for the embarked AH-64 aircrew. On 6th October the Commander in Chief Fleet, Admiral Sir Trevor Soar embarked with Vice Admiral Holloway, Commander of the US Second Fleet and Rear Admiral Fitzpatrick, Commander Strike Force Training Atlantic to provide the Americans with an opportunity to witness UK integrated operational training and a UK two-star battle staff in action. With only Apaches embarked *Ark* presented an unusual configuration to the US admirals but they nevertheless were left impressed by the flexibility and facilities that the ship could provide to joint operations.

During the second half of JOINT WARRIOR the warfare teams achieved significant interaction within the task group as the operations intensified, while the AH-64s conducted live firing missions on to the Cape Wrath ranges and progressed to integration within the Surface Warfare scenario. By the end of the exercise on 14th the Apaches were certified to have achieved their Initial Operating Capability (Maritime), while *Ark* was revalidated as a NATO Reaction Force two-star command platform. COMUKMARFOR and his principal staff disembarked via helicopter that day. *Ark* returned alongside at Portsmouth two days later, where the remainder of the battle staff disembarked. *Ark*'s planned programme for the rest of the month and early November included a maintenance period, before the Ship's Company would next go back to sea, and into the warm embrace of the FOST staff at Devonport.

As *Ark* exercised, the closing moves of the SDSR were being played out. The Treasury's demanded target of a 10% cut in the defence budget put the department at breaking strain. Symptomatic of the leaks and back-briefs that had plagued the process, Liam Fox's direct appeal to Prime Minister David Cameron found its way into the press and highlighted the breadth of the funding chasm still to be bridged. "*Frankly this process is looking less and less defensible as a proper SDSR and more like a "super CSR". If it continues on its current trajectory it is likely to have grave political consequences for us,*" warned Fox. "*Party, media, military and the international reaction will be brutal if we do not recognise the dangers and continue to push for such draconian cuts at a time when we are at war.*" The Royal Navy appeared to be most at threat by the range of options on the table. "*The impact on capability, particularly in the maritime domain, would be more substantial than one might imagine from the paper. The reduction in overall surface ship numbers means we will be unable to undertake all the standing commitments (providing a permanent Royal Navy presence in priority regions) we do*

today. Assuming a presence in UK waters, the Falklands and in support of the deterrent is essential we would have to withdraw our presence in, for example, the Indian Ocean, Caribbean or Gulf. Deletion of the amphibious shipping (landing docks, helicopter platforms and auxiliaries) will mean that a landed force will be significantly smaller and lighter and deployed without protective vehicles or organic fire. We could not carry out the Sierra Leone operation again. Deletion of the Nimrod MR4 will limit our ability to deploy maritime forces rapidly into high-threat areas, increase the risk to the Deterrent, compromise maritime CT (counter terrorism), remove long range search and rescue, and delete one element of our Falklands reinforcement plan." Understandably, Fox also foresaw that the "*potential for the scale of the changes to seriously damage morale across the Armed Forces should not be underestimated.*"

By the time *Ark Royal* returned to Portsmouth following JOINT WARRIOR, the die had apparently been cast in the final negotiations of the SDSR. With concessions made by the Treasury and a cap of 7.5% set on the budget cut, it looked like Fox's warning on the impact to the UK's maritime capability had been heeded and the Royal Navy would come out of the process better than expected. The 'big-ticket' future equipment programmes – the *Queen Elizabeth*-class carriers; Type-26 Global Combat Ship, Stanhope's "*future backbone of the Royal Navy*", and the remaining *Astute*-class SSNs - had been safeguarded. The difficult decisions on Trident's successor had been risk assessed and safely deferred until the next Parliament. Cuts would be expected to the existing fleet, including the Type-22s and remaining Type-42s, but timed to coincide with the Type-45s coming on stream so that the escort force degraded gracefully to nineteen units. Similarly, the amphibious force would be slimmed, with one of the two LPDs put in extended readiness and a Bay-class LSL put up for disposal, but enough capability would remain to be able to launch an operation on the scale of Sierra Leone. In any case, the predicted load for 3 Commando Brigade would continue in Afghanistan for the next four years. The Navy's carrier strike capability would be maintained by HMS *Illustrious* through to 2016, in time for the arrival of HMS *Queen Elizabeth*, with HMS *Ark Royal* back-filling the LPH role while HMS *Ocean* refitted, eventually going out of service in 2014. It seemed, at last, that the intellectual and financial arguments had been won and the Royal Navy should look ahead with optimism: belts would certainly be tighter and the service would be smaller, but it would be better equipped, balanced and sustainable within a carefully scaled set of commitments.

The apparent paradigm shift that took place in the last few days before the formal announcement of the SDSR dispelled that optimism. "*If you want the unofficial dark blue version, we did particularly well up until the Friday, then we lost it in the Prime Minister's office,*" said one senior, unattributed naval source. As expected the *Type-22*s would be scrapped, but the disposal of the *Type-42*s would be accelerated before the *Type-45*s were fully in service. Harrier GR-9 was out. With no aircraft to fly, HMS *Ark Royal* the strike carrier would be scrapped immediately and the Royal Navy would have to sustain a ten year gap in carrier strike capability until the second of the large carriers, HMS *Prince of Wales* came into operational service in 2020. Only one future carrier would ever operate at once; the other put into extended readiness or sold off. HMS *Illustrious* or HMS *Ocean* would be retained in the LPH role. The number of Joint Strike Fighters would be halved. The Nimrod MRA-4 would be cancelled, posing a significant threat to the protection of the deterrent SSBNs.

It appeared that the Government was ill-prepared for the backlash that followed the formal publication of the SDSR, despite attempts on the morning of its announcement in Parliament to pave the way for it. Deputy Prime Minister, Nick Clegg appeared at Rosyth and in an oblique reference to the future carriers promised "big announcements", seemingly unaware that behind him stood HMS *Illustrious* in refit and facing a very uncertain future. David Cameron visited service personnel at the Permanent Joint Headquarters at Northwood, accompanied by a grim-faced Liam Fox and Sir Jock Stirrup. Uncomfortable questions from Lieutenant Commander Kris Ward Royal Navy, a serving Harrier pilot whose father Nigel 'Sharkey' Ward DSC was the Falklands ace who commanded 801 Squadron flying from HMS *Invincible*, caused Cameron to fluff his lines, confusing the Tornado with the Typhoon. "*I have listened to all the military advice, and the military advice is pretty clear that when we have to make difficult decisions, it is right to keep the Typhoon as our principal ground attack aircraft, working in Afghanistan at the moment, and it is right to retire the Harrier.*"

All Captain Kyd and the Ship's Company of HMS *Ark Royal* could do was to listen to the radio and watch the news bulletins until the definitive answers were announced in Parliament. Bereft of any clear instructions in the face of a MoD-imposed communications embargo, Captain Kyd gathered his heads of department then ordered a Clear Lower Deck to present the facts as he knew them and to try to provide some reassurance to his Ship's Company. The covenant between a Commanding Officer and the Ship's Company of a warship was one of the enshrining principles on which the Royal Navy had been founded and on the morning of Tuesday 19th October 2010, with the gangways shut and in the privacy of the hangar, Captain Kyd reaffirmed the bond he had made with his Ship's Company of less than five weeks. If HMS *Ark Royal* was to go, then she would do so in the style that befitted the greatest ship in the Royal Navy. "*There was a sharp intake of breath and quite a few damp eyes I remember,*" recalled Captain Kyd. "*My message was that whatever was going to happen, Ark Royal – the Fleet's Flagship – would go out with dignity.*" That afternoon, as everyone feared, confirmation came that HMS *Ark*

Royal was to go.

In the cold light of the next day, it seemed extraordinary that the scrapping of a ship already twenty five years old with only four years left to serve should cause any great outcry. Similarly, scrapping a small, slow, forty-year old aircraft should hardly have caused many eyelids to bat. But the SDSR decisions failed to comprehend the overwhelming affection and reverence in which both HMS *Ark Royal* and the Harrier were held in the British psyche. *Ark Royal*, the most famous warship in the world since Nelson's *Victory*, defined both the best traditions of the Royal Navy and its enduring ability to stay at the leading edge. The Harrier, the most beloved aeroplane since the Spitfire and an example like Concorde of world-beating British technology, had won the air battle against a far superior force in the Falklands. The 'little' jet and the 'little' carrier, almost single handedly reignited the nation's belief in 1982 that Britain could still be taken seriously on the world stage, and since then had been ubiquitous players in UK operations around the globe.

The outcry was swift. In the midst of all of the other decisions taken, the loss of HMS *Ark Royal* and the Harrier were the only headlines. Furious questions were raised repeatedly in the Commons and Lords to understand why the Harrier had been given up instead of the more expensive Tornado. The savings of abolishing the GR-9 were only £1 billion while the Tornado could realise savings of anywhere between £3 billion and £7.5 billion. The capability arguments of keeping the Tornado seemed unclear. By all independent accounts, in what was supposed to be the pivotal decider, Afghanistan, the GR-9 had been more available, more reliable and more flexibly equipped during its five-year tour of duty from 2004-9 than the GR-4 was now proving to be. Although it lacked range, speed and a deep strike capability, the Harrier was regarded as the better CAS platform and this surely was the key role requirement, as David Cameron had spelled out, to "*support our troops in Afghanistan*"? Only the Harrier, deployed on a CVS, could provide a truly global, autonomous strike capability and was it not unwise to believe that friendly countries would always be willing to base British Tornados?

Among the most vocal opponents of the decision to cancel the Harrier was Lord West, former First Sea Lord and Labour security minister who on 27th October voiced his concern in the House of Lords. "*My Lords, the decision to get rid of the Harriers and not the Tornados is bizarre and wrong. It is the most bonkers decision that I have come across in my 45 years in the military and I can assure this House that I have been privy to some pretty bonkers decisions in that time.*" Implacable, on 10th November, Lord West joined by another former First Sea Lord, Sir Julian Oswald, *Ark*'s former Captain Jeremy Blackham and two other senior military figures wrote despairingly to The Times, "*Sir, We believe the Prime Minister has been badly advised to scrap the Harrier force and HMS Ark Royal and to rely entirely upon the Tornado. The decision to axe the entire Harrier force is strategically and financially perverse.*"

The Chiefs of Staff were unmoved, but the very public intervention demanded an equally public response. "*No-one would pretend that the SDSR has been painless. It has led to a range of decisions that we would not have otherwise chosen to make,*" they wrote in The Times the following day. "*The decision to withdraw Harrier from service and to retain a reduced Tornado force had to balance our current needs in Afghanistan with the intent to rationalise our fast jet fleets. After very careful consideration our military advice was to retain the more capable Tornado. Harrier's contribution has been huge but the decision to withdraw it is the right thing to do in the circumstances and a decision that we collectively agreed.*" On the emotive issue of the continued defence of the Falklands, the Chiefs sought to give reassurance that Britain had "*comprehensive defences in place, unlike 1982*", while reiterating the collective responsibility of the choices made.

"Tough decisions had to be made in the SDSR. It was delivered by a process in which we all played a part and although we voiced our reservations about particular conclusions robustly, as we should, the decisions made were collectively reached and supported. We stand by each of them. We must now move on with its implementation."

If the Chiefs of Staff had hoped that HMS *Ark Royal* would slip away quietly then circumstances did not play to their favour, since *Ark* was scheduled to be in the public eye throughout November, to celebrate, ironically, the 25th anniversary of her commissioning. The celebrations included a Ship's Company Dance at the Guildhall in Portsmouth at the end of October, a dinner onboard for her twelve Commanding Officers and *Ark*'s enduring friend, Sir Donald Gosling on the actual anniversary on 1st November, and a cocktail party for former members of the Ship's Company. But the ship's greatest coup was to be honoured with a visit by Her Majesty The Queen, at Portsmouth on Friday 5th November. Originally planned as a celebration, Her Majesty's visit took on a new and added poignancy, but there was no disguising the immense pride of the Ship's Company and thrill at seeing their Monarch onboard just once more. Over 1,000 family and friends gathered to watch the spectacle and see Her Majesty, who wore the *Ark* brooch originally given to The Queen Mother. Paying tribute to the ship's royal connection, and perhaps tempting fate, Captain Kyd told the Queen that it was only because of her mother that the ship bore the name *Ark Royal*. *"She was to be called the Indomitable, but at The Queen Mother's insistence the name was changed to Ark Royal. The politicians listened to her wisdom"*.

There was little sentiment within Fleet Headquarters for a farewell tour by their flagship, nevertheless HMS *Ark Royal* had real business still to undertake since her magazines needed to be emptied before she could begin paying off, and this would take place at Glen Mallen in Scotland. Calling in every last favour and making the case

that there needed to be some form of public 'closure', *Ark*'s planners constructed a final passage plan that would include a round trip of Britain, a last visit to the Tyne and one final foreign run ashore to Hamburg.

HMS *Ark Royal* sailed from Portsmouth on 9th November, just before the controversy of her cancellation was reignited by the Admirals' letter to The Times. Maintaining a dignified silence throughout her short passage, except to mark Armistice Day, *Ark* arrived at the Clyde on the 12th and made the slow approach up Loch Long to the ammunitioning facility at Glen Mallen. Amidst the bustle of deammunitioning, eighty of *Ark*'s Ship's Company led by the Executive Officer Commander Rob Bellfield took part in the annual remembrance parade at George Square in Glasgow. On the 15th the Wardroom held its final mess dinner, to celebrate the 70th anniversary of the Fleet Air Arm's finest hour, the routing of the Italian fleet at Taranto in November 1940. Admiral Andrew Cunningham, the Commander in Chief Mediterranean at the time considered that Taranto *"should be remembered forever as having shown once and for all that in the Fleet Air Arm, the Navy has its most devastating weapon"* and for the Navy's aviation community the annual celebration had taken on as great a significance as Trafalgar Night. For the pilots of No.1 (F) Squadron RAF who had embarked during the passage up the Irish Sea, the dinner was especially memorable since the guest of honour was one of *Ark*'s most famous sons, "Jock" Moffat. On 26th May 1941, Sub Lieutenant Moffat launched his Fairy Swordfish from the deck of *Ark Royal* III in atrocious conditions to make a desperate attack on a German surface raider. His target was the battleship *Bismarck*. In darkness, heavy seas and dodging a ferocious barrage of anti-aircraft fire, Moffat approached to within 1,000 yards of the ship before dropping his single torpedo. Having judged the release perfectly, Moffat's torpedo ran straight into *Bismarck*'s stern as the giant ship evaded to port, the explosion disabling her rudder and steering gear. Unable to manoeuvre, *Bismarck* circled until the following morning when the British battleships HMS *Rodney* and HMS *King George V* caught up and finished her off. The young RN and RAF pilots listening to Jock Moffat's account of that night could not help but reflect that in the right hands, a small, elderly aircraft launched from a carrier, could play a pivotal role in military history.

From Glen Mallen, *Ark Royal* sailed around the top of Scotland to her birth place at North Shields. Tynesiders came out in their thousands to greet the ship as she arrived on the 18th. For the Ship's Company, the reception was slightly overwhelming. *"The reception we got in Newcastle was phenomenal"* recalled Captain Kyd. *"Never before have I sailed a ship into harbour when there were thousands of people lining the jetty. It just shows the depth of feeling for the ship and the pride the country has for her"*. During the four-day visit over 10,000 people came onboard to say goodbye. The weather turned to Arctic conditions as the ship was due to leave and unlike the mass crowds that gathered to celebrate her arrival, only a few hardy souls ventured on to the dockside to bid farewell to one of the most famous names in British naval history as she set sail. But they nevertheless managed to bring a degree of jollity to the occasion, and as the tugs pulled the ship into the main channel for her final voyage down the Tyne, local ship workers played Rod Stewart's *"Sailing"* over their public address system.

The next leg of *Ark*'s final voyage would take her across the North Sea to Hamburg, but before she arrived at the German port, there was one last and historic operational evolution to complete; the final launch of a Harrier from a British aircraft carrier, on 24th November 2010. There were no crowds, no bands and no bunting. Instead, only the hardiest members of the Ship's Company and a handful of embarked journalists watched as four GR-9s launched against the forbidding back-drop of a stormy North Sea sky in freezing sleet. In many respects, it was an appropriate end to the

glittering career of one of Britain's most iconic warplanes, for no one who braved the sub-zero temperatures was in much spirits to celebrate the Harrier's last appearance on deck. One aircraft handler who talked to the visiting Daily Telegraph journalist summed up the mood, *"they've taken leave of their senses. You can't get a better fighting combination than this, and yet they are sending us all to the scrap yard."* As if to prove the point, the first two GR-9s provided a faultless display of their power and aeronautical dynamism before heading off to RAF Cottesmore.

At just after 09:00, the last GR-9 taxied to the end of *Ark*'s 400-foot runway as the ship steered headlong into a 45-knot wind, which was filled with intimidating flurries of snow. The pilot, Lieutenant Commander Jim Blackmore, who had qualified flying an FA-2 on *Ark* eight years before, applied full throttle to the aircraft's Pegasus engine, causing a sheet of sea spray to explode upon the deck as the aircraft hurtled towards the ramp. Seconds later it was soaring into the sky, causing the whole ship to reverberate with the roar of its engine. There were a few muffled cheers and waves from the frozen onlookers before the Harrier disappeared into the leaden, overcast skies. Even Jerry Kyd admitted there was a tear in his eye as the last Harrier made its dramatic exit from the nation's military landscape. *"For a ship like this, it is like taking the teeth from a tiger,"* he commented ruefully. Jim Blackmore who, like his RN and RAF colleagues faced an uncertain future was equally philosophical, *"I've wanted to be a Harrier pilot since I watched one hovering over Chatham Dockyard when I was eight years old,"* he said shortly before take-off. *"It's what every pilot dreams of when they join the Navy. I will absolutely miss it."*

From the Falklands to Afghanistan, via every major British conflict in between, the Harrier had played a vital role in defending the nation from a variety of threats. It saw action in both Gulf wars, as well as flying combat missions in Bosnia, Kosovo, Iraq and Sierra Leone. Its ability to provide close air support to ground troops had made it especially popular with the Army and Royal Marines, whether protecting UN convoys and fighting Serb army units, or during combat operations against the Taliban. But ultimately, Britain's most iconic jet of the past seventy years lost its final battle, with the Treasury.

General Sir David Richards, newly installed as the Chief of the Defence Staff had tried to close the book on the SDSR decisions on the day *Ark* sailed from North Shields, in a speech to the Policy Exchange think tank in London. The two lingering issues were the decision to purchase the new carriers and the decision to decommission the Harrier fleet and retain the Tornados; on both issues he gave a candid view. "*The case for carriers was not supported by everyone. Some argued that they were no longer necessary; that the range of modern jets, extended by a fleet of tanker aircraft, and our basing agreements mean they are part of yesterday's arsenal. I don't agree. Whilst I consider it an acceptable risk to be without carrier strike for the next decade, I do not think, and did not during the SDSR debate think, it prudent to assume a future that discounts ever requiring them again. The gap in carrier-based aircraft does not diminish our ability to defend the Falkland Islands. The situation in the South Atlantic is very different to that of 1982. Our strategy is based on deterrence and defence, i.e. for once learning the lessons of 1982. So today our defences are much greater with capable sea, ground and air presence. Furthermore the government in Buenos Aires is now a democracy, not a military dictatorship, based on the rule of law and tied into a network of alliances, both regional and international. The Argentine foreign minister emphasised in an interview this month that they would seek to take the islands through peaceful means. Once all this was understood and agreed, and given that our finances required us to remove a complete fast jet type, the issue of whether Harrier or Tornado could be based on current and anticipated operational need. In this,*

the choice was made for us some time ago. When the decision was taken in 2009 to reduce the Harrier fleet to 32 aircraft it became impossible to sustain operations in Afghanistan, and maintain an adequate contingent capability for the unexpected, with just the Harrier. The short delay to the first carrier, to allow it to be fitted with 'cats and traps', means that when it comes into service in 2019 it will be equipped with the hugely capable carrier variant of Joint Strike Fighter. That will mean we will have greater flexibility over their fifty years' lifespan and will ensure we are prepared for a less predictable future."

Despite the assurances by the new CDS, the headlines in the national press that followed the departure of the Harriers from *Ark* fanned the coals of the SDSR's fire that had been raked repeatedly for the previous month. "Plane Stupid" was the headline in the The Times editorial on 25th November.

In the collective mind of *Ark Royal*'s Ship's Company however, the departure of the last Harrier signalled finally the end of the ship's service life and, stoical as ever, that meant that the final run ashore in Hamburg should be savoured to the last drop. *Ark* arrived at the German port on 25th November for a five-day visit. The German public turned out en masse to see the carrier, with 3,000 visiting the ship on the Saturday, demonstrating her global appeal. The ship welcomed guests and dignitaries onboard for a final cocktail party on the Monday evening before saying 'auf Wiedersehen' at mid-morning the following day. In sub-zero conditions, *Ark* made her way up the river and out into the North Sea. The Ship's Company was sent out the next day to try in vain to clear the frozen flight deck as temperatures plummeted to -15°C. "*I can't feel my hands!*" remarked one sailor as he came in from the cold. "*I can't feel anything,*" replied his colleague, as if in a scene that could have been a living Tugg cartoon.

Covered in snow, *Ark* negotiated the shipping lanes of the English Channel as she made her way back to Portsmouth. Her penultimate day at sea was due to begin with a west to east transit through the Solent, allowing a rare opportunity for the people of the Gosport peninsular and on the Isle of Wight to catch a final glimpse of the ship before the final entry to her homeport. The plan had to be shelved due to thick fog and instead she followed her usual route via Nab Tower to anchor off Spithead overnight. With one last coat of polish applied and *Ark* looking pristine, she was ready to make the final, emotional entry to Portsmouth.

In bitterly cold temperatures, the ghostly image of HMS *Ark Royal* appeared through the thick fog. The conditions should have deterred anyone from pausing to watch through the gloom, but true to their old ship, and as they had done on numerous previous occasions, hundreds of well-wishers turned out to welcome *Ark Royal* home, cheering and shouting as she slipped past. As the ship passed the Round Tower, Commander Rob Bellfield's muffled tones came over main broadcast in an emotional goodbye. *"Thank you to everyone for showing your support. Thank you to the City of Portsmouth."* With that, Rod Stewart's "Sailing" played out one last time.

After 50,762 hours at sea and having sailed 621,551 nautical miles, at a few minutes past 10:00 on Friday 3rd December 2010, HMS *Ark Royal* V tied up alongside Victory Jetty. The most famous warship in the modern history of the Royal Navy was home for good. For her Ship's Company, *Ark*'s final homecoming was a hugely emotional affair. Some personnel, like Jerry Kyd, had served onboard through several appointments or drafts and the bond that had been formed with *Ark* was almost unbreakable. For the newer crew members, some of which had only just joined the ship after AURIGA and been onboard less than three months, the sense of passing of a Naval institution was equally palpable. The free champagne at the arrival reception, donated as ever by the ship's stalwart friend, Sir Donald Gosling, helped blunt emotions and offered a fitting means to celebrate end of an era.

Christmas leave came immediately for the Ship's Company and as they returned in the New Year of 2011 they faced the uncertainty of drafts to new ships and establishments throughout the Fleet. *Ark*'s sister HMS *Illustrious* survived the Strategic Defence Review primarily because the cost of her refit at Rosyth had already been spent and she was needed to fill a stop-gap while HMS *Ocean* went into dock. *Illustrious* was due to crew up in Spring and around 130 of *Ark*'s Ship's Company led by Jerry Kyd, her new Commanding Officer, cross-decked to bring her back into service.

Having only recently been refitted, *Ark* was in exceptionally good material state and all of her weapons, sensors, communications and auxiliary systems were in perfect order. Not surprisingly therefore, the cash-strapped planners within the Ministry of Defence took full advantage to use her as a donor for other ships. Parts were removed to go back into the spares loop, military task equipment was redeployed to ships heading east to the Gulf and entire systems, such as BOWMAN, Phalanx CIWS and the Precision Approach Radar were taken to help fit out brand new ships coming into service. Some equipment was even destined to be fitted in HMS *Queen Elizabeth*, *Ark*'s natural successor and the future hope for the Fleet Air Arm, due to enter service around 2015. In the meantime *Ark Royal* was destined to slip quietly from sight, however two enduring friends of the ship – her base port Portsmouth and her affiliated city Leeds – made sure that the final farewell would be anything but private. As part of the final goodbyes, both cities asked to host farewell marches for *Ark*'s Ship's Company.

Portsmouth honoured HMS *Ark Royal* with a farewell parade on 22nd January. Thousands lined the streets waving flags to pay an emotional farewell to the ship and its crew, as 250 members of Ship's Company marched with a Royal Marines Band to the city's Guildhall where a thanksgiving service was held. Council leader Gerald Vernon-Jackson said the vessel had a "very special" place in the hearts of the people of the city. He revealed he had written to the Queen and Prince Charles asking them to consider allowing one of the next generation of carriers, which were due to be named after them, to inherit the *Ark Royal* name instead, adding, "*I have probably broken every piece of naval etiquette there is.*"

Captain Kyd, in paying tribute to his crew, told the assembled dignitaries, "*It is with equal measure of sadness and a whole lot of pride that I stand here before you as the last Commanding Officer of Ark Royal. On behalf of Ark Royal's men and women, past and present, and for those who have given their lives while of this great ship, we would like to say how much Portsmouth has meant to us. There is a very close bond between the Royal Navy and this great maritime city - Portsmouth is the navy and the men and women of Ark Royal are proud to call Portsmouth their home port.*" With that, he presented the Lord Mayor, Councillor Paula Riches, with the ship's ensign. Following the ceremony, fifty members of the Ship's Company visited Portsmouth FC's ground at Fratton Park to say farewell on the pitch before Pompey's match, coincidentally against *Ark*'s other great friend Leeds United FC. While the teams played, some 5,000 visitors passed through the Naval Base and stepped onboard *Ark* for a final Ship Open to Visitors. The match ended 2-2; perhaps a fitting share of the spoils between *Ark*'s two great cities. Keen to keep an even score, Leeds' turn to pay a final tribute to the ship came in mid-February, with the traditional Freedom of the City march.

On 31st January, Greg Mulholland, Liberal Democrat Member for Leeds Northwest tabled an early day motion "*That this House welcomes the decision to commemorate HMS Ark Royal's unique and long-standing affiliation with Leeds by granting Freedom of the City to her crew on 12th February 2011, and holding a parade through the streets of the city to mark the raising of over £9 million in 1941 towards the cost of building another Ark Royal following the sinking of its predecessor; believes that these strong historical links make this tribute especially fitting; and*

further hopes that any future Ark Royal will once again have a similar affiliation with the city of Leeds." Twelve days later, 160 members of the Ship's Company marched for the last time through 'their' city, with bayonets fixed, Colour flying and drums beating, accompanied by a Royal Marines Band. Taking the salute, the Lord Mayor of Leeds, Councillor Jim McKenna said: "*The day is one of great celebration, but tinged with the sadness of the decommissioning of the ship.*"

The final farewell for HMS *Ark Royal* came on 11th March 2011 with the ship's decommissioning and by the end of May all but a handful of her Ship's Company remained. As with so many famous warships, numerous ideas were tendered on how she might be saved for the Nation or kept in some useful capacity out of service. Proposals included using her as a floating heliport moored in the Port of London near Greenwich, and her conversion to a floating school or nightclub based on the Mersey in Liverpool or in China. One proposal even suggested sinking the ship in Torbay to create an artificial reef that would attract scuba divers from all over the world. HMS *Ark Royal*'s eventual fate is still to be decided, but most likely she will follow her elder sister HMS *Invincible* to the scrap yard. Such an ignominious end is the fate of great ships, as befell *Ark*'s forebear in 1980.

The fifth HMS *Ark Royal* was born out of the compromise of the 1966 Defence Review; was very nearly still-born in the wake of the 1981 Review had the Falklands War not intervened; was reinvigorated by the 1998 Review as carriers once again claimed ascendency, but ultimately was killed prematurely by the 2010 Review on the same grounds of cost that put paid to CVA-01 twenty years before *Ark Royal* V entered service. "*In my beginning is my end,*" attributed to Mary Queen of Scots at her death, seems an equally fitting motto for *Ark*'s life, but for the men and women who served in her, only one reflects the 'Spirit of the *Ark*' that they helped ignite over the quarter of a century on active service -

"Zeal Does Not Rest"

Epilogue

HMS *Ark Royal* decommissioned on 11th March 2011 and after the final fanfares and farewells her last Ship's Company dispersed throughout the Fleet and took with them their stories of time served in the greatest warship of the modern Royal Navy.

The story of the fifth HMS *Ark Royal* is wrapped up in the wider struggle for the Royal Navy to retain its carrier capability. Forty four years separate the decisions made by Denis Healey and Liam Fox in considering the carrier question, but the circumstances in which those decisions were taken bear remarkable similarity. Bringing a burgeoning defence budget under control; rationalising the future 'joint' defence needs to meet an over-stretched set of commitments; wrestling the doctrinal question of land-based versus maritime aviation, and facing the looming cost of a future submarine-based nuclear deterrent were all challenges facing the governments of 1966 and 2010. In 1966, HMS *Queen Elizabeth* was cancelled because she was unaffordable, leaving the last conventional fixed wing capability to be flown from HMS *Ark Royal* IV and setting in train the decisions for her successor and the era of the Harrier. In 2010, HMS *Queen Elizabeth* was retained because it was unaffordable not to do so, but at the cost of HMS *Ark Royal* V and the end of the Harrier age. In both cases the Royal Navy lost the argument with the Royal Air Force of the supremacy of carrier-borne aircraft, with the politicians suitably convinced that land-based jets, flown from 'island bases' (1965) or 'friendly host-nations' (2010) could provide the needs of Defence. Ironically, the questions of 'size' and 'conventional versus STOVL' argued at length in the early 1960s and which led ultimately to the

'Through Deck Cruiser' and the Sea Harrier have now come full circle; the next generation carrier will be the largest warship ever built in Britain and the fifth generation aircraft that fly from it will be launched by 'cats' and recovered by 'traps'.

But it will be at least a decade before this full capability is realised and in the meantime the Royal Navy will sail uncharted waters. The Service has never before had to regenerate such a fundamental capability and the skill sets needed to do so will rely heavily on cooperation with those countries that have retained the big ships; indeed this is the central argument for retreading the steps along the 'conventional' path. Success will depend on the ability to master new technology and relearn old skills that were once commonplace among the Fleet Air Arm and on which some of the service's finest traditions and ethos were founded.

"Zeal Does Not Rest" would be a fine motto to capture the qualities that will be needed to achieve success in the fifth generation of carrier aviation and the history and ethos of the Fleet Air Arm are intertwined in the Spirit of a ship that has led the last four: HMS *Ark Royal*. In 1978, the Admiralty Board understood the value of the 'Spirit of the Ark', even if, so the story goes, they needed a gentle reminder from Her Majesty Queen Elizabeth the Queen Mother. Signalling Captain Anson onboard *Ark Royal* IV, as she sailed home for the last time, the Admiralty Board declared:

"The return to rest of another Great and Royal Ark marks the end of a glorious period in our naval history during which we have led the world in naval aviation techniques and efficiency. It also marks the beginning of a new and exciting epoch in which we can continue to demonstrate our determination and ability to remain in the forefront

of maritime aviation matters. It is particularly important therefore that the traditions, professionalism and dedication you have all demonstrated in the Ark Royal, Ship's Company and Squadrons alike, are carried forward into this new era, so maintaining the high standards expected of us. To remind the fleet and future generations of these high standards, it is intended that CAH-03 shall be named Ark Royal. Well done

and good luck to you all."

It is over thirty years since those words were written, but in the uncertain times for the Royal Navy of the 21st Century, perhaps therein lies the secret for its success. As the new carriers enter service, might yet the Admiralty Board consider the 'Spirit of the *Ark*' and turn to one faithful and absolute certainty, captured by the most famous name in its long history:

HMS ARK ROYAL

Chapter Notes

Professor Eric Grove has written twice about HMS *Ark Royal*. Chapters 2 to 7 of this book, covering the periods in command from James Weatherall (1985) to Terry Loughran (1994) are based on his original work "*Ark Royal*" written in 1994. Chapters 8 and 9, covering the ship's first refit at Rosyth and her emergence in 2001, are derived from Eric's second work "*Ark Royal*: a flagship for the 21st century" written in 2001. Both works have been substantially updated and added to from contemporary, declassified source material.

Eric Grove "*Ark Royal*" Fleet Publications, 1994   ©HMS *Ark Royal*/Crown Copyright (images), 1994
Eric Grove/Marjory Wood "*Ark Royal: a flagship for the 21st century*"
HMS Ark Royal/Catchline PR, 2001   ©HMS *Ark Royal*/Crown Copyright (images), 2001

HMS *Ark Royal's* complete Reports of Proceedings from 1985 to 1994 were obtained from the Naval Historical Branch. The Monthly Unit Records from July 2007 to December 2010 were retained onboard. The ROPs and MURs are ©Crown Copyright. The Navy News archive provided an abundance of stories, articles and photographs HMS *Ark Royal's* life; sadly they are too numerous to list them all individually. Articles sourced from The Naval Review are ©Copyright the author/Naval Review.

Research material for Chapter 1 -

NHB Studies –   All Naval Historical Branch ©Crown Copyright, 1997
62/1 1996 "The Carrier Controversy, British Aircraft Carrier Policy, Discussion and Decision 1945-1966"
62/4 1997 "The 'Invincible' Class CVS(G) – Escort Cruiser to Light Carrier"
62/4-1 1997 "Background, Concept and Design", 62/4-3 1997 "Early Experience"

Research material for Chapter 2 -

HMS *Ark Royal* 226/1 dated 28 November 1985 – Report of Proceedings 1 Jul – 1 Nov 1985
HMS *Ark Royal* 226/1 dated 10 April 1986 – Report of Proceedings 2 Nov 1985 – 20 Feb 1986
HMS *Ark Royal* 226/1 dated 14 July 1986 – Report of Proceedings 21 Feb – 19 Jun 1986
HMS *Ark Royal* 226/1 dated 20 November 1986 – Report of Proceedings 20 Jun – 13 Oct 1986
HMS *Ark Royal* 226/1 dated 3 February 1987 – Report of Proceedings 14 Oct 1986 – 3 Feb 1987
820 NAS Record Book February 1986 - January 1987   FAA Museum ©Crown Copyright, 1987
Neil McCart "*Three Ark Royals 1938-1999*" ISBN 190122502X   ©Neil McCart/Fan Publications, 1999

Research material for Chapter 3 -

HMS *Ark Royal* 226/1 dated 20 September 1987 – Report of Proceedings 3 Feb 1987 – 31 Aug 1987
HMS *Ark Royal* 226/1 dated 25 January 1988 – Report of Proceedings 1 Sep – 31 Dec 1987
HMS *Ark Royal* 226/1 dated 7 July 1988 – Report of Proceedings 1 Jan – 12 Jun 88
HMS *Ark Royal* 226/1 dated 3 Jan 1988 [err 89] – Report of Proceedings 13 Jun – 15 Dec 1988
HMS *Ark Royal* 226/1 dated 27 April 1989 – Report of Proceedings 16 Dec 1988 – 27 Apr 1989

Flag Officer 2nd Flotilla 225/7/14 dated 15 December 1988 – Report of TG318.1 6 Jun – 15 Dec 1988
HMS *Ark Royal* Commission Book Feb 1987 – Dec 1988   Navy News Archive ©HMS *Ark Royal,* 1988
820 NAS Record Book February – December 1987   FAA Museum ©Crown Copyright
You Magazine *"Want to Buy an Aircraft Carrier?"* Lee Wilson   ©Daily Mail newspapers, 1989

Research material for Chapter 4 -

HMS *Ark Royal* 226/1 dated 14 November 1989 – Report of Proceedings 27 Apr – 31 Oct 1989
HMS *Ark Royal* 226/1 dated 24 July 1990 – Report of Proceedings TU318.5.1 26 Apr – 5 Jul 1990
HMS *Ark Royal* 226/1 dated 24 July 1990 – Report of Proceedings 6 Jul – 23 Oct 1990

Research material for Chapter 5 -

Flag Officer 2nd Flotilla 225/100 dated 15 October 1991 – Report of TG313.1 9 Sep – 15 Oct 1991
HMS *Ark Royal* 226/1 dated 14 April 1992 – Report of Proceedings 7 Sep 1991 – 14 Mar 1992
HMS *Ark Royal* 226/1 dated 8 July 1992 – Report of Proceedings 15 Mar – 8 Jul 1992
UK national press cuttings 23 April 1992 and 3 September 1992 (accidental bombing, see pp50)

Research material for Chapter 6 -

HMS *Ark Royal* 226/1 dated 1 December 1992 – Report of Proceedings 8 Jul – 6 Nov 1992
HMS *Ark Royal* 226/1 dated 7 March 1993 – Report of Proceedings 7 Nov 1992 – 14 Jan 1993
UK national press cuttings 14/15 January 1993 (sailing for Op GRAPPLE, see pp62)
Soldier Magazine issues 16 November 1992 and 14 December 1992, Operation GRAPPLE reports
UK national press cuttings 5 February 1993 (Owen peace deal rejected, see pp65)

Stephen Prince & Kate Brett *"Royal Navy Operations off the Former Yugoslavia: Operation Sharp
Guard, 1991-1996"* Naval Historical Branch   ©Copyright Stephen Prince/Kate Brett, 2010

Cdr P A Jones RN *"Naval Poise Operations in the Adriatic"* The Naval Review 1994 Issue 1
Cdr D G Snelson RN *"Naval Poise Operations in the Adriatic – II"* The Naval Review 1994 Issue 2
RAdm Jeremy Blackham *"Maritime Peacekeeping"* Royal United Services Institute
Journal 138 No.4 August 1993   ©Copyright J J Blackham/RUSI, 1993

"Former Yugoslavia – UNPROFOR" Department of Public Information, United Nations, September 1996
                    open source at http://www.un.org/Depts/DPKO/Missions/unprof_b.htm

Research material for Chapter 7 -

Commander UK Task Group's 225/150 dated 13 July 1993 – Report of Proceedings of UK (Adriatic)
TG612.02 21 Apr – 13 Jul 1993
Commander UK Task Group's 226/3 dated 1 November 1994 – COMUKTG's Adriatic Report of
Proceedings 4 Feb – 28 Aug 1994
Eric Grove *"Navies in Peacekeeping and Enforcement: The British Experience in the Adriatic"*
International Peacekeeping 1, No.4 Winter 1994   ©Copyright Eric Grove, 1994

Capt T W Loughran RN "*Operational Effectiveness and Resource Constraints – HMS Ark Royal in Operations GRAPPLE and HAMDEN 1993/4*"
Royal United Services Institute Journal 140 No.1 February 1995   ©Copyright T W Loughran/RUSI, 1995

Research material for Chapter 8 -

Norman Friedman "*The Naval Institute Guide to World Naval Weapons Systems, 1997-1998*"
ISBN 1557502684   ©Copyright US Naval Institute, 1997

Select Committee on Public Accounts, 8 March 2000, Question 253-54 (Sir Robert Walmsley)
http://www.publications.parliament.uk/pa/cm199900/cmselect/cmpubacc/319/0030814.htm
Prepared 30 November 2000   ©Parliamentary Copyright, 2000

Research material for Chapter 9 -

George Robertson speech at Chatham House, 12 March 1998, "small aircraft carriers" (see pp107)
http://www.prnewswire.co.uk/cgi/release?id=10768

Cm3999 "*The Strategic Defence Review*" HMSO 1998 ISBN 10: 0101399928   ©Crown Copyright, 1998

Claire Taylor, Research Paper 04/71 "*The Defence White Paper*" 17 September 2004
International Affairs and Defence Section, House of Commons Library   ©Parliamentary Copyright, 2004

House of Commons Strategic Defence Review Debate 8 July 2008, Hansard vol 315 cc1073-96

BBC News "*Ark Royal memories of Queen Mother*" 1 April 2002   ©Copyright BBC News, 2002
http://news.bbc.co.uk/1/hi/england/1905052.stm

Lt Cdr 'Jack' London obituary, The Independent 7 December 2002   ©Copyright independent.co.uk, 2002
http://www.independent.co.uk/news/obituaries/ltcdr-martin-london-610170.html

800 NAS Record Book July 2001 – June 2002   FAA Museum ©Crown Copyright, 2002

Research material for Chapter 10 -

Various internet articles on background to and build up for Gulf War II
UNSCRs sourced from http://www.iraqwatch.org/un/Index_SecCounRes.html

Iraq Debate in House of Commons 24 September 2002, column 17   ©Parliamentary Copyright, 2002
http://www.publications.parliament.uk/pa/cm200102/cmhansrd/vo020924/debtext/20924-05.htm

Robin Cook, Personal Statement 17 Mar 2003: Column 726   ©Parliamentary Copyright, 2002
http://www.publications.parliament.uk/pa/cm200203/cmhansrd/vo030317/debtext/30317-33.htm

Alan Massey Operation TELIC War Diary extracts
Alan Massey recollection of Op TELIC April 2007, http://naval849.co.uk/AlanMassey.htm
800 NAS Record Book July 2002 – July 2003   FAA Museum ©Crown Copyright

Robert Fox "*Iraq Campaign 2003*" ISBN0954597206   ©Copyright Robert Fox/Agenda Publishing, 2003

Capt Alan Massey RN "Operation Telic – A Personal View" The Naval Review 2003, Issue 4

Jeremy Robbins "*Iraq and Al Faw Landings*", chpr XXXVI, "*Amphibious Assault - Manoeuvre from the Sea, Amphibious Operations from the Last Century*", 2005 Fleet Publications   ©Crown Copyright, 2005

Research material for Chapter 11 -

RAdm Scott Lidbetter "Joint Force 2000 – On Track or Coming Off The Rails?" Naval Review, 2003

Select Committee on Defence 4th Report "The Decommissioning of the Sea Harrier" paragraphs 71-96
http://www.publications.parliament.uk/pa/cm200102/cmselect/cmdfence/779/77908.htm
Prepared 10 July 2002   ©Parliamentary Copyright

House of Commons debate on Royal Navy Sea Harriers 8 May 2002, hansard vol 385 cc69-91
http://hansard.millbanksystems.com/westminster_hall/2002/may/08/royal-navy-sea-harriers

Select Committee on Defence, 1 May 2002, Question 180-199 (AM Jock Stirrup, DCDS(EC))
http://www.parliament.the-stationery-office.co.uk/pa/cm200102/cmselect/cmdfence/779/2050104.htm
Prepared 10 July 2002   ©Parliamentary Copyright, 2002

Research material for Chapter 12 -

HMS *Ark Royal* Rededication Book 22 March 2007, RN Graphics   ©HMS *Ark Royal*, 2007
ATC History published at http://en-gb.connect.facebook.com/note.php?note_id=148247081861245

Research material for Chapter 13 -

HMS *Ark Royal* 226/01 dated 11 July 2007 – Report of Proceedings 11 Jul 2006 – 10 July 2007
HMS Ark Royal Monthly Unit Records August 2007 – July 2008
Account of Narvik from http://en.wikipedia.org/wiki/Battles_of_Narvik#First_Naval_Battle_of_Narvik

Research material for Chapter 14 -

HMS Ark Royal Monthly Unit Records August 2008 – September 2010

Research material for Chapter 15 -

Malcolm Chalmers "A Question of Balance? The Deficit and Defence Priorities" RUSI Future Defence Review, Working Paper 7, June 2010   ©RUSI, 2010

Cm7948 "Securing Britain in an Age of Uncertainty: The Strategic Defence and Security Review" HMSO 2010 ISBN: 9780101794824   ©Crown Copyright, 2010

UK national press cuttings and articles October – December 2010 (comment on SDSR, HMS *Ark Royal*)

HMS Ark Royal Monthly Unit Records September 2010 – January 2011

Index

Acknowledgements

The authors are indebted to the following people whose contribution was invaluable in bringing together history of HMS *Ark Royal* V:

Jenny Wraight for granting access to the archive within the Naval Historical Branch, Portsmouth, and to Kate Brett for her patience and diligence in providing copies of the historical Reports of Proceedings and attempting to fill in the gaps!

Sarah Fletcher for granting access to the Navy News archives; Richard Hargreaves and Helen Craven for their advice on reconstructing the many *Ark Royal* stories that have appeared in Navy News since 1985; Sue Sullivan for her administrative support and, especially, to Trevor Muston for tirelessly finding images to illustrate *Ark*'s history.

The estate of Lieutenant C E A "Tugg" Willson MBE, for permission to reproduce the immortal cartoons that provided light relief through *Ark*'s history.

Becky McGibbon at the Marine Society for her research and assistance with Chapter 11.

Susan Dearing at the Fleet Air Arm Museum for her support in collating records of the Naval Air Squadrons that operated from HMS *Ark Royal*.

David Blackburn, Mark Trafford and Stephen Coltart for the personnel recollections of their time in *Ark Royal* and for images supplied.

The twelve Commanding Officers of HMS Ark Royal V who have generously given their time and advice, and whose original Reports of Proceedings have helped clarify much of the detail of Ark's history. If the authors have quoted out of context or misrepresented the contemporary record then the error is entirely theirs, for which sincere apologies are offered.

Commander David Hobbs MBE RN (rtd) and Mr Harry Graham for so diligently checking the proof, spotting the typographic errors that defied capture and for their encouragement and advice on the book's stylistic content.

Notes on the Authors

Lieutenant Commander Alastair Graham

Professor Eric Grove

Lieutenant Commander Alastair Graham joined the Royal Navy in 1992. He has served at sea as a weapons engineer in both submarines and surface ships, most recently as the Senior Weapon Engineer in HMS *Ark Royal* V, from 2008 to 2010.

With a diverse portfolio away from the front line, Alastair has worked at the heart of UK Defence policy-making, within the MoD central staff; conducted operational analysis and tactical development of complex submarine weapons, and managed a team providing core leadership to the largest Naval training establishment in Western Europe. From 2002 to 2004 he had the honour of serving as Equerry to HRH The Prince of Wales.

Alastair Graham is currently part of the Aircraft Carrier Allance, a joint partnership between the MoD and UK industry to design and build the new *Queen Elizabeth*-class aircraft carriers, due to enter service from 2015 onwards.

Eric Grove is one of two Professors of Naval History in the United Kingdom and has a worldwide reputation in the fields of naval history and contemporary maritime strategy, with research interests in nuclear weapons doctrine, strategy and British Defence Policy.

Eric often appears on television and radio as a commentator on these issues as well as wider matters of national and international security. He has published numerous books and articles including, "Vanguard to Trident, British Naval Policy Since 1945" (1987), "The Future of Sea Power" (1990), "The Royal Navy Since 1815" (2005) and has twice written a history of HMS *Ark Royal* V, first in 1994 and updated in 2001.

Eric Grove is a Fellow of the Royal Historical Society, Vice President of the Society for Nautical Research and a Member of the Council of the Navy Records Society